Holy War in Judaism

*About the cover:* Once upon a time in a field on the western edge of Jerusalem, I painted an image of a knight on a large piece of concrete rubble. This knight had somehow come from the burning fields of my parents' homeland in Ukraine and had fallen from the sky in a heap of noisy metal, feverish with the sickness of history.

From out of his armor emerged the memory of a life. This memory would now join me, here in our old-new homeland. A memory delivered by this guardian, which could protect but never attack.

He was a "good" knight.

And now, for this book, I've struggled to draw and understand the other side of power—the "holy" warrior knight. He too has fallen from the sky with a thud of noisy clanging metal. He too is burning with the fever of a sick history. But from his armor a world emerges, understood only in black and white—a world manipulated by fear, vengeance, and the certitude of his destiny.

Benny Ferdman, Artist
www.creativeways.org

# Holy War in Judaism

*The Fall and Rise of a
Controversial Idea*

REUVEN FIRESTONE

# OXFORD
UNIVERSITY PRESS

Oxford University Press, Inc., publishes works that further
Oxford University's objective of excellence
in research, scholarship, and education.

Oxford   New York
Auckland   Cape Town   Dar es Salaam   Hong Kong   Karachi
Kuala Lumpur   Madrid   Melbourne   Mexico City   Nairobi
New Delhi   Shanghai   Taipei   Toronto

With offices in
Argentina   Austria   Brazil   Chile   Czech Republic   France   Greece
Guatemala   Hungary   Italy   Japan   Poland   Portugal   Singapore
South Korea   Switzerland   Thailand   Turkey   Ukraine   Vietnam

Published by Oxford University Press, Inc.
198 Madison Avenue, New York, New York 10016
www.oup.com

Library of Congress Cataloging-in-Publication Data
Firestone, Reuven, 1952-
   Holy war in Judaism : the fall and rise of a controversial idea / Reuven Firestone.
      p. cm.
   Includes bibliographical references and index.
   ISBN 978–0–19–986030–2
   1. War—Religious aspects—Judaism.   2. War—Biblical teaching.
   3. War in literature.   4. Rabbinical literature—History and criticism.
   5. Arab-Israeli conflict—Religious aspects—Judaism.   I. Title.
   BM538.P3F57 2012
   296.3′827—dc23

                                            2011037959


9 8 7 6 5 4 3 2 1

Printed in the United States of America
on acid-free paper

# CONTENTS

# PREFACE

When I showed a Muslim academic colleague of mine a copy of my book on holy war in Islam shortly after it had just been released,[1] he chastised me for assuming that Islam had a concept of holy war. "How could you write this?" he said. "You know that there is no holy war in Islam!" His underlying concern, it seemed to me, was that my book would encourage a negative view of Islam in the public eye. Similarly, as I completed the manuscript for this book and showed parts of it to Jewish colleagues, I sometimes received a parallel response. Some were surprised, and some displeased. "You know that there is no holy war in Judaism," I heard. After continued discussion it appeared to me that they were particularly concerned about this book eliciting resentment against Jews, Judaism, and the state of Israel.

Yet both my Muslim and Jewish colleagues are technically correct in their denial of the phenomenon of holy war in Islam and Judaism. In fact there exists no *traditional* term for holy war in the vocabulary of either religion. "Holy war" is a slippery term, and some have cautioned against using it in scholarship because of its current politicization and because the traditional context for its discussion is within Christian thought and practice. Moreover, holy war in the Western imagination is war for conversion, while neither Judaism nor Islam condones engagement in war for that purpose.[2] But fear of criticism or political backlash should not hinder scholar-

---

[1] *Jihad: The Origin of Holy War in Islam* (Oxford U. Press, 1999).

[2] A famous *hadith* reports that Muhammad said, "I have been commanded to fight the people until they testify that there is no god but Allah; when they say that, they keep their life and their property safe from me..." (Abu Dawud *Sunan* [Cairo: *Dar al-Misriyya al-Lubnaniyya*, 1988/1408] *Kitab al-Jihad*, "Basis for Fighting Polytheists" [#2640]). This is a requirement for monotheism

ship, and the lack of a Hebrew term corresponding exactly to holy war or absence of conversionary wars in Judaism does not prove the nonexistence of the phenomenon as defined here. Judaism, Christianity, and Islam has each developed its own notion of divinely sanctioned war among several options or tactics available to protect the religious community, preserve the integrity of its religious tradition, or further its institutional goals.

What I mean by holy war is organized mass violence directed against rival communities based on what is considered to be God's approval or authority. This is the most fundamental definition of holy war: war that is justified by divine authority.[3] Although the authority for holy war ultimately derives from the divinity, that authority is communicated through a variety of media among the world's religions: scripture, dreams, visions, or audible messages conveyed through prophets, divination by religious leaders, natural signs and omens, or the interpretations of any of these by priests, sages, elders, shamans, or other religious experts. What makes holy war "holy" is its divine authority, and there is no major religion known to me that does not provide some kind of divine authority for mass violence.

Having said that, among the religious systems I have studied, Judaism has the least developed and least politicized ideology of holy war, and when it is invoked it has always applied to an extremely limited geographic scope.[4] This observation does not suggest to me that Judaism is intrinsically better able to resolve conflict peaceably or is more ethical than its

---

rather than conversion to Islam, though other, most likely later versions of this tradition (including the *hadith* that follows this one, #2641) add the requirement that the enemy also affirm that Muhammad is a prophet of God. War always involves excesses. Forced conversions of Jews and Christians to Islam occurred, but were not sanctioned according to Islamic jurisprudence.

[3] On definitions and categories of war, differences between "just war" and "holy war," and a range of definitions of holy war in scholarly literature, see James Turner Johnson, *Ideology, Reason, and the Limitation of War* (Princeton: Princeton University Press, 1975), 9–11; *idem*, *The Holy War Idea in Western and Islamic Traditions* (University Park, PA: Penn State University), 1997, 29–46.

[4] See Firestone, "Holy War Idea in the Biblical Tradition," in Palmer-Fernandez, G. (ed.), *Encyclopedia of Religion and War* (1st ed.). New York: Berkshire/Routledge, 2004, 180–85; *idem*, "Conceptions of Holy War in Biblical and Qur'anic Tradition," *The Journal of Religious Ethics* 24 (1996), 801–824. Much less has been written about holy war (or war in general) in post-biblical Judaism than in Christianity and Islam because of its limited ideological development and application in history until the 20th century. Most Jewish studies treat specific aspects of war and fighting in relation to the modern state of Israel rather than war in Judaism as a religious phenomenon. See Robert Eisen, *The Peace and Violence of Judaism: From the Bible to Modern Zionism* (New York: Oxford U. Press, 2011); Bradley Shavit Artson, *Love Peace and Pursue Peace* (NY: United Synagogue of America), 1988; Efraim Inbar, "War in Jewish Tradition." *The Jerusalem Journal of International Relations* 9 (1987), 83–99; Reuven Kimelman, "The Ethics of National Power: Government and War from the Sources of Judaism," in Daniel Elazar (ed.), *Authority, Power and Leadership in the Jewish Polity* (Lanham: University Press of America, 1991), 247–294; *idem*, "Laws of War and its Limits" (Hebrew), in Isaiah M. Gafni and Aviezer Ravitzky, *Sanctity of Life and Martyrdom* (Jerusalem: Zalman Shazar Center, 1992), 233–254; Cf. Kimelman, "Non-

sister religions, because I believe that the limits that Judaism has imposed on itself are fully explicable for historical reasons. In fact, the overwhelming influence of history on the religious formulation and application of holy war is one of the lessons I draw from this study. For the purposes of this study, I consider religion to be an institution constructed by humans in response to human comprehensions of the transcendent or divine.[5] The human element in the relationship is the interpretation and implementation of what is understood to be the divine message. The words of the message may be eternal and unchanging in the record of divine revelation, but their interpretation is always bound by history and changes accordingly.

My colleagues referred to earlier were concerned about my study of holy war in Judaism and Islam in part because they have observed how books with "holy war" in their titles have sometimes been used to reinforce bigotry and intolerance toward people simply because they are identified with a particular religion. The purpose of my work is neither to condemn nor praise, but rather to deepen my own understanding and, I hope, the understanding of others regarding this difficult and complex phenomenon.

War is only one of many tactics that human communities, polities, or states (including those defined by or institutionalized around religion) use to protect themselves and further their strategic goals.[6] Steven Weitzman has shown how Jews employed a variety of techniques in Antiquity to protect their communities and religious institutions. Among the tactics that Weitzman enumerates is holy war, though he refers to the wars of the Maccabees against the Greeks (and their sympathizers) and the Jews who revolted against Rome without further classification.[7] Nevertheless, the wars he describes fall into the category of classic holy wars because

---

Violence in the Talmud," *Judaism* 17:1 (Winter, 1968), 316–334, which is a hopeful projection cognizant of the rabbinic re-envisioning of war and violence.

[5] Cf. Max Weber, *The Sociology of Religion*, translated by Ephraim Fischoff (Boston: Beacon, 1963), 60–79; Emile Durkheim, *The Elementary Forms of the Religious Life*, transl. Joseph Ward Swain (London: George Allen and Unwin, 1915), 205–214, 416–447; Joachim Wach, *The Sociology of Religion* (Chicago: University of Chicago, 1944), 54–58, 109–112.

[6] Clausewitz famous dictum is appropriate for the perspective of this study: "War is...also a real political instrument, a continuation of political commerce, a carrying out of the same by other means" (Carl von Clausewitz, *On War*, transl. J. J. Graham [London N. Trübner, 1874]; new and revised edition with Introduction and notes by F. N. Maude, 1909 in three volumes), Vol. 1, #24, available at http://www.gutenberg.org/files/1946/1946-h/1946-h.htm#2HCH0001, checked 6.10.11. I define polity or state in general terms, following James Aho: "a relatively closed non-kinship group of armed persons that 'taxes' and 'protects' those residing in a fairly delimited territory..." (James Aho, *Religious Mythology and the Art of War: Comparative Religious Symbolisms of Military Violence* (Westport, CT: Greenwood, 1981), 3.

[7] Steven Weitzman, *Surviving Sacriledge: Cultural Persistence in Jewish Antiquity* (Cambridge, MA: Harvard), 2005.

they are considered by those fighting in them to be authorized by God for divine purposes.[8]

This book is a study of exegesis and history—the intellectual processes through which war, authorized and justified by the most sacred texts of Jewish scripture in the Bible, was virtually eliminated from the tactical repertoire of Judaism for nearly two millennia by the Talmud, after which it was subsequently revived.[9] Not all Jewish leaders or Jews in general followed this trend, and the program of the rabbis was never intended to remove war from Judaism or to transform Judaism into a pacifist religion. The purpose was, rather, to reduce the danger to the Jewish world that war had come to represent. This overall strategy intended to decrease the likelihood of militant uprisings among Jews. As such, it was not the elimination of war per se, but rather the elimination or at least reduction in the possibility of employing the powerful martial images of the Bible to promote violent movements that could become catastrophic. This does not represent a withdrawal from politics[10] but rather a re-alignment of priorities, which included strategic adjustments resulting from changes in the general perspective on the place of war among most Jews from Late Antiquity through the Middle Ages and into the modern period.

In a better world, war would never be an acceptable tactic, but the world we inhabit has not eliminated war from its political repertoire, nor has it removed holy war from its tactical inventory. Because of its ideological base, holy war is one of the more intractable expressions of war. When war becomes ideological, strategic issues and rational decision making tend to become blurred and weakened. Ideological rigidity, especially in the case of religious ideological warring under the unshakable faith that "God is on our side," allows for major contravention of human constraints. When the divinity is cited as the authority for mass violence, it is all the more difficult to halt its march. It is my deepest hope that my work on this difficult

---

[8] Weitzman and others have shown how wars in antiquity were generally considered to be sanctioned by the gods or transcendent powers of the day, even if the military leaders maneuvered their soldiers into believing so through their own manipulations (Weitzman, *Surviving Sacriledge*, 119–134; James Aho, *Religious Mythology*, 157–158; Bestenay Oded, *War, Peace and Empire: Justifications for War in Assyrian Royal Inscriptions* [Wiesbaden: Ludwig Reichert, 1992], 9–20). I distinguish between "holy war" and what might be called "mundane war," meaning war that is not considered specifically to be authorized by God, not only because of the modern distinction but also because, as shall be demonstrated below, the rabbinic sages held the same basic categorical distinction between "commanded (i.e. holy) war" and "discretionary (mundane) war."

[9] An early abbreviated inquiry into this subject is my "Holy War in Modern Judaism? 'Mitzvah War' and the Problem of the Three Vows," *Journal of the American Academy of Religion* 74.4 (2006), 954–982.

[10] See David Biale, *Power and Powerlessness in Jewish History* (NY: Schocken, 1986).

topic will contribute to a better understanding of the phenomenon of holy war, and perhaps will even contribute some small part to its elimination. The specific goal of this study, however, is limited to achieving a better understanding of the phenomenon of holy war in Judaism.

The initiation of my research for this book was funded by a fellowship from the National Endowment for the Humanities for travel and research in Israel during the 2000–2001 academic year, for which I am deeply grateful. Near the end of that year I was struck with a sudden medical emergency that would have been fatal without the immediate and brilliant diagnosis of Dr. Irena Krasilnikov, who served in the emergency room of Hadassa Ein Kerem in Jerusalem. I am further indebted to the expertise of Dr. Amir Elamy, who led the surgical team that saved my life at Hadassa. Lightning sometimes strikes twice, I have learned, so thanks goes out also to the surgical team led by Dr. Sharro Raissi at Cedars-Sinai Medical Center in Los Angeles for a repeat performance. This project would never have been completed without their caring expertise. A portion of my NEH–funded research has been published as "Holy War in Modern Judaism? 'Mitzvah War' and the Problem of the 'Three Vows,'" in the *Journal of the American Academy of Religion* 74(4) December, 2006, 954–982.

The Israel National Library was kind enough to allow me to spend much of the summer of 2003 in the basement stacks where I could leaf freely through journals and the newsletters of Zionist organizations and youth movements. The secretariat and archives of Hakibbutz Hadati also provided me with assistance and materials, and my work would have been impossible without the assistance of the librarians and staff of the Francis-Henry Library of Hebrew Union College in Los Angeles and the Zalman & Ayala Abramov Library of Hebrew Union College in Jerusalem.

Although the concept, contents, conclusions, and errors of commission or omission contained in this book are entirely my own, my task would have been impossible without the valued support and assistance of colleagues and experts with whom I consulted. I was guided in my work by the wise counsel of Dov Berkowitz, Eliezer don-Yehiyah, Aryeh Cohen, Lawrence Hoffman, Anita Shapira, Barry Walfish, Sharon Gillerman, Yair Sheleg, Ehud Sprinzak, Dvora Weisberg, Noam Zoar, George Wilkes, and John Kelsay. Rabbi Joseph Pollack first interested me in the topic through the dispute between Maimonides and Nachmanides over the commandedness of holy war.

# ABBREVIATIONS

ARN  *Avot deRabbi Natan*
BR  *Bereshit Rabbah*
BT  *Babylonian Talmud*
Deut  Deuteronomy
EJ2  *Encyclopedia Judaica (2nd ed. NY: Macmillan, 2007)*
Ex  Exodus
Gen  Genesis
IDF  Israel Defense Forces (this common acronym in Hebrew is Tzahal)
JBL  *Journal of Biblical Literature*
Lev  Leviticus
MT  *Mishneh Torah of Maimonides*
PRE  *Pirkei de'Rabbi Eliezer*
PT  *Palestinian Talmud*
ShB  *Shanah Beshanah*
TSP  *Torah Shebe`al Peh*
TVM  *Hatorah Vehamedinah*

Holy War in Judaism

# INTRODUCTION

HOLY WAR IS, BY definition, sacred. And the most obvious association of sanctity is with the divinity, however defined or understood. When war is authorized by God it is holy. That is the bottom line with holy war—it is authorized by God. Whether the fighter has faith while engaged in combat or whether the warrior is in a state of ritual purity in relation to the holiness of the camp[1] are related considerations, but the core issue is whether the combatants believe that their war is sanctioned by God.

But how does one know the divine will? Divine communication has been acknowledged by humanity through signs, oracles, priests, prophets, and revelation, and all of these media have authorized holy war at one time or another. As religions become established, institutionalized and standardized, however, fresh communication between God and humanity becomes limited, revelation becomes controlled through canonization into scripture, and prophecy is severely restricted or ended altogether.[2] Whatever is claimed by prophetlike individuals as divine inspiration is subsequently challenged by the religious establishments and either condemned altogether or tolerated only as strictly personal messages rather than public pronouncements.[3] With hardly an exception, it is only the record of previous divine revelation in the form of scriptural text that continues to represent the actual direct, public, and authoritative public communication from God.

---

[1] Gerhard von Rad, *Holy War in Ancient Israel,* Transl. and Ed. Marva J. Dawn (Grand Rapids, MI: William B. Eerdmans, 1991), especially 115–127; Susan Niditch, *War in the Hebrew Bible* (New York: Oxford University, 1993).

[2] BT. Yoma 9b, John 14:6 (but see Acts 11:27–30, Revelation 11:10); Qur'an 33:40, etc.

[3] Harvey Cox, *Fire From Heaven: The Rise of Pentecostal Spirituality and the Reshaping of Religion in the Twenty-first Century* (Jackson, TN: Perseus, 1994).

How, then, can religious leadership continue to make sense of the divine will through the passage and changes of history? The answer to this question, like the process through which the meanings and applicability of holy war itself have evolved, is quite simply through interpretation. The will of the transcendent and the meanings of religion are made intelligible through the medium of human understanding, usually via reading and interpreting God's word. In other words, we know what we know about God's will and design mainly through our attempts to decipher and make sense of the record of God's revelation in scripture. Religious leadership is always engaged in this process because it is charged to help its followers understand what God expects of them. Religious leaders thus translate, illuminate, and elucidate the demands of God to the community of believers.

But the processes of interpretation, the ways in which religious leadership decodes and deciphers divine revelation to provide contemporary meaning, are anything but simple. Among the three families of scripture-based monotheisms, complex interpretive strategies or hermeneutics have been developed in order to derive meaning(s) from revealed texts. Yet even when working with the same ground rules, different and often conflicting results emerge from the process. Some "stick" while others fall away and new interpretations arise, and the factions or communities that tend to form around them become more or less influential.

Various methods have been developed to determine and canonize authoritative interpretation. One well-known method is the unifying apostolic approach in the tradition of the Catholic Church.[4] Judaism, however, has tended not to produce any universal institutional approach but has relied on a more diffuse and by and large majority method that can be observed in the workings of traditional Rabbinic literature. The approach of the rabbis has been less prone than that of the Church to articulate principles that may lie behind the interpretive results.[5] Partly in response to this trend, methods of Jewish study tend to include attempts to suggest unarticulated reasons or concerns that were at issue in earlier interpretations, and this in turn has promoted more imaginative readings and explanations of prior interpretations of authoritative texts.

---

[4] Francis A. Sullivan, *Magisterium: Teaching Authority in the Catholic Church* (Paulist Press, 1984); James L. Heft, S.M., *John XXII and Papal Teaching Authority* (Edwin Mellen Press, 1986).

[5] Rabbinic tradition is more interested in case studies than in articulating general principles of law (although principles clearly can be derived from the study of cases). The same is true in rabbinic theology, which could be described as situational rather than systematic.

This book attempts to examine and make sense of the interpretive history of the notion of holy war in post-biblical Judaism. We shall observe in Part 1 that holy war is a common theme in the Hebrew Bible. Divinely legitimized through the authority of biblical scripture and its interpretation, holy war became a historical reality for the Jews of antiquity. Among at least some of the Jewish groups of the late Second Temple period until the middle of the second century, C.E., holy war was an operative institution. That is, Jews engaged in what is defined here as holy war.

Early Rabbinic Judaism, the base out of which has grown virtually all expressions of Judaism today,[6] began to emerge during this period in the region that is today the modern state of Israel and the Palestinian Authority lands. According to Rabbinic Judaism, God on certain occasions not only authorized but also commanded war. In fact, because the rhetorical articulation of proper ritual and ethical practice among the rabbis was understood in terms of divine commandment, the very term used by the rabbis for divinely sanctioned war (that is, "holy war") became "Commanded War" (*milchemet mitzvah*).[7] Three major Jewish wars were waged as holy wars during this period (though the term "commanded war" is not found in Jewish literature until later). These are the Maccabean revolt against the Seleucids in the second century B.C.E., the Great Revolt against Rome in the first century C.E., and the Bar Kokhba Rebellion in the second century. The first succeeded in repelling a powerful repressive foreign regime and establishing religious and national independence, but the second and third failed to produce victory. This was not merely an academic problem for the Jews of the day. The resulting destruction to human life and property when these wars failed was so overwhelming that they threatened to destroy Judaism and the Jewish people.

For the survival of Jews and Judaism, the Jewish leadership that became dominant during what is referred to by historians as the rabbinic period (from about 70 to about 600 C.E.)[8] engaged in certain exegetical strategies

---

[6] Including Karaite Judaism, which although not Rabbinic, emerged in part as a reaction to the hegemony of Rabbinic Judaism in the ninth century. See Leon Nemoy (ed.), *Karaite Anthology* (New Haven: Yale, 1952), Daniel Frank, *Search Scripture Well: Karaite Exegetes and the Origins of the Jewish Bible Commentary in the Islamic East* (Leiden: Brill, 2004), and Fred Astren, *Kara'ite Judaism and Historical Understanding* (Columbia, S.C.: University of South Carolina Press, 2004).

[7] For a synoptic overview of war in post-biblical Judaism, see Reuven Kimelman, "War," in Steven T. Katz, *Frontiers of Jewish Thought* (Washington, D.C.: B'nai B'rith Books, 1992), 309–332.

[8] The terminus ad quem for the period has been extended recently by current scholarship to the Arab/Islamic conquests of the seventh century.

to prevent the dangerous wild card of holy war to be easily played.[9] We shall observe in Part 2 how the rabbis of the Talmud, the small community of scholars that would become the most prominent leaders of the Jewish world, responded to the repeated catastrophic failures of military campaigns that were considered holy wars by their protagonists. They agreed that holy war was a genuine and perhaps even eternal divinely authorized institution, but they also made it virtually impossible for holy war to be an *operative* category in Judaism.

The rabbinic sages who led this charge had to contend with a massive and authoritative biblical literature that included many different and often glorious cases of victorious battle against the enemies of Israel. The strategy of the rabbis was to restrict the notion of divinely authorized warring to a simple and limited definition that would make it virtually impossible to apply in their own historical context. At the same time, they discovered through their analysis of scripture that God had established a series of agreements between the Jews and the gentile nations among whom they lived that were intended to avoid overwhelming violence directed by non-Jews against their community. As long as the Jews kept their part of the agreement, namely, to refrain from physical rebellion against the powers that established Jewish second-class status after loss of political independence, God would ensure that the gentiles would keep their part of the agreement to refrain from persecuting the Jews excessively. Subsequently, the rabbinic sages simply avoided engaging in meaningful discussion about holy war, thus effectively removing it from mainstream rabbinic discourse. It was as though the librarians of rabbinic literature took the complex notion of divinely authorized warring in ancient Judaism, packaged it up neatly, and then placed it deeply in the stacks of the library so that it could not be easily removed for detailed scrutiny.

But the biblical sources out of which the ideas of holy war were constructed always remained prominent in the library, even if discussion and analysis were placed far away from easy access. The notion of holy war (now called "Commanded War") was therefore revisited occasionally but actually quite rarely. It remained dormant for centuries, but even in its dormancy it continued to evolve. Some medieval rabbis, operating within the intellectual and political contexts of their own times, worked

---

[9] This was not the first time that Jewish leaders interpreted text and history to avoid the dangers of holy war. Half a millennium earlier in the face of Babylonia's overwhelming power, Jeremiah warned the Judeans that King Nebuchadnezzar was God's agent of punishment and that rebellion would be futile (Jer.25:1–11), but this view would not become accepted until centuries later.

with the notion of Commanded War. The dispute between Maimonides and Nachmanides on whether divinely authorized warring was an eternal divine commandment removed it briefly from the library shelf for open discussion. Their disagreement returned the old institution of holy war into the discourse of Jewish learning, even if peripherally. But although it was brought into the intellectual world of traditional study, holy war was far from a physical reality and was not examined in depth. The Jews of the world were without a polity and without even a distant hope of establishing one. Holy war thus remained academic, an institution, like the Red Heifer,[10] that could be studied but with the assumption that it would not be applied until the coming of the messiah.

With the emergence of modernity, examined in Part 3, it appeared to some Jews as though a messianic age—of sorts—was imminent. To many Jews in Western Europe during the nineteenth century, it seemed that the modern world itself was messianic. Within it humanity would produce a kind of man-made salvation in which Jews would be emancipated from their degraded status and accepted as equal to Europeans so they could integrate into the modern world individually, as members of the Jewish faith.

The Jews of Eastern Europe did not fare as well as their brethren in the West. Some who were unable to join in the liberal movements of Western Europe created their own neomessianic movements. One expression was Jewish nationalism, which emerged in Eastern Europe along with other neomessianic movements such as socialism and communism. These were largely nonreligious or even anti-religious developments in which a kind of "secular messianism" became part of their essential nature. The overwhelmingly secular movement of Zionism was the only successful expression of Jewish nationalism. It was led by nonreligious Jews, and most traditionally observant ("Orthodox") Jews never joined it. A few did, however, and they, like their secularist comrades, engaged in Zionism's pioneering settlement and development projects in Palestine.

Like their secularist brethren, religious Jews who joined the Zionist project were obliged to take up arms to defend themselves against Arab resistance to Jewish colonization. But unlike secular Zionists, the Orthodox religious Zionists were confronted with the traditional Jewish restriction against what the rabbis of the Talmud called "rebelling against the gentiles." This was part of the agreement or contractual arrangement just mentioned, which Talmudic sages understood to have been established by

---

[10] The Red Heifer is the animal described in Numbers 19, whose ashes were used in the ritual purification of persons and objects defiled by a corpse (See *Anchor Bible Dictionary* 3:115–116; EJ2 17:156–158).

God between the Jews and the gentiles of the world. Engaging in mass activities to reestablish Jewish political independence rather than waiting for God's messiah was understood by them as breaking the Jewish commitment to the contract, an act that was considered liable to bring about catastrophic divine punishment. Part 3 considers how those Orthodox Jews who were engaged in Zionism worked out a means to remain true to God's contractual agreements while remaining active in the Jewish national revival.

Holy war sources began to be shifted from deep within the library stacks toward its periphery after the Holocaust made it absolutely clear to Jews that they needed to be more aggressive in defending themselves. Henceforth, vigorous defense became a holy endeavor. When a formal Jewish military was formed in 1947–1948 to defend the new Jewish State of Israel, religious Zionists found themselves in a quandary. Talmudic sages had defined immigration en masse to Israel as "rebellion against the gentiles." Forming a Jewish military was also questioned. Once formed, even if only for defense, armies are sometimes required to initiate attacks as well as (or in order to) defend, and Jewish armed forces were no exception. Some religious Jews believed that initiating attacks would break the delicate balance of agreements established by God between Jews and gentiles. So although the sources were removed from the library shelf, their contents were only partially unpacked, for it was not at all clear whether engaging in war, apart from the most basic defense of Jewish communities, was divinely justified even after the establishment of the Jewish state.

Part 4 examines the struggle to make sense of the need to wage war in the period of Jewish statehood. It observes how after the 1967 War, the sources discussing holy war were opened wide, and a full range of meanings associated with divinely authorized war in Judaism was explored in religious Zionist discourse. During this period the notion and language of religious war also passed from the yeshivas and journals of Orthodox Jewry into the larger Israeli public discourse. By the early 1980s, to most religious Zionists and many Jews positioned outside that community, the modern wars of the State of Israel had attained an extraordinary status as having been divinely sanctioned—even commanded. Divinely commanded war is, in Jewish terminology, holy war. This study of the history of holy war's suppression and subsequent revival in Judaism ends, therefore, with the mid-1980s. Although the discussions and disagreements over messianism, the possibly transcendent meaning of the State of Israel, and divinely authorized war continue unabated in contemporary Jewish discourse, the revival of Jewish holy war has occurred for at least a significant segment of the Jewish world.

This book begins in the dark corridors of antiquity. It ends with the blinding explosion of the "Jewish underground" in the early to mid-1980s. Expressions of violence perpetrated by Jews who believe their acts to be divinely sanctioned have continued since then, including even the assassination of the Prime Minister of the State of Israel, Yitzhak Rabin, in 1995. Although continued research into these developments is of great interest, it falls outside the parameters of this study of the history of holy war's containment and subsequent revival in post-biblical Judaism. The goal here is to make sense of the conceptual journey of the holy war idea in Judaism from its vigorous days in Early Antiquity, failure and suppression in Late Antiquity, dormancy in the Middle Ages, and revival in the modern period. By the mid-1980s the revival of holy war in modern Judaism had been complete, and therefore also this study.

## A Note About Methodology

This book is not a history of Judaism or of Zionism but rather a historical study of a common religious phenomenon as it is manifest in Judaism. The nature of such a project requires one to work through a long span of history and in a broad range of scholarly disciplines ranging from the study of history to religion to literature to hermeneutics. There are a number of ways to approach this topic. I have taken an interest in religious phenomenology and the historical contextualization of interpretation, so I base my work on how people of religion read and interpret their sacred texts in relation to their contemporary environment. More original texts and commentaries are included in this study than is usual for a history. Although this may seem a bit tedious for some, it is necessary in order to track the sometimes subtle changes in the reading and interpretation of traditional sources.

For the ancient and medieval periods, there is little alternative to the study of ancient texts and artifacts. But for the contemporary period making up fully one-fourth of this book, many of the actual players in the drama could have been interviewed. I chose not to do that, even though I have written much of this book while in Israel and with access to many of those engaged in the debates and actions. I have refrained from interviewing for the following reasons. When engaging in an interview, the interviewer has a certain advantage in directing the nature or path of the discussion toward her particular interests, but that can skew the relative weight of any part of the information received. It is possible that the subject, if left to his or her own choice, would engage more fully in another topic or angle that is thus lost by the interviewer. The interviewer also conveys nonverbal messages (purposefully or inadvertently) in the process of interviewing, and the interviewee may respond to these cues in ways that might differ from another interview context. The interviewee may also be influenced by an issue of immediate concern or have a particular agenda that may or may not be relevant to the issue at hand, thus skewing the data collected.

I have chosen only written sources for this study. They come from traditional Jewish texts and from modern books, scholarly journals, and movement newsletters. These sources tend to reflect carefully articulated views that have been considered deeply before being committed to writing. Ideas or views put into writing are reviewed and edited prior to final submission, often by an editor as well as the author. They are rarely immediate, impromptu responses to questions or angles that may not have been considered deeply prior to their asking. Such a methodology loses out on the freshness and immediacy of the journalistic approach, but I believe that it provides a more reliable articulation of ideas.

The primary sources examined for this study derive primarily from the traditional library of Judaism. They include the Hebrew Bible, Talmud, and Midrash, and some of the more important medieval Jewish thinkers whose ideas have had a powerful impact on Jewish thinking and action. For the modern and contemporary periods, I have chosen journals, newsletters, and the collected works of religious scholars and activists who represent the major ideological trajectories of Religious Zionism and that have been demonstrated to have had a powerful impact on the development of religious Zionist ideology related to war.[11] I chose not to concentrate on radical individuals and fringe groups and their publications (though I do refer to some), but rather on the leading intellectual edge within the mainstream of Religious Zionism, because it is these people who best represent the thinking that has resulted in the revival of Jewish holy war. It is true that extremists such as Rabbi Meir Kahane influenced religious Zionism by moving the center toward the right, but his ideas are of interest only after they are repeated by rabbis who are accorded greater authority in the larger religious Zionist community.

---

[11] I examined all of the national journals published by Orthodox Jewish communities in Israel that were available to me in the Israel National Library in Jerusalem, including those published by communities or institutes that are not necessarily Zionist, and I include material from them when relevant. I also examined the major Orthodox religious journals published in the United States, though they have not stood in the vanguard of discussion on the topic at hand.

Textual interpretation cannot be studied adequately without an eye to the historical contexts in which they are written. This book, therefore, includes a fair amount of discussion of historical context, and especially general Zionist history and thought as it has influenced the Jewish ethos of war in the modern period. As a longitudinal study spanning more than two millennia, this book cannot attend to every source that might be considered important to specialists in particular periods or literatures. That is simply the nature of such a study, but I hope to have covered the most important bases.

And although this book makes no attempt to be a history of Judaism or Zionism, it does touch on some central and controversial Jewish and Zionist issues aside from war. One is the question of the meaning of the centrality of the Land of Israel to Jews and Judaism in history, an issue that continues to be a subject of debate among historians, politicians, theologians, and political and religious ideologues. No one would doubt the central importance of the Land of Israel to Jews and Judaism throughout history. Its centrality is readily apparent from any familiarity with Jewish ritual, law, prayer, home customs, and all genres of Jewish literature. The sides of the debate have developed, rather, over Jewish attitudes and historical responses to that centrality—namely, did Jews act on that centrality through historical immigration movements? Or to put it differently and more directly in terms of the current problematic, is the modern Zionist movement to settle the Land of Israel and gain political control over it a natural response to Judaism and Jewish history, or is it a synthetic movement that is more in line with other nationalist movements of nineteenth century Europe and inconsistent with Judaism?

One school asserts that Jews have consistently and actively sought to live in and physically develop the Land of Israel throughout history and actually encouraged and engaged in immigration movements to realize this concrete aim. The only reason that more Jews could not be found living in the Land of Israel prior to the emergence of Zionism was that gentile powers prevented them from realizing their aspirations. The other school takes the position that traditional Jewish notions of divine redemption and the return of Jews to the Land of Israel remained in the abstract and were spiritualized, to be realized in some far-off time but not to be considered actionable in history. This study will certainly be examined by some parties in light of the debate, but my intent here is not to take a position on the question.[12]

---

[12] The debate is spelled out succinctly by Arie Morgenstern, "Dispersion and the Longing for Zion, 1240–1840," *Azure* 12 (2002), 71–132. His list of individuals and groups who tried or succeeded in immigrating to the Land of Israel is not adequately contextualized in relation to the Jewish communities at large. It is difficult to know from the sources how significant they

Finally, this book is not a study of halakhah. That is to say, there is no intent here to evaluate whether any particular position is correct or even consistent from the standpoint of Jewish law and tradition. I leave that entirely up to experts in halakhah. This work is, rather, a study in Jewish history and the broad discipline of religious studies. Its purpose is to trace the history and evolution of a powerful and influential religious institution.

## A Note About Terminology

In a study such as this, terminology can carry a lot of baggage. A classic case in point is the names that are applied to wars. To Jews, the Jewish-Arab war of 1947–1948 is the War of Independence (*milchemet ha`atzma'ut*). To Arabs, and especially Palestinians, it is the *nakba*, or calamity. I therefore refrain from assigning names to wars. Unless for a specific and intentional nuance of meaning, I refer to the wars between the State of Israel and its Arab and Palestinian neighbors according to their dates: 1948, 1956, 1967, 1973, and 1982.[13]

But terminology is often at the center of interpretation. The definition and explication of terms is sometimes the core of exegesis. Accordingly, we will examine the evolution of meaning of certain critical terms. Given the sensitivity of the issue, I feel the need to clarify some of my own terminology here. In traditional Jewish texts, the Jewish People is generally referred to as Israel. The geographical region that most Arabs call Palestine and many Christians call the Holy Land is referred to in traditional Jewish texts and by most Orthodox Jews as the Land of Israel (*eretz yisra'el),* meaning the land that is considered by Jewish tradition to belong to or to have been divinely promised to the *people* Israel. This is often distinguished from the State of Israel, which consists of the institutions of the nation-state and the land within its political borders. The Land of Israel is much larger in area than the State of Israel. Sometimes the Land of Israel is simply referred to as "the Land" *(ha'aretz).* Because we are working with traditional Jewish texts and Jewish thought, we will follow the Jewish terminology used in that discourse.

This book is about Jewish holy war. As previously mentioned and as examined in greater detail in the rest of the book, "holy war" is defined

---

were in relation to what would appear to be the overwhelming majority of Jews who did not engage in them or support them. Additional synchronic studies would help resolve the problem.
[13] I do not include the so-called "War of Attrition" of 1968–1970 because it had no significant impact on the topic of this study.

in the traditional Jewish context as "Commanded War"—war commanded by God. A second category of war, called "Discretionary War" *(milchemet reshut)*, is also a legitimate form of war according to the sages of the Talmud and Jewish tradition. Its legitimacy is proven at least in part by the fact that the great King David engaged in Discretionary War according to the sages and by the fact that even in wars "...fought to expand the biblical boundaries or to enhance the prestige of the king, the warriors had to ensure that their camp would be 'consecrated'" according to certain rules of biblical purity.[14] Some might include Discretionary War within the definition of "holy war" because it is a category discussed in the Talmud that refers to certain wars found in the sacred scripture of the Bible. I do not accept this position because the discretionary nature of the category allows for a ruler to engage in war, as did King David, for personal gain or aggrandizement rather than in order to fulfill the divine command.[15] But although Commanded War is understood as prescribed by God (a Jewish way of saying divinely sanctioned), war is prosecuted by human beings. Historically, therefore, even Commanded War is a human institution, and human institutions have no meaning outside of human historical contexts and the meaning that is applied to them. Contextualization is critical.

Before the modern period, traditional Jewish categories of war were accepted by all rabbinic Jews everywhere because, although the Jewish world was divided into different groups that had many disagreements about practice and theology, they all agreed on the absolute authority of scripture and tradition. They simply interpreted scripture and tradition in somewhat different ways. Since the modern period and especially after the Holocaust, however, most Jewish groups (and most Jews) do not automatically accept the traditional sources of authority as absolute guides to behavior and belief. In fact, most Jews today do not observe religious behaviors and practices in a recognizably traditional manner. Many are avowedly secular and follow few religious practices at all.

---

[14] George R. Wilkes, "Religious War in the Works of Maimonides and Its Reception Amongst Jews in Christian Lands," in Sohail Hashmi, ed. *Just Wars, Holy Wars, and Jihads: Christian, Jewish, Muslim Encounters and Exchanges* (Oxford: Oxford University Press, 2012).

[15] The term "discretionary" is not preferred by some scholars, perhaps because although the term presumes that the decision may be virtually arbitrary, this category is also assumed to be divinely sanctioned. "Authorized" has thus also been used to translate the Hebrew term, *reshut* (Michael J. Broyde, "Just Wars, Just Battles and Just Conduct in Jewish Law: Jewish Law is Not a Suicide Pact!*," in Lawrence Schiffman and Joel B. Wolowelsky, *War and Peace in the Jewish Tradition* [New York: Yeshivah University, 2007], 12).

The minority of Jews that continue to rely on the absolute authority of Jewish tradition are referred to by both insiders and outsiders as Orthodox Jews, and they are divided into a number of different configurations. One important consideration in identifying different Orthodox groups is to distinguish between those who are Zionist and those who are non-Zionist or anti-Zionist. It is the Orthodox Jews who are Zionist for which the category of Commanded War is most important today. It is usually a nonissue for the anti-Zionist Orthodox Jews (except when they argue the point with Zionist Orthodox Jews), because the anti-Zionist Orthodox do not accept the possibility of Commanded War, at least until the clear and unmistakable advent of the messiah, for which they see no signs in modern history. The non-Zionist Orthodox, perhaps better identified as those Orthodox Jews who are ambivalent about Zionism, are somewhere in between the Zionists and the anti-Zionists with regard to the categories of Jewish war-making examined here.

Those responsible for the revival of Jewish holy war derive from the community of Orthodox Jews who are avowedly Zionist and who believe deeply in a transcendent meaning to the return of the People of Israel to the Land of Israel and the creation of the State of Israel. We will observe how their involvement in the Zionist project would seem impossible without the revitalization of holy war paradigms. But there is no truly accurate and nonpoliticized terminology to define these Jews. They are generally called "religious Zionists," and the ideological perspective that they represent "Religious Zionism," to distinguish them from the overwhelming majority of Zionists who have been secular or secularist ("secularist" meaning in this book actively anti-religious). But "Religious" Zionism suggests that there is no religiosity in "secular" Zionism or that there is no form of religious Zionism other than Orthodox religious Zionism. However, the so-called "religious Zionists" who practice Orthodox Judaism are not the only religious Jews who are Zionists, for Reform, Conservative, Reconstructionist, and other religious Jews are Zionists who live in Israel and in the Diaspora, and their communities are growing. "Secular" Zionism is not really adequate either, because Zionism has always carried a spiritual element and continues to do so among many non-Orthodox Jews today. Yet there seems to be no other term to adequately describe the religiously Orthodox Zionists that is not awkward.[16] For purposes of clarity, therefore, and for lack of a more appropriate term, I will reluctantly continue the tradition by referring to the religiously Orthodox Jewish community that is Zionist as religious Zionists.

---

[16] "Orthodox Zionists" appears as if it refers to an orthodox political ideology, and "religiously Orthodox Zionists" is an awkward term.

## A Note About Hebrew Transliteration

In the interest of readability, I do not employ the standard technical system of diacritic marks in Hebrew transliteration for either vowels or consonants. The Hebrew *khaf* (soft "k") is rendered with *kh*, the hard *kaf* as *k*. The guttural Hebrew *ḥet (chet)* is rendered as *ch* except in common English spellings of names and terms such as Rav Hisda (not Rav Chisda). No distinction is made in transliteration of long and short vowels.

# PART I | The Ancient Jewish World
## *Holy War in Practice*

# CHAPTER 1 | Holy War in the Bible

The Lord is a Man of War

EXODUS 15:3

The hebrew bible is full of stories, references, and commands through which God sanctions mass violence against the enemies of Israel.[1] Heroes such as Joshua, Gideon, Saul, David, and even Moses lead Israel into wars that devastate Israel's enemies in response to God's command. The People of Israel are sometimes referred to as "armies of God" (Ex. 7:4, 12:41) and Israelite warriors as "armies of the living God" (1 Sam. 17:26). God gives advice to the warriors and provides strategy in some cases.[2] In others, God commands genocide against Israel's adversaries.[3] In still others, God even engages in the fray himself.[4] This is classic "holy war"—that is, war that is holy because it is sanctioned or even commanded by God.

According to biblical historiography, Israel's holy wars were successful when the people obeyed their God. They fell short when the people failed to heed the divine command. This can be expressed in the simple equation of obedience = success/disobedience = failure. We thus observe in the Book of Numbers 14:39–45 (retold in Deuteronomy 1:42–44) how

---

Parts of this chapter first appeared in my article "Conceptions of Holy War in Biblical and Qur'anic Tradition," *The Journal of Religious Ethics* 24 (1996), 801–824.

[1] The traditional Jewish term, "Israel," is a shortened form of "the People of Israel" (`am yisra'el`), not a reference to a modern nation-state. The actual name of the modern Jewish state is *Medinat Yisra'el*, "the State of [the People of] Israel." In this book I use the traditional vocabulary of "Israel" to refer to the Jewish people from the biblical to the modern periods.

[2] Yigal Levin, "The wars of Joshua: Weaning away from the divine," in Yigal Levin and Amnon Shapira, *War and Peace in Jewish Tradition* (London: Routledge, 2012), 37–50.

[3] Deut. 3:6, 7:2, 20:17, Josh. 6:17, 10:28–40.

[4] Ex. 15:3; Deut. 1:30; Josh. 1:5, 28:41; Isaiah 42:13; Ezek. 38–39, Psalm 24:8, etc..

Israel failed in its first collective attempt to fight its mortal enemies, the Canaanites and Amalekites, at Hormah, because the people transgressed the divine command. All subsequent failures and defeats, as well as victories, were understood in biblical depictions as divinely determined, including the destruction of the Jerusalem Temple in 586 B.C.E. and the associated massacres and population transfers by the Babylonian armies.[5]

In the overarching worldview of the Hebrew Bible, the course of history is determined by the divine will. God even directs the Babylonian Empire to destroy the kingdom of Judah. But God then commands the Persian King Cyrus to rebuild the Jerusalem Temple and bring the Judeans back from Babylonian captivity.[6]

Some of Israel's wars are successfully prosecuted by Israelite leaders with no reference to God. One such war, which will be of interest to us later, was David's war against the Arameans that resulted in the conquest and subsequent vassalage of a region outside the borders of the Land of Israel called Aram Zobah.[7] In light of such cases, it is evident that not all wars depicted in the Bible are explicitly commanded or forbidden by God. Some simply "happen," prosecuted without direct reference to any divine command.

Overwhelmingly, however, Israelite wars in the Hebrew Bible, like all human history, are understood within the context of divine authority. Yet no consistently recurring term can be found there to distinguish between divinely authorized fighting—what we identify here as holy war—and fighting that is independent of divine concern. The latter category might be called mundane or discretionary wars that seem to occur without reference to any divine command or caution. The term "wars of God" does occur occasionally, but it is rare (Numbers 21:14, 1 Sam.18:17, 25:28) and is remarkable only for its absence from nearly all the numerous references in the Bible to divinely authorized warring.

Most Israelite wars are fought by God or with God and, indirectly, for God. References to these many wars may be found from Exodus to the latest books of the Hebrew canon. Whether the biblical war texts represent an actual accounting of these wars or are merely memories or even fantasies generations later, most Israelite wars are understood by scripture to be phenomena that transcend the simple contest of human combatants for status, power, material wealth, or any kind of achievement of mundane goals.

War as depicted in the Bible has been a popular topic of study ever since Julius Wellhausen pointed out its overwhelming significance in his

---

[5] These are described in 2 Kings 24:1–4; Jeremiah 36:27–31, 38:2–3, 39:15–17; 2 Chron. 36:11–21.
[6] Described in Isaiah 44:26–45:6; Ezra 1:1–8; 2 Chron. 36:22–23.
[7] 2 Sam. 10.

*Prolegomena to the History of Ancient Israel* in 1885.[8] Various approaches and conclusions have been suggested, from Friedrich Schwally's coining of the term "holy war" (*heilige Krieg*) in his monograph of that name in 1901 to Rudolf Smend's "Yahweh war" more than half a century later.[9] Publication continues apace on the subject of war in the Bible to this day and, as one can imagine, interest in the topic is motivated by religious and political inclination, as well as scholarly goals.[10]

Much of the scholarly discussion centers on the evolution of the notion of holy war in ancient Israel because of the very long and complicated textual tradition of the Hebrew Bible. Questions are posed such as: When and under what circumstances did the concept first develop in ancient Israel, and as a result of what historical, political, and sociological stimuli did it mature into its latest expressions? Much of the argument regarding these questions rests upon the dating of biblical texts, the reconstruction of historical events, cultic practices and ancient theological concepts, and the discovery of extrabiblical ancient Near Eastern texts containing literary and conceptual parallels.

Because of the variety of scholarly approaches, the acknowledged uncertainty regarding the dating, arrangement, and structure of biblical texts, and the differences in interpretation of the meaning and function of ancient Israelite cultic practice, agreement regarding the question of holy war in ancient Israel remains elusive. Real consensus may be found only in the certainty that the concept of holy war developed and changed as the people of Israel evolved from patriarchal to tribal to national organization.

---

[8] Originally published in German in 1883 as *Geschichte Israels*, and then as *Prolegomena zur Geschichte Israels* (1883), translated into English by J. Sutherland Black and Allan Menzies as *Prolegomena to the History of Ancient Israel* (Edinburgh: Adam and Charles Black, 1885, repr. New York: Meridian Books, 1957).

[9] Friedrich Schwally, *Der Heilige Krieg in alten Israel* (Leipzig: Dietrich Stolz, 1901); Rudolf Smend (*Yahweh War and Tribal Confederacy: Reflections upon Israel's Earliest History* (the first German edition appeared in 1963) 2nd ed. Trans. M. G. Rogers [Nashville: Abingdon, 1970]). The most important approaches to the topic have been developed by Schwally, Gerhard von Rad (*Holy War in Ancient Israel*, orig. *Der Heilige Krieg im alten Israel* [Göttingen, 1951] trans. Marva Dawn [Grand Rapids: Eerdmans, 1991]) and Smend. See also, Susan Niditch, *War in the Hebrew Bible: A Study in the Ethics of Violence* (NY: Oxford, 1993). For a good accounting of the major studies of biblical war since Wellhausen, see Niditch, 3–27 and Ben Ollenburger's introduction with Judith Sanderson's representative bibliography in the Eerdmans reprint of von Rad, *Holy War in Ancient Israel*, (Grand Rapids, 1991).

[10] Scholars treat the subject in accordance with their interest in theology, law, or the history of religion, while religiously or politically motivated writers also write on the topic. Some examples of the latter categories include Lois Barrett, *The Way God Fights: War and Peace in the Old Testament*. Peace and Justice 1 (Scottdale, PA: Herald, 1987); Peter Craigie, *The Problem of War in the Old Testament* (Grand Rapids, MI: William B. Eerdmans, 1978); and Karen Armstrong, *Holy War: The Crusades and Their Impact on Today's World* (New York: Doubleday, 1988).

According to the broad outline of this consensus, Israel's God, like the deities of other peoples in the ancient Near East, fought on behalf of his people.[11] The biblical concepts of holy war evolved out of the earlier notion of a tribal god associated with one tribe or people and warring on behalf of its human followers against the peoples and gods of foreign tribes. In the ancient Near East, the gods of all the tribal nations fought with or on behalf of the groups they represented. The notion of God's wars for Israel therefore developed in parallel with the evolution of Israel's theology and the evolution of Israel's self-concept of a "folk" or nation that was unified out of a loose grouping of ethnically similar, migratory tribes after they gained control of their own land.

God's wars on behalf of Israel, or Israel's wars in which God is depicted as fighting or determining the outcome, tend to be associated in the Bible with protection of the national unit or the acquisition and sanctification of its divinely given territorial holdings. The array of biblical holy wars begins, therefore, with the Exodus from Egypt and destruction of Israel's first national enemy, the Egyptians. Holy war would then appear to end with the defeat of those enemies of Israel that tried to prevent the nation from realizing its divinely ordained corporate goals of consolidation and settlement, some time around the turn of the first millennium, B.C.E.

But as the history of Israel became mythologized in the biblical record, virtually all wars that profoundly affected that history were understood to have been ordained or determined by God. As previously noted, these include wars destructive to Israel, such as the catastrophic destruction of the kingdom of Judah by the Babylonians in 586 B.C.E. Lest anyone get the idea that Marduk, the god of Babylon, defeated the God of Israel, even that catastrophe came to be understood as divinely authorized on account of Israel's sins by virtue of the fact that God, as the one great God of the entire world, ordained the outcome. Not exactly a category of war, the Babylonian debacle is seen as an act of divine punishment realized through war, although punishment could also be administered through plague, drought, lack of fertility, or other "acts of God."

---

[11] For tribal or national gods in the ancient East, see Jeremiah 2:11. See also, Johannes Pedersen, *Israel: Its Life and Culture* III–IV. London: Cumberlege: Oxford University Press, 1940 (translated and reprinted from the Danish edition of 1934), 18; William Foxwell Albright, *Yahweh and the Gods of Canaan* (Garden City, NY: Doubleday, 1968); Moshe Weinfeld, "Divine Intervention in War in Ancient Israel and in the Ancient Near East," in *History, Historiography and Interpretation: Studies in Biblical and Cuneiform Literatures*, ed. Moshe Weinfeld and Hayim Tadmor. Jerusalem: Magnes, 1983, 121–147; Gwilyn H. Jones, "The Concept of Holy War." In *The World of Ancient Israel: Sociological, Anthropological and Political Perspectives*, ed. R. E. Clements. Cambridge: Cambridge University, 1989, 299–302.

Most studies of war in the Bible assume a linear evolutionary progression through the various stages of biblical history. They presume a unity of belief and worldview within the Israelite polity as a whole at any one time. These two assumptions have led many scholars to the pursuit of an overarching theory of biblical war. It appears at least as likely, however, as Susan Niditch points out in her book, *War in the Hebrew Bible*,[12] that the concept evolved not only chronologically but also geographically, demographically, and/or politically. The variety of depictions of holy war in the Bible attests to its complexity. A search for a single overarching solution to the problem of biblical holy war would appear, therefore, to be futile.

Nevertheless, an accurate though less universal understanding of the subject may be gained if study is carefully restricted to specific contexts. Certain passages, while not representing all of the varied depictions found in scripture, nevertheless depict points of view that were prominent or dominant in certain places during specific periods. The notions portrayed in these texts provide an intelligible basis for raising questions about the meaning and function of holy war as found in general within scripture.

Notwithstanding the many and varied biblical portrayals of direct divine involvement in Israel's wars and the likelihood that other expressions also represent a consensus of opinion at particular times, most scholars agree that the book of Deuteronomy represents the most fully developed and theologically "canonized" expression of holy war in ancient Israel.[13] Deuteronomy functions as a kind of internal biblical exegesis providing explanations or reformulating laws, customs, and concepts known from older biblical texts.[14] War is one important item among the many that it treats. Whether scholars consider the deuteronomic expression of holy war to be a late reinterpretation of earlier historical events[15] or the record of an early concept evolving either independently within Israel[16] or in parallel

---

[12] New York: Oxford University Press, 1993.

[13] The idealized expression of holy war in the later Prophetic books tends to be seen more as a literary phenomenon than a cultural or religious construct informing policy decisions (see Von Rad 1991, 74–114; Lind 1980, 132–144; Niditch, 48–49, 66–68).

[14] Ya'ir Zakovitch, *Introduction to Internal Biblical Commentary* (Hebrew). Even-Yehuda, Israel 1992, Michael Fishbane, *Biblical Interpretation in Ancient Israel*. Oxford: Clarendon. 1985, 164, 201–202, 206–208.

[15] Schwally 1901, Pedersen 1940, von Rad 1991, Patrick Miller, Jr., *The Divine Warrior in Early Israel. Harvard Semitic Monographs* no. 5 (Cambridge, MA: Harvard University Press, 1971).

[16] Smend 1970, Stolz 1972, Lind 1980.

with other ancient Near Eastern peoples,[17] a coherent and authoritative formulation may be found there.[18]

The deuteronomic depiction of holy war is the most systematic and comprehensive in the Hebrew Bible. It therefore has the greatest likelihood of representing a consensus at any period—in the case of Deuteronomy, late in the seventh century B.C.E.—despite the probability that because of its formulation long after the consolidation of the nation, fighting based on its specific formulation may never have taken place.[19] Deuteronomy therefore cannot be relied upon as an actual case study of contemporary legislation on war because as a reading back into history, it was likely to have served more as a guide to "what should have been" than as a guide to "what should be." It nevertheless organized and reworked earlier concepts and ideas in a systematic fashion in order to provide a conceptual model from which later policies may be and have been drawn. And in fact, as will be examined in some detail in Part II, the rabbis of the Talmud and throughout the medieval period construct their views on divinely sanctioned war out of the famous "rules of engagement" found in Deuteronomy chapter 20.

The classic "holy war" texts of Deuteronomy mention two major aims, which serve also as justifications for the wars of Israel. The first is possession of the land promised by God to Israel (Deut.1:6–8; 2:25–37; 3:1–22; 6:10–12; 7:1; 9:1–3; 11:23–25; 20:1–18; 29:6–8; 31:3–6). God promised lands to Israel, but not all lands. Deuteronomy also notes that certain adjacent lands were specifically forbidden to Israel because these lands had already been given by God to other peoples (2:4–5, 18–23). The second aim is to make sure that Israel, the inheritors of the land, will remain true to God. Israel's loyalty can be proven only by ensuring that the national patrimony remain free of idolatry—which means that the land remain free also of those *peoples* practicing idolatry (7:1–5, 16–26; 12:1–3; 12:29–13:1; 13:2–19; 16:21–22; 17:2–7; 18:9–14). Deuteronomy calls quite explicitly and repeatedly for the destruction of both the idolatrous practices throughout the sacred land and those people who practice them. There are mentioned, however, certain national or ethnic groups that are more acceptable than others and with whom Israelites may intermarry, although these nations are not permitted a corporate existence within the borders of the Land of Israel (23:8–9).

---

[17] Manfred Weippert, " 'Heiliger Krieg' in Israel und Assyrien: Kritische Anmerkungen zu Gerhard von Rads Konzept des 'Heiligen Krieges im alten Israel'," *ZAW* (*Zeitschrift fur die altestamentiche Wissenschaft*) 82 (1972):460–493.

[18] Jones 1989, 314; Lind 1980, 24–32.

[19] Michael Walzer, "The Idea of Holy War in Ancient Israel." *Journal of Religious Ethics* 22.2 (1992), 215–227. The division of Deuteronomy into parts which can be identified as "original" Deuteronomy and "late Deuteronomic historian" remains unresolved, but scholarly consensus has it that the final form of the book was redacted in the late 7th to mid-sixth century B.C.E.

Lurking behind the destruction of idolaters within the land is the warning that despite the fact that God has chosen Israel above all other nations (Deut.7:6), even God's own chosen people will be destroyed if they forsake their God and practice the abominations of the idolaters (7:1–4, 9–11; 8:19–20; 11:16–17; 11:26–28; 28:1–68; 29:15–27; 30:17–18). Israel will succeed in possessing and keeping its land only if it obeys God's will (11:22–25; 11:26–28).

Deuteronomy thus links other biblical expressions of divinely authorized war in Exodus, Joshua, Judges, Samuel, and Kings to the sacred history of Israel and its destiny to possess the Land of Israel. The command of possession, in turn, is intimately linked to Israel's special relationship with God. The subsequent command to destroy all traces of idolatry within the consecrated land is a direct result of that relationship and is a deuteronomic reformulation of the older concept of the tribal god fighting opposing peoples and their gods.

It must not be overlooked, however, that destruction of the idolatrous peoples could be effected only within the consecrated land. No deuteronomic command extended this ruling beyond the boundaries of the Land of Israel, and Deuteronomy 20:10–18 specifically limits the wholesale destruction, known in the Bible as *cherem*, to within those borders (10:16).[20] Moreover, the capital prohibition against idolatry in the sacred land is directed as harshly against Israel as it is against the Canaanite nations. Idolatry is directly related to loyalty to God. Individual Israelites or even entire Israelite cities must be destroyed if they are found to be involved in idolatrous practices (13:2–9).

In contrast to Exodus 14–15 and some of the earlier depictions of war in the books of Joshua and Judges, the late, distilled view of holy war depicted in Deuteronomy virtually eliminates the physical defense of the still-forming polity of Israel from outside attack as a justification for war. By the period of Deuteronomy, the Israelite people had become a consolidated national-religious entity enjoying a long history of settlement in its land. The major issue that confronted Israel at this time was less from outside than from inside. It was the danger of religious syncretism and political strife, which threatened to destroy the unity of the nation as it had evolved into its monarchic form within the Land of Israel. The text of Deuteronomy continues to presume and indeed stresses the divinely ordained possession of the land. The subtext, however, is the unity of the people demonstrated by obedience to God through the destruction of

---

[20] For a summary of the scholarly views on the *cherem*, see Philip Stern, *The Biblical Herem: A Window on Israel's Religious Experience* (Atlanta: Scholars Press, 1991).

the syncretistic and idolatrous practices that continued to thrive within the consecrated land, even long after the successful establishment of Israelite political authority there (See 2 Kings 23:4–24).

The allure of idolatry and the attraction of non-Israelite religious practice represented a powerful threat to the Israelite system and subsequent unity of the people. The nation, which had already been divided into two separate and fractious political entities, was in a position of cultural and military decline. A major message embedded within the deuteronomic expressions of holy war, therefore, is that if the nation of Israel will obey God's religio-national dictates, then God will continue to fight on behalf of the nation and ensure its viable existence in its own land (4:1–40; 6:1–25; 7:1–8:20, etc.). The land given to Israel is therefore secure only as long as it is free from foreign or syncretistic religious practices and its people obey the divine will.

According to the deuteronomic view, and consistent with what is known of late monarchic history and ancient Near Eastern religious perspectives in general, God's dictates regarding war on behalf of Israel could hardly represent a universalist stance. The purpose of war in Israel never included bringing "right religion" to other nations. On the contrary, Israel's wars served to isolate Israel from the religions of the neighboring peoples and their attractive cultic practices.

Holy war as expressed in Deuteronomy, therefore, was not to "propagate the faith," the commonly assumed purpose of holy war envisioned by the West. It was not by any means outward-looking and had no interest in seeking converts, either through physical force or through persuasion. It served, rather, as a conservative means to unify and strengthen a minority people and its religio-political system through withdrawal and isolation from other peoples. That could take place only within defined borders of a particular geographic locale consecrated to the survival of its own religio-cultural expression.[21]

It is possible that biblical depictions of the battles of Israel against the Canaanites, Philistines, Assyrians, and even Babylonians were a later reading back into ancient history. Given the social structure and political history of the region, however, it is clear that fighting couched in the language of holy war certainly did occur, and occasional parallel references to some such wars can be found in the Bible and extrabiblical literatures.

---

[21] The one exception to this is the case of the Amalekites, who were condemned to destruction for their insidious acts against the Israelites as they were trying to escape the wrath of the Egyptian Pharaoh by fleeing into the desert (Exodus 17:8–16; Numbers 14:43–45; Deuteronomy 25:17–19). The case of the Amalekites may reflect an earlier, dialectical concept of holy war than that set out in Deuteronomy (Jones 1989, 307).

A classic case of war described from both sides of the battle is that between the Israelite King Jehoram (or Omri) and the Moabite King Mesha, described both in 2 Kings chapter 3 and a stone plaque written in Moabite called the Mesha Stele.[22] But while wars were certainly fought by the Israelites, it is not certain how they were viewed by those who actually engaged in the battles. We cannot know, for example, whether they were necessarily considered "holy wars" authorized by God at the time that they were fought, or even exactly what that might have meant in various biblical contexts. This is a question of compelling interest but need not detain us here.

What is of critical importance, for the purpose of this study, is the vision of these wars centuries later. Whether or not the Israelites who battled against the various peoples depicted in the Hebrew Bible thought that they were fighting holy wars, their Jewish descendants certainly believed that they had been. As a record of Israel's sacred national history, the Bible depicts paradigms of relationships, behaviors, and expectations representing truth and transcendence that, because they are embedded in scripture, remain relevant one way or another for all times and all places. According to the Hebrew Bible, divinely authorized and guided warring, when prosecuted with determination to follow God's will and obey the divine command, resulted in overwhelming success against the enemy. For the believer living generations after the battles depicted in the Bible, there is no reason to doubt the veracity of the message that such war-making can bring the same kind of success in one's own day. Such was the conclusion of a group of zealous Judean traditionalists during the Hellenistic period in their battle against an enemy that they perceived as trying to undermine and destroy their religious faith and observance.

---

[22] Translated in James B. Pritchard, *The Ancient Near East: An Anthology of Texts and Pictures, Vol. I* (Princeton: Princeton University Press, 1958), 209–210.

# CHAPTER 2 | Jewish Holy War in Practice
## *Early Success*

You delivered the mighty into the hands of the weak, the many into
the hands of the few, the wicked into the hands of the righteous, the
unclean into the hands of the pure, and the arrogant into the hands of
those who were devoted to Your Torah

—AL HANISIM PRAYER

## The Maccabean Revolt and the Festival of Hanukkah

How Jewish communities celebrate the festival of Hanukkah is an indica-
tion of their particular collective worldview about political and military
activism. Hanukkah, meaning "dedication," refers to the Jewish rededication of the Jerusalem Temple after its ritual defilement by the Seleucid
Greeks. It is a holiday that originated in second century B.C.E. Judea and
has taken on—and discarded—various levels of meaning through the
ages.[1] Hanukkah is not a "biblical holiday" because no verse from any
part of the canonical Hebrew Bible refers to it; this is despite the generally
accepted dating of chapters 7–12 of the biblical *Book of Daniel* to the reign
of the Seleucid King Antiochus IV, the self-same evil king of the Hanukkah
story. But *Daniel* is essentially a pietistic work, has no references to war,
and is unsupportive of activist movements. At any rate it does not refer
directly to contemporary events or personages. Reference to the festival of
Hanukkah cannot be found in the canonical Hebrew Bible, but only in the

---

[1] For a charming study of this topic with particular emphasis on how various contemporary and
historical Jewish communities find meaning in the festival, see Noam Zion and Barbara Spectre,
*A Different Light* (NY and Jerusalem, Shalom Hartman Institute, 2000).

apocryphal books of *First* and *Second Maccabees*, original Jewish compositions excluded from the canon that was finally closed by Jewish leaders shortly after the destruction of the Jerusalem Temple by the Romans in 70 C.E.[2] The reasons for the exclusion of Hanukkah from the Hebrew Bible need not concern us, although it may be observed that aspects of these works had to have been contrary to the views of those determining the canon.[3] Nevertheless, they express ideas that were popular enough to warrant their publication and dissemination among Jews for quite some time. Their views therefore reflect a significant Jewish contemporary viewpoint, countered later by rabbis who wished to establish a different paradigm, but nonetheless of great importance for the history of war in Judaism.

The Jewish leaders who canonized the Bible excluded the Books of Maccabees, but they did not forbid the celebration of the festival first described in them. Instructions for the celebration may be found in rabbinic literature (Babylonian Talmud *Shabbat* 21b), and it is mentioned also in the New Testament (John 10:22). The rabbinic concept of the festival and the miracle associated with it, however, paint a very different picture than that portrayed in the Books of Maccabees that were written much closer to the actual historical occasion. In short, while the Maccabean texts celebrate the divinely wrought military victory of the small Judean forces over the vastly more powerful pagan enemy, the rabbinic material ignores the military victory and celebrates, in its place, a different miracle. This is the "miracle of the oil," which will be examined shortly.

The successful war against the Greeks was prosecuted by Jewish warriors who were known as Maccabees or Hasmoneans.[4] "Maccabean"

---

[2] *I Maccabees* is placed either during the early administration of John Hyrcanus (soon after 135 B.C.E.) or during the time of Alexander Jannaeus (after 103 B.C.E.), while *II Maccabees* appeared later, perhaps in the mid-70s, B.C.E.

[3] One of the significant problems with *I Macc.* is the complete lack of mention of resurrection despite the multiple occasions for such mention in the narrative. Another is the author's claim that God had chosen Mattathias's line to be both priests and kings, contrary to the traditional Davidic line of non-priestly kings. The later problematic history of the Hasmonean kingdom would bear out the error of the author's view and would easily render the book unacceptable to the Jewish canon, though it may have remained beloved by many for the wonderful exploits depicted in it. *II Maccabees'* candidacy for the canon is less problematic conceptually, since it does include resurrection (7:9, 13–14), and, although adoring of Judas, does not extol the Hasmonean family as does *I Macc.* Its appearance in Greek, however, would render it invalid for the rabbinic canon. See Gedalia Alon, "Did the Jewish Nation and Its Sages Cause the Hasmoneans to be Forgotten?" in Gedalia Alon, *Studies in Jewish History* (Hebrew), Vol. 1 (1967), 15–25, translated in Alon, *Jews, Judaism and the Classical World* (Jerusalem: Magnes Press, 1977), 1–17 (Cf. Abraham Ya`ari, "Has the Heroism of the Hasmoneans been Truly Forgotten?" (Hebrew) *Machanayim* 63 (1962), 138–149).

[4] For a recent military history of the wars, see Bezalel Bar Kokhva, *Judas Maccabaeus: The Jewish Struggle Against the Seleucids* (Cambridge, England: Cambridge University Press, 2002).

and "Hasmonean" are often interchanged terms today, though Maccabean refers most often to the warrior sons of one Mattathias who became an early figurehead of the revolt leading to a large mobilization in 167–166 B.C.E., and Hasmonean to the ruling dynasty deriving from him. Both were an additional name (*cognomen*) added to a given name (*praenomen*) in order to better identify the individual, since only relatively few given names were used by Jews during the period. Judah "Maccabee" (or Judas Maccabeus) was applied to the Judas who became the military leader of the revolt in order to distinguish him from the many other Judases of the day. "Mattathias had five sons: John, nicknamed Gaddi; Simon, called Thassi; Judas, called Maccabaeus; Eleazar, called Auaran; and Jonathan, called Apphus" (*I Macc.* 2:2–5). Perhaps because of Judas' major role, his *cognomen* was extended. "Hasmonean" does not appear in *I Maccabees*, but only in later sources.[5]

First Maccabees chronicles the rise of the Hasmonean dynasty from its first hero Mattathias, to John Hyrcanus (died 104 B.C.E.). Written originally in Hebrew but preserved only in Greek, the anonymous work notes how God favored the zealotry of the Jewish military uprising against the pagan Hellenists based in what is today Syria (the Seleucids). It suggests throughout that God assured the success of the war because of the piety and heroic fortitude of the Hasmonean family. Despite many setbacks, including the deaths of the sons of Mattathias, their piety, bravery and perseverance always earned them ultimate collective success. They regularly prayed to God for help before going into battle, equating their fighting with the battles of biblical heroes (3:46–57, 4:8–11, 30–34, 7:40–42). Attempts by other Judeans to lead battles independently of the Hasmoneans resulted only in disaster (5:55–62), but God's favor for the Hasmoneans would result in their ultimate victory. I Maccabees rarely includes outright divine miracles in the sense of direct supernatural intervention (a notable exception is a reference in Judah's prayer found in I Macc.7:41, where he calls on God to crush the enemy like God's angel struck down 185,000 blaspheming followers of a certain king), nor does it claim that its contemporary history was a fulfillment of prophesy. On the other hand, it describes events in a way that would suggest the likelihood of divine intervention, such as the agonizing death of the Hellenizing Jewish priest, Alcimus, after he had begun his blasphemous demolition of part of the sacred Temple (9:54–56). The hero Judah is depicted as relying entirely on God's deliverance in his

[5] Jonathan A. Goldstein, *I Maccabees*; Anchor Bible series (Garden City, NY: Doubleday, 1976), 17–19, 229–231.

battles against overwhelming odds, exclaiming, for example, "It is easy for many to be delivered into the hands of few. Heaven sees no difference in gaining victory through many or through a few, because victory in war does not lie in the weight of numbers, but rather strength comes from Heaven." (*I Macc.* 3:18–19).

Like the book of Joshua, I Maccabees exudes great confidence in divine providence. It sometimes parallels biblical renderings of divinely sanctioned, inspired, and assisted war. One unmistakably intended correspondence is the I Maccabees (3:55–56) parallel with the rules of war outlined in Deuteronomy 20, referring specifically to the deferments that could be taken in order to remove oneself from fighting.[6] On the other hand, unlike the purpose of war for the Land as expressed by biblical (First Temple Period) sources, the purpose for war repeatedly articulated in I Maccabees was for the sake of the people, the city of Jerusalem, the Temple and the Torah.[7] I Maccabees expresses the conviction that divine favor would assure ultimate military success for the Hasmoneans. The narrative stresses that the people of Judea would clearly benefit from Hasmonean leadership, and indeed, the book is considered a source of authority and validation for the rule of the Hasmonean dynasty.[8] Its claim of divine support for the war of course provides authority for the rule of the Hasmonean House itself, despite its usurpation of the previous priestly family, its lack of claim to Davidic descent, and its (later?) unpopular combination of religious priesthood with the political authority of kingship.[9]

I Maccabees is a complex document that cannot occupy us further here, aside from examining its account of the events of the awesome day of rededication. In preparation for the day the priests built a new and undefiled altar, repaired the sanctuary, purified the despoiled interior, made new and unblemished equipment required for the sacrifices, burned incense and set

---

[6] It is interesting to note that while the wars of the Maccabees are depicted as divinely authorized and under the category later to be articulated by the rabbis as "commanded war" (*milchemet mitzvah*), the deferments established in Deut. 20 are considered actionable only in the case of "discretionary war" (*milchemet reshut*). More will be said about this below, but this contradiction was troublesome to some of the medieval rabbis, some of whom went to great lengths to demonstrate that the Maccabean wars had to have been discretionary if they allowed deferments (Yehuda Gershuni, "Discretionary War and commanded war" [Hebrew], *Shanah Beshanah* 1971, p. 154). Others considered the Maccabean wars to have clearly been commanded wars (that is, "holy war"), and made efforts to account for the issue of deferments in such a war (Rabbi Shlomo Goren, "Army and War in the Light of the Halakhah," [Hebrew] *Mahanayim* 121 [1969], p. 12).

[7] 1Macc. 2:27, 49; 3:43, 59; 13:3; 14:29; 15:17 (Weinfeld, 1993, 204–205).

[8] Weitzman, 40; Goldstein, *I Maccabees*, 62–89.

[9] On the issue of the priesthood during this period, see Elias Bickerman, *The Jews in the Greek Age* (Cambridge, MA: Harvard University Press, 1988), 140–147.

the sacred loaves on the table, hung undefiled curtains and lit the lights of a multi-flamed candelabrum "so that they illumined the nave" (4:47–51). The unblemished priests who were "lovers of Torah"

> rose early on the morning of the twenty-fifth day of the ninth month, that is the month of Kislev, in the year 148 (of the Seleucid calendar, correspond-ing to December 15, 164 B.C.E.), and they brought a sacrifice according to the Torah upon the new altar of burnt offerings which they had built. At the very time of year and on the very day on which the gentiles had profaned the altar, it was dedicated to the sound of singing and harps and lyres and cymbals. The entire people prostrated themselves and bowed and gave thanks to Heaven Who had brought them victory. They celebrated the dedication of the altar for eight days, joyfully bringing burnt offerings and sacrificing peace offerings and thanks offerings. They decorated the front of the nave with golden cornices and bosses and restored the gates and the chambers and fitted them with doors. The people were overjoyed as the shame inflicted by the gentiles was removed. Judas and his brothers and the entire assembly of Israel decreed that the days of the dedication of the altar should be observed at their time of year annually for eight days, begin-ning with the twenty-fifth of the month of Kislev, with joy and gladness. At that time they also fortified Mount Zion, surrounding it with a high wall and strong towers to prevent the gentiles from ever coming and trampling it as they had done before. —[I Maccabees 4:52–60][10]

This depiction, probably the earliest extant and closest to the events themselves, describes the rededication as a day of sacrifice and prayer with singing accompanied by instrumental music, and mass prostration of those in attendance in "thanks to Heaven Who had brought them victory." We do not know the identity of the author of I Maccabees, nor do we know whether the purpose of his writing may have distorted the accuracy of his description. On the other hand, it is not really important for us whether the account is an accurate record of what really happened. Our purpose is not to reconstruct the actual event, but to understand the significance of the event as depicted by the sources. I Maccabees portrays the day as one of great joy, celebration, and thanks to God for the Jewish victory over gen-tile defilement and the attempt to end the autonomous Jewish sacrificial system. I Maccabees is concerned with issues of purity and reestablishing

---

[10] Translation by Jonathan A. Goldstein, *I Maccabees*, Anchor Bible, NY: Doubleday, 1976, 272–273.

the proper system of worship "according to the Torah." It is a statement of obedience to the divine will as established by scripture. And this obedience and piety was rewarded with a miraculous, divinely wrought victory over the overwhelming power of the enemy. Why an annual eight-day celebration was decreed by the Hasmonean house is never explained by the text (though explanations may be found or alluded to in II Maccabees and later rabbinic literature).[11] In fact, however, such an unprecedented act of commemoration from the Jewish perspective was common among the Greeks, who memorialized important historical occurrences by establishing annual commemorative events.[12]

The depiction of the Temple's rededication is sandwiched between many and far longer accounts of the Maccabees' battles against the Seleucid Greeks and descriptions of internal religious, social and political issues within the Judean community. It is part of a much longer depiction of a forty-year period from the accession of the enemy Antiochus Epiphanes in 175 B.C.E. to the death of Simon in 135–134, the last of the five Maccabee brothers and the first Hasmonean to establish the full independence of Judea. The day of rededication is an important part of this longer narrative, but is not of prime importance. The larger message of I Maccabees is the piety and unwavering bravery of the Hasmonean House in resisting the Greeks and their traitorous Jewish supporters, thereby proving their righteous position as leaders of the Judean community.

II Maccabees is an entirely different work, written originally in Greek and in the style of Greek historians. It claims to be an abridgement of a much larger work of Jason of Cyrene, an otherwise unknown author (II Maccabees 2:19–32). Unlike the sober prose with occasional poetic inserts of I Maccabees, II Maccabees is highly emotional throughout, and despite its obvious Greek cultural setting, it expresses a strong condemnation of Hellenization, including the tendency of the pre-Hasmonean Judean priesthood to serve the alien Greek powers. The Greeks are represented as barbarians bent on plunder and pillage, while the Jews are urged to fulfill God's commandments and thus avoid divine punishment. Powerful stories of Jewish suffering and martyrdom are found in the account of Eleazer (6:18–31) who suffered terrible tortures rather than eat forbidden food, the

---

[11] *II Maccabees* 5:27, 6:6 and 10:6, Midrash Pesikta Rabbati, piska 2 (in William Braude translation [2 Vols. New Haven: Yale, 1968]) 2:50–58.

[12] Van Henten, "II Maccabees as a History of Liberation," in *Jews and Gentiles in the Holy Land in the Days of the Second Temple, the Mishnah and the Talmud*, ed. Menachem Mor and Aharon Oppenheimer, Jack Pastor and Daniel Schwartz (Jerusalem: Yad Ben-Zvi, 2003), 79–82; idem, *The Maccabean Martyrs*, 296.

tale of the anonymous woman and her seven sons who suffered agonizing deaths for sanctification of the Divine Name (chapter 7), and the story of Razis, the Jewish official who killed himself rather than submit to the Seleucid general Nicanor by plunging a sword into his stomach, jumping off a balcony, and finally tearing out his own entrails (14:37–46). Their martyrdom has a measure of efficacy, for the acts of martyrdom are depicted as having a positive effect on the Hasmonean victories. Unlike I Maccabees, II Maccabees includes many miracles and repeatedly mentions its belief in resurrection.[13] Judas and his soldiers are portrayed as scrupulously observing the divine commandments and as praying for and receiving divine aid, which is repeatedly depicted as the cause of Judas's many victories. II Maccabees' depiction of the Temple rededication follows.

> [Judas] Maccabaeus and his men, with the Lord leading them, recovered the sanctuary and the city. They destroyed the illicit altars which the foreigners had built around the marketplace and also the illicit shrines. After purifying the temple, they made another altar. Using fire they got by igniting stones, for the first time in two years they offered sacrifices and incense and installed the lights and set out the showbread. That done, they prostrated themselves and prayed to the Lord that they never again would come to suffer such disasters. Rather, if they should ever sin, let them be chastised by the Lord himself, with clemency, and not delivered over to the hands of blasphemous and barbarous gentiles. On the very same date on which the temple was profaned by foreigners occurred the purification of the temple, on the twenty-fifth of the ninth month, that is, Kislev). Joyfully they held an eight-day celebration, after the pattern of Tabernacles, remembering how a short time before they spent the festival of wreathed wands, and branches bearing ripe fruit, and palm fronds, they offered songs of praise to Him Who had victoriously brought about the purification of His Place. By vote of the commonwealth they decreed a rule for the entire nation of the Jews to observe these days annually.[14] [10:1–8]

This depiction of the dedication feels farther removed from the event than does that of I Maccabees, though the large number of parallels has suggested to some scholars that they derive, at least in part, from a common source. God is mentioned as leading the Maccabean victory, but the immediacy of battle is not as keenly felt, nor is the depiction of the purification

---

[13] For a comparison of the two, see Goldstein, *I Maccabees*, 3–36.

[14] Translation by Jonathan A. Goldstein, *II Maccabees, Anchor Bible*, NY: Doubleday, 1989, 374.

as detailed. II Maccabees exhibits a concern for what will happen in the future when the people should sin, suggesting a consciousness of the declining position of the Hasmonean House as it, too, succumbed to some of the very sins of Hellenization that it fought to eradicate at the outset. It also explicitly and ritually relates the eight-day celebration of rededication to the eight-day celebration of Sukkoth (Tabernacles) with the holding of fruit and branches associated with prayers, something that is not articulated in the earlier account.[15] And finally, the statement that the celebration of the festival was decreed by a vote of the commonwealth seems odd for either a biblical or rabbinic text, although a parallel might be found in Hellenistic material treating community celebrations decreed by voting citizens of the *polis*. What is clearly evident from both representations, however, is the divine association with military victory. God leads the virtuous soldiers to victory, allowing them to recover and purify the Temple of God. Pious zealotry was rewarded with divinely-wrought military triumph, which in turn brought about the purification of God's Temple and, eventually, national independence. This was all possible because of the pious activism of the Jewish heroes.

The wars of the Maccabees took place from 168–160 B.C.E., but independence of the Jewish state was proclaimed only two decades later in 143/2. As depicted in I and II Maccabees, the Hasmoneans not only defended Judaism against the excesses of the Greek authorities, but also engaged in religious wars that find remarkable parallels in biblical depictions of the destruction of pagan cults. Judas burned down the temple of the Syrian goddess Atargatis (Ashtoret) in which his escaping enemy sought shelter, (I Macc. 5:44; II Macc. 12:26) and went out of his way to destroy the altars and graven images in the district of Ashdod (Azotus in I Macc. 5:68). During the war Jews not infrequently referred to God's promise of the Land, even before the reestablishment of Jewish authority.

But pious militancy was not the only position contained in the Books of Maccabees. Non-military tactics were employed by devout quietists who opposed the militant activism of the Maccabee family. The quietists are depicted in the sources as retreating to the desert to escape the evil decrees of Antiochus rather than fight against them (I Macc. 2:29–38, II Macc. 6:11). Unlike the militants who escaped to the mountains lightly

---

[15] *II Maccabees* describes an eight-day festival of dedication during Solomon's day and depicts it as properly following the earlier dedication of Moses (2:9–12; on the complexity and dispute over this passage, see Goldstein *II Macc.* 157–188).

packed and ready for action, these fled to the wilderness, burdened with their entire families and even cattle. They choose neither to desecrate the Sabbath nor to defend themselves against the Greek army detachment sent out to destroy them. And destroy them they did. I Maccabees depicts Mattathias drawing the conclusion from this that Jews must, contrary to contemporary practice, fight defensively on the Sabbath,[16] assuming that this group refused to fight precisely because of the Sabbath prohibition. That the group did not fight because of the Sabbath prohibition is not explicit in the narrative. Only in II Maccabees (6:11) does it suggest that they refrained from fighting for this reason, although the entire incident is mentioned there only in passing.

The account by Josephus, written more than two hundred years after the events, finds many parallels with both Books of Maccabees.[17] Like the Maccabean works, it was not included within the canon of Jewish sacred literature, and like Maccabees, it reflects an authentic current in Jewish thinking about war. Josephus defended the honor of the Hasmoneans and claimed to be a descendant of the Hasmonean house himself. He shows that he was proud of the martyrs who gave their lives for the honor of God and nation, and he believed in the value of martyrdom.[18] Although he himself gave up the life of a soldier during the Great Revolt against Rome in 66, he was no pious quietist. His mission included, rather, an attempt to influence his Greco-Roman audience with a positive depiction of Jewish history and achievements through his writing.

> And now that the generals of King Antiochus had been defeated so many times, Judas assembled the people and said that after the many victories which God had given them, they ought to go up to Jerusalem and purify the temple and offer the customary sacrifices. But when he came to Jerusalem with the entire multitude and found the temple desolate, the gates burned

---

[16] Fighting defensively on the Sabbath became codified in Maimonides' Law Code (*hilkhot shabbat* 2:23) and was considered obligatory after the destruction of the Jerusalem Temple. Not only was defensive war prosecuted on the Sabbath, but war initiated by Jews was permitted to be fought on the Sabbath as well according to the BT *Shabbat* 19a and *Tosefta `Eruvin* 4, 7 (Moshe Herr, "The Problem of War on the Sabbath in the Second Temple and the Talmudic Periods" (Hebrew), in *Tarbiz* 30 [1961], 242–256, 342–356). A large literature on war and war preparedness on the Sabbath has developed in halakhic journals since 1948.

[17] Ralph Marcus, *Jewish Antiquities* [Greek/English text], vol. 7 (London: William Henemann, LTD, 1943 and reprinted 1961), 163–169. On comparisons of Josephus with I Maccabees, see Louis Feldman, "Josephus' Portrayal of the Hasmoneans Compared with I Maccabees," in Fausto Parente and Joseph Sievers (eds.), *Josephus and the History of the Greco-Roman Period: Essays in Memory of Morton Smith* (Leiden: Brill, 1994), 41–68.

[18] Goldstein, *I Maccabees* 55–56; Feldman, "Josephus' Portrayal," 47.

down and plants growing up by themselves in the sanctuary because of the desolation, he began to lament with his men in dismay at the appearance of the temple. Then he selected some of his soldiers and commanded them to keep fighting the men who guarded the *Akra* until he himself should have sanctified the temple. And when he had carefully purified it, he brought in new vessels, such as a lamp stand, table and altar, which were made of gold, and hung curtains from the doors, and replaced the doors themselves; he also pulled down the altar, and built a new one of various stones which had not been hewn with iron. And on the twenty-fifth of the month Chasleu, which the Macedonians call Apellaios, they kindled the lights on the lamp stand and burned incense on the altar and set out the loaves on the table and offered whole burnt offerings upon the new altar. These things, as it chances, took place on the same day on which, three years before, their holy service had been transformed into an impure and profane form of worship. For the temple, after being made desolate by Antiochus, had remained so for three years; it was in the hundred and forty-fifth year that these things befell the temple, on the twenty-fifth of the month Apellaios, in the hundred and fifty-third Olympiad. And the temple was renovated on the same day, the twenty-fifth of the month Apellaios, in the hundred and forty-eighth year, in the hundred and fifty-fourth Olympiad. Now the desolation of the temple came about in accordance with the prophecy of Daniel, which had been made four hundred and eight years before; for he had revealed that the Macedonians would destroy it.

And so Judas together with his fellow-citizens celebrated the restoration of sacrifices in the temple for eight days, omitting no form of pleasure, but feasting them on costly and splendid sacrifices, and while honouring God with songs of praise and the playing of harps, at the same time delighted them. So much pleasure did they find in the renewal of their customs and in unexpectedly obtaining the right to have their own service after so long a time, that they made a law that their descendants should celebrate the restoration of the temple service for eight days. And from that time to the present we observe this festival, which we call the festival of Lights, giving this name to it, I think, from the fact that the right to worship appeared to us at a time when we hardly dared hope for it. Then Judas erected walls around the city, and having built high towers against the incursions of the enemy, he placed guards in them...

As in both previous works, Josephus demonstrates great concern for the repurification of the Temple and its appurtenances. All three sources note the serendipity of the date of the rededication as well, occurring as it did on the same date that the sanctuary had been defiled three years earlier.[19] This was taken as a sign of divine assistance with the victory, though Josephus, in opposition to the two Maccabees sources, tends to de-emphasize the role of God in his depiction.

In an interesting comment, Josephus notes that the name for the annual festival is "Festival of Lights," but his candidly uncertain attempt to explain this name fails to make any connection whatsoever with the kindling of lights in the refurbished Temple, despite the fact that he notes their kindling in verse 319. It is apparent that by the time of Josephus, the holiday is associated with light, perhaps because of its calendrical location at or near the winter solstice when pagan holidays associated with light took place. But the later, rabbinic explanation had not yet evolved to explain the popular association that is assumed today. Unlike II Maccabees, Josephus fails to mention any parallel with the fall holiday of Sukkoth (Tabernacles). Perhaps the association had fallen out of the popular understanding by his day, though some medieval rabbis explained the eight-day festival in a manner similar to that of II Maccabees.

Thus far we have examined Jewish depictions and explanations for the Hanukkah festival found in sources that were excluded from the rabbinic canon. Official rabbinic discourse on the festival is entirely different. The Mishnah, published around the year 200 C.E., for example, though containing material regarding Hanukkah and indeed referring to it by that name,[20] gives no account whatsoever of the purification and rededication of the Temple at Hanukkah, despite its great interest in Temple ritual.[21] It attests to the fact that Hanukkah was observed as a minor festival during the "tannaitic period," roughly the first and second centuries, C.E., but unlike all the earlier Jewish works that refer to Hanukkah, the Mishnah refrains from noting the heroism of the Jewish warriors or the power of the God of Israel to enable Jewish armies to be victorious over the pagan Greek foe. In fact, the Mishnah omits any explanation for the holiday whatsoever. This is certainly influenced by the close association between the festival and the Hasmonean family, which defied the tradition of exclusive Davidic rule adhered to by the rabbis by establishing a dynasty of kings outside the

---

[19] *II Maccabees* erroneously has two rather than three years separating the two events. The date of the rededication historically was probably not serendipitous at all, since Judah was in possession of the Temple from the early spring but did not rededicate it until the approximate time of the winter solstice (Goldstein *I Macc.* 273–280).

[20] Bikkurim 1:6, Rosh HaShanah 1:3, Ta'anit 2:10, Megilah 3:4, 6, Mo'ed Qatan 3:9, Baba Kama 6:6.

[21] Most of the Mishnah *Tahorot* is dedicated to purity and defilement in the context of the Temple service.

Davidic family. But it was likely to have been influenced also by discomfort with Hanukkah's militant origins and associations.

The only explanation for the holiday in the Jewish canon is the short but famous passage in the Babylonian Talmud that was codified sometime around the end of the sixth century but made up significantly of earlier material. The story is found in a passage called a *barayta* dated to sometime no later than the second century. A *barayta* is a tannaitic passage, meaning material that originated contemporary to the Mishnah but excluded from the final edition of that collection.[22]

> What is [the reason for] Hanukkah? As our rabbis taught, on the twenty-fifth of Kislev [begin] the eight days of Hanukkah, during which eulogies and fasting are not permitted, for when the Greeks entered the Temple they defiled all the oils that were in the Temple, and when the Hasmoneans prevailed and defeated them, they sought but found only one container of oil with the seal of the High Priest, containing only enough to light for one day. But a miracle occurred in which they lit [the lamp] from it[s oil] for eight days. The following year they established those [days] as a festival with songs of praise and thanksgiving. [BT Shabbat 21b].[23]

This single, codified rabbinic view of Hanukkah is radically different from the three earlier sources cited above. Reference is indeed made to the Hasmonean triumph over the Greeks, demonstrating that the rabbis did not intend (or were not able) to erase the memory of the Hasmoneans from Jewish history,[24] but no mention is made of any thanksgiving offering or prayers offered by the conquerors, no victory celebration. The entire passage focuses on the need to rekindle the Temple lights with undefiled oil and the potential crisis associated with the lack of proper oil for that purpose. The miracle in this passage lies entirely in the fact that one container of oil was sufficient to keep the Temple light ignited until properly prepared oil could be manufactured. This is the reason, according to the Talmud, for the eight-day festival of Hanukkah. Neither militant zealotry, fighting for religious freedom, nor any kind of heroism is even mentioned. The focus has shifted entirely to a kind of pious and obedient quietism that

---

[22] Although the Babylonian Talmud was not finally redacted until at least the sixth century, C.E., it is composed of earlier traditions. "Tannaitic" refers to material deriving from the tannaitic period of the 1st–2nd centuries.

[23] Nearly the identical text is found also in *Megillat Ta`anit* (Lichtenstein), ch. 9.

[24] Cf. Alon, "Did the Jewish People and Its Sages Cause the Hasmoneans to be Forgotten?" in Gedalia Alon, *Jews, Judaism and the Classical World* (Jerusalem: Magnes Press, 1977), 1–17.

ignores the most important issues around which are constructed the passages in the Books of Maccabees and Josephus.

In fact, Judah Maccabee, the greatest hero of the Maccabee family, is nowhere even mentioned in the Talmud. His person and significance were largely excluded from the rabbinic canon. It was only after the mid-tenth century with the composition of the popular *Sefer Josippon*, a work that relied on the works of Josephus and Maccabees, that Judah and his heroic activism were reintroduced to the rabbinic Jewish world.[25]

The biblical equation of obedience = success/disobedience = failure is maintained in the Hanukkah narratives, but the nature of the actions to be rewarded varied between the Hellenistic Jewish texts and the rabbinic texts. The foundational texts of rabbinic Judaism played down the militancy and glorious heroism that was so much a part of the Books of Maccabees' and Josephus' depictions of Hanukkah. Their interest, to use Jacob Neusner's terminology, was in sanctification rather than salvation.[26] As we shall observe below, the canonical rabbinic sources of Talmud and Midrash played down the option of militant activism that was thought by some to lead to salvation.

One important rabbinic liturgical text, however, relates to Hanukkah in a manner that would seem to contradict this tendency. This is the `Al hanisim ("On account of the Miracles") prayer recited in the Jewish prayer service (and grace after meals) during the Hanukkah period. The earliest extant version is found in the ninth century *Seder Rav Amram,* [27] which, although originally redacted around the middle of the ninth century, contains many later additions and adjustments.

On account of the miracles and on account of the mighty deeds and the victories and the wars,[28] redemption and deliverance that you wrought for our ancestors in ancient days during this season during the days of

---

[25] David Flusser (ed.), Sefer Yosifon (Jerusalem: Mercaz Zalman Shazar, 1978); Elias Bickerman, *From Ezra to the Last of the Maccabees.* New York: Schocken, 1947, 134.

[26] Jacob Neusner, *Messiah in Context: Israel's History and Destiny in Formative Judaism* (Philadelphia, Pennsylvania: Fortress Press, 1984), throughout. It is worth noting that the special biblical *haftarah* reading assigned by tradition to the Sabbath liturgy for Hanukah ends with the words of Zechariah 4:6: "Not by might, nor by power, but by My spirit—said the Lord of Hosts."

[27] *Seder Rav Amram Gaon* (Warsaw, 1865), 35–36; cf. *Seder Rav Amram Gaon*, ed. Daniel Goldsmith (Jerusalem: Mosad Harav Kook, 1971), 97–98.

[28] The liturgical commentary of David Abudarham (1340) of Seville is exceptional in that he has "consolations" (*hanechamot*) here in place of "wars"(*milchamot*), perhaps influenced by the assonance of the two Hebrew words (Ismar Elbogen, *Jewish Liturgy: A Comprehensive History*, translation by Raymond Scheindlin based on the 1913 German edition and 1972 Hebrew edition [Philadelphia: Jewish Publication Society, 1993]), 52.

Mattathias son of Yohanan the Hasmonean High Priest and his sons when the wicked Greek kingdom rose against them, against your people Israel, to make them forget your Torah and to make them transgress the statutes of your will. But you, in your abundant mercy, stood by them in their time of trouble. You fought their battle, judged their case, and wrought their vengeance. You delivered the mighty into the hands of the weak, the many into the hands of the few, the wicked into the hands of the righteous, the unclean into the hands of the pure, and the arrogant into the hands of those who were devoted to your Torah. For you yourself, you made a great and holy name for yourself in your world and for your people Israel you won a great victory and deliverance on this very day. Thereafter, your children came to the inner shrine of your House and cleansed your Temple, purified your sanctuary and kindled the lights in your holy courts, and established these eight days to praise and thank your name. Just as you made a miracle, so make for us, Lord God, miracles and great wonders at this time, and we shall thank your great name.[29]

This is more a liturgical recitation than benediction or even supplication, omitting many of the markers of the traditional forms for these types of prayer. In the Ashkenazic liturgy, the petition in the last line does not occur.[30] This recitation extols a militant God who brings victory to Israel and vengeance to Israel's enemies. The importance of this canonical composition plainly indicates that the rabbis did not expunge reference to violence and revenge from the canon. But in typical rabbinic fashion and in unambiguous contrast to both Books of Maccabees and to Josephus, there is no mention of Jewish heroes and no reference to the bravery and valor of Jewish warriors. It is God, and only God, who destroys the enemies of Israel. The destruction is removed from "real time" and rendered transcendent. It is carefully couched in terms that would not easily be read as condoning armed military insurrection, but rather, in terms that would release anger and bitter frustration but not encourage rebellion against the ruling powers.

---

[29] *Seder Rav Amram, seder hanukkah.* [Hebrew text from the Bar Ilan University *Responsa Project* (version 9)]. The earliest reference to the prayer is found in *Masekhet Sofrim* 20:4, one of the non-canonical treatises (so-called "minor tractates") of the Talmud that were not included within the official Talmudic canon. While some consider these to have been composed in the late Geonic period, Michael Higger considers them to have been early Palestinian material, perhaps completed as early as 400 C.E. and containing earlier material (Michael Higger, *Sheva Massekhtot Ketanot* [NY: Bloch, 1930], 5).

[30] The Ashkenazic rite evolved largely under Christianity. The Romaniot rite that was extant under the Byzantine Empire also omits the petition, which is found in the Sephardic and Roman liturgy.

It has been suggested that the `Al hanisim prayer was composed during the Hasmonean period itself[31] and became canonical against the will of the rabbis (or their predecessors) who wished to expunge such violent expression from the literary and liturgical canon. According to this view, the people loved it because its recitation served as a form of release for anger and pain under oppression, and their overwhelming support defeated the rabbinic desire to expunge it. Reciting `Al hanisim was a way to take spiritual and emotional revenge against oppressors, but with God the agent of violence—not humans.

But `Al hanisim is not an exception. Such expressions of violence and vengeance can be found elsewhere in rabbinic tradition.[32] Rabbinic Judaism, once it became a canonical system, was by no means a non-violent tradition. It tends, rather, to be quietist in that it is inclined to eschew *military* activism and *collective* zealotry, while not infrequently extolling individual zealotry and even acts of individual violence, such as the rabbinic extensions of the biblical story of Pinchas from Numbers 25:1–8 and the stories of sages who battle against enemies of Israel.[33] Pinchas in particular, who is also praised exceedingly in Psalm 106:28–31, became a model for the Maccabees[34] and the image of his absolute zealousness was internalized by the Zealots in their rebellion against Rome, the next great power after the Greeks to overwhelm Judea. He is rewarded by God in Numbers 25:11–13 for turning away the divine wrath through "his being zealous with My zealous passion in the midst [of Israel],"[35] from which the standard name of rebellious groups, "zealots," is derived.[36]

---

[31] Goldstein *I Macc.* 18f.

[32] Examples in the Talmud, particularly with regard to the Romans, can be found in the early pages of Avodah Zarah in the Babylonian Talmud. See also Michael Walzer, Menachem Lorberbaum, Noam Zohar and Ari Ackerman, *The Jewish Political Tradition* Vol. 2: *Membership*. New Haven: Yale University Press, 2003, 20–21, 82–83, 446–447, 480–482.

[33] See Louis Ginzberg, *Legends of the Jews.* 7 vols. Transl. Henrietta Szold (Philadelphia: Jewish Publication Society, 1911), vol. 3, 383–391, 408–411 and notes for original sources, and vol. 7, 371–372,

[34] See, for example, I Macc. 2:26: "So Mattathias showed his fervent zeal for the law, as Phinehas had done when he killed Zimri son of Salu;" 2:54: "Pinehas, our forefather, never flagged in his zeal, and his was the covenant of an everlasting priesthood." Many other references in I Macc., less in II Macc. refer indirectly to Pinchas.

[35] *Beqan `o et qin `ati betokham.* In Sanhedrin 82a-b, Pinchas is a "super zealot" (*qana`i ben qana'i*), a zealot born of a zealot, who turns away God's wrath by his zealous, violent act. In *Pirkey DeRabbi Eli`ezer* (chapter 47), "he was seized with a great zealousness" (*qine` qin`ah gedolah*), so he grabbed Moses' lance from his hand and hurried to run the guilty parties through with it. He then proceeded single-handedly to kill the guilty among Israel, for which he and his descendents were rewarded and the plague stopped.

[36] On the connection between Pinchas and Jewish militant and military zealotry in antiquity, see Martin Hengel, *The Zealots: Investigations into the Jewish Freedom Movement in the Period from Herod I until A.D. 70,* transl. by David W. Smith (Edinburgh: T & T Clark, 1989),

Emerging rabbinic Judaism was not entirely unified in its ultimate vote for quietism. The tension between militant activism and quietism reflected in the Hanukkah texts simply indicates the reality of Jewish life during the three or more centuries after the Maccabean rebellion. Responses to the two critical historical watershed rebellions against Rome in 66 and in 132 also reflect this tension. As we shall observe below, rabbinic Judaism would eventually express preference for the quietist heroism of Rabban Yohanan Ben Zakkai over the militant activism of Eleazer ben Ya'ir, and the piety of Rabbi Elazar Hamoda`i over the military exploits of Bar Kochba. And it would largely de-militarize the image of Rabbi Akiba, the influential rabbinic authority behind the military revolt known as the Bar Kokhba rebellion. But the victory of rabbinic quietism over militant activism was far less a statement of reasoned ethics than a reactive repositioning in response to the overwhelming and catastrophic failure of rebellion.

---

146–183. Hengel also notes, however (pp. 168–171), rabbinic criticism of Pinchas and Elijah, the other biblical character often associated with zealous violence on behalf of God (1 Kings ch. 18). On the importance of Pinchas in Philo, Pseudo-Philo and Josephus, see Feldman, *"Remember Amalek!" Vengeance, Zealotry, and Group Destruction in the Bible According to Philo, Pseudo-Philo, and Josephus* (Cincinnati: Hebrew Union College, 2004), 193–216.

## CHAPTER 3 | Holy War Fails

With the coming of the month of Av, happiness is decreased.

MISHNAH TA'ANIT 4:6

## The Great Revolt

The "Great Revolt" (*hamered hagadol*) against Rome broke out in the year 66 C.E., triggered by a combination of events in Caesarea and Jerusalem that provoked a clash between Jews and the Roman army.[1] The Jews initially had the upper hand. They destroyed the Roman garrison in Jerusalem, suspended the usual sacrificial offerings for the welfare of the Roman people and emperor, and set up a provisional Jewish government that attempted to unify the traditional Land of Israel under its rule.

The Roman response under Emperor Nero was overwhelming as he dispatched Vespasian with an immense army to crush the rebellion. Internal complications accompanying the death of Nero in 68 and Vespasian's victorious succession a year later delayed much of the fighting, but by the year 70, the Jerusalem Temple had been burned by Vespasian's son, Titus, and the only lingering active resistance remained in the desert fortress of Masada, which held out until 73.

The Jewish revolt against Roman rule in 66 was no surprise. Josephus, the New Testament, and Greco-Roman as well as rabbinic sources note how the communities of Judea chafed under Roman rule and that "zealots" (Hebrew, *kana'im*) were counted among a number of Judean communities.

---

[1] For a schematic portrayal of the foundational changes in Jewish thinking that resulted from the confrontation with Rome see Nahum Glatzer, "The Attitude Toward Rome in Third-Century Judaism," in Nahum Glatzer, *Essays in Jewish Thought* (Tuscaloosa, AL: University of Alabama Press, 1978), 1–14.

Even Simon, one of Jesus' disciples, was known as a zealot,[2] and when executed for sedition, Jesus was crucified between two zealots (Greek, *lestai*), thus suggesting that the Romans considered Jesus to be associated with zealot bands.[3]

A "zealot movement" had already emerged in the year 6 C.E. when Judea was first incorporated into the Roman Empire under Emperor Augustus. According to Josephus, one Judah the Galilean (or in Greek, Judas, or Judas of Gamla) had already participated in the widespread disturbances that followed Herod's death in 4 C.E. and seized control of a government armory in Sepphoris. When the Roman governor of Syria arrived in Judea in the year 6 to take a census in order to process the area into a Roman province, this Judah encouraged the Judeans to refuse to pay tribute or to acknowledge the Roman emperor. Josephus refers to Judah and his followers as outside the three main sects or philosophies of the Judeans: the Pharisees, Sadducees, and Essenes. Josephus usually refers to them as *lestai* (brigands)[4] or *sicarii* (dagger-men), though he occasionally calls them by the name they used to refer to themselves, *kana'im* (zealots), and finally considers them to be a fourth philosophic sect.[5]

It appears that the leadership of Judah's movement was, like that of the Maccabee/Hasmonean movement in the rebellion against the Seleucids,

---

[2] Matthew 10:4, Mark 3:18, Luke 6:15, Acts 1:13.

[3] Mark 15:27, John 19:18. But it should be noted that the Hebrew word *kana'im* denotes zealousness, whereas the Greek *lestai* means, simply, "robbers." The Jewish texts might refer to rebels as zealots, the Christian texts as simple bandits, thus suggesting something like the aphorism that one person's terrorist is another's freedom fighter. Hebrew and Aramaic actually borrowed from the Greek to create the Hebrew *listim*, Aramaic *lestaya'* to denote robbers. An additional rabbinic term, *biryonim,* has the sense of "roughnecks" or "hooligans" and is also used with reference to the zealots that fought against Rome. The variety of terminology in the rabbinic sources conveys the variety of perspectives and complexity of Jewish positions regarding the uprising.

[4] Modern scholarship is not in agreement over which category of troublemakers this term refers to. The arguments vary from political revolutionaries to social bandits, "Robin Hood-like heroes of the downtrodden," desperate people who have fallen through the cracks of a strained economy, or a combination of these (Seth Schwartz, *Imperialism and Jewish Society, 200 B.C.E. to 640 C.E.* [Princeton: Princeton University Press, 2001], 89–90).

[5] On Judah the Galilean and the Fourth Philosophy, see Hengels, *Zealots*, 76–145. Some recent scholarship considers the Sicarii to be descendants of the unnamed "fourth philosophy" mentioned by Josephus and unconnected to social bandits, Zealots, or other groups (S. Cohen, *From the Maccabees to the Mishnah* [Philadelphia: Westminster, 1987], 164–166).This Judah may also be confused with Judah ben Tziporai (Judas son of Saripheus) who, along with Mattathias son of Margalot (Matthias son of Margalothus), led a group to pull down the golden eagle that symbolized Rome during Herod's fatal illness but who were captured and burned alive by Herod's orders (Josephus, *Wars* 2:4, 2:8, *Antiquities* 17:6, 18:1). On Josephus' reference to what the zealots called themselves, see *Wars* 4:3 (trans., William Whiston, Grand Rapids: Kregel, 1960). Cf. Mary Smallwood, "Bandits, Terrorists, Sicarii and Zealots" (appendix A) Josephus, *The Jewish War*, transl. G. A. Williamson (NY: Dorset, 1981), 461–462.

a family affair. The demise of Judah the Galilean in the uprising of 6 C.E. may have been referred to in Acts 5:37.[6] Josephus mentions that Judah's two sons, James (or Jacob) and Simon, continued the rebellion and were slain by Tiberius Alexander.[7] A third son, Menachem,[8] and another heir of the family, Eleazer, were included among the most prominent leaders of the Great Revolt. The close kinship relations of the leadership and the confusion of Judahs (or Judases) suggests the possibility of a well-known template of successful and divinely sanctioned rebellion—that of another Judah (even the name epitomizes the identity, "Jew"), Judah the Maccabee, and his brothers. In any event, when the tide turned in favor of Rome, Menachem was killed by a Jewish functionary of the Temple.[9] Eleazer retreated to Masada after the fall of Jerusalem and died in a collective suicide rather than submit to the Romans. Josephus reproduces Eleazer's haunting speech to the leaders of the Masada community, an oration that has been repeated to hundreds of graduating Israeli army units when they finish their basic training in a symbolic climb to the top of the desert fortress.[10] "Since we, long ago, my generous friends, resolved never to be servants to the Romans, nor to any other than to God himself, who alone is the true and just Lord of mankind, the time is now come that obliges us to make that resolution true in practice . . . "[11]

The leadership of the revolt may indeed have been centered around a family or narrow leadership group of zealots, but it would never have been as successful as it was against Roman power without a significant degree of loyalty and support among the general public. Although Josephus' figures are often exaggerated, there were certainly large numbers of Jewish fighters, though he repeatedly blames a small group of zealots for destroying the entire community.[12] Hengel rightly calls this uprising a "holy war," as was the previous Maccabean rebellion and the following rebellion under the leadership of Akiba and Bar Kokhba.[13] The fighters

---

[6] According to Samuel Brandon (*EJ* 16:948), although it seems more likely that this refers to the messianic Theudas who arose under the procurator Fadus and was beheaded in 45 or 46 C.E.

[7] *Antiquities* 22:5.

[8] Listed by Josephus as Judah the Galilean's son (*Wars* 2:17). If Judah were killed in the year 6, it seems unlikely that his biological son would have been alive sixty years later, though it is not uncommon in rabbinic literature for a man to be referred to as "son" of a distinguished ancestor (see Yohanan ben Zakkai's famous statement, cited later, in the name of Zechariah ben Ido, in which Ido was Zechariah's grandfather).

[9] Josephus, *Wars* 2:17.

[10] On the Israeli military association with Masada, see Ben-Yehudah, *The Masada Myth*, 147–162.

[11] Josephus, *Wars* 7:8.

[12] As does BT Gittin 56a. For casualty figures from the Great Revolt and the Bar Kokhba Rebellion, see Seth Schwartz, *Imperialism and Jewish Society*, 108. n. 11.

[13] Hengel, *Zealots*, 282–290.

presumed that they were fighting for God and his Temple, and that God would intervene as in ancient days. But the Jews were divided into political or religious factions at the time—they did not merely portion themselves out into passive philosophic schools or sects as Josephus's terminology might suggest—and groups were also divided in loyalty and interest based on geographic location, as well as class, so there was a decided lack of unity. Some divisions appear to have formed around notions of nationhood or peoplehood, which were also influenced by geography. The profound difference between the groups that favored fighting and those that devoted their energies to nonmilitant resistance is not only of interest to historians of Late Antiquity but also has been the source of a major divide among Zionist leaders and ideologues since the beginning of the Zionist movement. In modern Zionist discourse it is often described as the difference between Yochanan Ben Zakkai and the zealots, or alternatively, between Yavneh and Jerusalem.[14]

## Rabban Yohanan ben Zakkai and the Zealots

The story of how Rabban Yohanan ben Zakkai was spirited out of Jerusalem under Roman siege hidden in a coffin by his students appears several times in rabbinic literature.[15] The sources maintain that the subterfuge was the only way he could pass the zealot guards of the city gates without being killed for treason. As the zealots in Jerusalem were making their last stand against Rome, Rabban Yohanan ben Zakkai negotiated with the Roman general, Vespasian, for permission to build an academy in the Judean town of Yavneh (Jamnia).

In the 1940s, Gedaliyah Alon collected the Jewish and Greco-Roman literary sources that treat this narrative about Yohanan Ben Zakkai and set out to reconstruct the likely historical events from the often contradictory

---

[14] One set of factions with textual traditions to support their positions are those known from the texts discovered in the caves near Qumran and the Dead Sea, commonly known as the "Dead Sea Scrolls." I have not included those writings in this study because they are noncannonical and it is not clear what communities they even represent. A number of texts from this large corpus, such as the "War Scroll" or the "Damascus Rule," include interesting material about war, messianism, and prophecies, but they are not directly relevant to the purpose of this book because, unlike the books of Maccabbees, they have had little impact on the *longue durée* of Jewish history. I have excluded other noncanonical Jewish materials that include notions of holy war (such as the Ethiopian Enoch, Testament of the Twelve Patriarchs, etc.) for the same reason.

[15] Avot de Rabbi Natan (ARN[1] chapter 4, ARN[2] chapter 6), BT Gittin 56a-b, Midrash Lamentations Rabba 1:5, no.31, Midrash Mishle 15 which is virtually identical to ARN[2].

data presented in the sources.[16] Three major issues concerned him: whether Yohanan sympathized with the zealot revolt or opposed the war from the beginning and wished the Jews to submit to the Romans without reservation, whether Yohanan was communicating with Vespasian in some manner during the siege and was therefore welcomed by Vespasian upon his escape, and whether he requested to be allowed to build a school in Yavneh or whether he was taken there as captive only to be released to build an academy there after the end of hostilities. These issues are of significant interest for the historian of Late Antiquity, but the actual historicity of events does not interest us directly here.

Our concern, rather, centers on the meaning that the narrative in its various recensions represents for rabbinic Judaism. It seems evident from the canonical Jewish sources represented by Talmud and Midrash[17] that the rabbis' view of the zealots was more favorable than that of Josephus. However, all four canonical Hebrew versions of the narrative praise Yohanan for abandoning the rebellion and dedicating himself to establishing a safe haven for the transmission of Torah and tradition.

Yohanan ben Zakkai was forced to exit Jerusalem through subterfuge because anyone attempting to flee the war zone would have been killed on the spot by the zealots. In two versions of the story, however, a zealot leader (though also Yohanan's nephew) assists the rabbi in the deception.[18] At the end of the day, it is not the zealots but Yohanan ben Zakkai and his students who survive the destruction and reestablish Jewish life in the Land of Israel, thus guaranteeing Jewish survival even if as a depressed people and under the dictatorial rule of Rome. This is the bottom line of the narrative.

One needs to keep in mind that in the ancient Near East, the temples of ethnic religious centers were considered the dwelling places of the gods, who were the protectors of the people. This was the case also in ancient Israel, with some differences associated with the transition to monotheism, throughout the period until the destruction of the Jerusalem Temple in 70 C.E. It is difficult, so far removed from the period, to imagine the symbolic power of the Temple and the catastrophe of its destruction. Virtually

---

[16] Gedaliah Alon, "Rabban Johanan B. Zakkai's Removal to Jabneh," in Gedaliah Alon, *Jews, Judaism and the Classical World* (Jerusalem: Magnes, 1977), 269–313 (translations of the four Hebrew sources are provided there in an appendix).

[17] This literature is treated in the following chapter.

[18] The role of this protagonist is examined by Galit Hasan-Rokem, *Web of Life: Folklore and Midrash in Rabbinic Literature*, translated by Batya Stein (Stanford, CA: Stanford University, 2000), 176–177. The version in the Babylonian Talmud (Gittin 56a) refers to him as Abba Siqra (not Bar Siqra as in Hasan-Rokem), meaning "dagger-man" (lit. "father of the dagger").

all the ethnic religions of the ancient Near East disappeared after the destruction of their cultic centers. Only Judaism and its people survived.[19]

This is not to suggest that Yohanan ben Zakkai represents the triumph of a form of Judaism that is non-Temple or anti-Temple oriented. Whether Yohanan is represented as desiring to hold out in siege against Rome, as depicted in one source (Lamentations Rabba parallel to the Babylonian Talmud: Gittin), or as opposed to resistance altogether, as depicted in another (ARN), his acts nowhere indicate disregard for the Temple and the sacrificial system. On the contrary, he is depicted in rabbinic sources as being deeply engaged in issues of sacrificial practice and Temple authority while the Temple stood. "When Rabbi Yohanan ben Zakkai saw that the Temple was destroyed and the sanctuary burnt, he stood and tore his garments, took off his *tefillin*, and sat weeping, as did his students with him."[20]

Yet he is credited with solving the overwhelming existential problem of community survival when the mode for atonement through sacrifice had been cut off with the destruction of the Temple. When one Rabbi Yehoshua laments that the means for atonement had been destroyed, Yohanan replies, "My son, be not grieved; we have another atonement as effective as this. And what is it? It is acts of loving-kindness, as it is said, *For I desire mercy and not sacrifice*" (Hosea 6:6).[21] Traditional commentators take great pains to point out that his exegesis does not condemn Temple sacrifice or claim that the power of kindness to atone for sin is greater than the Temple offerings. It is only a substitution because of the severity of circumstances. The issue is simply that Yohanan Ben Zakkai's strategy, as constructed by rabbinic tradition, held that the survival of the people and the religious system of Judaism, however defined, lay in the survival of an independent spiritual and educational center rather than an independent political center. He is a transitional figure, as Galit Hasan-Rokem points out,[22] and he represents the transition from Temple-centered religion to that of the House of Study.

---

[19] Mendels, 107–110, 190–192; Seth Schwartz, *Imperialism and Jewish Society*, 105–106. But one must also keep in mind that the Hellenization of biblical Judaism represented another form of survival for biblical religion. The version that eventuated in Christianity was neither temple-oriented nor organized around human kingship, but rather on "the kingdom of God" (Gk. *basileia tou theou*—Heb. *malkhut shamayim*) (Mendels, 202, 228–229), Cf. Jonathan Z. Smith, *To Take Place* (Chicago: University of Chicago, 1987).

[20] ARN[2] chapter 7. He is depicted elsewhere as knowing or predicting that the Temple would be destroyed, based on Zech.11:1: "Open your doors, O Levanon, that the fire may devour your cedars." (*Yoma* 39b).

[21] ARN[1], 4 (transl. Judah Goldin, *The Fathers According to Rabbi Nathan* [New Haven: Yale University Press, 1955], 34.)

[22] Hasan-Rokem, *Web of Life*, 180–181, 188–189. See 171–189 for a literary and folkloristic analysis of the narrative as it appears in Lamentations Rabba.

According to two of the four Hebrew renderings of the story, Yohanan seemed opposed to the revolt altogether,[23] but according to the other two, he decided to leave Jerusalem only after the stores of food were destroyed and all hope of holding out through the Roman siege was ended. This is quietism, not pacifism, and it is born out of the sense of the futility of resistance to the overwhelming power of Rome. Some historians argue that there were rational reasons from the Jewish perspective to have gone up militarily against Rome. The Jews were well aware of Rome's power, but they were also mindful of the long biblical history of God's defeat of other powerful enemies such as Egypt and Assyria. Holy war remained on option until it ceased to produce results.

Unlike the noncanonical accounts of the Maccabean victory that highlight the glory of a military solution, all the extant accounts of the Great Revolt convey that the war was futile and the survival of Jews and Judaism required, in the end, the loss of political independence. All the same, the Jews lost badly to the Romans, and that loss was calamitous. According to the line of thinking that became dominant in rabbinic tradition, life, even under oppression and humiliation in exile, is preferable to glorious death in the homeland; there was always a hope that the future would bring a better life.

Some early modern Jewish historians took this view another step by claiming ultimate Jewish victory over Rome. "Since the Roman commander, who respected only palpable physical strength, was unable to apprise the manifold consequences resulting from the seemingly inconsequential action that Rabban Johanan intended to take, he acceded to his 'humble' request, without sensing that he was at that moment destroying with his own hands the fruit of his victory by permitting a wretched and outcast fugitive to create a new spiritual Judaism, which was destined to outlive the victorious Roman Empire."[24]

Secular Zionist thinkers representing various political positions, such as Theodor Herzl and Max Nordau, Ahad Ha'am, Micah Berdichevsky and Yonatan Ratosh, have argued about the dichotomy between Yavneh and Jerusalem from the earliest days of the movement.[25] The cultural Zionist Ahad HaAm favored the sages of Yavneh over the zealots of Jerusalem because, according to him, the former put their energies toward long-term rather than short-term goals (*chayey `olam velo chayey sha`ah*). That is, the

---

[23] Both recensions of Avot de Rabbi Natan.

[24] The historians Heinrich Graetz and Simon Dubnow, as cited by Gedalia Alon, "Rabban Johanan..." 269.

[25] Ehud Luz, *Wrestling with an Angel: Power, Morality, and Jewish Identity* (New Haven: Yale, 2003), throughout, but especially 55–56.

state is not enough in and of itself but only as part of a much larger entity that is Jewish culture and history, which can and must survive beyond independent political existence. The practical Zionist Berdiczewsky took the "Jerusalem" position, claiming that Ahad HaAm's view did not really reflect the overwhelmingly militant expressions of historic Israel. The historic Israel knew that only a people willing to fight for its land deserves to remain on it. Like Berdiczewsky, the Revisionist Abba Ahimeir in the 1940s claimed that all the nations that gave in to Rome perished. Only the Jews, who resisted at Jerusalem, Masada, and Beitar, remain alive and strong. According to him, "a nation that does not give in is everlasting...but a nation that gives in will be destroyed."

According to this position, Yohanan ben Zakai was thus a traitor who prepared the future for exile. The right-wing Irgunist Yonatan Ratosh, along with leftist activist Yitzhaq Tabenkin, also rebutted the traditionally dominant view that Yohanan Ben Zakkai saved the people, for to them it was the heroism of the zealots and their memory that saved the people. Yehezkel Kaufman, the acclaimed biblical scholar, however, held that Yavneh was not entirely quietest, for it produced Akiba and the *biryonim* who would resist Rome at a later time. Both expressions would continue to exist in tension there, at least through the Bar Kokhba Rebellion, for even after the destruction of the Jerusalem Temple in 70 C.E., many still hoped that Israel would finally triumph militarily against Rome.

The Jewish resistance to Roman occupation held out at the Masada fortress for three years after the destruction of the Temple. Masada, located on a nearly impregnable cliff overlooking the Dead Sea, was the location of the last and most enduring resistance to Rome. The Jewish military resistance at Masada was left unrecorded in the canonical Jewish sources but, as we shall observe, became a powerful symbol of modern Zionism. Its story has been preserved only by Josephus and recycled in the ninth to tenth century *Sefer Josippon*.[26]

More recently, and particularly since the 1980s, the dominant Zionist narrative extolling and glorifying heroic resistance has been reexamined by some for what its critics claim has created Zionism's distorted attitude toward power. The argument is symbolized by the term "Masada Complex"[27] and considers whether the heroic image of the Masada fighters

---

[26] *The Book of Jossiphon ben Gurion* 2 vols. (Hebrew), Jerusalem: Oraita, 1999, vol. 2, 371–380.

[27] The term first appeared in an article in the newspaper, *Haaretz* (April 22, 1973), 16 as cited in Zerubavel, "The Death of Memory and the Memory of Death: Masada and the Holocaust," *Representations* 45 (Winter, 1994)," 99 n.86 (full article, 72–100). On the "Masada Complex,"

committing collective suicide rather than submit to the tyranny of Rome promotes courage and a stubborn will to fight until victory in the context of modern Israel, or rather a feeling of despair that defeat is ultimately inevitable along with a willingness to commit national suicide. Although Israel is far and away the most powerful military power in the Middle East, does a fixation on the symbols of Jerusalem and Masada create an anxiety that distorts an accurate reading of reality? These are enduring and critical questions, but they tend to be argued among Jewish Israelis (and other Jews) who are in the secular camps, or among those Orthodox Jews (especially academics) who are fully engaged in "secular-nationalist" paradigms of thought. These are self-reflective questions of strategy in a secular world of power-politics rather than questions of transcendent religious meaning. It is the latter category that produces theories of sacred power and divinely authorized warring that have increasingly dominated political discourse within the religious Zionist camp.

One other serious Jewish revolt against Rome occurred between the Great Revolt of 66–70 and the Bar Kokhba Rebellion that shall be examined presently. It took place in the Hellenized Jewish Diaspora in Alexandria of Egypt, Cyrenaica (today's Libya), and Cyprus, though the violence spread to other areas as well.[28] Led by one Lukuas (sometimes referred to as Andreas), who may have been a messianic figure, Jews purportedly destroyed many pagan temples. It is sometimes called the "Kitos War" for the Roman general, Lusius Quietus, whom Trajan sent to quell the revolt and who did so ruthlessly. Unfortunately, we have little information about this war, but we can assume that it was another, even if not well documented, case of a Jewish rebellion that might fit our definition of holy war. Because of the lack of data there is little reason to dwell on this militant uprising.

## The Bar Kokhba Rebellion 132–135 C.E.

Bar Kokhba is the *nom de guerre* of the military leader named Simon Bar Kosiba who commanded the Jewish revolt against Rome in 132–135 C.E.

---

see Robert Alter, "The Masada Complex," *Commentary* 56, 1 (July, 1973), Bernard Lewis, *History Remembered, Recovered, Invented* (Princeton: Princeton University Press, 1976), Charles Leibman and Eliezer Don Yehiya, *Civil Religion in Israel* (Berkeley: University of California Press, 1984). Nahman Ben-Yehuda provides a thorough study of the history of the events under the Jewish resistance at Masada and the reconstruction of that history into a mythic tale of heroism that omits the problematic aspects in *The Masada Myth: Collective Memory and Mythmaking in Israel* (Madison: University of Wisconsin Press, 1995).

[28] Gedaliah Alon, *The Jews in Their Land in the Talmudic Age*, translated and edited by Gershon Levi (Cambridge, MA: Harvard University, 1980), 382–405.

The details of the revolt do not concern us here, aside from the fact that it was serious enough to have been a source of real concern to the Roman rulers. According to the Roman historian Cassius Dio, the Roman forces suffered so many losses that the victorious "…Hadrian in writing to the senate did not employ the opening phrase commonly affected by the emperors, 'If you and your children are in health, it is well; I and the legions are in health…' "[29] The rebellion precipitated a Roman response to ensure that no future uprisings would be attempted. Statistics from ancient reports are notoriously unreliable, but it is likely that tens or perhaps even hundreds of thousands of Jews were killed in the fighting or died from starvation and illness in the chaos that followed.[30]

Outraged by Jewish defiance, the Romans obliterated the most notable historic markers by which Jews identified their land. They renamed Judea *Syria-Palestina*, that is, the Palestine of Syria. Jerusalem was depopulated of Jews, and its sacred shrine, which had already been destroyed in the Great Revolt of 66–70 C.E., was replaced with a temple to Jupiter. The city was turned into a pagan Roman colony and the ancient name by which the city had been known was replaced by Aelia Capitolina after the Emperor Titus Aelius Hadrianus. Jewish practices such as circumcision, Torah study, and even prayer were evidently banned for a short period.[31]

---

[29] Dio Cassius, *Roman History* 69, 12:1–14:3, cited in Menahem Stern, *Greek and Latin Authors on Jews and Judaism* 3 vols. (Jerusalem: Israel Academy of Sciences, 1974, 1980, 1984), vol. 2, 391–393. On the geographical and military scope of the rebellion and its threat to the empire, see Menahem Mor, "The Geographical Scope of the Bar-Kokhba Revolt," in Peter Schäfer, *The Bar Kokhba War Reconsidered*, 107–131.

[30] For a variety of perspectives on the history of the rebellion, see Geza Vermes and Fergus Millar's revision of Emil Schurer, *The History of the Jewish People in the Age of Jesus Christ* (NY: Continuum, 1987); Yigal Yadin, *Bar Kokhba* (NY: Random House, 1971); Shimon Applebaum, *Prolegomena to the Study of the Second Jewish Revolt* (Oxford: British Archaeological Reports, Supplement 7, 1976); Aharon Oppenheimer, *The Bar Kokhba Revolt* (Hebrew) (Jerusalem: Zalman Shazar Center, 1980); Aharon Oppenheimer and Uriel Rappaport, *The Bar Kokhba Revolt: New Studies* (1984); Menachem Mor, *The Bar Kokhba Revolt: Its Extent and Effect* (Jerusalem: Yad Ben-Tzvi, 1991); Peter Schäfer, *The Bar Kokhba War Reconsidered: New Perspectives on the Second Jewish Revolt Against Rome* (Tübingen: Mohr/Siebeck), 2003. On views regarding the image of Bar Kokhba in rabbinic literature, see Ephraim Urbach, *The Sages* (Cambridge, MA: Harvard University Press, 1987), 593–603; Richard G. Marks, *The Image of Bar Kokhba in Traditional Jewish Literature* (University Park, PA: Pennsylvania State University Press, 1994). On attitudes of Talmudic rabbis toward the Romans in relation to the revolt, see Richard Kalmin, "Rabbinic Traditions about Roman Persecutions of the Jews: A Reconsideration," in *Journal of Jewish Studies* 54, no. 1 (spring 2003): 21–50.

[31] Peter Schäfer, "Hadrian's Policy in Judaea and the Bar Kokhba Revolt: A Reassessment," in Philip R. Davies and Richard T. White (eds.), *A Tribute to Geza Vermes. Essays on Jewish and Christian Literature and History* (Sheffield: JSOT Press, 1990), 281–303. For the problem of dating of the founding of Aelia Capitolina (whether it was the cause of or the result of the revolt), see Peter Schäfer, "The Causes of the Bar Kokhba Revolt," in Jakob Peuchowsky and

Most Jewish survivors in Judea were forced to emigrate due to a combination of Roman military and political restrictions, on the one hand, and economic destitution on the other. By an act of the Roman senate, it was decreed "that it is forbidden to all circumcised persons to enter and to stay within the territory of Aelia Capitolina; any person contravening this prohibition shall be put to death."[32] Many moved east to Persia or north to the Galilee, and Jewish Judea did not recover until the twentieth century. The revolt is remembered in Jewish sources both in references to its military leader, Bar Kokhba, and to the location of his last stand in the city of Beitar. Its disastrous results were of such importance to the evolving rabbinic self-concept that it was listed in the Mishnah along with four other great disasters that befell the Jews on the ninth day of the month of Av.

> Five things occurred to our ancestors...on the ninth of Av....On the ninth of Av, it was decreed [by God] that our ancestors would not enter the Land [of Israel], the First and Second Temples were destroyed, Beitar was captured and the city was plowed under. With the coming of Av, happiness is decreased (Mishnah Ta`anit 4:6).

The Bar Kokhba Revolt was the last great Jewish military action until the advent of modern Zionism in the twentieth century. There were, of course, occasional Jewish military actions that had no historical impact, such as the revolt against Gallus Caesar in the fourth century,[33] the uprising of Abu `Isa al-Isfahani against the Caliphate in the eighth century,[34] and the militant Jewish Khazar nation.[35] But the revolt against Gallus is not even mentioned in Jewish sources,[36] the militant uprising of Abu `Isa barely echoed in Jewish history (his story is found in Islamic sources), and the Jewishness of the Khazars remains uncertain and, aside from very few

Ezra Fleischer (eds.), *Studies in Aggadah, Targum and Jewish Liturgy in Memory of Joseph Heinemann* (Jerusalem: Magnes, 1981), 81–84.

[32] Michael Avi-Yona, *The Jews of Palestine: A Political History from the Bar Kokhba War to the Arab Conquest* (New York: Schocken, 1976), p. 50.

[33] Günter Stemberger, *Jews and Christians in the Holy Land*, transl. Ruth Tuschling (Edinburgh: T & T Clark, 2000), 161–184.

[34] See Aaron Aescoly, *Jewish Messianic Movements* [Hebrew] (Jerusalem: Bialik Institute, 1956), 123–124, 139–141; Salo Baron, *A Social and Religious History of the Jews* 18 vols. (New York: Columbia University Press, 1952–1983), vol. 5, 184–194; Steven Wasserstrom, *Between Muslim and Jew* (Princeton, NJ: Princeton University Press, 1995), 71–82.

[35] Douglas Dunlop, *The History of the Jewish Khazars* (Princeton, NJ: Princeton University, 1954); Peter B. Golden, *Khazar Studies* (Budapest: Akadémiai Kiadó, 1980); Kevin Alan Brook, *The Jews of Khazaria*, 2nd ed. (Lanham, MD: Rowman & Littlefield, 2006).

[36] Stemberger, 163.

references by Spanish Jews, Khazar military prowess had virtually no impact on Jewish history or thought per se.

The rebellion known by the name of the military general Bar Kokhba had the backing if not coleadership of Rabbi Akiba, arguably the most important religious leader of his generation.[37] The very name, Bar Kokhba, meaning "son of the star," hints at the messianic associations with the revolt. According to the Palestinian Talmud[38] (Ta'anit 4:5) and Midrash Lamentations Rabba (2:4),[39] Rabbi Akiba referred to Bar Kokhba as the King Messiah (*malka meshicha*) and supported his view with an interpretation of Numbers 24:17 that is viewed by the rabbis as a clear messianic statement.[40]

Rabbi Shim'on b. Yohai[41] taught: "Akiba my teacher would expound (Num.24:17): *A star will step forth out of Jacob*[42] as follows: Koziba will step forth from Jacob. Rabbi Akiba, when he saw Bar Koziba, would say: 'This is the King Messiah.'" R. Yohanan b. Torta[43] said to him: "Akiba, weeds will grow out of your cheeks and the son of David will still not have come!"[44]

The star (*kokhav*) rising out of the Jacob was none other than Bar Kokhba, according to Rabbi Akiba, and the name Bar Kokhba in Aramaic

---

[37] Israeli scholars have generally assumed that most if not all the rabbinical leadership of the time backed the rebellion; see Y. Ben-Shalom, "The Status of Bar Kokhba at the Head of the Nation and the Support of the Sages for the Rebellion" (Hebrew), *Cathedra* 29 (1984), 13–28; Gedalia Alon, "The Bar Kokhba War" (Hebrew), in Gedalia Alon, *A History of the Jews in the Land of Israel During the Period of the Mishnah and the Talmud* (NP: HaKibbutz HaMe'uhad, 1957), 41, translated into English by Gershon Levi in Alon, *The Jews in their Land in the Talmudic Age* (Jerusalem: Magnes, 1984), 630. This is unlikely. As mentioned above, Seth Schwartz (*Imperialism and Jewish Society*) has shown that the amount of power and influence of the rabbis at this time is really unclear, and it is likely that the community was divided just as it was during earlier periods of military conflict with imperial powers (Schäfer, "The Causes of the Bar Kokhba Revolt," 93–94).

[38] This is the standard English name for this work, called the "Jerusalem Talmud" in Hebrew.

[39] On Lamentations Rabba, see Hasan-Rokem, *Web of Life*, 8–9, 12–15.

[40] See Targum Onkelos and Pseudo Yonatan s.v. Num.24:17.

[41] Mid-second century C.E. sage in the Land of Israel. He was one of only four students of Rabbi Akiba who survived the Bar Kokhba revolt (BT Yevamot 62b). According to the traditions attributed to him, his hatred of the Romans remained with him throughout his life.

[42] The full verse is, "I see it, but not now, I behold it, but it is not near: a star (*kokhav*) will step forth out of Jacob, a scepter will rise out of Israel. It will smash the brow of Moab, the foundation of all the children of Seth. Edom will become a possession, yea, Seir a possession of its enemies..."

[43] Little is known of this figure aside from his opposition to Akiba over the status of Bar Kokhba given in this passage. The only other statement given in his name gives the reasons for the destruction of the two Temples (Tosefta, *Menahot* [Tzukermandel Ed.] 13:22; BT Yoma 9a-b).

[44] For textual analysis of this and the Bar Kokhba citations to follow, see Peter Schäfer, "Bar Kokhba and the Rabbis," in Peter Schäfer, *The Bar Kokhba War Reconsidered*, 1–7.

means exactly that: "star man." Moreover, Edom, referred to in the continuation of the Numbers passage, is a code throughout rabbinic literature for Rome.[45] According to Akiba's understanding, then, Bar Kokhba was destined by divine authority to lead the Jewish people in a successful revolt to retake possession of the Land of Israel, if not to destroy the evil empire of Rome altogether. Akiba's view is countered in this source by that of Rabbi Yohanan ben Torta, an otherwise insignificant tannaitic sage, who does not take Bar Kokhba to be a messianic figure.[46] Bar Kokhba is twice referred to in the passage as "Bar Koziba." In fact, neither Bar Kokhba nor Bar Koziba was the general's real name.

We know that his actual name was Simon Bar Kosiba (or Bar Kosba). Two puns seem to have evolved in relation to the name, depending on how he was viewed: Bar Kokhba ("star man") among those who attributed messianic status to him (in relation to Num.24:17),[47] and Bar Koziba ("son of lies" or "liar") among those who opposed him and later, those who suffered from the failure of the revolt. In our texts and throughout traditional Jewish literature, his name is written Bar Koziba, reflecting the obvious conclusion reached by the rabbis that he was a false messiah who succeeded only in bringing terrible destruction to his people.[48]

This passage, then, begins by laying out the divergent Jewish positions regarding the revolt. It is a long narrative, as Talmudic passages go, and continues by adding further layers of information that demonstrate the

---

[45] Gerson Gohen considers the origin of the association of Esau/Edom with Rome to be the Bar Kokhba Revolt and identifies Rabbi Akiba as the likely source (Gerson Cohen, "Esau as Symbol in Early Medieval Thought," in *Jewish Medieval and Renaissance Studies* ed. Alexander Altmann [1967], 20–22). Louis Feldman sees that identification already in Josephus, and perhaps even in the Testaments of the Twelve Patriarchs (*Remember Amalek*, 63–64). After the Christianization of the Roman Empire in the fourth century, Edom became a code name for Christianity.

[46] The earliest reference to Bar Kokhba by his messianic name is found in a contemporary, Justin Martyr, who wrote in Greek and seems not to have known that it was his *nom de guerre* (Richard Bauckham, "Jews and Jewish Christians in the land of Israel at the time of the Bar Kochba war, with special reference to the *Apocalypse of Peter*," in Graham Stanton and Guy Stroumsa, *Tolerance and Intolerance in Early Judaism and Christianity*, 228–229).

[47] Marks, *The Image of Bar Kokhba*, 14–15. Bauckham concludes from Justin Martyr's innocent reference to him by his messianic nickname that it was standard usage and that Jewish support for the revolt was virtually universal except for Jewish Christians. It seems unlikely that support for Bar Kokhba would have been so overwhelming, given the fractious nature of the Jewish community during this period, the variety of positions held by Jews regarding the earlier Great Revolt observable in Josephus and rabbinic literature, and the harsh rabbinic critique found in the texts cited here which, although edited into earlier messianic material by later redactors, conform to points of view that would be contemporary to Akiba/Bar Kokhba.

[48] Yael Zerubavel, "Bar Kokhba's Image in Modern Israeli Culture," in Peter Schäfer [ed.], *The Bar Kokhba War Reconsidered* [*Tübingen*: Mohr/Siebeck], 2003, 281.

complexity of the rabbinic attitude toward Bar Kokhba and a revolt that took place only two generations after the catastrophic revolt of 66 that ended with the destruction of the Temple.[49]

Rabbi Yohanan[50] said: "Eighty thousand pairs of [Roman] trumpeters had surrounded Beitar, and every single one of them was appointed over a few regiments. Ben[51] Koziba was there, and he had two hundred thousand [fighters, each one] with a finger cut off. The sages sent and asked him: "How long will you make Israelite men unfit?"[52] He answered: "How else is it possible to test them?" [The sages] replied to him: "Any one who cannot ride his horse and uproot a Cedar of Lebanon will not be enrolled in your army." So he had two hundred thousand of these and two hundred thousand of those. When he went into battle he said: "God of the universe, do not help us and do not shame us. (Ps.60:12) *Have you not rejected us [or, made us fall], God, by not going out with our armies?*"

For three and a half years, Hadrian besieged Beitar while Rabbi Elazar HaModa`i[53] would sit in sackcloth and ashes, praying every day and saying: "Master of the universe! Do not sit in judgment today! Do not sit in judgment today!" When Hadrian [finally gave up and] began to leave off [from the siege], a certain Cuthean (*Kutai*)[54] said: "Don't leave, because I see what to do in order to force the city to surrender to you." He went into the city through a [drainage] pipe and found Rabbi Elazar HaModa`i standing and praying. He made as if he were whispering in [Elazar's] ear. The inhabitants of the city saw him and brought him to Bar Koziba. They told [Bar Koziba]: "We saw this old man chatting with your friend." He said [to the Cuthean]: "What did you say to him, and what did he say to you?" He answered: "If I tell you the [Roman] king will kill me, and if I don't tell you, you will kill me. Better for me that the king kill me and not you." So [the Cuthean]

[49] For a study of the rabbinic sources, see Marks, *The Image of Bar Kokhba in Traditional Jewish Literature.*

[50] Yohanan ben Nappaha (died c. 279 C.E.) was from Sepphoris and one of the most important Palestinian Talmudic sages.

[51] The words *ben* and *bar* both mean "son of," the former in Hebrew and the latter in Aramaic. It is not uncommon for the two languages to be mixed in a single Talmudic passage.

[52] Unfit for certain ritual priestly duties without all one's fingers. Cutting off the finger was a test of fortitude for his warriors.

[53] As his name, "Ha-Moda`i" notes, he was from the Hasmonean center Modi`in. According to some rabbinic sources, he was the uncle of Bar Kokhba (PT Ta`anit 4:68d; Midrash Lamentations Rabba 2:2)

[54] A member of a sect of Samaritans, but also sometimes used to denote a Jewish sectarian or Gnostic.

said to him: "He told me that I should surrender the city." [Ben Koziba] went to Rabbi Elazar HaModa`i and said to him: "What did this Cuthean say to you?" He said to him: "Nothing." [Ben Koziba] said: "What did you tell him?" He answered: "Nothing." [Ben Koziba] gave him one kick and killed him. Immediately a Heavenly Voice went out and announced (Zachariah 11:17): *"O the worthless shepherd who abandons the flock! Let a sword fall upon his arm and on his right eye! His arm will certainly shrivel and his right eye go blind!* You killed Rabbi Elazar HaModa`i, the arm of all Israel and their right eye. Therefore, the arm of the man [who did that] will shrivel and his right eye be blinded!" Immediately, Beitar was captured and Ben Koziba killed.

[Roman soldiers] brought his head to Hadrian. [Hadrian] asked them: "Who killed this one?" A Cuthean said to him: "I killed him." He said: "Bring me his corpse [as proof]." He brought him his corpse, around which was curled a big snake. [Hadrian] said to him: "If God did not kill him, who could have killed him?" And he recited in regard to him (Deut.32:30): *If their Rock had not sold him, the Lord had [not] handed him over.* [The Romans] killed [the Jewish soldiers and inhabitants of Beitar] until their horses sunk in the blood up to their noses, and the blood [was deep and swift enough to] roll boulders for forty *se'ah*s until the blood flowed four miles into the sea.... [PT Ta`anit 4:5]

The narrative picks up after noting Akiba and Yohanan B. Torta's disagreement with a statement about the magnitude of the great battle over Beitar. Tens of thousands of warriors faced each other over the walls of the city. Bar Kokhba's way of testing his warriors displeased the rabbis, who suggested an alternative that was accepted, and Bar Kokhba's startling battle prayer begging God to stay out of the fray is virtually a statement of heresy in rabbinic Judaism. Despite the hero's great flaws, however, Hadrian was unable to conquer the city. But the actual reason behind Beitar's safety was not what it seemed, because it had nothing to do Bar Kokhba's military prowess or messianic status. On the contrary, the reason for the failure of the greatest army on earth to conquer this single Jewish town is that one man, the righteous Elazar HaModa'i, prayed daily in sackcloth and ashes that God not deliver Beitar to Rome. Bar Kokhba is not the real hero. The real hero is the rabbi, Elazar Hamoda'i, but Hadrian the pagan Roman (like Bar Kokhba and even Rabbi Akiba) is unable to recognize where the power in Beitar really lay. Bar Kokhba remained tragically ignorant of Elazar's critical role. It was the Cuthean (of which, more follows) who figured out where Beitar's Achilles' heel lay, and only he was able to put an end to the rebellion.

We find a similar role in the previous narrative treating Rabbi Yohanan ben Zakkai's exit from a doomed Jerusalem. In the rendering found in Lamentations Rabba, the very presence of one weak and emaciated Rabbi Tzadok in Jerusalem prevented the Roman army from conquering it. In this case it is not prayer, per se, but rather teaching in the rabbinic academy which is the source of his strength (Lamm. Rabba 1:3). Rabbi Tzadok is a minor character in the narrative, however, and does not appear in all versions. It is Yohanan ben Zakkai in this story who epitomizes the rabbinic concern for alternative ways to respond to the Roman threat.[55]

The parallel version of the Bar Kokhba story in Midrash Lamentations Rabba 2:4 is quite similar to that of the Palestinian Talmud, but noting some of the differences helps to unpack the issues embedded in the narrative. In the midrash passage, it is the people of Beitar and not only Bar Kokhba who pray that God neither hinder nor help them in their battle against Rome, and this fact helps contribute to the city's downfall. Bar Kokhba is literally a physical superhero in the midrashic version. With his knees he personally catches the very missiles hurled into the city by the great Roman catapults and flings them back against the enemy soldiers, killing many of them. This is why, according to this midrash, Akiba believed Bar Kokhba to be the messiah. The midrashic version thus appears more sympathetic to Akiba's mistaken opinion regarding Bar Kokhba's messianic status. However, this midrash also stresses Bar Kokhba's uncontrollable fury that leads to his killing of Elazar with one kick of his foot, suggesting a less sympathetic view of the would-be messiah. The same powerful legs that caught the Roman missiles put an end to the real protection of Beitar.

The midrashic version is also more explicit that the Cuthean knows how Rabbi Elazar was single-handedly protecting Beitar through his prayers. The Cuthean, though a sectarian and enemy of Israel, understood the extraordinary efficacy of the prayers of a few exceptional, righteous men.

A certain Cuthean came and found [Hadrian] and said: My lord, every day that that hen rolls around [on her eggs] in the ashes, you will not conquer it. Wait for me to do something to enable you to conquer it today!

---

[55] See Hasan-Rokem, 174–175, 186–187. Note also the meaning of the names of these two heroes. Tzadok means "righteous" and ben Zakkai means "pure, meritorious."

He immediately went into the city through a [drainage] pipe and found Rabbi Elazar HaModa`i who was standing and praying.

Lamentations Rabba also suggests a slightly different reason than the Talmudic version for the subsequent fall of the city. In the Talmudic rendering, the heavenly voice announced to Bar Kokhba, "You killed Rabbi Elazar HaModa`i, the arm of all Israel and their right eye. Therefore, the arm of the man [who did that] will shrivel and his right eye be blinded!" Bar Kokhba must be punished for his sin, and that punishment indirectly causes the destruction of the entire city and the rebellion. In the midrashic version, however, the heavenly voice proclaims, "You bound the arm of Israel and blinded your own right eye! Therefore, your arm will be withered and your right eye will be blinded." Here the narrative suggests that it was Bar Kokhba's act of ending the protective prayer of Elazar that caused the tragedy, and not his act of murder per se. When Bar Kokhba killed Elazar, he removed the source of the city's protection. Thus it was not the need to bring recompense to Bar Kokhba that destroyed the last holdout of the rebellion, but rather, the tragic end of the real protection of Israel: the true prayer of the righteous.[56] This becomes even more evident when we compare the last lines of the two sources (see Table 3.1).

What, then, was the real function of Elazar's prayer? Its purpose was to bring atonement for the sins of the people.[57] Elazar's prayer was so powerful that its atoning quality had a cosmic impact that protected the people from the divine punishment normally resulting from sin, even though that punishment was to be delivered by the most powerful army on earth.[58] By praying successful prayers of atonement for Israel's sins, Elazar could hold off the combined legions of the Roman army, and he was so successful that the emperor himself was ready to give up and return to Rome. It was

---

[56] Hasan-Rokem notes the gender imagery between the "brooding hen" associated with Rabbi Eleazar and the brute male strength of Bar Kokhba. "As opposed to the megalomanic pole of a forceful hero, R. Eleazar represents the power latent in motherly warmth, while still appealing to God out of the impotence of humanity.... Thus, R. Eleazar can be seen as the embodiment of God's motherly compassion, and as long as this feeling is alive within the city, there is hope. Ben Kozbah, who seeks to win by force, invalidates the power of divine compassion represented by the praying sage" (166–167).

[57] We have already cited the famous statement of Rabbi Yochanan Ben Zakkai found in ARN (version 2, chapter 4) that subsequent to the destruction of the Jerusalem Temple, prayer would be efficacious like sacrificial offerings in atoning for the sins of Israel. Rabbinic literature is full of references to the efficacy of true prayer for atoning for Israel's sins.

[58] Rabbinic sources regularly consider the Roman emperor and his armies to be the tools of God that can do nothing more than God's bidding. It was therefore God's decision to end the rebellion, to destroy the Temple, and to exile the Judeans from the vicinity of Jerusalem.

TABLE 3.1

| Palestinian Talmud: | Midrash Eikha Rabba: |
| --- | --- |
| [Ben Koziba] gave him one kick and killed him....Immediately, Beitar was captured and Ben Koziba killed. | Immediately, sins caused the capture of Beitar, and Ben Koziba was killed. |

only the Cuthean's knowledge of where the *real* power lay that saved the Romans from humiliation and defeat and destroyed the Jewish rebellion.

What is particularly striking about this narrative is that while the Cuthean, representing apostasy from Israel, knew where the real power was hidden, Rabbi Akiba, Bar Kokhba's powerful rabbinic supporter and the acknowledged rabbinic master of his generation, did not. Akiba was fooled by Bar Kokhba's incredible strength, but he wasn't entirely wrong in his assessment, for even the emperor is made to confirm in the following paragraph that Bar Kokhba was protected by the divine will until he made the mortal error of killing Elazar. The snake curled around his body was to make clear to the emperor that it was the power of God that destroyed him and not any Roman soldier. In rabbinic literature, deaths caused by snakes represent divine retribution, and this is confirmed by the citation of Deuteronomy 32:30 in the text: "If their Rock[59] had not sold him, the Lord had [not] handed him over...."

On the other hand, it was indeed the Cuthean and his clever trick that destroyed Bar Kokhba and his rebellion. "Kuti" (Kutai in Aramaic) is a common designation for Samaritan, the sectarian group living in the northern section of the Land of Israel, whose roots are a mélange of old Israelite religion and the Assyrian introduction of foreign culture and religion to the conquered Northern Kingdom.[60] The term is often used in rabbinic literature to refer to Jewish sectarians in general or to heretics having Gnostic, Christian, or other unacceptable leanings.

Whether Samaritan or sectarian, the Cuthean represents a threat to Judaism by virtue of his status as being Jew-like but not truly Jewish. The pagan Romans were of course incapable of knowing the secret of Elazar's prayer, but it is surprising that Bar Kokhba and even the great Rabbi Akiba were also ignorant of the real center of power in Beitar. They thus symbolize the last remnants of the old school represented by physical prowess and

---

[59] "Rock" (*tzur*) here is parallel to "the Lord," and is quite commonly used in poetic biblical material to denote God (see Deut. 32:15, 1 Sam. 2:2, 2 Sam. 22:32, 47, Isaiah 26:4, 30:29, Ps. 18:32, 89:27, 94:22, 95:1, etc.).

[60] The term probably derives from *Kuta*, one of the towns or areas from which the Assyrian king brought populations to Samaria in the Northern Kingdom (2 Kings 17:24, 30).

warring that was an integral part of Jewish culture, certainly during the Hasmonean and Hadrianic periods during the twilight of the Second Temple.[61] But the tale shows that the militant approach is now out of place. It resulted in horrendous destruction. Henceforth, teaches the story, it is not might or power but quietism and strength of spirit that will preserve the Jews and their religious civilization.

These texts move away from the political context of Israel versus Rome and redefine the threat to Jewish survival through inward-looking examples, one of proper religious behavior and the other of apostasy. It was the Cuthean who represents the real threat to Jewish survival in the story. The insidious Cuthean easily crossed the boundaries between the Romans and the Jews; he knew both worlds intimately, spoke the languages of both peoples, and even knew how to get into the city of Beitar through the drainage pipes. The Cuthean easily defeats Bar Kokhba, without even touching him. Only the Cuthean was capable of bringing down the last stronghold of Jewish resistance against Rome.

Henceforth, the rabbis of the Land of Israel would strive to rid themselves of such Cuthean threats by consolidating rabbinic Judaism and eliminating the most threatening foreign elements [of course, rabbinic Judaism was rife with Hellenistic and other ideas itself]. They would concentrate on the spiritual world of prayer and righteous behavior as determined by *halakhah*, the body of rules and practices that Jews are bound to follow. It was not military might that would bring the messianic redemption, but piety. The messiah will arrive when the Jews carry out God's will through obedience to the Torah and the divine commandments. Armies and independent polities are not necessary for this. Emphasis, rather, must be concentrated on cultivating those behaviors that will build a positive relationship with God in this world and the world to come.

The story of Bar Kokhba and the fall of Beitar encapsulate the ambivalence of rabbinic views regarding this military hero and his rebellion. We know, of course, that Bar Kokhba was a historical figure. Personal letters written by him or for him have been found hidden in caves in the Judean Desert, and these indicate that he regarded himself as having jurisdiction over Judea.[62] Many Jews supported him, perhaps even the majority at the beginning of the revolt, and although it is certain that rabbinic Judaism

---

[61] Other sources, however, such as PT Hagigah 3:1, suggest that supporters of Rabbi Akiba continued to hold significant power after the failed revolt (A. I. Baumgarten, "The Akiban Opposition," *HUCA* 50, 1979), 179–197.

[62] Schäfer, "Bar Kokhba and the Rabbis," 13–16.

was not yet dominant during the second century,[63] even rabbinic texts associate the greatest rabbi of Bar Kokhba's generation, Akiba ben Josef, to have backed him fully.

While the rabbinic material treating the Bar Kokhba Rebellion cannot be relied upon for providing historically accurate data, it certainly expresses the rabbinic sages' real concerns. It is not absurd for rabbis to have backed Bar Kokhba initially because he had, it would seem from his initial success expressed through portrayals of his extraordinary strength, at least a modicum of divine help and protection. He would have appeared to be a great hero. And at least according to the perspective of our rabbinic texts, Rome never succeeded in destroying him.

Yet he is also portrayed in these texts as a reprehensible sinner who murdered the real hero of Beitar, and for this he is destroyed by God via the snake—not by Rome. Surprisingly, given his great stature in the Talmud, Rabbi Akiba was mistaken. The real power of protection for Israel lay not in the might of war heroes, but in the cosmic, spiritual power of the sages— that is, the rabbis. Neither kings, priests, prophets, nor the military leaders known as judges represent the saving future. According to the rabbinic perspective that became dominant and that was read back into the story of the Bar Kokhba Rebellion, leadership would now be filled by righteous, pious men.

Bar Kokhba and Elazar represent virtual opposites. The soldier Bar Kokhba fought physical battles, while the sage Elazar, perhaps the greatest Torah interpreter of his generation according to the Talmud (Shabbat 55b), fought and struggled over the meaning of Torah. Bar Kokhba, on the one hand, relied solely on human strength and military might. He did not wish God's involvement at any level in the conflict. Elazar, on the other hand, relied entirely on God's help, and it was Elazar the pious rabbi, rather than the mighty warrior Bar Kokhba, who was called by the heavenly voice "the power (arm) of all Israel."[64] His humility stands in stark contrast to Bar Kokhba's arrogance.

---

[63] Hannah Cotton lays out the evidence from the many papyri found among the Bar Kokhba caches to show how surprisingly little known rabbinic institutions and language seem to be included within them ("The impact of the documentary papyri from the Judaean Desert on the study of Jewish history from 70 to 135 CE," in Aharon Oppenheimer [ed.], *Jüdische Geschichte in hellenistisch-römischer Zeit. Wege der Forschung: Vom altern zum neuen Schürer* [Munich, R. Oldenbourg, 1999], 221–236 and especially 235–236).

[64] The term "arm" or "limb" is commonly used in the Bible to denote might or strength and takes on the meaning of power and capacity (Ex. 6:6, Deut. 4:34, 5:15, 26:8, Isaiah 51:9, 53:1, 62:8, Jeremiah 21:5, 27:5, Psalm 89:11, 136:12, etc.).

In a discussion about the qualities of the awaited messiah based on Isaiah 11:2–3, the Babylonian sage, Rava (d. 325), remarked:

> [The messiah] can judge by sensing,[65] as it is written (Isaiah 11:3–4) *He shall not judge by seeing with his eyes…He will judge the humble with righteousness and adjudicate the poor evenly.* Bar Koziba ruled for two and a half years. He said to the rabbis, 'I am the messiah.' They answered, 'about the messiah it is written that he senses and judges. We will see whether he senses and judges.' When they saw that he did not sense and judge, they[66] killed him. [BT Sanhedrin 93b].

Note that this passage records a decisive view toward the military leader, with unambiguous disregard for any messianic pretensions. Situated in the Babylonian Talmud, it is likely to be the latest in the series of references to him (or the latest to have been redacted). And it is also the most dismissive. Both earlier and from the Land of Israel, the accounts in the Palestinian Talmud and Lamentations Rabbah naturally may have taken greater consideration of Akiba's stature in his support of Bar Kokhba.[67]

The Bar Kokhba Rebellion marks a watershed in both the history of Israel and in the history of Jewish thought. After its horrendous failure, Jewish activists engaged in guerrilla activities henceforth would be described in rabbinic literature as criminals *(listim, biryonim)* rather than freedom fighters *(qana'im)*.[68] As a watershed event, it marks a change in attitude based on real history, a reaction to the reality of events. Rabbinic Jewish wisdom would henceforth teach that it is not physical acts of war that would protect Israel from its enemies, but rather spiritual concentration in righteousness and prayer. The militant messianic uprisings and military confrontations that occurred from the Maccabees to Bar Kokhba were to be superseded by a far more quietist messianism. Consequently, the rabbinic sources that emerged after the failed revolt teach that, unbeknownst to Bar Kokhba or even Akiba, Rabbi Elazar Hamoda'i was the real hero who had been protecting Beitar against the Roman siege those

---

[65] Literally, "he smells and judges."

[66] According to Jewish sources the rabbis did not kill him. Jewish commentators suggest that "they" refers to the Romans.

[67] The Palestinian Talmud and Midrash Lamentations Rabba were redacted in the Land of Israel.

[68] Aharon Openheimer, "Sanctity of Life and Martyrdom in the Wake of the Bar Kokhba Revolt" (Hebrew), in Yesha`ya Gafni and Aviezer Ravitzky (eds.), *Sanctity of Life and Martyrdom* (Jerusalem: Zalman Shazar Center, 1993), 89.

three and a half years. It was the pious sage and not the great warrior who was the true hero, and his heirs among the rabbis rather than the mighty warriors would henceforth lead the people of Israel and bring them, eventually, to redemption.[69]

---

[69] The controversy over the status of Bar Kokhba and the meaning of his rebellion would be revived with the emergence of Zionism (see chapter 11), and then again with the discovery of Bar Kokhba artifacts in 1960–61 in the "Cave of Letters" (see chapter 13).

# PART II | The World of the Rabbis
## *Holy War Interrupted*

# CHAPTER 4 | Rabbinic Responses to War's Failure

Have you not rejected us, God, by not going out with our armies?

PSALM 60:12

We recall from chapter 1 that according to biblical historiography, Israel's wars were successful when the people obeyed their God, but they fell short when the people failed to heed the divine will. After the successful Maccabean Revolt, this equation of obedience = success/disobedience = failure began to break down. The Temple's destruction in the failed Great Revolt against Rome (66–70 C.E.) could still be explained for a time through recourse to the belief that success and failure are related to obedience to God. Josephus and as well as rabbinic literature blamed the destruction on the sins of certain Jews. Jewish bandits and hooligans (Gr. *lēstēs*/Heb. *listim*) were roaming the countryside of Roman Judea at the time, and the activists at the core of the rebellion were a group that Josephus called [terrorist] dagger-men (*sicarii*). Rabbinic Jews would call them thugs (*biryonim*). According to both rabbinic and other sources, these were not heroic freedom fighters, but rather outlaws who not only killed foreign members of an oppressive and illegal occupying force but also their own innocent coreligionists.[1]

There was one critical difference, however, between the destruction of the First Temple and that of the second. Unlike the first destruction, ostensibly justified by Jewish sin but forgiven seventy years later with the annihilation of the Babylonian Empire and subsequent return of Jews from Babylonia, the destruction of the Second Temple was not followed by a return. Following the chronological paradigm of the first destruction

---

[1] Josephus, *Wars* 4:3–9; Lamentations Rabbah (Buber) 1:3; BT Gittin, 56a-b, Nidah 61a.

almost exactly, the Bar Kokhba Revolt began in the year 132, nearly seventy years after the destruction of the Second Temple in 70 C.E. In fact, had it succeeded the pattern of a seventy-year restoration might have actually occurred. But even though the revolt was led by Akiba ben Joseph, who was considered the most righteous and pious rabbi of his generation, it failed to destroy the evil empire. A story is related in the Talmud how some disciples of Rabbi Akiba were once overtaken by Jewish robbers. When they were asked whose disciples they were, they replied: " 'Rabbi Akiba's,' whereupon the robbers exclaimed, 'Happy are Rabbi Akiba and his disciples, for no evil person has ever done them harm.' "[2]

That observation did not prove accurate, for as we noted in the previous chapter, one of Rabbi Akiba's disciples was Bar Kokhba. We observed how Akiba considered Bar Kokhba to have been the messianic war-hero who would deliver Israel from the Romans, just as Judah Maccabee delivered Israel from the Greeks. But it turned out that *this* disciple of Akiba was *not* safe from harm, nor were most of his warrior followers. The Bar Kokhba rebellion failed, and the results were devastating. Both Bar Kokhba and Akiba were destroyed, and the massacres, disease, famine, and human dislocation that followed were so great that the surviving rabbis felt the need to find a way to overturn, abrogate, or cancel the dangerous paradigm that expected militant piety to lead to military success. Henceforth, Judaism would turn inward. History now dominated by Roman power would have little significance to the rabbis. The study of Torah and Tradition would develop into the primary Jewish pursuit, and a life of quietist sanctity and piety would become the "national" goal of the Jews. We shall observe how this was accomplished, but the world of the rabbis and their intellectual strategies must first be established in its historical and literary context.

## The Emergence of Rabbinic Judaism and Its Canonical Texts

Rabbinic Judaism is called such because the leadership of this movement was made up of a scholar class called rabbis, meaning "masters" or "teachers." But as Shaye Cohen has put it, "the expression 'rabbinic period' reflects the fact that we are well informed about the rabbis and about no one else."[3] What he means is that while other, nonrabbinic expressions of Judaism existed for centuries into what we call the rabbinic period in the Land of Israel and in the Diaspora, we know very little about them. Some

---

[2] BT Avodah Zarah 25b.
[3] Shaye Cohen, *From the Maccabees to the Mishnah*, 225.

forms of Judaism in the eastern Mediterranean are now called Hellenistic Judaism by historians.[4] A different set in Mesopotamia were subsumed under various names that were eventually lumped together to be identified as Kara'ite Judaism,[5] but in fact we know little about the internal communal organization and history of the Jews in the Land of Israel and Babylonia in the first centuries, C.E.

The status and title of rabbi has no precedence in biblical religion.[6] The title emerges into history within the Land of Israel around the turn of the millennium and appears in writing only with the publication of the Mishnah in about 200, though a probable Greek translation occurs in the New Testament in reference to Jesus (Matt. 26:25; Mark 9:5; John 3:2, etc.). The rabbis completed the long process of canonizing the "Written Torah" (the Hebrew Bible) and were responsible also for the canon of the "Oral Torah," that library of rabbinic works represented most obviously by the Talmud. The rabbinic Talmud (and a parallel genre of biblical interpretive literature called Midrash) became *the* post-biblical Jewish literature, while other Jewish works collected into the Apocrypha, Pseudepigrapha, and the compositions of Philo and Josephus, as well as many others, were not preserved by Jews.

The consensus of current scholarship considers rabbinic Judaism to have begun to emerge in the Land of Israel toward the end of the Second Temple Period, and most historians associate it with the earlier surfacing of Pharisaic Judaism beginning with the Maccabees/Hasmoneans in the mid-second century, B.C.E. The literature of emerging rabbinic Judaism began to develop at about the same time as other genres of Jewish literature representing different expressions of Judaism, such as the large and varied assortment of Hellenistic Jewish compositions. Soon after 70 C.E., however, with the destruction of the Second Temple, along with its authority structures of priesthood and kingship, new leadership schemes emerged and vied for influence. These were based on the authority of kinship, congregational structures of village synagogues, economic status (landed aristocracy), and writing skills, along with knowledge of Torah. Rabbinic leadership based on scribal skills and Torah knowledge eventually dominated, and this leadership absorbed or

---

[4] Erich S. Gruen, "Hellenistic Judaism," in David Biale (ed.), *Cultures of the Jews* (New York: Schocken, 2002), 77–132; Fergus Millar, "The Jews of the Graeco-Roman Diaspora Between Paganism and Christianity, AD 312–438," in Judith Lieu, John North, and Tessa Rajak (eds.) *The Jews Among Pagans and Christians in the Roman Empire* (London: Routledge, 1992), 97–123.

[5] Meira *Polliack, Karaite Judaism: A Guide to Its History and Literary Sources* (Leiden: Brill), 2003; Fred Astren, *Kara'ite Judaism and Historical Understanding* (Columbia, SC: University of South Carolina, 2004); Leon Nemoy, *Karaite Anthology* (New Haven: Yale University, 1980).

[6] Catherine Hezser, *The Social Structure of the Rabbinic Movement in Roman Palestine* (Tübingen: Mohr Siebeck, 1997), 53–77.

rejected other forms of Jewish thinking and practice to eventually become the prevailing Jewish expression of biblical monotheism.

The record of that transition from biblical monotheism to rabbinic Judaism is virtually unknown, something of a black hole of Jewish history. This is quite different from the transition within a closely related community from biblical monotheism to Christian monotheism, which is celebrated in the New Testament as a break from and fulfillment of the old religious system. The obvious severance claimed by the Christians may have actually influenced the perspective of the rabbis, who claimed in opposition to their Christian brethren that they were more faithful to the authentic, unaltered meaning of the Hebrew Bible. And yet, with the destruction of the Temple system of worship and all the institutions and assumptions based upon it, rabbinic Judaism in fact carried out many changes in order to function in a post-Temple world. And the leadership that became known as the rabbis had to compete with other Jewish factions that had their own ideas about how to carry on God's word and law with the Temple no longer standing.

Until recently, the transition and domination of rabbinic Judaism was assumed to have taken place in the first two to three centuries, C.E. Today, scholars such as Seth Schwartz are questioning the presumed early ascendancy of the rabbis and have pushed it forward by a number of centuries.[7] Whether the rabbis became dominant in the second to third centuries or the sixth to seventh centuries, the literature that gave them authority reflects radical changes regarding war.

The rabbinic works examined here are the Talmud and Midrash, neither of which is easily datable. The Talmud represents a number of different layers of literature, the earliest of which is referred to as "tannaitic" because it is associated with the *tannaim*. *Tannaim* roughly means "teachers," and refers to the rabbis living in the Land of Israel from roughly 100 B.C.E. through about 200 C.E. who appear in the texts of the Mishnah. The Mishnah is written in Hebrew and represents the organizational and conceptual core of the Talmud. It is a collection of teachings that include discussions about ritual behavior, civil and criminal law, and morals and ethics expressed in a variety of ways ranging from brief stories or situational examples to aphorisms, and even includes household wisdom and medical advice, all of it organized according to its own internal principles and not based on direct exegesis of the Bible. The Mishnah was originally an independent collection of tannaitic literature that was published around the second century.

---

[7] Seth Schwartz, *Imperialism and Jewish Society, 200 B.C.E. to 640 C.E.* (Princeton, N.J.: Princeton University, 2001).

Other tannaitic material known as *baraitot* (meaning "outside materials" because they were not included in the Mishnah) are closely related to it but found in other parts of the Talmud.

When the Mishnah was published and made accessible, scholars studied it with great deliberation and discussed it in great detail. The language they spoke at the time was Aramaic, and as their discussions expanded over time they began to record them so as to remember them. A written record of these discussions was eventually edited and placed in relation to the Mishnah material they addressed. This became known as the Gemara, meaning "completion," because it was understood (at least for a time) to have completed or at least augmented the discussions of the Mishnah. Typically, in the Talmud, a paragraph of the Mishnah on any given topic is followed by a longer set of paragraphs of Gemara, after which appears the next Mishnah, followed by its own extension in Gemara.

There exist two versions of this compilation of Mishnah with its extended Gemara discussion. One was assembled in the Land of Israel and is called the *Talmud Yerushalmi*, meaning the Jerusalem Talmud (though it was not actually assembled in Jerusalem). In English it is usually called the Palestinian Talmud. A later, somewhat different and more complete version was assembled in Iraq, which Jews have always referred to as Babylon (*Bavel* in Hebrew). That collection is called the *Talmud Bavli* or Babylonian Talmud. While the mishnaic core of both Talmuds is virtually identical, the Gemaras of the Jerusalem and Babylonian Talmuds are essentially different compositions, despite the fact that they include many parallels and even much of the same material. The Gemara of the Palestinian Talmud is significantly shorter than that of the Babylonian, and it is the Babylonian Talmud that is always indicated when one refers to *the* Talmud.

Both the Mishnah and the Gemara are made up of thousands of short statements made by or in the name of rabbis. Although it is known when and where most of the rabbis named in the Talmud lived, it is difficult to date Talmudic material because statements are often attributed to more than one rabbi or are given anonymously; moreover, the text is often so complex and vague that it may be difficult to determine which named rabbis were the ones to whom statements are actually attributed.

Midrash, like the Talmud, is composed of many thousands of short rabbinic statements, some of which are identified and others of which are anonymous. And there is a significant amount of overlap between Talmud and Midrash in that many rabbinic statements are found in both. Although the term "Talmud" refers to a single composition (or two editions of the same composition, the Jerusalem and Babylonian Talmuds), "Midrash" refers to a *genre*—that being of the earliest collections of rabbinic tradition dedicated to direct exegesis of the Hebrew Bible. Dozens of collections of Midrash span the ages from the late Second Temple period into the Middle Ages. "Classical" Midrash refers to the earliest collections that were assembled between the fourth to about the tenth centuries, C.E., and it is to these anthologies that we refer in this chapter.

Not only is rabbinic Judaism post-biblical in chronology, it represents a complex of worldviews that reflect a post-biblical reality. While it is true that Talmud and Midrash provide much detail of Temple practice that cannot be found anywhere else, including the Bible, most of the contents of rabbinic literature treat aspects of Jewish life that could be lived anywhere. Most of the particular behaviors enumerated in the Bible that are required within the borders of the Land of Israel became impossible because they were associated with institutions such as the Temple that no longer existed. Thus rabbinic Judaism became a Judaism of Diaspora, even within the borders of the Land of Israel.

Rabbinic Judaism developed in a period during which it was not in political control of its national destiny. The rabbis had no true polity and, aside from a very few rare and short-lived exceptions, Jews had no armies.[8] To this reality must be added that the last independent and semi-independent Jewish governments that began with the Maccabean/Hasmonean revolt soon became politically and religiously corrupt. In fact, the turmoil of this period was a major factor in the emergence of rabbinic Judaism.

There has always been an assumption, expressed in the Talmud and Midrash and reinforced in the daily liturgy and home ritual, that the Temple would again be rebuilt and Jewish control would again be reestablished over the sacred lands. By the time of the codification of the Talmud, however, an assumption that achieved the level of virtual doctrine had it that God would determine the time and the method of the great Return to the Land of Israel. God, not human leaders, would initiate the Return. As a result, military, political, and even migratory movements intending to accomplish that goal were determined to be dangerous and were ultimately forbidden by law and tradition. We have observed in the previous chapter how Jewish militant movements against Rome had ultimately failed and how the

---

[8] Rare exceptions essentially proved the rule. One was the previously mentioned independent Khazar kingdom, which became Jewish in the ninth century and was destroyed in the tenth. Another was the messianic warrior Abu Isa al-Isfahani (eighth century Iran), but neither seem to have been part of the normative world of rabbinic Judaism, and neither had any impact on the development of war ideas in Judaism.

failure had brought catastrophic destruction. The calamity was so devastating that even centuries later, when that rabbinic literature was canonized into the Talmud, activist militancy had been suppressed and replaced by a general worldview of pious quietism in relation to outside powers.

The change to quietism did not occur overnight, nor was it universal. There remain strands within the weave of rabbinic Judaism that are more or less politically activist, and the sages of the Talmud were certainly not known collectively as pacifists, nor were they empty of violent rage.[9] In fact, a large body of apocalyptic literature developed in Judaism that spans from the Bible to the present in which war, to use Lawrence Schiffman's words, "was considered an instrument by which God would bring about the redemption of His people."[10] This literature had a profound influence on modern thinkers such as Abraham Isaac Kook and his disciples, and it was no less influential among the Jews of Late Antiquity. It took a long period of struggle and argument among the many (and some still unknown) factions and circles within formative rabbinic Judaism for the transition to have been made. Certainly by the middle of the third century, however, the overwhelming weight of rabbinic thinking was resigned politically, if not always spiritually, to quietism in relation to the ruling powers. It eventually became codified in rabbinic literature, and this has had a deep and long-lasting impact on the Jewish attitude toward war, as well as violent actions in general, despite the well-known and beloved biblical descriptions of Israel's great military victories achieved under divine providence.[11]

## The Abolition of a Biblical Institution

The rabbis succeeded in their suppression of militancy by establishing two symbolic paradigms to counter the expectation of divinely authorized military success. One defined divinely authorized warring—"holy war"—in a way that made it virtually impossible to apply. The other constructed a delicate relationship between exile and redemption in which the Jews had

---

[9] There are stories about rabbis, for example, who with their very gaze burned up those who derided the words of the sages (BT Berakhot 58a, Shabbat 34a, Baba Batra 75a, Sanhedrin 100a), and one case in which a rabbi was so enraged that everything he looked at caught fire (Baba Metzi`a 59b).

[10] "War in Apocalyptic Thought," in Lawrence Schiffman and Joel Wolowelsky, eds., *War and Peace in the Jewish Tradition* (New York: Yeshivah University, 2007), 492.

[11] See Joseph Isaac Lifshitz, "War and Aesthetics in Jewish Law," in Yigal Levin and Amnon Shapira, *War and Peace in Jewish Tradition* (London: Routledge, 2012) 107–110.

virtually no option other than to accept their divinely ordained fate to live under the political hegemony of gentiles. These two symbolic paradigms will be examined in detail in the following chapter but will be outlined briefly here.

In the first construct, found at the end of the eighth chapter of the Mishnah tractate called Sotah, the rabbis condense the dense, complex, and varied expressions of holy war in the Bible into two sentences, and within those two sentence they distill them into two types: "Discretionary War" (*milchemet reshut*) and "Commanded War" (or "war of *mitzvah*"—*milchemet mitzvah*). One the one hand, Discretionary Wars according to the Talmud allow for so many deferments that they could be understood as mercenary ventures. Commanded Wars, on the other hand, are sacred endeavors commanded by God for which there can be no deferments. As the Mishnah states in Sotah 8:7, "everyone must go forth [to Commanded War], even a bridegroom from his chamber and a bride from her bridal pavilion."

This construct established extremely narrow parameters for discussion of war in rabbinic Judaism. The Talmuds expand the Mishnah only slightly, and they do so by limiting Commanded War to the divinely commanded wars of conquest led by Joshua in antiquity.[12] This essentially eliminated the dangerous wild-card of holy war because Commanded War was associated with a historical occasion that had long passed. A new conquest of the Land of Israel was never to be initiated by Jews, but only by the Holy One, who was the single power with the authority to determine when the time was right.

According to the Palestinian Talmud, war of defense requiring full mobilization was also considered Commanded War, which allowed the possibility of Commanded War at any time and place as a defensive act. This position is absent from the Babylonian Talmud, out of which authoritative Jewish law is constructed, but the great medieval legalist and philosopher, Moses Maimonides (d. 1204), nevertheless formalizes the notion of defensive war as a category of Commanded War in his *Code of Jewish Law*.[13]

The second construct that emerged from the rabbinic repertoire is the "Three Vows." through which the rabbis discouraged mass-movements that might instigate a backlash by the gentile powers under which the Jews lived.[14] These vows refer to a phrase occurring three times in the

---

[12] The terminology in the two Talmuds is quite specific: "the wars of Joshua to conquer" in the Babylonian Talmud, *Sota* 44b, and "Joshua's war" in the Palestinian Talmud, *Sota* 8:1.

[13] *Hilkhot Melakhim* 5:1.

[14] In Maimonides' famous *Epistle to Yemen* he chronicles a number of cases in which failed Jewish messianic movements instigated violent backlashes by non-Jews in both the Muslim and

Song of Songs, *I make you swear, o daughters of Jerusalem, by the gazelles and by the hinds of the field, do not wake or rouse love until it is wished.*[15]

The interpretation of consensus on this verse among the rabbis is that God is making the daughters of Jerusalem (a metaphor for Israel) swear not to wake or rouse love (attempting to bring the messiah) until it is wished—meaning until God decides the time is right. Attempting to bring messiah by human means through rebellion, war, or revolution rather than waiting patiently for God to bring the messiah himself is "forcing God's hand."[16] This is an act of disobedience that would only bring further divine wrath and additional disasters for the Jewish people.

Combined, the two constructs convey the divine command that Israel not ascend to the Land of Israel en masse,[17] nor rebel against their inferior position under the rule of gentiles. In response, God will not allow the gentiles to persecute the Jews "overly much" (Hebrew: *yoter middai*). But if the Jews would not agree to these terms, then they would be subject to divinely authorized violence at the hands of the gentiles, permitting their "flesh [to be consumed] like [that of] gazelles or hinds of the field."

The biblical construct of Israel's wars succeeding when the people obeyed their God, but failing when the people refused to heed the divine will (obedience = success/disobedience = failure), was thus retained in rabbinic Judaism but with one major innovation. That innovation was, in essence, a lesson derived from history. After the destruction of the Second Temple and the failure of the Bar Kokhba Rebellion, Jewish leaders were no longer to be considered qualified to determine when the time is ripe for war.[18] War is still theoretically possible but impossible to put into actual

---

Christian worlds (Abraham Halkin and Boaz Cohen, Moses Maimonides' *Epistle to Yemen: The Arabic Original and the three Hebrew Versions* [NY: American Academy for Jewish Research, 1952], xvi–xx.) Maimonides follows his references with a strongly worded caution against following such messianic pretenders by citing the Three Vows (ibid, xx).

[15] *Song of Songs* (in Christian Bibles, "The Song of Solomon") 2:7, 3:5, 8:4. The last rendering of the sentence, in 8:4, does not contain "by the gazelles and by the hinds of the field," but the rabbis include it there also by analogy.

[16] Or more literally, "pressing the End" (*dochin et haqetz*). For an early appearance of this idiom, see *Leviticus Rabba* 19:5; Gershom Scholem, *The Messianic Idea in Judaism* (London: George Allen & Unwin, 1971) 14.

[17] "Ascension" or "going up" refers to moving from outside the Land of Israel to within the biblical borders (from whence the modern Hebrew term for emigration to the state of Israel, `*aliyah*). Many religious scholars considered this a collective prohibition but not a prohibition against individuals who wished to move their families to the Land of Israel.

[18] The role of the leadership body of the Sanhedrin, according to rabbinic sages, will be discussed below.

practice. In other words, the "default position" would judge Jews incapable of knowing whether or not they were spiritually fit enough to engage the enemy successfully. The rabbis ruled, therefore, even if somewhat indirectly, that Jewish wars for all intents and purposes were no longer an option. The only one capable of deciding when the time is ripe is God, and "the time" is represented by the coming of the messiah.

# CHAPTER 5 | Rabbinic Typology of War

Why are there these three vows? One teaches that Israel should not go up [to the Land of Israel] in a wall, in one the Holy One made Israel swear that they would not rebel against the nations of the world, and in one the Holy One made the nations of the world swear that they would not subjugate Israel too harshly.

BABYLONIAN TALMUD KETUBOT IIIA

## First Construct: Categories of War

### In the Mishnah

The rabbis exhibit relatively little interest in biblical wars and the behavioral expectations or rules (*halakhot*) that might be derived from them, devoting far more attention to other issues. The Mishnah (redacted sometime after 200 C.E.), which establishes the agenda for all subsequent rabbinic discussion of Judaism, only twice mentions the difference between what we shall observe is a critical distinction between "discretionary" war and "commanded" war.[1] One occurs in the discussion of authority for the king to muster troops for war found in tractate *Sanhedrin* and examined in the next chapter. The other occurs in a discussion of military deferments in tractate Sotah, which is the current topic of discussion. In the brief account

---

[1] In a related collection of tannaitic material called the Tosefta (meaning "supplement" to the Mishnah), the term for Discretionary War does appear a few more times (*Sanhedrin* 2:4, *Eruvin* 2:7, 3:7, *Megillah* 3:25, *Sota* 7:24), therefore presupposing more thinking about the dichotomy between the two categories of war that will be examined in detail later in the chapter.

found at the end of the eighth chapter of tractate Sotah (Sotah 8:7),[2] the broad range of warring in the Bible is distilled into a simple, if initially confusing, classification system.

The discussion is stimulated by a set of rules and procedures treating war in Deuteronomy 20. The title of Mishnah chapter eight is "The Anointed for Battle" (*mesuach milchamah*), which refers to the priest who addresses the Israelite troops before battle (Deut. 20:1–4). The term, "The Anointed for Battle," is a rabbinic idiom and not found in the Bible, but the rabbis assumed that the priest referred to in Deuteronomy 20:2–4 was specifically appointed (and anointed) for the purpose of encouraging the troops and assuring them that God would go out with the warriors and actually engage in the fray for God's people (*haholekh `imakhem lehi-lachem lakhem*).

After a very brief discussion about this official in the first *mishnah*, the following four *mishnah*s treat the deferments from battle listed in Deuteronomy 20:5–9. The Mishnah is not the first Jewish text to treat war deferments. Some three centuries earlier, I Maccabees depicts Judah the Maccabee following the biblical deferments listed in Deuteronomy: "In accordance with the law, he ordered back to their homes those who were building their houses or were betrothed or were planting vineyards or were faint-hearted."[3] The rabbis, however, felt the need to probe these deferments in some detail. They note in Deut. 20:5, for example (*Is there anyone who has built a new house but has not dedicated it?*), that it is not clear whether "new house" *(bayit chadash)* refers only to a human habitation or may refer also perhaps to a structure for cattle or to store feed or wood. The Hebrew word *bayit* can range in meaning from a physical structure to a tribal kinship community, and it appears in the Bible in reference to tents (Numbers 16:32, Deut. 11:6), animal shelters (1 Sam. 6:7, 10), and even a spider's web (Job 8:14). What, then, ask the rabbis, might qualify as a "new house" for this deferment? Such questions are asked about the other deferments listed in Deuteronomy as well.

After interrogating the war deferments listed in Deuteronomy in some detail, the seventh and final *mishnah* then proceeds to define the types of wars for which the deferments would or would not apply.

---

[2] The Mishnah (capitalized here) will henceforth refer to the work as a whole, called *the* Mishnah, while *mishnah* (lower case and italicized) will refer to the numbered paragraphs or subsections of every chapter found within the Mishnah. Chapter and *mishnah* may also be represented as "8:7"—meaning chapter 8 *mishnah* 7.

[3] *I Macc.* 3:56.

To what (types of wars do these deferment) instructions apply? To a Discretionary War (*milchemet ha-reshut*),[4] but in a Commanded War (*milchemet mitzvah*) everyone must go forth, even a bridegroom from his chamber and a bride from her bridal pavilion.[5] Rabbi Yehudah[6] said: "To what (types of wars) do these (deferment) instructions apply? To a Commanded War (*milchemet mitzvah*), but in an Obligatory War (*milchemet chovah*) everyone must go forth, even a bridegroom from his chamber and a bride from her bridal pavilion."

This *mishnah* is made up of two parts. The first is an anonymous statement. The second is nearly identical but given in the name of Rabbi Yehudah. The two statements agree in their division of Israel's wars into two categories, but they disagree on the terminology applied to them. The first category allows for all the deferments listed in Deuteronomy 20 and amplified by the Mishnah. The second category does not allow for any deferments whatsoever. Even the bride and bridegroom about to consummate their marriage must cease immediately and join the troops.[7] A hierarchy is thus established here in the Mishnah, with war category #2 requiring the participation of all Israel with no exceptions.

The Mishnah treats two issues. The first is to establish a typology of war, which is accomplished by dividing all biblical wars into two types according to whether or not deferments apply to them. The second issue appears to be a conflict between rabbinic sages over terms used to label the two types, or perhaps a conflict over what kinds of war allow or forbid deferments. According to the anonymous statement, the first category of war allowing for deferments is called "discretionary," while the first category according to Rabbi Yehudah is called "commanded." The second category of war allowing for no deferments is called "commanded" in the anonymous statement, but it is called "obligatory" by Rabbi Yehudah.

---

[4] I capitalize these three categories of war because they become technical terms here and in all subsequent discussion.

[5] The phrase, *a bridegroom from his chamber and a bride from her bridal pavilion* is a direct citation from Joel 2:16, derived from a context of an imagined End of Days described in language reminiscent of war: raging and devouring fire, horsemen and chariots, marching hordes, weeping and mourning.

[6] Yehudah bar Ilai, who lived during the middle of the second century, C.E. in the Land of Israel. He is an important sage whose opinions are cited often in tannaitic literature.

[7] This surprising statement appears to suggest that women should join in such wars, but this is actually a rhetorical use of the biblical verse from Joel 2:16 (it is unlikely that the rabbis would ever have considered that women should participate in war). Modern halakhic literature on rules of war treats this topic in some detail.

While this *mishnah* establishes a typology for war, it never explains what wars might or might not allow deferments, nor is an explanation provided anywhere else in the Mishnah. Moreover, it should be noted here that the Mishnah's division of the wars of Israel into those for which deferments apply and those for which deferments do not apply seems to go against the plain meaning of the biblical text. The section of Deuteronomy that mentions deferments (Deut. 20:1–9) represents a discrete section and does not suggest that they might not apply to one type of war or another.

However, the following section in Deuteronomy 20:10–18 distinguishes between two categories of war, though it does so with regard to an entirely different issue. That issue is what we call today "rules of engagement." Two sets of rules of engagement apply to two categories of enemy, respectively, which are determined in Deuteronomy 20:15–16 by according to where the enemy is located: "[the enemy living in] towns that lie very far from you, the towns that do not belong to the local peoples," and "[the enemy living in] the towns of these [local] peoples." According to Deuteronomy's categorization of rules of engagement, the enemy in "towns that lie very far from you" may survive as subject peoples, while the enemy in "the towns of these [local] peoples" must be entirely destroyed.

The Mishnah does not openly express interest in the nature of Deuteronomy's two categories. It neither discusses rules of engagement nor geographical location of the enemy. On the other hand, it is likely that Deuteronomy provided the impetus for the Mishnah's classification into two categories based on whether or not deferments apply. Both Deuteronomy and the Mishnah divide war into two categories, but their divisions are based on different criteria. To summarize, the Mishnah distills the wide range of Israelite war into two categories derived from a single passage in the book of Deuteronomy: one for which deferments apply, and one for which they do not. It recognizes that there is some disagreement over the terms used to identify these categories.

Two questions raised but not answered by this *mishnah* are (1) to what difference between the two types of war does the Mishnah refer, and (2) why is different terminology employed by the anonymous statement and Rabbi Yehudah?


In the Gemara(s)

Both questions are taken up by the Gemaras of the Jerusalem and the Babylonian Talmuds, the two compendia containing records of some of the continuing discussion of the rabbis subsequent to the canonization of the Mishnah. The earliest to be redacted was the Palestinian Talmud, which can be dated to sometime before 500 C.E.

> RABBI YOHANAN SAID: There is [only] a terminological difference (*mashma'ut*) between [the anonymous statement and Rabbi Yehudah]. Rabbi Yehudah called the Discretionary War [of the anonymous statement] a Commanded War. However, [they all agreed that] everyone [was required] to go out for an Obligatory War, even a bridegroom from his chamber and a bride from her bridal pavilion.
>
> RAV HISDA[8] SAID: There is a conceptual dispute (*machloqet*) between them. The rabbis [represented by the anonymous statement][9] contend that a Commanded War would be David's war, while an Obligatory War would be Joshua's war; but Rabbi Yehudah called a Discretionary War one that we initiate against them [i.e., the enemy], and an Obligatory war one which the [enemy] initiates against us.[10]

> It is written (1 Kings 15:22): "Then King Asa mustered all of Judah; no one was exempt *(ein naqi)*". What is the meaning of *no one was exempt*? Rabbi Simon [differed with] the rabbis. Rabbi Simon [said: a man is] not exempt [to leave fighting in order] to go home [even] for one hour. The rabbis said: [Even] a rabbi of an eminent rabbinical house is not [exempt]. (PT Sota 8:1)

In this *gemara*, Rabbi Yohanan resolves the difficulty of the Mishnah by suggesting that two terms refer to the same thing. Rabbi Yehudah and the anonymous statement referred to the same two categories—they simply used different terms to refer to them. The rabbis' Discretionary War and Rabbi Yehudah's Commanded War referred to wars for which the

---

[8] One of the most frequently quoted sages of the Babylonian and Palestinian Talmuds, Hisda was a third-generation Babylonian (d. c. 309 C.E.) and head of the academy at Sura.

[9] According to the usual rhetoric of this discourse, when two opinions are stated, one being anonymous and the other named, the anonymous is considered to be the majority opinion, while the named opinion is identified because it goes against the majority. Reference to the anonymous statement is therefore often given as "the rabbis."

[10] In the manuscript tradition, an otherwise unnamed Vatican ms. cited by Goren, has: "Rabbi Yehudah called Commanded War, such as when we go against them, Required War, such as when they come against us." Shlomo Goren, "Commanded War and Discretionary War" (Hebrew), *Mahanayim* 69 (1962), 6. Another version found in the *Qorban Ha'edah* cited by Tekhoresh has, "Rabbi Yehudah said: Commanded War is the war of David. Obligatory is the war of Joshua. The rabbis said: Discretionary War is one in which we go out against them. Obligatory War is one in which they come against us." K. P. Tekhoresh, "Discretionary, Commanded and Required War" (Hebrew), *Hatorah Vehamedina* 2 (1950), p. 92.

deferments apply. And the rabbis' Commanded War and Rabbi Yehudah's Obligatory War (both referred to by Rabbi Yohanan as Obligatory War) allowed no deferments. Despite Rabbi Yochanan's logical resolution, his explanation does not explain Rabbi Yehudah's preference for the term "commanded" over "discretionary" and "required" over "commanded."[11]

In the following section, Rav Hisda resolves the difficulty differently. He understands the difference between the rabbis and Rabbi Yehudah as one of substance rather than merely semantics. According to Rav Hisda, the rabbis' two categories (represented in the anonymous statement) relate to specific wars or types of wars found in biblical history. The first category of Commanded War refers to the war of King David for which deferments apply, while the second category of Obligatory War with no deferments refers to the war of Joshua.[12] Rabbi Yehudah's categories, however, distinguished between two generic categories of war. A Discretionary War (with deferments) is one that is initiated by Israel, while an Obligatory War without deferments is a defensive war. This response explains the difference in terminology used by the rabbis and Rabbi Yehudah by suggesting that the two parties are referring to two different typologies.

It is not clear from Rav Hisda's reference to David's and Joshua's wars whether he is referring to specific wars or categories of war typed according to those waged by David and Joshua. The former possibility would of course be much more limited than the latter. The reference to "David's war" is understood in rabbinic literature to refer to King David's subjugation of a region of Syria called Aram in 2 Samuel 10 and known by the rabbis as David's conquest of Aram Zobah (2 Sam. 10:6). The rabbis considered this area to be outside the official borders of the Land of Israel. "Joshua's war" refers to the conquest of Canaan (Joshua 1:1ff). War deferments would then apply to David's personally initiated wars of expansion beyond the biblical

---

[11] Later commentators would explain that the difference of terminology reflects Rabbi Yehudah's view that serving in a Jewish army exempts a Jew from engaging in certain other commandments, while the rabbis (represented by the anonymous statement) were not concerned about that issue. Both parties, however, would agree that deferments listed in Deuteronomy 20 and Mishnah Sotah 8 would apply to category one, but not to category 2. In both cases, say the commentators, the rabbis are clarifying through the use of different terminology that there is a hierarchical difference between the two categories of war, and that the second category is more stringent and does not allow deferments.

[12] The same examples of David's and Joshua's wars found here in the Gemara of the Palestinian Talmud are also given in the Babylonian Talmud, as we shall observe (BT *Sotah* 44b), but in the Babylonian Talmud the descriptions are more explicit: "the wars of the House of David for expansion" and "the wars of Joshua for conquest."

borders of the Land of Israel, but not to Joshua's divinely prescribed wars of conquest.

Rav Hisda continues by contrasting this anonymous typology with a typology he associates with Rabbi Yehudah based on whether war is initiated by Israel or is purely defensive. Category one, then, is a Discretionary War allowing deferments according to Rav Hisda's reading of Rabbi Yehudah, because it is initiated by Israel against its enemies, while category two allows for no deferments because it is a war of defense against enemy attack. Rav Hisda's comment significantly expands the range of thinking about the wars of Israel. It should be noted, however, that he meant to clarify what he considered to be a conceptual difference between Rabbi Yehudah and the rabbis by their use of different language in the Mishnah. His comment was not intended to determine which side was correct. When a difference of opinion occurs between the rabbis, on the one hand, and a single named source, on the other, the rule of thumb is that the correct position is that of the rabbis.[13]

The passage concludes with an example of a specific battle described in the Bible for which no deferments were allowed. One might have thought that bringing this example (as usual in the form of an argument) was an attempt to prove the correctness of either the anonymous rabbis or Rabbi Yehudah with regard to the *type* of war for which no deferments are allowed, since the language of the verse makes explicit that nobody was exempt from the fighting. But the discussion moves in a rather different direction. It forbids deferments, but treats the topic from an entirely different angle than found in either of the passages in Deuteronomy or the Mishnah. The argument revolves around whether the restriction is one of time or of person. Rabbi Simon suggests that the emphasis is meant to preclude anyone from returning to his home even for one hour, while the rabbis hold that it forbids even eminent rabbinic leaders from military exemption.

The next layer of rabbinic literature to take up the categorization of wars is the Babylonian Talmud (*Sotah* 44b). The discussion begins with the opening words of *mishnah* 7: "To what do these instructions apply?" and continues with a statement attributed to Rabbi Yohanan that parallels that of the Palestinian Talmud.

---

[13] The hermeneutical principle is formulated as follows: "when there is [a difference between an opinion of] a single sage and the majority of sages, the *halakhah* follows the majority."

RABBI YOHANAN SAID: Discretionary [War] according to the rabbis is Commanded [War] according to Rabbi Yehudah. Commanded [War] according to the rabbis is Obligatory [War] according to Rabbi Yehudah.

RAVA[14] SAID: The wars of conquest of Joshua everyone agrees is Obligatory, while the wars of the House of David for [territorial] expansion everyone agrees is Discretionary. They differed over weakening idol worshippers so that they would not march against them. One considers this Commanded while the other considers it Discretionary.

The [halakhic] difference [between the two positions] is that one who is engaged in the performance of a commandment is exempt from [the performance] of a [different] commandment.

Rabbi Yochanan's statement here is parallel to the statement attributed to him in the Palestinian Talmud, but more concise. As in the Palestinian Talmud, he claims that the rabbis (who represent the anonymous statement of the Mishnah) and Rabbi Yehudah are working with the same typology but with different language. The rabbis' Discretionary War is the same as Rabbi Yehudah's Commanded War, and the rabbis' Commanded War is the same as Rabbi Yehudah's Obligatory War.

A statement by Rava follows, which finds a parallel with that of Rav Hisda in the Palestinian Talmud. Like Rav Hisda, he provides examples of the types of wars that would apply to each of these two categories, though he reverses the order found in the Mishnah by placing the more stringent category for which there are no deferments (category 2) before category 1. Rava explains that both parties would agree that category two, for which there are no deferments, would include the divinely authorized wars of conquest of the Land of Israel by Joshua. Here as in the Palestinian Talmud, it is not clear whether Joshua's wars of conquest are cited as a specific and limited reference to a single occasion or as an example of a type that might incorporate others as well. And in an important formulation, Rava notes that all (the rabbis) would consider the wars of Joshua "required," even the party (i.e. the rabbis) that did not use that specific term in their original formulation in the Mishnah (the importance of these terms will be examined shortly).

---

[14] An abbreviation of Rav Abba (d.325), Rava lived and taught at Mahoza in Babylonia and was one of the most important sages of his generation.

All parties agree that there exists a hierarchy between two kinds of wars, but they use different terminology to refer to them. To the rabbis, "commanded" is more stringent than "discretionary" and to Rabbi Yehudah, "obligatory" is more stringent than "commanded." Rava refers to the more stringent category in the strongest formulation possible: "obligatory." Rava then gives the example of the wars of King David for territorial expansion as the ideal type of category 1: wars for which deferments would be accepted by both parties, the rabbis and Rabbi Yehudah. And true to his method, he refers to this category in its least stringent formulation—"discretionary"—when he states that everyone (even Rabbi Yehudah, who did not use the term) would consider it so.[15] It should be noted here that Rava's division corresponds closely with the division in Deuteronomy 20:10–18 between "towns that lie very far from you . . . that do not belong to the local peoples," (category one: David's territorial expansion) and "the towns of these [local] peoples" (category two: Joshua's conquest of the Land of Israel).

Since Rava notes how the rabbis and Rabbi Yehudah are in agreement about these basic categories, it is asked what exactly they *disagree* about. The answer provided here, and it is not clear whether this is a continuation of Rava's statement or an inserted comment of the editor/redactor, is that there is indeed an essential disagreement between the rabbis and Rabbi Yehudah, and this concerns a third type of war not previously considered. In parallel with the comment attributed to Rav Hisda in the Palestinian Talmud, the Babylonian Talmud then introduces a new category of war not mentioned in the Mishnah. This third type is what we would today call a "preemptive strike," an attack against the enemy to weaken it so that it would not be able to mount its own pending attack against Israel. As said in the Gemara, one of the two parties would call it Commanded and the other would call it Discretionary. The first party would be Rabbi Yehudah because he did not use the term "discretionary" at all, and the second party would be the anonymous statement of the rabbis.[16]

The passage ends with a final comment by the redactor, which explains that the disagreement over whether a given battle should be considered

---

[15] We shall observe that elsewhere in the Talmud, a context for David's Discretionary War is given that associates it with plunder, with a personal decision of the king to go to war, and with the requirement to consult with the Sanhedrin and the Temple oracles (the Urim and Tumim).
[16] The issues are much more complex from the *halakhic* perspective, which does not concern us here, because of the different ways to understand individual and public or universal responsibility. Rabbi Shaul Yisraeli, "*Milhemet Mitzvah and Milhemet Reshut*," *Torah Shebe'al Peh* 10 (1968), p. 50. For the major issues surrounding preemptive war, see J. David Bleich, "Preemptive War in Jewish Law." *Tradition* 21 (spring, 1983), 3–41.

a Discretionary War or Commanded (or Obligatory) War boils down to a different issue entirely. According to Jewish law and practice in general, no particular religious obligation takes precedence over another, but in certain cases when one is involved in carrying out a commandment it may be difficult or even impossible to observe certain other commandments. One of those all-encompassing activities is engaging in war. Therefore, according to the last, anonymous statement, the disagreement between the rabbis and Rabbi Yehudah had to do with whether a category of war would exempt fighters from responsibility to fulfill other commandments.

When compared in columns, the parallels and differences between the two Gemaras are easier to notice (Table 5.1).

TABLE 5.1

| PALESTINIAN TALMUD | BABYLONIAN TALMUD |
| --- | --- |
| Rabbi Yochanan said: There is [only] a terminological difference *(mashma`ut)* between them. Rabbi Yehudah called the "Discretionary War" a "Commanded War." However, [they all agreed that] everyone [was required] to go out for an Obligatory War, even a bridegroom from his chamber and a bride from her bridal pavilion. | Rabbi Yochanan said: Discretionary [War] according to the rabbis is Commanded [War] according to Rabbi Yehudah. Commanded [War] according to the rabbis is Obligatory [War] according to Rabbi Yehudah. |
| Rav Hisda said: There is a conceptual difference *(mahloqet)* between them. The rabbis contend that a Commanded War would be David's war, while an Obligatory War would be Joshua's war, but Rabbi Yehudah called a Discretionary War one in which we initiated against them [i.e. the enemy], and an Obligatory War one in which the [enemy] initiates against us. | Rava said: The wars of conquest of Joshua everyone agrees is Obligatory, while the wars of the House of David for [territorial] expansion everyone agrees is Discretionary. They differed over decreasing the idol worshippers so that they would not march against them. One considers this Commanded, while the other considers it Discretionary. |
| It is written (1Kings 15:22): *Then King Asa mustered all of Judah no one was exempt.* What is the meaning of *no one was exempt?* Rabbi Simon [differed] with the rabbis. Rabbi Simon [said: a man is] not exempt [to leave fighting in order] to go home [even] for one hour. The rabbis said: [Even] a rabbi of an eminent rabbinical house is not [exempt]. | The [halakhic] difference [between the two positions] is that one who is engaged in the performance of a commandment is exempt [from the performance] of a [different] commandment. |

TABLE 5.2

| | DISCRETIONARY | COMMANDED | OBLIGATORY |
|---|---|---|---|
| | *RESHUT* | *MITZVAH* | *CHOVAH* |
| **MISHNAH:** | | | |
| Rabbis | Deferments | No deferments | |
| Yehudah | | Deferments | No deferments |
| **P. Talmud** | | | |
| **Hisda:** | | | |
| Rabbis | | David's wars | Joshua's wars |
| Yehudah | Israel initiates | | Defensive wars |
| **B. Talmud** | | | |
| **Rava:** | | | |
| All agree | David's wars of expansion | | Joshua's wars of conquest |
| Yehudah | | Preemptive strike | |
| Rabbis | Preemptive strike | | |

To summarize thus far, the Gemara of the Palestinian Talmud tries to understand possible criteria for the two-fold typology of war found in the Mishnah by introducing two ways of thinking about the Mishnah categories. One is to think about them according to recognizable historical wars mentioned in the Bible. The other is to think about them as either initiated by Israel or as wars of defense against an attacking enemy. Neither of these schema is explicit in the Mishnah. The Gemara of the Babylonian Talmud then introduces a third way of thinking about the Mishnah dichotomy, through the notion of a preemptive strike. The opinions expressed in the three texts are delineated in Table 5.2.

Unlike any of the preceding material, the Babylonian Talmud concludes with a halakhic rule: "one who is engaged in the performance of a commandment is exempt from other commandments."[17] This then compels the reader to reevaluate the entire series of statements according to this idea, thus enabling a completely different reading that is not concerned with engaging in war at all. In this reading, war becomes nothing more than a theoretical example of a case in which a person engaged in fulfilling a commandment might be exempt for engaging in other commandments. Reading the passages through this interpretive lens allows the foundational issue to move from the specific problematic of war to the observance

---

[17] This idea is not unknown elsewhere in rabbinic literature (e.g. BT *Sukkah* 25a–26a).

of commandments in general, thereby transferring the discussion from engaging in war to simply observing God's commandments.

One last reference should be mentioned here. Elsewhere in the Babylonian Talmud (Berakhot 3b) a context for David's Discretionary War is provided that associates it with plunder, the personal decision of the king to go to war, and the requirement to consult with the Sanhedrin and the Temple oracles of the Urim and Tumim (Num. 27:21).

> [David] immediately rose and studied Torah until the break of dawn. When dawn broke, the wise men of Israel entered and said to him: "Our lord the king, your people Israel need sustenance!" He replied, "Go and make a living from one another." They said to him: "A handful cannot satisfy a lion, nor can a pit fill itself up of its own accord." He replied to them: "Stretch out your hands in a troop to plunder." They immediately took counsel with Achitofel, consulted the Sanhedrin, and asked of the Urim and Tumim.

This passage acknowledges and sanctions economic or material motivations for engagement in war, and it serves as a source for discussion about who has the authority to initiate wars. In the particular situation described here, which all commentators place at the lowest end of the hierarchy regarding war (usually Discretionary, sometimes Commanded), the king's permission (or command) to go to war for material gain is followed up by consultation with three ancient authorities: the royal counselor (Achitofel), the largest court of rabbinic decision makers (the Sanhedrin),[18] and the divine oracle managed by the priests (Urim and Tumim).[19] In other words, wars for economic gain are permitted by virtue of their association with the divinely beloved and great warrior-king, David, but since such mundane and worldly (as opposed to absolutely sacred) acts require that at least a portion of the able population engage in battle in which they may be killed, they cannot be commanded to do so simply by royal fiat. Such wars require approval from other sources, including the judicial and priestly branches.

These short passages lay the foundation for subsequent Jewish thinking and discussion about the obligation to engage in war. All discussion

---

[18] The Sanhedrin (from the Greek, *synedrion*) was the supreme Jewish court of seventy-one rabbis that tradition understood to have functioned during the period of the Second Temple (placing it at the time of David as in this story is clearly reading it back into history).
[19] Ex. 28:30, Lev. 8:6–8, Num. 27:21.

in Orthodox communities about Jewish participation in modern wars for Israel, from the earliest Jewish skirmishes with local Arabs to the War of Independence to the latest *intifada,* refer to them. It needs to be stated here that based on the sacred biblical precedent for all these categories of war, including David's wars of conquest and fighting for material gain, they all carry a sense of divine sanction at some level. Some wars, however, have more authority than others. These foundational texts establish, at the very least, that Joshua's wars of conquest of the Land of Israel were obligatory for every individual Israelite. Whether called "Commanded" or "Obligatory" wars, they were authorized by the divine will, for which there were no deferments.

Jewish tradition likewise considers these Bible and Talmud passages as proof texts confirming that wars of expansion initiated by Israelite leaders beyond the divinely established boundaries of the Land of Israel were Discretionary Wars for which military exemptions applied. The battles of Joshua to conquer the Land of Israel were Commanded and countenanced no deferments. The battles of David for expansion were Discretionary, for which deferments were allowed.

The texts do not clarify, however, into which category a conquest of the Land of Israel subsequent to that of Joshua would fall. Was reference to the wars of Joshua intended to single out only one specific war, or did Joshua's wars represent a category that we might call "wars for the conquest of the Land of Israel?" Therefore, should the Hasmoneans' reconquest of parts of the Land of Israel be considered a Commanded War or a Discretionary War?[20] Would modern Israel's War of Independence be considered a Commanded War because it represents a conquest of the Land of Israel? Or could it be so considered because, according to the Palestinian Talmud ("in which [the enemy] initiates against us"), it is a war of defense against attacking Arab armies? These are questions that the traditional sources do not readily answer. In any case, a second rabbinic construct is employed to constrain the possibility of initiating Commanded War in post-biblical Jewish history.

---

[20] Notice that Judah the Maccabee allowed for deferments according to I Macc. 3:56. This has disturbed some modern Orthodox commentators because the situation described in I Macc. 3:38–44 appears to be a response to an invasion, therefore a defensive war for which there would be no deferments (Rabbi Shlomo Goren, "Army and War in the Light of the Halakhah [Hebrew], *Mahanayim* 97 [1965], 10–15; idem, "Army and War in the Light of the Halakhah," *Mahanayim* 121 [1969], 12).

## Second Construct: The Three Vows

The second standard that entered the rabbinic repertoire is the story of "The Three Vows,"[21] which refers to a phrase occurring three times in the Song of Songs, "I make you swear, o daughters of Jerusalem, by the gazelles and by the hinds of the field, do not wake or rouse love until it is wished"[22] (BT *Ketubot* 110b–111a, cf. *Song of Songs Rabbah* 2:7). The general rabbinic understanding of the repeated phrase is that God is making the daughters of Jerusalem, a metaphor for Israel, swear not to wake or rouse love—understood as attempting to bring the messiah—until it is wished, meaning until God decides the time is right. Attempting to bring messiah through human initiation rather than waiting patiently for God to do so is sometimes called "forcing God's hand," which would only bring God's wrath and further disasters for the Jewish people. The discussion articulated in this Talmudic passage became symbolic for Jews for well over a millennium.

Through this construct, the rabbis discouraged mass-movements that might have instigated a backlash by the various gentile powers under which the Jews lived after the destruction of the Second Jerusalem Temple. The narrative is often cited by those who have opposed movements of Jews to settle or live in the Land of Israel. As Aviezer Ravitzky has shown, the construct of the Three Vows has acted as a kind of brake or governor to such inclinations. Even those believing that every Jew is commanded to settle in the Land of Israel are required to refer to the Three Vows as a means of assuring potential critics that they are not attempting to go against God's will.[23] The Three Vows became a major weapon of Orthodox Jews who opposed Zionism and the State of Israel and who do not believe that its wars have transcendent meaning.

Ironically, perhaps, the Three Vows passage occurs within a longer section stressing how important it is for Jews to live *within* the biblical borders of the Land of Israel. The extended passage includes such dicta as, "One should always live in the Land of Israel even in a city where most of the inhabitants are pagans, and not live outside the Land of Israel even in a

---

[21] *Ketubot* 110b–111a, paralleled in the midrash, *Song of Songs Rabbah* 2:7. For an examination of the impact of this symbolic paradigm in Jewish history, see Aviezer Ravitzky, *Messianism, Zionism, and Jewish Religious Radicalism*, transl. Michael Swirsky and Jonathan Chipman (Chicago: U. of Chicago Press, 1997), 211–234.

[22] *Song of Songs* 2:7, 3:5, 8:4. The last rendering of the sentence, in 8:4, does not include "by the gazelles and by the hinds of the field," but the rabbis include it also in 8:4 by analogy.

[23] Ravitzky 1996, 22–26, 211–234.

city where the majority is Israel." Nowhere in the passage is there any suggestion, however, that Israel should try to take over political control of the Land of Israel. After a section in which the Gemara denigrates living outside the Land of Israel,[24] a story is told about Rabbi Zeira,[25] who wished to move to the Land of Israel against the wish of his teacher, Rav Yehudah.[26] The story illustrates the ambivalence that pervades the issue and details the strategies its two protagonists use by reading identical biblical texts to support their opposing positions.

Rabbi Zeira wished to go up to the Land of Israel and tried to avoid Rav Yehudah, for Rav Yehudah said: Anyone who goes up from Babylonia to the Land of Israel transgresses a positive commandment, as it says (Jeremiah 27:22): *They shall be brought to Babylon and there they shall remain until I take note of them—declares the Lord of Hosts.* [But Rabbi Zeira obviously could not avoid Rav Yehudah, for] Rabbi Zeira [said:] this [verse] refers to the equipment used in the Temple [service and not to the Jews themselves]. Rav Yehudah [answered]: But it is written in another place (Song 2:7): *I make you swear, o daughters of Jerusalem, by the gazelles or by hinds of the field: do not wake or rouse love until it is wished.* Rabbi Zeira [responded]: This [verse teaches only] that Israel should not go up [to the Land of Israel] in a wall.[27] Rav Yehudah: There is another "*I make you swear.*" Rabbi Zeira: That one needs to be explained according to the view of Rabbi Yose in the name of Rabbi Hanina who said: Why are there these three vows [in the Song of Songs]? One [teaches] that Israel should not go up [to the Land of Israel] in a wall, in one the Holy One made Israel swear that they would not rebel against the nations of the world, and in one the

---

[24] According to Michael Avi-Yonah, these passages were an attempt by the Jews of Palestine, following the foiled Bar Kokhba rebellion and resultant Hadrianic persecutions, to discourage emigration to Babylonia (*The Jews of Palestine*, 25).

[25] Zeira (d. c. 300) is mentioned frequently in both the Jerusalem and Babylonian Talmuds. He was a Babylonian who later emigrated to the Land of Israel, therefore referred to as both rav and rabbi, the respective rabbinic titles of Babylon and the Land of Israel. His attempt to avoid his teacher Rav Yehudah while deciding to leave Babylon is recorded also in BT Shabbat 41a.

[26] Yehudah bar Yehezkel (d. 299), the Babylonian sage who founded the academy of Pumbedita after the destruction of the academy of Nehardea in 259. Not only Zeira, but also Abba, was forced to sneak into the Land of Israel without Yehuda's knowledge (Berakhot 24b).

[27] The great medieval commentator known as Rashi glosses this as "together, by force." The parallel in Song of Songs Rabba 2:7 has "and that they will not ascend the wall from Exile." Elsewhere in the Talmud (Yoma 9b) the idiom is explained as: "If you had made yourselves 'like a wall' and had ascended altogether as in the days of Ezra...." The intent of the phrase is certainly understood by the interpretive tradition to mean "together as a large group or movement."

Holy One made the nations of the world swear that they would not subjugate Israel too harshly. Rav Yehudah: It is written, *Do not wake or rouse love*. Rabbi Zeira: This must be explained according to Rabbi Levi who said: Why are there these six vows?[28] Three we just mentioned, and [three] others: That they shall not reveal the End, not postpone the End, and not reveal the secret to the gentiles. [It is written] *by the gazelles or by hinds of the field*. Rabbi Elazar said [with regard to this phrase that God intended the following]: If you carry out the vow, good. But if not, I will permit your flesh [to be consumed] like [that of] gazelles or hinds of the field.[29]

This complex passage requires some historical background. Both Yehudah and Zeira were Babylonian sages, but Zeira was committed to moving to the Land of Israel and absorbing the wisdom of its own population of Jewish sages. According to a tradition recorded in the Talmud, when he finally arrived in the Land of Israel he took on 100 fasts in order to forget the Babylonian method of study so that he could absorb the technique employed by the local sages without naturally falling back into the approach to which he was accustomed.[30] His teacher Yehudah did not want him to go, and Yehudah attempted to convince him to remain by employing typical and well-known rabbinic exegesis to biblical verses. Zeira was no longer a young student at this time, and he was familiar with the interpretations offered by Yehudah. Like Yehudah, he was acquainted with a mass of exegetical traditions and exegesis, so the two rabbis engaged in a battle of interpretation, each one attempting to prove the correctness of his own position. It is this kind of battle of wits for the sake of heaven, rather than a physical battle with arms, for which the sages of the Talmud were referred to as "shield-bearers" (*ba`aley trisin*)[31] engaging in oral rather than physical battle to prove their intellectual rather than military mettle.

---

[28] Ravi Yehudah is observing that the doubled phrase *do not wake* and *do not rouse* represent two separate commands, and they are included in the phrase three of the four times that the phrase appears in Scripture. According to this interpretation, with which all the rabbis in the passage appear to agree, God therefore requires a total of six vows. According to Yehudah, then, one of the six surely forbids Israel to move as individuals to the Land of Israel.

[29] Ketubot 110b.

[30] Zeira was known in the Talmud for engaging in fasts for other purposes as well (BT *Baba Metzi`a* 158b).

[31] BT Berakhot 27b, 36a. See also Sanhedrin 93b, where David's warrior qualities described in 1Sam.16:18 are reconstructed as intellectual prowess and being "well versed in the battle of Torah."

Yehudah commences by citing a verse from the Prophets and warning his former student that his emigration would transgress a divine commandment. Zeira parries by noting that the contextual meaning of the verse cited by Yehudah refers to ritual objects of the Temple rather than people. Yehudah then thrusts with a verse from the Song of Songs whose interpretation was familiar to both rabbis: God made the Jews promise not to try to bring the messiah themselves. Human endeavor to bring messiah rather than waiting patiently for God to do so is "forcing God's hand," which could only rouse divine wrath and bring further disasters for the Jewish people. Zeira's decision to move to the Land of Israel was understood by Yehudah to be just that—or at least to appear to be just that (appearance could also be dangerous): a foolhardy attempt to "bring messiah" through human self-actualization. But then Zeira immediately counters Yehudah with the argument that the prohibition is commonly understood as a collective rather than an individual prohibition. That is, Israel is forbidden to move to Israel "in a wall" (collectively), but individuals such as he would not be forbidden from personally making the move.

Yehudah then reminds his former student that the divine adjuration is given more than once. Because the phrase is repeated, rabbinic interpretive discourse assumes that it appears each time as an independent message. Hence, if the first appearance of the phrase teaches that the Jews should not move to the Land of Israel collectively, a second appearance of the identical phrase would teach something else. It would therefore be reasonable to understand that the second appearance teaches that Jews are also forbidden to move to the Land of Israel individually. This explains Yehudah's comment that "there is another *I make you swear*." Zeira responds by citing the tradition of Rabbi Hanina taught by Rabbi Yose, that each of the three citations of the phrase, *I make you swear, o daughters of Jerusalem... do not wake or rouse love until it is wished* is already accounted for exegetically.[32] Because each case is already explained by Rabbi Hanina, suggests Zeira, there is no room for Yehudah's now extraneous interpretation that one of the repeated citations prohibits him from moving to the Land of Israel.

Yehudah then counters this position by pointing out that in each of the three citations, God makes two demands. This is based on the phraseology, *do not wake or rouse*. Rather than three adjurations, therefore, God has actually made six! Since one of the six is certainly unaccounted for,

---

[32] While the phrase "I make you swear daughters of Jerusalem" occurs four times in the Song of Songs, the following phrase, "do not wake or rouse love until it is wished" occurs three times.

Yehudah can use it to prove his interpretation. But Zeira again counters his master's position, this time by citing a tradition associated with Rabbi Levi, that there are six vows and each one is accounted for.

This is the end of the argument. Yehudah has nothing more to say. The discussion is then concluded with a tradition given in the name of Rabbi Eleazar that explains the odd form of swearing *by the gazelles or by the hinds of the field*. Explains Rabbi Eleazar, " If you carry out the vow, good. But if not, I will permit your flesh [to be consumed] like [that of] gazelles or hinds of the field," meaning to impress upon Israel the gravity of failing to keep their promises forced upon them by God for their own good.

We have observed the rhythm of argument in the passage. Now we must examine its overall message. The cultural assumption of rabbinic Judaism and the literary and topical context of the passage is that a hierarchy exists that places the Land of Israel above all other lands. The very essence of living there has transcendent value, as these statements on the same Talmud page attest: "Rabbi Elazar said: Anyone who lives in the Land of Israel lives without sin." "Rav Anan said: Anyone who is buried in the Land of Israel is as if he were buried underneath the [Temple] altar."

This overwhelming praise for the Land of Israel and its merits is tempered, however, with a caution lest the Jewish people decide to relocate there en masse and bring disaster upon themselves. During the age of Ezra and Nehemiah in the fifth century B.C.E. a large group of Judeans returned to the Land of Israel from Babylon and successfully rebuilt the Jerusalem Temple. In the wake of the catastrophic Bar Kokhba Revolt, however, the rabbinic leadership became extremely cautious. They tried to discourage any mass migration or attempt to establish an independent Jewish commonwealth in the Jewish homeland.

The Three Oaths of our passage became symbolic of this position; they establish a delicate balance between God, Israel, and the nations of the world that would characterize the essence of Jewish life in exile. God forces Israel, the "daughters of Jerusalem," whose very name attests to their delicate nature and their eternal attachment to the Holy Land, to swear oaths in relation to the world. First, they must not go up to the Land of Israel en masse, though individuals might do so. Second, they must never try to rebel against the nations of the world, never organize an army or polity to fight the great empires that control and oppress them. In exchange for doing their part, God forces the nations of the world to swear that they will not subjugate Israel too harshly. The terms of the relationship are conditional and work like a mathematical formula. If Israel does not live up to the terms of the relationship, then the nations of the world will subjugate them cruelly. If Israel sticks to the terms of the agreement, they will be protected from overwhelming cruelty and destruction in exile.

Why such a delicate balance? It establishes a kind of carrot and stick arrangement to protect Israel from endangering itself by engaging in collective political or military opposition to the ruling powers. Such acts were identified as sinning against God and endangering Israel's own collective redemption, blasphemous efforts to decide for God when or where the messiah will come to redeem Israel and the world. Only God decides the time for Redemption, and God's ways are beyond human understanding. Israel must have faith that the Endtime will inevitably come, for one day God's love for Israel will indeed be roused and awakened. Some argued that the messiah will come when all Jews return to traditional Jewish religious practice, but the timing will always remain unknown. One thing is certain. "Forcing God's hand" will only bring disaster.

The literature arguing against organized emigration to the Land of Israel tends to cite "the Three Vows." But another Talmudic passage refers to "four vows," and it is in response to the latter that Rabbi Jacob Emden, the famous eighteenth century central European Talmudic scholar, composed the following prayer: "Master of the Universe, be for us a God of salvation from exile, for through four vows You have made us swear not to do anything ourselves to force the Endtime—only to await Salvation."[33]

The "four" undoubtedly refers to the fact that four vows are actually found in the Song of Songs, but the passage in question is of interest here for two other reasons. First, it specifically condemns the militant Bar Kokhba Revolt, and second, it cites what it considers to be a true historical case in which failure to uphold the vow resulted in disaster for the Jewish People. The passage is referred to as that of the Children of Efrayim.[34]

> RABBI HELBO SAYS: There are four vows here; [God] made Israel swear that they not rebel against the governments, that they not try to bring the End early, that they not reveal their mysteries to the nations of

---

[33] Cited in Ravitzky, *Messianism*, 299.

[34] Song of Songs Rabbah 2:7. See also Midrash Mekhilta deRabbi Yishmael *masekhta devayehi beshallach, petichta* (Horovitz-Rabin [Jerusalem: Wahrman, 1970], 76–77/Lauterbach [Philadelphia, Jewish Publication Society, 1936], vol. 1, 172–173). Not only does the name Efrayim refer to one of the tribes of Israel, it is also a collective noun in biblical and rabbinic idiom to refer to the ten tribes that made up the Northern Kingdom known as "Israel" and their descendants, and even to the People of Israel as a whole (Isaiah 7:5, 8; Jeremiah 31:17, 20; Hosea 5:3, 5, etc.). The context for citing this verse in the Midrash tends to be the failure of the Israelites to have faith in God's redemption when they decided themselves to charge the combined forces of the Canaanites and Amalekites at the battle of Hormah [Num. 14:39–45//Deut. 1:42–44].

the world, and that they not go up [as] a wall from the Exile. If they do, then why should the King Messiah come to gather the exiles of Israel? Rabbi Onia said: [God] made them swear four vows in relation to the four generations that tried to hasten the End and failed, which are: one in the days of Amram, one in the days of Dinai, one in the days of Ben Koziba, and one in the days of Shutelach b. Efrayim, as it says (Ps.78: 9) *The children of Efrayim were as archers carrying bows [who turned back in the day of battle. They kept not the covenant of God and refused to follow his Torah...]*[35] ... What did they do? They gathered together and went to war, and many of them fell and were killed. Why? Because they did not believe in God and did not trust in His salvation, because they transgressed the Endtime and transgressed the vow, *do not wake or rouse love* (Song 2:7). [Song of Songs Rabbah 2:7]

This interpretation is even more forceful than the previous, and its powerful message reflects the philosophy of political quietism that was the operating principle of most of Jewish historical life until the nineteenth century. There was of course plenty of Jewish activism within the community, and sometimes even in relation to outside powers through attempts to influence by persuasion and payments, but any other means was virtually impossible. As Moses Maimonides' father observed in his "Letter of Consolation" written in the twelfth century, "While the current destroys walls and sweeps along rocks, the soft thing remains standing. Thus the Exile destroys and breaks and uproots great pillars and enormous walls, but the Holy One, blessed be He, saves the weak and soft nation, that the current not sweep it along."[36]

It appears clearly from the material presented cited here that the rabbinic sages sought to downplay the importance of militant behaviors in relation to the Land of Israel. As Yitzhak Baer put it, "Only after stubborn resistance was the lesson learned: that love cannot be prematurely aroused, that the kingdom of God cannot be set up by force, that one cannot rise in rebellion against the overlordship of the nations."[37] Yet despite its policy of quietism, rabbinic Judaism never abdicated the right of the People of Israel to return to its homeland under God's providence at some future time and regain control of the Land. Rabbinic literature, which is so

---

[35] Brackets indicate the continuation of the verse assumed by the passage but not explicitly cited.
[36] Cited in Ravitzky, *Messianism*, 16.
[37] Yitzhak Baer, *Galut* (NY: Schocken, 1947), 13.

deeply concerned with the pious life of commandment, stressed that many of God's commandments were impossible to perform outside its borders. This fact of Judaism ascribed great sanctity to the Land that continued to exist both theoretically and yet practically, even after the destruction of the Jerusalem Temple. Dozens of proof texts may be found scattered throughout rabbinic and medieval sources demonstrating the right of Israel to be in possession of the land, based on the laws of legal acquisition, inheritance, or conquest.

In summary, we have observed how rabbinic Judaism developed two interpretive constructs to avoid self-destructive militarism after the disastrous Jewish military failures against Rome. One established an abbreviated taxonomy of wars that simplified and often ignored the many examples of divinely ordained war-making in the Bible. The other established a formula to protect the Jewish people from accidental destruction through God's imposition of demands for Jewish quietism and faithful patience that would be rewarded ultimately with divinely redemption. Community survival would not occur through political independence, but by means of sanctification through engagement in divine commandments. The constructs of the war typology and the three vows were tactics in an overall strategy to protect Jews and Judaism. The goal of the rabbis was not the elimination of war per se, but rather the elimination of the possibility of initiating war in history. Neither was it an abdication from the creedal centrality of Jerusalem in Judaism. Jerusalem remained no less sacred under the authority of the three vows. What the rabbis had developed was a political strategy, not a withdrawal from politics. The two rabbinic constructs examined in this chapter represent a strategic political re-alignment of priorities.

The program required that the community of Israel redefine itself indefinitely as a community of Diaspora, even among those Jews living in the Land of Israel.[38] But the self-definition always included a deep and abiding memory of the Land and of a powerful ritual and theological centeredness on the Land, often symbolized by Jerusalem, or the Temple in Jerusalem, or the Holy of Holies in the Temple. Jewish ritual is saturated with references to Jerusalem and the Land of Israel, the origin and homeland of the Jewish People, and it is saturated with the desire and hope for the great Return. Writings in virtually all genres of Jewish literature express a deep

---

[38] This is realized in Jewish law, since after the destruction of the Jerusalem Temple even Jews living in the Land of Israel could not observe all the special practices specific to the Land of Israel.

and abiding faith that there will be a future return to the days when the Temple stood, when Jews would again live in their own land under their own control through the direct authority of the Divine Presence.

A profound tension thus exists in Judaism. It is a tension between "Diaspora" and "Center," meaning between the reality of Diaspora and the (often fantastic) memory of Center, and a tension between a humbled present and a glorious messianic future that will inevitably come—when God deems the time is right.

# CHAPTER 6 | Who Is the Enemy?

You shall blot out the memory of Amalek from under heaven.
Do not forget!

DEUTERONOMY 25:19

We noted in chapter 1 that all wars depicted in the Hebrew Bible, whether initiated by or against Israel, are considered to have been directed or determined by God. That does not mean, however, that all wars have the same status. They are not all *authorized* by God.[1] We noted in the previous chapter how the rabbis of the Talmud differentiated between Commanded War and Discretionary War. These are established as general categories in the earliest layer of the Talmud and later concretized through certain examples. While both Talmuds clearly establish an association between the category of Commanded War and war for the conquest of Canaan, the Palestinian Talmud also includes war of defense in the same category. But this extension remains general. No attempt is made to identify an enemy.

Elsewhere, however, the rabbis follow the Bible by paying special attention to wars against Amalekites and against the "Seven Canaanite Nations." The Bible expresses a distinct hatred toward these two communities and commands their absolute destruction. This exceptional position with regard to two particular peoples, both of which have no obviously identifiable living descendents, has had a profound impact on rabbinic thought and has come to influence the discourse of war in the modern State of Israel.

---

[1] Numbers 14:39–45 (retold in Deuteronomy 1:42–44).

## Wars Against Amalek

The Amalekites, often referred to in the singular "Amalek" as a kind of personification of an entire tribe or people, epitomize the absolutely evil "other" in both biblical and rabbinic tradition. "Remember what Amalek did to you on your journey, after you left Egypt—how, undeterred by fear of God, he surprised you on the march, when you were famished and weary, and cut down all the stragglers in your rear."[2]

Amalek is an everlasting enemy in the Bible and turns up just as relentless and persistent in rabbinic literature. The Amalekites are associated in the Bible with desert areas to the south of the Land of Israel (that is, in the Sinai Peninsula).[3] They appear as enemy throughout the early history of Israel but are never destroyed, despite the divine command to do so in Deuteronomy 25:19 and the divine promise that God will do the deed in Exodus 17:14. Early in the wanderings of Israel after the Exodus from Egypt, Amalek initiated a battle at Refidim (Exodus 17:8–13). Moses told Joshua to engage the Amalekites, but the warrior leader was successful only as long as Moses was able to hold his hands aloft with the help of his assistants Aaron and Hur, thus indicating that God was engaged in assisting the Israelites against their enemy. Joshua led the battle from the Israelite side and "overwhelmed" them[4] but did not destroy them. God then dictates to Moses the divine words, "I will utterly blot out the memory of Amalek from under heaven!" (Ex. 17:14). This sentiment is conveyed again in Deuteronomy 25:17–19, but in the form of a command to Israel: "Therefore, when the Lord your God grants you safety from all your enemies around you, in the land that the Lord your God is giving you as a hereditary portion, you shall blot out the memory of Amalek from under heaven. Do not forget!" Amalek nevertheless lives on.

Saul is commanded by God through the prophet Samuel centuries later to destroy the Amalekites entirely because of their previous perfidious behavior. "Thus said the Lord of Hosts: I am exacting the penalty for what Amalek did to Israel, for the assault he made upon them on the road, on their way up from Egypt. Now go, attack Amalek, and proscribe all that

---

[2] Deuteronomy 25:17–18 (New JPS Transl., Cf. 1 Sam. 15:2).

[3] There is a "city of Amalek" (1 Sam. 15:5). Given the biblical references to Amalekites as a nomadic people, it is more likely that `ir `Amalek refers to a major camp.

[4] Or variously translated as "harried," "defeated," or by Everett Fox, "weakened," which is probably the most accurate rendering of the Hebrew in verse 13, *vayyachalosh yehoshua` et `amalek* (Everett Fox (transl), *The Five Books of Moses* (New York: Schocken, 1983).

belongs to him. Spare no one, but kill alike men and women, infants and sucklings, oxen and sheep, camels and asses!" (1 Sam. 15:2–3). But Saul fails to obey the divine command in its entirety by sparing the booty, even if to be dedicated to God, and by sparing the Amalekite leader Agag as well. Samuel rebukes Saul harshly for his sin, whereupon Saul admits his failure to carry out the divine command and asks forgiveness. But the deed has been done. Saul fails to carry out the divine command, for which he loses the kingship: "You have rejected the Lord's command, and the Lord has rejected you as king over Israel." (1 Sam. 15:26).

David, who replaced Saul over this fatal error, then pursued the Amalekites from Ziklag, which they had despoiled (1 Sam. 30). Despite Saul's decimation of the Amalekites, David found the enemy in such great number that they are described as being spread throughout the land. "David attacked them from before dawn until the evening of the next day; none of them escaped, except four hundred young men who mounted camels and got away" (verse 17). Ever able to survive and multiply, Amalek came to personify, first in the Bible and then in subsequent Jewish tradition, the eternal enemy of Israel. Even Haman, the great villain of the Book of Esther who plotted to do away with all the Jews, descended from the Amalekite leader, Agag, of 1 Samuel 15.[5] In Holocaust literature to this day, Hitler is not infrequently associated with Amalek.[6]

The rabbis associate Amalek with unredeemable evil. No other biblical enemies of Israel achieve this level, including even the Edomites and Egyptians, who tormented the Israelites greatly. "When you enter the Land, remember to repay the good according to his decency and the bad according to his malevolence. How? It is written (Deut. 23:8), 'You shall not abhor an Edomite, for he is your kinsman.' Whether good or evil, he is [still] your kinsman. 'You shall not abhor an Egyptian, for you were

---

[5] He is identified in the Book of Esther as Haman son of Hamedata the Agagite (Esther 3:1–6).

[6] Elliott Horowitz, "From the Generation of Moses to the Generation of the Messiah: The Jews Confront 'Amalek' and His Incarnations," (Heb). *Zion* 64 (1999), 425–454; Gerald Cromer, "Amalek as Other, Other as Amalek: Interpreting a Violent Biblical Narrative," *Qualitative Sociology* 24.2 (2001), 191–202; Norman Lamm, "Amalek and the Seven Nations: A Case of Law vs. Morality," in Lawrence Schiffman and Joel Wolowelsky (eds.), *War and Peace in the Jewish Tradition* (New York: Yeshivah University, 2007), 215–224. On the image of Amalek in late antique Jewish literature, see Louis Feldman, *"Remember Amalek!" Vengeance, Zealotry, and Group Destruction in the Bible According to Philo, Pseudo-Philo, and Josephus* (Cincinnati: Hebrew Union College, 2004). On major trends in halakhic responses to the commandment to destroy Amalek, see Avi Sagi, *Judaism: Between Religion and Morality* (Hebrew) (Tel Aviv [?]: Hakibbutz Hameuchad, 1998), 216–229.

a stranger in his land.' Whether good or evil, you lived with them for a number of years. But Amalek? 'Remember what Amalek did to you!' "[7]

According to the biblical narrative in the Book of Esther, the Amalekite line was finally destroyed in Persia. By way of typical rabbinical exegesis playing on Hebrew words derived from the letters *alef, mem, nun*,[8] the midrash called *Pesiqta Rabbati*[9] asks: "When did [Amalek's] sun set, [and when was] his egg crushed and his seed uprooted from the world? When the one came,[10] about whom it is written, 'and he was the one to adopt *(omen)* Hadassah [who is Esther]' (Esther 2:7).[11] It is written (Ex.17:12), 'thus [Moses'] hands remained steady *(emunah)* [until the sun set].' What does 'until the sun set' mean? [It means] When the faithful adopter *(omen)* comes, his [Amalek's] sun will set."

This exegesis connects the final fall of Amalek in the Book of Esther with the first confrontation between Amalek and Israel in the Book of Exodus through the parallel use of the Hebrew root. The meaning of this root in biblical and rabbinic Hebrew ranges from "steadfastness" to "being a guardian of" to "faith." Moses' hands remained *steadfast* until the setting of the sun. So too, many centuries later, the coming of the *steadfast* one (Mordecai) to *serve as the adoptive guardian (omen)* and teach *steadfast-ness (emunah)* to Esther would finally spell the doom of Amalek through the destruction of Haman and his ten sons. This is the setting of Haman's sun, symbolizing the end of the Amalekite genealogical line.

The sages used similar exegetical tools to demonstrate that Amalek succeeded in permanently weakening the image of Israel in a predatory world, thus serving as the ultimate cause of all subsequent attacks and tragedies perpetrated against Israel by the nations.[12] At the same time, the rabbis did not remove reproach from Israel. For example, unethical behavior, symbolized by unfair weights and measures, is an "abomination to God" (Prov. 11:1), and such practices would bring divine punishment upon Israel. The rabbis connect the *abomination to God* in Prov. 11:1 with *abomination to God* in the verse preceding the narration of Amalek's predation of Israel in Deuteronomy 25. The result: "If you see a generation whose [weights and] measures are false, know that the kingdom will come and punish that

---

[7] Midrash Pesiqta Rabbati 12: "Remember what Amalek did to you!" (section 3). See also, Midrash Pesiqta deRav Kahana, *pisqah, Zakhor* (3).

[8] The key words in this passage, *omen* and *emunah,* are considered by the rabbis to be related terms and are spelled with these three letters.

[9] *Pesiqta* 12: "And Moses' hands were heavy." (section 8).

[10] Referring to Mordecai.

[11] *Vayhi omen et hadassah hi esther.*

[12] Midrash Pesiqta deRav Kahana, *Zakhor* (3:10)

generation.... What is written [to demonstrate this at the end of the argument]? 'Remember what Amalek did to you...' "[13]

Amalek, therefore, although destroyed physically, lives on and becomes a metaphor for both the external and internal weakening of Israel. However, his terror and sin is turned inward by the rabbis. Amalek becomes the enemy within, the evil inclination within the heart. But this internalizing of the Amalek metaphor never removed a concrete identification of Amalek, functioning both as metaphor and as a tangible reality, from association with the enemies of Israel. Even if Amalek is physically no more, the Amalekite inclination for plunder and predation exists in the evil found among those who would destroy Israel. We will observe in the following chapter how Maimonides states that the seven Canaanite nations are no longer identifiable, so the commandment to destroy them has lapsed. But he does not say the same regarding Amalek.

The inclination to identify Amalek as Israel's quintessential enemy and Israel's enemies as Amalek continues to this day. The Maharal of Prague Rabbi Judah Loew (d. 1609), considered all enemies of Israel throughout the generations of their Dispersion to be genealogical descendents of Amalek.[14] Rabbi Chaim Soloveitchik of Brisk (d. 1918) declared that the commandment to destroy Amalek extends not merely to the genealogical descendents, but also to all who embrace the ideology of Amalek by trying to destroy Israel. This applies to the Arab nations seeking to destroy the people of Israel. According to Rabbi Joseph B. Soloveitchik (d. 1993) in the name of his father, Rabbi Moshe Soloveitchik (d. 1941), the commandment with regard to Amalek is two-fold: (1) the obligation of each individual Jew to destroy the genealogical descendants of Amalek, based on Deut. 25:19: "you shall erase the memory of Amalek," and (2) the communal obligation of all Jews to defend the Jewish people against any enemy threatening its destruction, based on Exodus 17:16, which speaks of "the war of God against Amalek."[15] According to Shear Yashuv Cohen, the Chief Rabbi of Haifa, "Every nation that conspires to destroy the community of Israel becomes Amalek according to the *halakhah*...and Amalek exists even now after the mixing up of the nations."[16] Not only is Hitler accused by Jewish leaders of being Amalek, but so is Yassir Arafat and others;[17]

---

[13] Midrash Pesiqta deRav Kahana, *Zakhor* (3:5).

[14] Rabbi Judah Loew, *Or Hadash* 54a, in J. David Bleich, *Contemporary Halakhic Problems* (New York: KTAV, 1977), p. 17, note 6.

[15] J. David Bleich, *Contemporary Halakhic Problems*, p. 17.

[16] Shear Yashuv Cohen, "The Call for Peace in Israelite Wars," *Torah shebe`al-peh* 1980, p. 89.

[17] "Pikuach Nefesh," an association of rabbis opposed to returning territories that came under Israeli control after the 1967 war, said that "the day of Arafat's death should be a day of

sometimes collectives of contemporary Palestinians, have likewise been vilified as the seed of Amalek.[18] "In each generation we have those who rise up to wipe us out; therefore each generation has its own Amalek. The Amalekism of our generation expresses itself in the extremely deep hatred of the Arabs to our national renaissance in the land of our forefathers."[19] This absolute condemnation of Israel's enemies through identification with the hated Amalek is not reserved only for gentiles. As will be examined in chapter 9, some of the most strident anti-Zionist rabbis even referred to Zionists as Amalek.[20]

## Wars Against the Seven Nations

In the Bible, the main enemy of Israel in relation to the Land is the Canaanites. "Canaanites" appears to be a general or collective term that is used to designate the various peoples—kinship groups or tribes, village communities, or perhaps dialect groups—living in the area that corresponds roughly to what becomes the Land of Israel in the biblical narrative.[21] Canaanites are often listed in the Bible along with other groups, such as the Kenites, Kenizites, Kadmonites, Hittites, Perizzites, Refa'ites, Emorites, Girgashites, and Jebusites (Genesis 15:18–19),[22] but the biblical

---

rejoicing," as Arafat was "the Amalek and the Hitler of our generation" (*Haaretz*, November 12, 2004: http://www.haaretz.com/news/right-wing-groups-welcome-arafat-s-death-1.139977).

[18] Elliot Horowitz, *Reckless Rites: Purim and the Legacy of Jewish Violence* (Princeton: Princeton University, 2006), 1–4, 109–109.

[19] Haim Tzuria, "The Right to Hate," *Nekudah* No. 15 (August 29, 1980), as cited in Ehud Sprinzak, *The Ascendance of Israel's Radical Right* (New York: Oxford, 1991), p. 123. See also Yehudah Gershuni, "Discretionary war and commanded war," (Hebrew) *Torah shebe`al-peh* 1971, 151, where he identifies Germans and Arabs "desiring to destroy Israel" as Amalek, and Cf. idem, "On the Issue of the Command to Wipe Out Amalek," *Hatorah Vehamedinah* #9 (1958), 76–81.

[20] Rabbi Yoel Teitelbaum, *On the Redemption and Recompense* (Hebrew), Jerusalem, 1982 (5th printing), section 46, p. 87, and see Aviezer Ravitzky, "Religious Radicalism and Political Messianism in Israel," in Sivan, Emmanuel, and Friedman, Menachem (eds.), *Religious Radicalism and Politics in the Middle East*. Albany, New York: SUNY Press, 1990, p. 16. On rabbinic, medieval and modern associations of Amalek with Jewish enemies, see Horowitz, *Reckless Rites*, 107–146. The most recent published discussions on identifying Amalek to date may be found in Kalman Neuman, "The Law of Obligatory War and Israeli Reality," in Yigal Levin and Amnon Shapira, *War and Peace in Jewish Tradition: From the Biblical World to the Present* (London: Routledge, 2012), 195–196, note 14.

[21] Occasionally the term Amorite (*emori*) designates the conglomerate of groups (Gen. 15:16, 1 Sam. 7:14). For current perspectives on their origin and identity, see Niels Peter Lemche, *The Canaanites and Their Land* (Sheffield, England: JSOT, 1991); Jonathan Tubb, *Canaanites* (Norman, OK: U. of Oklahoma, 1998); Ann Killebrew, *Biblical Peoples and Ethnicity* (Atlanta: SBL, 2005), 93–148.

[22] For other lists, see Exodus 3:8, 17, 13:5; Deut. 20:17, Joshua 3:10, 9:1, 12:8, 24:11; Judges 3:3; Ezra 9:1, etc.

narrative most often refers to the Canaanites as the local peoples living in the "Land of Canaan" that has been promised by God to become the Land of Israel (Gen. 12:6–7; 1 Sam. 13:19; 2 Kings 5:2, etc.). The famous war text of Deuteronomy 7:1 authorizes conquest of the local peoples in the following language: "When the Lord your God brings you to the land that you are about to enter and possess, and He dislodges many nations before you—the Hittites, Girgashites, Amorites, Canaanites, Perizzites, Hivites, and Jebusites, seven nations.... " The rabbis often refer to the local peoples from this verse as the "Seven Nations."

The Bible is unambiguous in its directive to drive out (Numbers 33:50–53) or destroy (Deuteronomy 7:1, 20:17) the local inhabitants of the Land. It is equally unambiguous in its complaint that neither of these tactics was successfully employed, for Ezra complains that the Israelites were intermarrying with local peoples "whose abhorrent practices are like those of the Canaanites, the Hittites, the Perizzites, the Jebusites, the Ammonites, the Moabites, the Egyptians, and the Amorites" many centuries after the great conquest and its harsh wars of extermination and ethnic cleansing were supposed to have taken place (Ezra 9:1–2). For many centuries, even according to the biblical narrative, Israel lived among Canaanite peoples and intermarried with them, contrary to the command given in Deuteronomy 7: 2b–3. Over time, however, while Israel retained a distinct identity, the identities of the local peoples disappeared as they mingled and intermarried with one another and were absorbed into the neighboring peoples, including Israel.

As early as in the Mishnah, which was assembled in about 200 C.E. but contains much earlier material, the rabbis concluded that "ever since Sennacherib came and mixed up all the peoples," massive intermarriage made it impossible to identify the local nations of the Land.[23] Maimonides makes the case in his *Book of Commandments* that Canaanite identity disappeared earlier, despite the evidence from Ezra. "The seven nations are no longer in existence... They were finished and cut off in the days of David, when the remainder was dispersed and intermingled with the nations to the extent that no root remained."[24]

Therefore, whereas Amalek still exists, at least metaphorically or abstractly among all those enemies who would attempt or even wish to destroy Jews, the Seven Nations have disappeared. As we will observe in

---

[23] Mishnah, *Yadayim* 4:4; Tosefta, *Kiddushin* 5:4 (Leiberman); *Yadayim* 2:17 (Zuckermendel); BT *Berakhot* 28a.

[24] Moses Maimonides, *Book of Commandments, with the commentary of Nachmanides* (Hebrew, Ed. Charles B. Chavel, Jerusalem: Mosad Harav Kook, 1981) positive commandments 187 [p. 227].

Maimonides, however, the end of the Canaanites does not spell the end of the commandment to destroy them. This becomes an issue in the modern Middle East when Palestinians maintain that they trump the historical claims of Jews by claiming direct descent from the "original" indigenous peoples of the area, whom some of them have called the Canaanites.

## The Authority to Send Fighters Off to War

The sages of the Talmud discussed the issue of authority for declaring war and for inducting soldiers who would very possibly be killed in battle. The discussion is brief, however, and relatively superficial compared to many other issues. In the Mishnah's opening discussion of the various types of law courts, distinguished by the number of judges sitting on them, a list of cases is provided that can only be decided by the highest court in the land. This is the court of seventy-one sages that is often called the Great Sanhedrin.

One of these cases treats the authority to send fighters out to a Discretionary War: "They may not send forth [fighters] to a Discretionary War except on the authority of a court of seventy-one."[25] The same message is given in the positive in the following chapter in reference to an Israelite king: "He may send forth [fighters] to a Discretionary War on the authority of a court of seventy-one" (Sanhedrin 2:4). The Gemara (Sanhedrin 20b) asks why the same message is offered twice, and answers that one is given in relation to the authority of the rabbinical courts, the other in relation to the authority of the king. Although not stated there, later commentators will derive from this that even the authority of the king is not great enough to send out fighters for a Discretionary War. The additional authority of the Great Sanhedrin, the court of seventy-one, is required.

What is not articulated in the brief Talmudic discussion is the source of authority for sending forth fighters for the Commanded (or Required) War. Later commentators will derive from the silent argument that in the case of such a war, the Sanhedrin's authority is not necessary. The king has enough authority without the Sanhedrin to muster an army for defense or for conquest as defined by the parameters established for these categories.

We have previously mentioned a Talmudic tradition, given in reference to a topic unrelated to war, in which a group of Israelite leaders (lit. "wise men of Israel") visit with King David early one morning. When

---

[25] Sanhedrin 1:5.

they inform David that the economy is bad and the people need a source of income, he tells them to go out and engage in plunder. They immediately consult David's advisor and the Sanhedrin, but they also consult the divine oracle called the *urim vetumim*, which was located on the breastplate of the uniform of the High Priest.[26] The same discussion is found elsewhere in the Talmud, but it is framed by a Gemara discussion on Discretionary War.[27] Rabbi Abbahu derives from Numbers 27:21 (and following) that a Discretionary War requires sanction from the king, the priest ordained for war discussed in the previous chapter, the Sanhedrin, and also the *urim vetumim*. Later discussions about the authority to declare war therefore treat the issue of the divine oracle as well.

At issue for some Orthodox Jews, as we shall observe below in relation to the establishment of the State of Israel, is whether the government of a modern Jewish nation-state has the authority to declare war and require the induction of Jews into a national army. Governmental authority for a modern nation-state is invested in a parliament and a prime minister or president. Do these bodies, individually or collectively, inherit the authority of an Israelite king? How do courts of law established by a modern civil government fit the paradigms described in rabbinic literature for the rabbinical courts? Also, how do the rabbinical courts in the modern state of Israel, which were established independently of the civil authorities, fit into these paradigms? And is there a parallel in authority between the priest anointed for war or the *urim vetumim* and contemporary religious leaders in the state? Might the institution of the Chief Rabbinate of the State of Israel have this authority?

These issues have not been resolved among the religious communities of the State of Israel. Orthodox Jewish Zionists have often taken the default position of submitting to the secular political and military authority of the modern state, but this has sometimes placed them in a bind, as we shall observe in subsequent chapters, when the demands of the secular institutions appear to conflict with the expectations and demands derived from Jewish tradition and law.

---

[26] Berakhot 3b. The topic that frames this story is the timing of prayer, and an example is made of King David's night prayers, after which he is approached and asked the question by the sages of Israel.

[27] Sanhedrin 16a.

## CHAPTER 7 | Maimonides' Counting of the Commandments

When the peoples of the world say to Israel: 'You are robbers because you took the lands of the seven [Canaanite] nations,' Israel replies to them: 'All the earth belongs to the Holy One blessed be He. He created it and gave it to whom He pleased. When God wished, He gave it to them [i.e. the Canaanites]; and when God wished, He took it from them and gave it to us!'

RASHI, ELEVENTH CENTURY

After the catastrophic results of the Bar Kokhba Rebellion, Jewish religious and political life began a long process of reorganization. The process was long, and uncertainty remains among scholars about the details and length of time for that development. Certainly by the early Middle Ages, a Jewish leadership referred to vaguely as "the rabbis" gained ascendancy, and that Jewish leadership accepted, for lack of an alternative, political domination of non-Jews. Although it took some centuries after the Temple's destruction and the failed Bar Kokhba Rebellion, the center of Jewish political life was eventually forced out of the land of its biblical forebears. The Land of Israel nevertheless remained at the core of rabbinic Judaism liturgically, conceptually, halakhically, and theologically, even during the many centuries when the Jews would lack any semblance of political and military control over it. This irony may be difficult to comprehend and cannot be treated here in any kind of systematic manner. At the end of the day, however, Judaism was able to survive as a landless people despite its consideration of the Land of Israel as its own patrimony and central to its identity. It has been suggested that Jewish civilization survived *because* of its never-ending regard for the Land of Israel, but it survived as a Diaspora religion even among Jews who lived within the very land that they considered to be their own birthright.

The period of Late Antiquity ends with the Muslim conquest in the seventh-eighth centuries. By that time Jews had spread throughout the Mediterranean lands, most of Europe, the Middle East, and on through the silk road into Central and East Asia. During most of the Middle Ages there was little Jewish interest in emigration to the Land of Israel.[1] One might expect discussion of political and military issues to be associated with activist movements to achieve greater corporate rights or independence, but there was hardly interest in either during the Medieval Period. Marc Saperstein shows how the rabbis of the Middle Ages walked a fine line between maintaining the spiritual importance and centrality of the Land of Israel on the one hand, with support for continued creative Jewish material life in the Diaspora on the other.[2]

Jews evolved a highly developed corporate organization under Christian and Muslim rule, but despite semi-independent courts of law, and even rare periods when Jewish communities could carry out corporal punishment against their own members, Jews did not govern themselves in independent polities and had no standing armies. In rare cases, we learn of Jewish involvement in rebellions on the side of one power or another, but these references are infrequent and it is often impossible to reconstruct, whether from Jewish or non-Jewish sources, whether or not the references are rhetorical.[3]

In the medieval Jewish literature to which we have access, theoretical discussion about war does not advance much beyond the brief discussions established in the earlier classical rabbinic literature, and for this reason I will not dwell long on this period. The paucity of discussion on war is consistent with the tendency among Jews to consider their existential situation in exile to be normative until the expected arrival of the messiah at some undetermined future time. In the meantime, Jews must obey the commandments of Torah and live out their lives under the political, social, and military control of the gentile nations.

---

[1] Baer, even in his essay on the degradation of exile, cites only minimal and short-lived interest in immigration to the Land of Israel (*Galut*, especially 55, 69).

[2] Marc Saperstein, "The Land of Israel in Pre-Modern Jewish Thought: A History of Two Rabbinic Statements," in Lawrence A. Hoffman (ed.), *The Land of Israel: Jewish Perspectives* (South Bend, Ind: Notre Dame, 1986), 188–209.

[3] For a partisan survey, see Josef Braslavi (Braslavski), War and Defense among the Jews of the Land of Israel from after the Bar Kokhba Rebellion to the First Crusade (Hebrew) (Ein Harod, 1943).

In a survey of the literature on Jewish emigration to the Land of Israel during the Middle Ages, Aviezer Ravitzky concludes that, aside from rare exceptions, there was little interest among European Jews to immigrate to the Land of Israel until the thirteenth century,[4] and even then the interest was minimal. The thirteenth century emigrations of French Tosafists, sometimes called "the ascension of the three hundred rabbis," were not inspired by messianic or neomessianic (political) impulses, but rather by an interest in increasing halakhic observance by moving to a place where more of the divine commandments would apply.[5] Not until the eighteenth century was there a significant immigration with messianic expectation among disciples of the Vilna Gaon, which appears to have influenced a larger messianic movement to the Land of Israel in the mid-nineteenth century.[6]

The great exception to the general trend was in the person of Rabbi Moses ben Nachman, known as Nahmanides (d. 1270).[7] Not only did he immigrate personally to the Land of Israel, as did a few other notable exceptions to the general rule such as the philosopher and poet, Judah HaLevy (d.1141), but he also wrote quite firmly that moving and settling in the Land of Israel is a commandment incumbent upon every individual in every age. He held, moreover, that "We are commanded to come to the land and conquer the nations in order to return our tribes [to the Land of Israel]."[8]

Nahmanides was exiled from his native Spain toward the end of his life, and it was only then that he made his way to the Land of Israel. Most Jewish leaders in the following centuries did not follow his lead. Certain other exceptions may be found. Ravitzky points out Isaac ben Sheshet Perfet of Barcelona, known to Jewish tradition as the *Ribash*, a refugee of the Spanish persecutions of 1391 who ruled like Nachmanides that "Emigration to the Land of Israel is a commandment," though he also cautioned "not to ascend the wall."[9]

---

[4] Ravitzky, *Messianism*, 214–220. As noted earlier, Morgenstern considers messianic movements to the Land of Israel to be more significant ("Dispersion...").

[5] Contra Morgenstern, and according to Ravitzky, even this seems to have been countered with a harsh condemnation by the leading Ashkenazic pietist leader, Eliezer ben Moshe of Wurzburg (Ravitzky, *Messianism*, 216).

[6] Arie Morgenstern, *Messianism and the Settlement of Eretz-Israel in the First Half of the Nineteenth Century* (Hebrew) (Jerusalem: Yad Yitzhak ben Tzvi, 1985).

[7] Isadore Twersky (ed.), *Rabbi Moses Nahmanides: Explorations in His Religious and Literary Virtuosity* (Cambridge MA: Harvard University, 1983); Charles Chavel, *Ramban, His Life and Teachings* (New York: Feldheim, 1960).

[8] *Addenda* to Maimonides' *Book of Commandments*, positive commandments 4 (printed with traditional editions of Maimonides' *Book of Commandments*). The full text will be examined in the next chapter.

[9] Ravitzky, *Messianism*, 220–221.

When asked about emigration to the Land of Israel in the fifteenth century, Solomon ben Simeon Duran of Algiers (the *Rashbash*), the child of Spanish refugees, responded: "It is incumbent upon every individual to go up to live [in the Land of Israel]...However, this is not an all-inclusive commandment for all of Israel in their exile, but is withheld from the collectivity....For it is one of the oaths which the Holy One, blessed be He, has adjured Israel, that they not hasten the End, and not go up in the wall. Consider what happened to the children of Ephraim when they forced the End prematurely."[10]

The rule of the Three Vows was effective as a means of encouraging Jewish communities in the Diaspora to develop their own communities of support as best they could in the Middle Ages. The variety of Jewish political and community organization during the period is astonishing, ranging from a centrist and nearly empire-like arrangement of the Geonim of Baghdad under the Abbasid Caliphs to tiny independent communities scattered in Northern Europe or Central Asia. In rare cases of semi-autonomy, Jewish courts ruled on capital crimes and even carried out capital punishment.[11] Generally, however, Jewish courts were limited to ruling on cases of religious and family law, with criminal law the responsibility of the political-military power.

In one famous but extremely exceptional case, one Shmuel ha-Nagid (Isma`il b. Naghrela, d. 1056), poet, rabbi, physician, and scholar, served as general of the Granadan army for sixteen years. He was a great strategist and victorious commander—for the gentile kings of Granada (not for a Jewish hegemon). He had no need to consider rabbinic rulings and discussions regarding "commanded" or "discretionary" wars in his role of military leader of the kingdom, for he served as a faithful servant to his Muslim king.

There is, in general, little discussion of war in medieval Jewish sources, even among the commentaries on the Talmudic discussions reviewed in the previous chapter. This is consistent with the far greater concern among Jews for ritual, economic, civil, and even criminal issues than for military and political issues. The one exception to the rule is Maimonides (d. 1204), the great twelfth century Spanish polymath who lived most of his adult life in Fostat, Egypt. Before we turn to him, however, we must examine the positions of one influential medieval thinker who preceded him.

---

[10] Ravitzky, 1996, 221.

[11] Salo Baron, *A Social and Religious History of the Jews*, vol. 5 (Philadelphia: Jewish Publication Society of America, 1957), 45–46.

# Rashi

Rabbi Shlomo Yitzhaqi (d. 1105), known universally by his acronym "Rashi," is the most widely read commentator on both the Bible and Talmud.[12] He lived in Troyes in northern France, where he was spared the destruction of the Ashkenazi Rhineland Jewish communities during the First Crusade in 1096. Rashi made his living as a vintner and lived in an environment where Jews and Christians interacted regularly. He never organized his views into systematic essays or independent works, so they must be constructed from his extensive commentaries. Rashi begins his comprehensive Bible commentary with the following remark on the first Hebrew phrase of the Bible, "In the beginning."

> *In the beginning* (Gen.1:1). Rabbi Isaac said: The Torah should have begun with (the verse), *This month shall be the first of the months* (Ex.12:1) which is the first [collective] commandment given to Israel.[13] Why then did [the Torah] begin with Creation? Because *He declared the power of his works* [i.e. Creation] *in order to give to* [Israel] *the heritage of the nations* (Ps.111:6). So if the peoples of the world say to Israel: "You are robbers because you took the lands of the seven (Canaanite) nations," Israel can reply to them: "All the earth belongs to the Holy One blessed be He. He created it and gave it to whom He pleased. When God wished, He gave it to them [i.e. the Canaanites]; and when God wished, He took it from them and gave it to us!

As Rashi himself notes, the core of this commentary is derived from Rabbi Isaac, in the midrashic collection called *Tanchuma*.[14] But Rabbi Isaac's comment in *Tanchuma* ends with the Psalms citation. The reader can then make any connection desired to the Psalm verse. Rashi makes his own by linking the statement of divine power with a familiar Christian

---

[12] Maurice Liber, *Rashi* (Philadelphia: Jewish Publication Society, 1906/1938); Herman Hailperin, *Rashi and the Christian Scholars* (Pittsburgh: University of Pittsburgh, 1963); Chaim Pearl, *Rashi* (New York: Grove, 1988).

[13] God commanded individuals, but Exodus 12:1 is the first time that God addressed the community of Israel as a whole to articulate communal commands. *This month shall be will be the first of the months* is taken as a commandment to begin counting the religious ritual calendar from this date onward.

[14] Midrash Tanchuma (Buber), *Bereshit*, section 11. The same tradition is found in Midrash Yalqut Shim'oni, which is roughly contemporary with Rashi (Exodus section 12 [Jerusalem: Mosad Harav Kook, 1977, Exodus volume, p. 115]). An earlier Midrash, *Song of Songs Rabbah*, section 1, first uses the exegesis that Jewish religious logic would not expect the Bible to begin with an exposition on Creation, but *Song of Songs Rabbah* arrives at a different conclusion.

polemic against the Jews—that scripture describes Israel pillaging and plundering their way into the Land of Canaan in their conquest, thereby depicting a Jewish religion of violence and war as opposed to the Christian religion of love and grace. Rashi's message is one of justification and consolation.[15] The justification is that God is the true owner of all creation. Because God has power over all things under creation, it was God rather than the Jews who authorized the conquest of the Land of Israel. Rashi lived during the period of the Crusades, when Christian and Muslim armies were engaged in war for possession of that same land. And ironically, the Jewish communities of both Europe and the Land of Israel were devastated by the Crusader warriors. Rashi's consolation might have included the sentiment that despite the Crusaders' power and armies, God would return the People of Israel to their rightful possession of the Land of Israel.

Alone, Rashi's comment might be construed as justifying Israelite war in general as divinely authorized. Any successful Jewish war of conquest could be construed, simply by virtue of its success, as being ordained by God.[16] Elsewhere in his commentaries, however, Rashi severely limits divinely sanctioned wars of conquest to the past, the period of conquest under Joshua.

In Rashi's commentary on the Talmud, he responds to the first reference to Commanded War in Sotah 44b with the following: *Commanded War,* "Such as the conquest of the Land of Israel in the days of Joshua." This definition is similar to those found in the Gemaras. Recall from chapter 5 that the Mishnah did not give examples for either Discretionary War or Commanded War. The Palestinian Talmud defined the category of war for which no deferments are allowed[17] in two ways, as either "the war of Joshua" or defensive war. The Babylonian Talmud defined such war as "the wars of Joshua to conquer." Rashi's definition in Sotah and those offered by both

---

[15] Rabbi Chayim Dov Chavel, *Rashi's Commentaries on the Torah* (Hebrew. Jerusalem: Mosad Harav Kook, 1995), p.2; Grossman, *Rashi,* 36–38.

[16] The weakness of this argument is, of course, that it can be reversed: the loss of the Land of Israel would have also been ordained by God, and perhaps this loss is permanent! This was not lost on modern religious Zionist thinkers. In reference to Rashi's commentary here, Rabbi Yehudah Herzl Henkin lectured in a dedication ceremony marking the establishment of the new Orthodox religious settlement, Matityahu on the West Bank (named after the zealot patriarch of the Maccabees, Mattathias, mentioned in chapter 2), "It is said to the nations that the Holy One gave the Land to whom He willed, and they say to us: 'If so, then when we conquer the Land back from your hands, this will be proof that our God (*lehavdil*) gave it to us.'" The answer to this in the tradition is that the primary sanctity applied to the Land (*kedushah rishonah*) derived from the conquest of Joshua. This was temporary and lost through conquest. The second sanctity (*kedushah sheniyah*), which is derived from settlement, is forever ("On Settling the Land of Israel," *Shanah Beshanah* 1983, 332; the difference between these expressions and the sanctities they represent will be examined in chapter 13).

[17] "Commanded" or "Required," depending on the authority (see chapter 5).

Talmuds refer to the conquest of Joshua as an example of war for which no deferments applied (whether called "Commanded" or "Required"). Rashi's language construes the conquest of Joshua as an example, but not a limitation. In other words, the category is not necessarily limited to the days of Joshua. Other wars that fit this category might be implied by the Talmudic examples, including wars of conquest in some future time.

Elsewhere, in his Talmud commentary, however, Rashi defines the difference as follows: "All war is considered discretionary except for the war of Joshua to conquer the Land of Israel."[18] Rashi limits the category of nondiscretionary war here to the conquests of Joshua. He uses no language like "such as" (*kegon* in the Hebrew) in this definition, so it appears here that he is not citing Joshua's wars as an example, but rather as a limit.[19] This sentiment is also evident from his comment on the same term in *Eruvin* 17a: "[This is] simple Discretionary War from [the time of] Joshua's war onward, [Joshua's war being] Commanded War ."

It should be mentioned here that by the time of Rashi in the eleventh century, the terms used to define the typology of war were standardized to what is still used today: Discretionary War as opposed to Commanded War: "Everyone [now] discusses it according to [the terminology of] "commanded" versus "discretionary."[20]

Rashi has nothing significant to add to these comments. One of his remarks may be read to suggest that divinely commanded war to conquer the Land of Israel might still be possible. Elsewhere his language seems to limit the category to the historical wars of Joshua. The students of the Ashkenazi schools of the Rhineland known collectively as the *Ba`alei tosefot* had nothing of significance to add. It would be the minimalist position of Maimonides on the issue of war that would stimulate surprise and then reaction, first in the century of his death, and then continuing on and off until the present day.

## Maimonides' Counting of the Commandments

Moses Maimonides (d. 1204) was a brilliant thinker and prolific writer who engaged in most of the intellectual disciplines available to Jews

---

[18] Sanhedrin 2a.

[19] Many rabbis in the modern Nationalist-Zionist camp would disagree, as will be demonstrated in Part Four. Rabbi Shaul Yisraeli, for example, did not consider this a limitation when he wrote, "It appears from [Rashi's] language that he takes [from this] that the only example of commanded war is the war for conquest of the Land." (Rabbi Shaul Yisraeli, "Commanded war and Discretionary War" [Hebrew], *Torah Shebe`al Peh* 10 [1968], 46.)

[20] Rashi on *Sota* 45b s.v. *mitzvah derabbanan.*

during the Middle Ages.[21] Born in Cordoba in 1138, he and his family fled Spain soon after his tenth birthday in the face of the conquest of that city by the repressive Muslim Almohad movement in 1148. Nothing is known of the family for the next few years, and it is assumed that they wandered in various parts of Spain and perhaps also Provence. In 1160 they settled in Fez in today's Morocco, which was also under the control of the Almohads. They fled Fez five years later, perhaps in response to the martyrdom of Maimonides' teacher there, Yehuda ibn Susan, who chose death over forced apostasy, and arrived in the port of Acre on the coast of today's Israel, then under the control of the Fatimid Caliphate based in Fostat (old Cairo). They remained in the Land of Israel for about half a year until they finally made their way to Fostat. Maimonides' family settled there and prospered, although it would take some years before he would achieve his great fame.

In order to arrive at a full sense of Maimonides' views on any given subject, a number of his major works must be consulted. We begin with his early *Commentary on the Mishnah* that he composed while in his twenties, where he first discusses the issue of war in relation to the passage we examined previously in Mishnah Sotah 8.[22]

> [Mishnah: To what (types of wars) do these instructions apply? To a Discretionary War, but in a Commanded War everyone must go forth, etc.]

> There is no disagreement between them [the rabbis and Rabbi Yehudah] that war against the seven (Canaanite) nations and war against Amalek is obligatory. And [furthermore] there is no disagreement between them that war against[23] the people of the other nations is discretionary. There is a difference of opinion only about war against those who [come to] fight them in order to weaken them so they will not initiate war against Israel

---

[21] Literally thousands of academic articles and books have been written on Maimonides. See Jay Harris' preface in his (ed.) *Maimonides After 800 Years: Essays on Maimonides and His Influence* (Cambridge, MA: Harvard University, 2007), vii–xi, and following articles; see also Isadore Twersky, *Introduction to the Code of Maimonides* (New Haven: Yale University Press, 1980).

[22] Sotah 8 (end), translation to Hebrew from the Arabic by Yosef David Qafih, *Mishnah with the Commentary of Our Rabbi Moses b. Maimon* 6 v. (Jerusalem: Mosad Harav Kook, 1965), v. 3 *Seder Nashim*, p. 185.

[23] The Hebrew translation in the traditional printed editions has *harigat* (הריגת), which may be a mistranslation from the original Arabic, which I suspect is *qitaal* (قتال), meaning "fighting." The error would be a mistranslation via the similar-sounding Jewish Aramaic *qetal(a)* (קְטָלָא), meaning killing, which would be equivalent to the Arabic *qatl* (قتل).

and attack their land.[24] The rabbis[25] consider this discretionary, while Rabbi Yehudah calls this type of war commanded. According to Rabbi Yehudah, whoever was engaged in this [category of preemptive] war or in activities supporting it is exempt from the [other] commandments because our principle, as you know, is that one who is engaged in commandments is exempt from [other] commandments. According to the rabbis, he [who is involved in preemptive fighting] is not engaged in a commandment. Jewish law (the *halakhah*) does not follow Rabbi Yehudah.

Maimonides defines the two categories established by the Mishnah differently from earlier sources. Most strikingly, he drops the explanation given in the Palestinian Talmud, in the name of Rav Hisda, and in the Babylonian Talmud, in the name of Rava, that Joshua's wars of conquest define Obligatory (or Commanded) war.[26] In the position of Joshua's wars of conquest, he places wars against the seven Canaanite nations and Amalek, two categories of war that were not treated as such by the Talmudic discussion(s). We shall observe below how this substitution served to extend the category of Commanded Wars beyond the limited, particularistic case of the wars of conquest of the Land of Israel.[27]

Maimonides also extends the Talmudic example of David's wars to the more general definition of "other nations"—any peoples living in any location other than the seven nations and the Amalekites. This would include David's wars against the Arameans of Aram Zobah but would extend the category far beyond it. Like Rashi a century before him, Maimonides agrees with Rava's explanation that the difference between the two parties of the Mishnah may be reduced to the rule that one who is engaged in a commandment is exempt from other commandments, and then concludes by establishing the *halakhah* according to the majority "rabbis" rather than Rabbi Yehudah.

---

[24] That is, what is called today a preemptive attack.

[25] He uses the term, *tanna kamma*.

[26] We will show below that Maimonides redefines Commanded War to exclude the idea or example of conquest of the Land of Israel from his legal definition of the notion. However, he does not dissociate Joshua's conquest entirely from the notion. In his discussion of fighting on the Sabbath, he mentions that Joshua's conquest of Jericho, which he notes is well known to be Commanded War, occurred on the Sabbath (*hilkhot shabbat* 2:24).

[27] According to George Wilkes, Maimonides' views on war develop from his early *Commentary on the Mishnah* to his *Mishneh Torah*, and that development reflects the change in his intellectual environment from his youth in Almoravid and Almohad Spain to his adulthood in Fatimid and then Ayyubid Egypt. In this case, however, his extension of the Talmudic position seems consistent (George R. Wilkes, "Religious War in the Works of Maimonides and the 'Maimonideans': An Idea and Its Transit Across the Medieval Mediterranean," in S. Hashmi, ed., *Just Wars, Holy wars, and Jihads: Christian, Jewish, Muslim Encounters and Exchanges* (New York: Oxford, 2012).

Maimonides extends this thinking in his *Code of Jewish Law* (completed 1180), in the section, "Laws Concerning Kings and Wars." He follows the line established by the Mishnah when he responds to the question regarding the types of war to which deferments apply.

> To what (types of wars) do these instructions about discharging people from battle apply? To a Discretionary War, but in a Commanded War everyone must go forth, even a bridegroom from his chamber and a bride from her bridal pavilion (Kings & Wars 7:4).

Elsewhere in the tractate he defines the categories of war.

> The primary war that the king wages is a Commanded War. Which may be considered a Commanded War? War against the seven [Canaanite] nations, war against Amalek, and aid to [deliver] Israel from an attacking enemy. Secondarily he [may] fight a Discretionary War, which is war against the other nations to extend the borders of Israel and to enhance his greatness and prestige (Kings & Wars 5:1).[28]

This understanding of the Mishnah's two categories of war extends the views expressed in the Palestinian and Babylonian Talmuds (like Rashi, he uses "discretionary" for category one, and "commanded" for category two, leaving out the definition of "obligatory" from discussion). Maimonides' reference to Discretionary Wars "against the remaining nations to extend the borders of Israel and to enhance his greatness and prestige" parallels but generalizes and extends the category of expansionary wars, which are limited in the two Talmuds to David's wars of expansion. His definition of Commanded War against the local peoples living in Canaan also extends the categories of the Talmud, which refer specifically and only to Joshua's wars of conquest. It is true, of course, that Joshua's wars were directed against the peoples of Canaan, the "seven Canaanite nations" of Deuteronomy 7, but the examples cited by the Talmuds were limited to the conquest. The Talmuds did not generalize their reference to include wars in general against Canaanites, which could have occurred long after the conquest since Canaanites remained living in the area. Following the Palestinian Talmud, Maimonides includes defensive wars within the category of Commanded Wars,[29] and as in his *Commentary to the Mishnah*, also wars against the

---

[28] All translations of the *Mishneh Torah* are mine, based on that of Abraham Hershman, *The Code of Maimonides* (New Haven: Yale University Press, 1949).

[29] Original to the Palestinian Talmud as "obligatory."

TABLE 7.1

|  | DISCRETIONARY<br>רשות | COMMANDED<br>מצוה | OBLIGATORY<br>חובה |
|---|---|---|---|
| MISHNAH: |  |  |  |
| Rabbis | Deferments | No deferments |  |
| Yehudah |  | Deferments | No deferments |
| P. Talmud |  |  |  |
| Hisda: |  |  |  |
| Rabbis |  | David's wars | Joshua's wars |
| Yehudah | Israel initiates |  | Defensive wars |
| B. Talmud |  |  |  |
| Rava: |  |  |  |
| All agree | David's wars of<br>expansion |  | Joshua's wars of<br>conquest |
| Yehudah |  | Preemptive strike |  |
| Rabbis | Preemptive strike |  |  |
| Maimonides (Mishneh<br>Torah) | Other nations, to<br>extend borders for<br>prestige | Seven (Canaanite)<br>nations, Amalek,<br>defense. |  |

Amalekites. It is striking that he omits "Joshua's wars" entirely from both his *Commentary on the Mishnah* and his *Code of Jewish Law*. Table 7.1 adds Maimonides' schema to our earlier chart (Table 5.2).

Maimonides' choice of terminology denotes a significant conceptual change from that of the rabbinic period. Most important, he takes the discussion about war out of the particularistic context of the Talmud and builds out of it a universal Jewish theory of war patterned after the universal Muslim theories of war that were issues of discussion in his contemporary environment living under the Caliphate.[30] By removing Joshua's wars of conquest from the typology, he removes from his system the chronological and geographical limitations established previously by the Jerusalem and Babylonian Talmuds. In Kings & Wars 5:6, he extends the meaning of the borders of the Land of Israel by considering any legal Jewish conquest equal to the conquest by Joshua as long as the additional lands are conquered after all the Land of Israel, as defined by the Torah, is already under Jewish political control.

---

[30] Maimonides' Muslim contemporary, Muhammad Ibn Rushd ("Averroes," d.1198), for example, wrote a chapter on war *(jihad)* in his legal handbook, *Kitab bidayat al-mujtahid wanihayat al-muqtasid fil-fiqh* (translated in Rudolph Peters, *Jihad in Classical and Modern Islam* [Princeton: Markus Wiener, 1996]), 27–42. By the twelfth century, Islamic theories of government and war had been well established.

All lands that Israel conquers through [the leadership of] the king at the decision of the court are deemed national conquest *(kibbush rabbim)* and become in all respects an integral part of the Land of Israel conquered by Joshua, provided that they are conquered after the whole of the Land of Israel specified in the Bible (Kings & Wars 5:6).

This provides a legal foundation for a theoretical Jewish conquest of territories extending far beyond the limited biblical borders of the Land of Israel.[31] Maimonides defines "national conquest" elsewhere in the following way:

The Land of Israel is defined as those lands that were conquered by a king of Israel or a prophet with the authorization of the majority of Israel; this is what is called "majority [in effect, national] conquest" *(kibbush rabbim)*. But any individual, family or tribe of Israel that goes and conquers a place for themselves, even if within the Land that was given [by God] to Abraham, is not considered the Land of Israel for the purposes of observing all of the commandments. This is why Joshua and his court divided all of the Land of Israel into tribal divisions even though it was not yet conquered—in order that there would be no individual conquest through the acts of each tribe to conquer its own territory.[32]

This should not be misconstrued to suggest that Maimonides was advocating a military conquest to reestablish Jewish hegemony over the biblical Land of Israel and beyond. There is nothing known to me in his writings that would suggest this. The purpose of this grand vision is, rather, to demonstrate the universal ideology that he understood to lie behind the commands for war found in the Torah. The following citation indicates how the core of that ideology, in parallel with a core component of the war ideologies of Islam, is intended to eliminate all idolatry from the world.[33]

---

[31] The "biblical borders" of the Land of Israel vary considerably, depending upon the biblical text, but even the largest biblical delineated areas are small in relation to the universalizing trend apparent from this section (see Israel Ariel, *Atlas of the Land of Israel: Its Boundaries according to the Sources* [Hebrew], Jerusalem: Cana, 1988).

[32] *Hilkhot Terumot* 1:2. See also *hilkhot Terumot* 1:3, 1:5, 1:10.

[33] On this ideological underpinning and its parallel with Islam, see Gerald (Yakov) Blidstein, "Holy War in Maimonidean Law," in Joel L. Kraemer, ed., *Perspectives on Maimonides* (New York: Littman Library and Oxford University Press, 1991), 209–220 and Isaak Heineman, "*Maimuni und die arabischen Einheitsleher*" *MGWJ* 79 (1935), 133ff. Much in Blidstein's article is expanded in his more detailed *Political Concepts in Maimonidean Halakhah* (Hebrew) 2nd and expanded edition (Ramat Gan: Bar Ilan University, 2001).

Moses our teacher bequeathed the Torah and commandments only to Israel, as it is said (Deut.33:4), *the heritage of the congregation of Jacob*, and to all those who wish to become Jewish *(lehitgayyer)* from the other nations, as it is said (Num.15:16), *(the same ritual and rule shall apply) to you and to the resident alien (ka-ger)*. But no coercion is applied to those who do not wish to accept the Torah and commandments. Moses was commanded by the word of the Most High, therefore, to compel all human beings to accept the Noahide laws,[34] and anyone who does not accept them is put to death (Kings 8:10).[35]

Maimonides does not simply follow Islamic norms in this position, though Gerald Blidstein has noted how Maimonides' views were influenced by the war ideologies known from his Islamic intellectual environment.[36] That Moses was commanded to compel all human beings to accept the Noahide laws is a significant extension of Talmudic war ideology, though it remains significantly less developed than the position of Islam. Maimonides' position would eliminate idolatry through the less rigorous requirement to follow the simpler Noahide laws rather than to convert entirely to Judaism,[37] while Islam would require idolaters, but not monotheists, to convert to Islam.[38] His insistence in compelling the Noahide laws is consistent with his repeated critique of idolatry and his call to destroy it.[39]

---

[34] For Noahide law and Noahides, see Aaron Lichtenstein, *The Seven Laws of Noah* (NY: Z. Berman, 1987); David Novak, *The Image of the Non-Jew in Judaism: An Historical and Constructive Study of the Noahide Laws* (NY: Edwin Mellen, 1983).

[35] For Islamic parallels, see Majid Khadduri, *War and Peace in the Law of Islam* (Baltimore: Johns Hopkins, 1955) 55–69.

[36] *Political Concepts*, 254–255.

[37] Kings & Wars 8:10.

[38] Monotheists fall into the Qur'anic category of the "peoples of the book," also known in later juridical literature as "protected peoples" or *dhimmis* (Claude Cahen, "Dhimma" in Encyclopaedia of Islam (2nd Ed.), 2:227–231, Muhammad b. Jarir al-Tabari, *Jami` al-bayan `an ta'wil ayat al-Qur'an* (Beirut: Dar al-Fikr, 1984), 10:77–78, 109–110. For a full discourse on the topic in Arabic, see Shams al-Din Ibn Qayyim al-Jawziyya [d.1350], *Ahkam ahl al-dhimma* [ed. Sabhi Salih, Beirut, 1983]).

[39] Others, such as the twelfth century Andalusian philosopher, Abraham b. Daud (d.1180), did not consider acceptance of the Noahide commandments a requirement for making peace with other peoples (*Hasagot lemishneh torah*, chapter 6 [Jerusalem: Naor, 1984] as cited in Abraham Tzvi Rabinowitz, "Ethical Considerations on the Topic of War," in Blum, Eli, Shlomo Bar-On, et. al., *Values under the Trial of War: Morality and War in the View of Judaism* (Hebrew) Jerusalem: Hamakor/Har Etzion, n.d., p.44.) Cf. Nahmanides' commentary on Deut. 20:10; discussion in Betzalel Naor, *Hasagot Haravad lemishneh torah: sefer mada vesefer ahavah* (Jerusalem: Zur-Ot, 1984), 132–133; and discussion in the *Or Sameach* (Meir Simchah of Dvinsk, d.1926, commentary on the *Mishneh Torah*) hilkhot milah 1:6 s.v. *aval im lo qibel `alav sheva mitzvot yehareg* [Bar Ilan Responsa Project, version 14].

However, Maimonides requires only the destruction of the seven Canaanite nations and the tribe of Amalek. He notes that the command to destroy these two groups is eternal, even though the peoples in question no longer exist.[40]

It is a positive command to absolutely destroy the seven nations, as it is said (Deut. 20:17), *You must utterly destroy them*, and anyone who fails to kill any of them who fall into his hands transgresses a negative command, as it is said (Deut. 20:16), *You must not let a soul remain alive.* But their memory has long perished.

So, too, is it a positive command to obliterate the memory of Amalek, as it is said (Deut. 25:19), *you shall blot out the memory of Amalek.* It is a positive command always to bear in mind his evil deeds and ambushes so as to keep alive enmity toward him, as it is said (Deut. 25:15), *Remember what Amalek did to you.* The oral tradition teaches, "*Remember* (Deut. 25:15) by word of mouth, *do not forget* (Deut. 25:19) in your mind," in order to forbid forgetting hatred and enmity toward him (Kings & Wars 5:4–5).

Destruction of the seven Canaanite nations and Amalek symbolizes for Maimonides the destruction of idolatry and the immorality that is innately associated with it. This is in keeping with the position of Islam articulated as early as the Qur'an that idolatry and immorality are in direct relationship.[41] The Maimonidean extension of Canaanism to idolatry in general extends to a universal view regarding repentant idolaters (which also finds a parallel in Islam).[42] For Maimonides, the way must always be left open for repentance from idolatry, even among Canaanites and Amalekites, and, therefore repentance from their immoral behaviors. In Islam such renunciation requires conversion to Islam; to Maimonides, it is sufficient that they become Noahides. Such a position with regard to Canaanites and Amalekites would appear to fly in the face of the explicit Torah command to annihilate these two groups through the biblical institution of

---

[40] *Book of Commandments*, positive 187. Maimonides continues: "One might think that this commandment is not binding for all time, since the seven nations have long ceased to exist.... as long as descendants of Amalek exist they must be exterminated.... Thus we did until their destruction was completed by David and this remnant was scattered and intermingled with the other nations so that no trace of them remains." (*The Commandments* 2 vols. transl. Charles Chavel [London: Soncino, 1967]), 200. Cf. *Guide for the Perplexed*, part III, chapter 29 (Friedlander translation [NY: Dover, 1956]), p. 320.

[41] Qur'an 4:116; 6:148–153; Q. 89.

[42] Qur'an 9:5–6.

the ban *(cherem),*[43] but Maimonides states in Kings and Wars 6:1 that the rule allowing those Canaanites and Amalekites who accept the Noahide laws to live, applies to both Discretionary and Commanded War *(echad milchemet hareshut echad milchemet mitzvah).*

> One may not wage war against anyone in the world unless a peace offer is made first. This applies to Discretionary Wars and Commanded Wars, as it is said (Deut. 20:10): *"When you approach a town to attack it, you shall offer it terms of peace.* If they surrender and accept the seven Noahide commandments, not a single soul is killed. But they become tributary, as it is said (Deut.20:11): *all the people present there shall serve you at forced labor..."* (Kings & Wars 6:1).

Maimonides nowhere mentions the option of going to war against any peoples who are already following the Noahide laws. He is even more explicit later on in the same chapter.

> If they refuse to surrender, or if they surrender but do not accept the seven [Noahide] commandments, war is made against them. All adult males are killed and all their money and children are taken as plunder, but no woman or child is killed, as it is said (Deut. 20:14): *[take as your booty] the women and the children.* "Children" refers to male minors. To what does this [rule] apply? To a Discretionary War against the other nations [that do not surrender or accept the Noahide laws]; but if the seven [Canaanite] nations and Amalek do not surrender, no one is spared, as it is said (Deut.20:15–16), *Thus you shall deal with all [the towns that lie very far from you]...only of the towns of these* [neighboring] *peoples...you shall not let a soul remain alive.* So too, with respect to Amalek it says (Deut. 15:19), *You shall blot out the memory of Amalek.* From where do we derive that this refers only to those who have not surrendered? As it says (Josh.11:19–20), *Not a single town surrendered to Israel apart from the Hivites who dwelt in Gibeon; all were taken in battle. For it was the Lord's doing to stiffen their hearts to give battle to Israel in order that they might be utterly destroyed.* We infer from this that [Israel] offered them [all—even the Canaanites and Amalekites] the option of surrender but they did not accept it (Kings & Wars 6:4).[44]

---

[43] Deut. 7:1–2, 20:16–17, 25:17–19, and see Philip D. Stern, *The Biblical Herem: A Window on Israel's Religious Experience* (Atlanta: Scholars Press, 1991).

[44] The surrender of the Hivites who dwelt in Gibeon proves the rule, therefore, that all had the option and those who surrendered were not destroyed.

Maimonides thus finds biblical proofs to justify his universal position on idolatry, and in so doing, universalizes the extinct Canaanites and Amalekites by making them into eternal symbols of idolatry and its associated evils. According to his reading, even the idolatrous Canaanites and Amalekites were offered terms of peace by Joshua, but they refused, thus justifying the divinely commanded wars to destroy them. By emphasizing the universal nature of the issue, Maimonides removes the discussion from the particularity of the Land of Israel. He thus portrays the biblical wars against the Canaanites and Amalekites more as a reflection of the divine will to bring humanity to right religion than for Israel to take possession of the Land. His universalizing, with the resulting negation of the centrality of the Land of Israel in his war ideology, is repeated in his *Book of Commandments* that enumerates all of the commandments found in the Torah.

Positive commandment 187 is that God commanded us to kill the seven [Canaanite] nations and to exterminate them, for they were the root and original foundation of idolatry. This [command] is [in] His (may He be exalted) statement (Deut. 20:17), *You must utterly destroy them.* [God] has explained to us in many Scriptural texts that the reason [for their destruction] is so that we not learn from their apostasy.[45] Now there are many Scriptural passages that strongly urge killing them. War against them is Commanded War. One might think that this commandment is not binding for all time, since the seven nations no longer exist. But one could only think this who does not understand the difference between things that are eternally binding and those that are not.... Thus have we been commanded to kill the seven nations and to destroy them; this is a Commanded War through which we are required to root them out and pursue them throughout all the generations until they are destroyed without even a single survivor. And thus we did until they were brought to a complete end by David, while the survivors were scattered and assimilated among the nations until no trace of them survived. It does not follow that, although they have been destroyed, the command to kill them is no longer in force throughout the generations, just as it cannot be said that war against Amalek is not in force throughout the generations even though they have been absolutely

---

[45] Some contemporary religious Zionist thinkers read Maimonides to teach that the essence of the command is for the Canaanites to repent from idolatry—in traditional language "to make *teshuvah.*" This is why he did not include within the definition of commanded war, the wars of Joshua to conquer but, rather, the destruction of the Seven Nations (Rabbi Shlomo Goren, "Commanded War and Discretionary War" [Hebrew], *Mahanayim* 69 [1962] 13).

destroyed. This is because these commandments are not bound by time or by place... (Positive Command #187).

Maimonides repeats that war against the Canaanites and Amalekites is a Commanded War, but here he explains their symbolic significance and their transition to the abstract. Although they no longer exist, the command to destroy them remains in force. His view is clarified further in his great philosophical work, the *Guide to the Perplexed* (1:54), where the Canaanite nations represent impediments to the knowledge of God. Although it is not stated here explicitly, it is evident from the repeated biblical association (as well as his direct reference in positive command 187) that their addiction to idolatry is the underlying problem.

> You have no doubt noticed in the Torah when it commanded the destruction of the seven nations with [the verse] *you shall not let a soul remain alive* (Deut.20:16), that joined to these words is *lest they lead you into doing all the abhorrent things that they have done for their gods and you stand guilty before the Lord your God*? That is to say: Do not think that this is cruelty or an act of vengeance. Rather, it is an act required by human reason to remove all who would deviate from the path of truth and remove all obstacles that impede the realization of perfection, which is the knowledge of God, may He be exalted. [46]

This corroborates further how Maimonides universalizes certain commands that in the Torah were directed specifically against two groups that had threatened Israelites in and immediately around the Land of Israel. Maimonides views the purpose of the commandments to be the universal elimination of the theological and moral threat of idolatry. But the biblical commands are limited to the Land of Israel, and the Talmud does not extend them.[47] Maimonides' expansion of the notion reduces the relative importance of the Land of Israel as he extends Jewish responsibility to eradicate idolatry to a universal scope.

In his *Book of Commandments*, Maimonides lists the traditional 613 divine commandments derived from the Torah according to his counting of the 248 positive and 365 negative Torah commandments mentioned in the Talmud (Shabbat 87a). "Positive" commandments are "thou shalt" commands, referring to acts that are commanded according to God's words

---

[46] *The Guide of the Perplexed*, part I, chapter 44 (Samuel Ibn Tibbon edition with four commentaries including that of Isaac Abarbanel; Hebrew. Jerusalem, 1969), 81b.
[47] Blidstein, *Political Concepts*, 255.

in the Torah. "Negative" commands are the "thou shalt not" commands, those acts and behaviors that are specifically forbidden in the Torah.

Maimonides lists the destruction of the Canaanites and the Amalekites in war as distinct positive commands (#187 and #188) because they are, as he points out numerous times, Commanded Wars. Even Discretionary Wars are considered by Maimonides to be positive commands, based on Deuteronomy 20:11: *[all the conquered people] shall serve you and pay you taxes.*[48] But nowhere, to my knowledge, does Maimonides refer to Joshua's conquest of the Land of Israel as a binding divine command. Two terms that gain a great deal of importance in later discussions, "Conquering the Land" *(kibbush ha'aretz)* and "Settling the Land" *(yishuv ha'aretz)* are known to Maimonides, but he does not list them as commandments in his compendium or even refer to them elsewhere as divinely authorized acts.[49]

Like the rabbis of the Talmud before him, he expresses little interest in the reconquest and settlement of the Land of Israel. Even his views on messianism do not emphasize the role of the Land of Israel (Kings & Wars chapters 11–12). He does write that the messiah will restore Israel's sovereignty and the kingdom of David, rebuild the Jerusalem Temple, and gather the dispersed of Israel. But these conclusions are already so clearly spelled out in earlier rabbinic texts that it would be remarkable to have excluded them. He nevertheless minimizes the centrality of Jerusalem and the Land of Israel in the messianic future. He also notes that the prophets and sages did not hope for the messianic era in order to increase their power or prestige, but rather, to devote themselves to the Torah and its wisdom. The goal is neither political freedom nor sovereignty, but rather a world in which all will know God and in which Israel will attain the deepest and most complete understanding of God possible for the human mind (Kings & Wars 12:4–5).

Rashi and Maimonides remain true to the agenda of the rabbis of the Talmud. Although the Talmudic sages neither rejected the basic biblical equation of obedience = success/disobedience = failure, nor the extraordinary nature of the Land of Israel and the expectation that one day the Jewish people would again be in control of their own sacred trust, they created

---

[48] The translation of 20:11 as an imperative is based on Maimonides' interpretation of the verse rather than the plain meaning, which is a conditional sentence: "If it responds peaceably...then they shall serve you and pay taxes." The opening verse of the section (20:10) establishes a context that does not command the fighting. Cf. Positive Commandment 190.

[49] See *Mishneh Torah, Shemitah* 10:2, 12:15, *De'ot* 7:8, *Shekhenim* 4:10, 14:1; *Guide* 3:24; *Book of Commandments*, Negative 46, 353.

powerful barriers to prevent Jews from engaging personally in the realization of those goals. Maimonides does not move exactly along the same trajectory as the rabbis, but his thinking advances the same basic thrust. The rabbis remain highly particularistic in their view of the commandments. They identified Commanded War as the wars of Joshua to conquer the Land of Israel. Maimonides, while not rejecting the particularism of the People of Israel and the Land of Israel, universalized the commandments requiring the destruction of the Seven Nations and Amalek that had until then been associated with political and military control of the Land. By extending those commands to indicate the worldwide elimination of idolatry, along with its natural association with immorality and unethical behavior (that association was part of the general Muslim ethos of the culture in which he lived), he essentially spiritualized Commanded War. Unlike the rabbis, he dissociated it from conquest and the geography of the Land of Israel. In so doing, he took a different tack from the rabbinic sages of the Talmud, but the result with regard to the research of this book was largely the same. Both Maimonides and the rabbis distanced Jewish holy war from any possible application to political or military action by Jews.

# CHAPTER 8 | Nahmanides' Critique, and Other Thinkers

We are commanded to engage in the conquest in every
generation. . . . It is an eternal positive command, obligating every
single individual even during the time of Exile.

MOSES BEN NACHMAN

The great thirteenth-century spanish scholar Moses ben Nachman of Gerona (d. 1270), known as Nahmanides, began his life during a period of relatively liberal Christian rule over Spanish Jewry. Toward the end of a long and productive career in Catalonia he would be required to confront publicly the ugly side of Christian authority. In 1263, at the age of sixty-nine, Nahmanides was forced into a public disputation in Barcelona against the Jewish convert to Christianity, Pablo Christiani. Protected by King James I and allowed to speak freely during the course of the disputation, he was nevertheless brought to trial two years later in 1265 for supposed public abuses of Christianity.[1] He escaped prosecution but not persecution, fleeing to the Land of Israel at the age of seventy-three. After living for a short time in Jerusalem, he settled in Acre where, unlike his predecessor Maimonides a century earlier, he remained and became the religious leader of the Jewish community.

---

[1] The best study of the disputation and references to all important earlier studies is Robert Chazan, *Barcelona and Beyond* (Berkeley and Los Angeles: University of California, 1992). On the question of whether his trial was a result of his presentation at the disputation or his subsequent record of the proceedings published nearly two years later, see ibid, 91–99. For a more general study, see Nina Caputo, *Nahmanides in Medieval Catalonia: History, Community and Messianism* (South Bend, IN: University of Notre Dame, 2008).

Nahmanides' decision to move to the Holy Land was exceptional, though it is not clear whether the "emigration could have been the result of the discomfort occasioned by the Dominican efforts [against him] or, alternatively, of spiritual factors that had nothing to do with his involvement in the Barcelona debate."[2] In any case, his departure for the Land of Israel broke with the mystical and halakhic principles of his school of Gerona Kabbalists.[3] Throughout the late Antique and Medieval periods, Jews tended not to immigrate to the Land of Israel; rarely did they do so en masse, and never as a political movement.[4]

A physician by trade, Nahmanides was a polymath who wrote glosses on the entire Talmud, a popular Bible commentary found in most standard Rabbinic Bibles, and works of Jewish law. These include a critique of Maimonides' *Book of Commandments*, which may be found in traditional printed editions of Maimonides' opus.[5] Among other issues, he criticizes Maimonides' universalizing tendency regarding war because he believed that it ignored undeniable and specific divine commands to conquer and settle the Land of Israel. In a famous comment that is often cited by activists and ideologues among Orthodox religious Zionists today, Nahmanides censures Maimonides for not including conquest of the Land of Israel as one of the 613 commandments. Nahmanides' critique is rather long, but I cite it in full because his argument becomes an essential element of modern thinkers involved in the revival of the holy war paradigm of Commanded War.

The fourth commandment is to inherit[6] the land that God, may He be praised and exalted, gave to our ancestors, to Abraham, Isaac and Jacob, and not to

---

[2] Chazan, *Barcelona*, 99.
[3] Ravitzky 1996, 24.
[4] The few cases of significant immigrations can be counted on one hand: the Karaite *Avelei Tsiyyon* in the tenth century, French Tosafists in the "aliyah of 300 rabbis" in the thirteenth century (the descendents of whom Nahmanides probably knew), and the establishment of the mystical community of Safed in the sixteenth. Occasional movements of Jews from Eastern Europe and other areas became more prominent in the early modern period. See Fred Astren, *Kara'ite Judaism and Historical Understanding* (Columbia, SC: University of South Carolina Press, 2004) 66–72 and references there; Ephraim Kanarfogel, "The Aliyah of the 'Three Hundred Rabbis'" *Jewish Quarterly Review* 76 (1986): 191–212; H. H. Ben-Sasson, *History of the Jewish People* (Cambridge, MA: Harvard University Press, 1994), 66–67; and especially, Arie Morgenstern, "Dispersion and the Longing for Zion, 1240–1840," *Azure* 12 (2002), 71–132.
[5] It is referred to as Nahmanides' "Critique" (*hassagot*), which was first published in Constantinople in 1510 and strongly influenced subsequent works such as the *Sefer hachinnukh* that attempt to identify the 613 commandments mentioned in the Talmud as enumerated in the Torah. The passage below is Nahmanides' Critique #4, which is printed in relation to Maimonides positive commandment #187 in traditional printed editions.
[6] Or "possess" (Hebrew: *lareshet*).

leave it in the hands of any other nations or to allow it to become desolate. This is what [God] said to them (Num.33:53): *You shall take possession of the land and settle it, for I have assigned the land to you to possess. You shall apportion the land among yourselves.* The message of this command is repeated in other places, as in (Deut. 1:8), *Go and possess the land that the Lord has sworn to your fathers.* [God] detailed for them its borders and boundaries in this command, as He said (Deut. 1:7), *Start out and make your way to the hill country of the Amorites and to all their neighbors in the Aravah, the hill country, the Shefelah, the Negev, the seacoast,* etc., so that they do not leave any part of it. The proof that it is a command is His words in reference to the scouts (Deut. 1:21), *Go up, take possession, as the Lord, the God of your fathers, promised you! Fear not and be not dismayed!* He said, furthermore (Deut. 9:23), *And when the Lord sent you out from Kadesh-barnea, saying, "Go up and take possession of the land that I am giving you!"* When they did not obey by going up, it is written (ibid), *you flouted the command of the Lord your God; you did not put your trust in Him and did not obey Him.* This instruction is a command—not [merely] a statement of destiny or a promise. This is what the sages call Commanded War. This is what they said in Sota (44b): "Rav Yehudah said, 'the wars of conquest of Joshua everyone agrees is required, while the wars of the House of David for [territorial] expansion everyone agrees is discretionary.' "[7] And in the language of the [Midrash] Sifrei (17:14), *"You will dispossess it and settle it* (Deut. 26:1). By virtue of you dispossessing it, you shall settle it!"[8]

Do not be confused and say that this commandment [only] obtains regarding war against the seven [Canaanite] nations whose destruction is commanded, as it is said (Deut. 20:17), *Utterly destroy them.* This is not the case, for we are commanded to kill these nations when they war against us; but if they desire to surrender we allow this and leave them [alive] according to the known conditions; but we do not leave the Land in their hands or in the hands of any other from among the nations in any generation. If these nations fled from us and went their way, as in the [rabbis'] saying, "The Girgashites left and went their way, and the Holy One gave them a good land in Africa like their [own] land,"[9] we are commanded to come to the land and conquer the nations in order to return our tribes [from them]. After we have destroyed the aforementioned nations, if our tribes desire then to leave the Land and conquer the Land of Shin`ar or the Land of Ashur or

---

[7] Note how this differs from our Sotah 44b text examined above in chapter five, which has Rava in place of Rav Yehuda.

[8] Midrash Sifrei Devarim, *shoftim* 13, but with slightly different wording.

[9] Midrash Deuteronomy Rabbah, *shoftim* 5:5.

the like, they are not permitted because we are commanded to conquer [the Land of Israel] and to settle it. On the basis of the [rabbis'] statement that the war of Joshua to conquer [is commanded, you must] understand that the commandment is through conquest. This is what they said in the *Sifrei*[10] [in relation to Joshua 1:3], *Every spot on which your foot treads I give to you, as I promised*: "[God] was saying to them: All the places you conquer other than these are yours, or it is your privilege to conquer outside the Land [only] after you have conquered the Land of Israel." Thus it teaches (Deut. 11:23), *You will dispossess nations greater and more numerous than you*. And only afterwards [does it say], *Every spot on which your foot treads*.

[The rabbis in the Midrash just cited] said: If you ask why David conquered Aram Naharaim and Aram Zobah where the commandments [of the Torah regarding the Land of Israel] do not apply, they answer, David did something that was not in accordance with the Torah. The Torah said: After having conquered the Land of Israel you are free to conquer outside the Land. But he did not do thus.

We are commanded to engage in the conquest in every generation. Now I say that the sages emphasized living in the Land of Israel to the point of hyperbole, even to the point of saying that anyone who leaves [the Land of Israel] and lives outside the Land is as if he has engaged in idolatry, as it is said (1 Sam. 26:19), *They have driven me out today from sharing in the Lord's Possession* [as if] *I am told, "Go worship other gods."*[11] They made many other such hyperbolic statements regarding this positive commandment that we are commanded to possess the Land and settle it. It is therefore an eternal positive command, obligating every single individual even during the time of Exile as is known from the Talmud in many places. In the language of the Sifrei,[12] "It once occurred that Rabbi Yehudah ben Batira, Rabbi Matya ben Harshuni, Hananya ben Achai, Rabbi Yehoshua, and Rabbi Natan had left the Land [of Israel]; [when] they came to Puteoli[13] they remembered the Land of Israel, lowered their eyes, cried rivers of tears, tore their clothes [in mourning], and recited this verse (Deut. 11:31–32),[14] *When you take possession of it and settle in it, take care to observe all the commandments...*" They concluded: Settling [in] the Land of Israel

---

[10] Midrash Sifrei Devarim, `eqev 16. Here also the wording is somewhat different.

[11] Midrash *Torat Kohanim behar* 5:4, TB *Ketubot* 110b.

[12] Midrash Sifrei Devarim, *re'eh* 28. See also Midrash Yalkut Shim`oni, *re'eh* 485.

[13] A well-known port in Italy at the time (Jastrow 1179, s.v. *paltum*, as in *Sifrei*).

[14] The wording in Nahmanides is slightly different from that of the Deuteronomy text and of *Sifrei Devarim*; it follows the *Yalkut* text more closely.

(*yeshivat eretz yisra'el*)[15] is equal to all of the commandments in the Torah![16] [*Hassagot*, positive 4]

Nahmanides' position is clear. God's command to destroy the seven Canaanite nations is not a universal declaration against idolatry as Maimonides suggests, but rather a specific directive to take possession of the Land of Israel. God commanded the People of Israel to both conquer and settle the Land of Israel. "This," as he notes, "is a command and not [merely] a statement of destiny or a promise." Conquest and settlement require dispossession of the prior inhabitants by expulsion or destruction. He is careful to emphasize the term "dispossession" *(horish)* found in Numbers 33:53 (and elsewhere) with which he begins his discussion, because Num. 33 does not specify particular peoples as do those passages that require the destruction of the Canaanite nations. This allows him to consider the commandment directed expressly and eternally toward the Land of Israel, as it refers to any and all peoples rather than only the Canaanite nations that once occupied the Land but that have since disappeared. "Do not be confused and say that this commandment [only] obtains regarding war against the seven [Canaanite] nations whose destruction is commanded."

However (and in this he agrees with Maimonides), the nations in the Land need not be destroyed if they surrender and accept certain conditions. In any case, control of the Land of Israel must remain in the hands of the People of Israel. The command to conquer and possess the Land of Israel is not bound by time but is in force forever. "We are commanded to engage in the conquest in every generation... It is therefore an eternal positive command, obligating every single individual even during the time of Exile."[17] That eternal command is realized through conquest.

At the very end of his comment Nahmanides offers an interesting alternative to the eternal divine command for *military* conquest, and his articulation of an interpretation that he found in the Midrash called Sifrei has made a deep impact on religious Zionists more than six hundred years after

---

[15] "Settling" [in] the Land of Israel may be rendered *yeshivat* or *yishuv*. The former is the wording of the Sifrei, which is the source for the commandment (Israel Schepansky, *Eretz-Israel in the Responsa Literature* (3 Vols. Hebrew) (Jerusalem: Mosad Harav Kook, 1978), Vol. 3, 1). Schepansky indicates in his collection of responsa that some medieval thinkers understood the two forms of the idiom to convey different meanings, but the subtleties are not important here.

[16] Cf. *Tosefta Avodah Zarah* 5:2 (Zuckermandel edition, 4:3),: "A man should live in the Land of Israel even in a city whose inhabitants are mostly idolaters [Zuckermandel: "non-Jews" *goyim*] and not outside of the Land even in a city that is all Israel. [This] teaches that settling in the Land of Israel is equal to all of the commandments in the Torah."

[17] See also, Nahmanides' commentary on Numbers 33:53 s.v. *vehorashtem*, Deut. 20:10 s.v. *ki tiqrav el `ir*, etc.

his death: "Settling [in] the Land of Israel is equal to all of the command-ments in the Torah." Consequently, it is not necessarily through military triumph that one fulfills one's divine obligation of conquest, but alterna-tively by settling it—establishing Jewish communities and developing the Land. Nonmilitary forms of conquest also satisfy the requirement.

To Nahmanides, then, conquest of the Land of Israel is an eternal, unde-niable, and irrevocable commandment. But Jewish military conquest was inconceivable in his world of the thirteenth century, not only impracti-cal, but impossible, even suicidal. Nahmanides therefore provides a new understanding based on an interpretation of the sages in the Midrash: the requirement of conquest can be fulfilled through settlement. This reduces the scope and the danger of the act, it remains within the parameters of the Talmudic sages to discourage dangerous political movements, and it preserves the eternal commandment and makes it practical.

It is often impossible to determine whether ideology is the prime mover behind behavior or whether behavior is justified after the fact by ideology, but one cannot help but note the parallels and distinctions between the lives and views of the two great medieval masters examined here. Maimonides, on the one hand, was exiled with his family from his native Spain and moved to the Land of Israel in his young adult years, but soon left with his family for Fostat, the capital of the Fatimid Empire in Egypt. Fostat was the thriving urban center of a powerful land, and Maimonides ended his years as the personal physician to the ruler of Egypt and the respected prince of Egyptian Jewry, a powerful and respected Diaspora Jew.

Nahmanides, on the other hand, was forced from his native Spain dur-ing the twilight of his life. Bitter and unhappy, he made his way to the Land of Israel and settled in Jerusalem; but he soon left and became the leader of the small Jewish community of Acre, where he died a few years later. Exiled from exile, the unequaled leader of Catalonian Jewry was forced out of Diaspora life and found an uneasy shelter in an undeveloped Land of Israel. Maimonides was also exiled from exile, but his Diaspora life became stable after initial difficulties, even if not always good. Maimonides did not list the conquest or settlement of the Land of Israel in his accounting of the 248 positive commandments, while Nahmanides considered the conquest and settlement of the Land of Israel an obvious and eternally valid decree.

In a famous New Year's sermon that he gave in Acre in the year before his death,[18] Nahmanides reveals some of his feelings about his final move

---

[18] Chayim Dov Chavel, ed., *The Writings of our Rabbi Moses ben Nachman* (Hebrew, 2 vols. Jerusalem: Mosad Harav Kook, 1964), 2: 214–252.

to the Land of Israel at the end of his days. While citing the passage in Midrash Sifrei Devarim (*re'eh* 28) that he had already quoted in his critique on Maimonides' *Book of Commandments*, he repeats the sages' observation that "Settling in the Land of Israel is equal to all of the commandments in the Torah." He adds, furthermore, that a similar statement may be found also in the Tosefta, tractate *Avodah Zarah* (5:3). He then concludes his sermon.[19]

And what has taken me out of my [native] land and has moved me from my place? *I have abandoned my home, I have deserted My inheritance* (Jeremiah 12:7). I have become like a raven to my sons, cruel to my daughters. Because of my wish to uproot, I have put [them] in the lap of their mother....The designated Torah portion states (Lev. 18:3), *[do not copy the practices of] the land of Egypt*,[20] but [Egypt] did not vomit out its inhabitants, nor did the rest of the lands of the [foreign] nations [vomit out] their inhabitants. Rather, all [these data demonstrate] the unique quality of the Land of Israel and its sanctity.[21] The splendor of the world lies in the Land of Israel, the splendor of the Land of Israel in Jerusalem, the splendor of Jerusalem in the Temple, the splendor of the Temple in the Holy of Holies, the splendor of the Holy of Holies in the place of the cherubim wherein resides the Divine Glory....[22]

The difference between Maimonides and Nahmanides on the issue of whether or not conquest of the Land of Israel is an eternal divine command would become a classic dispute or Torah debate (Hebrew: *machloqet*) to be cited, discussed, and argued in the curriculum of study among traditional Jewry to this day. Nahmanides became the hero of the religious Orthodox Zionist school, which cites his comments regularly in order to support their view of the critical importance of settling and controlling the Land of Israel in the contemporary period. At the same time, this school has spilled seas of ink in attempting to understand why Maimonides, considered the greatest Jewish mind of the Middle Ages, did not also stress the importance of conquering and setting the Land of Israel (Table 8.1).

---

[19] Ibid, 251–252.

[20] The verse continues, *nor shall you follow their laws. My rules alone shall you observe and faithfully follow My laws.* He is emphasizing the importance of observing the religious commandments of Judaism and making repentance for any infringements before the upcoming Day of Atonement.

[21] Which would spit out its inhabitants if they would not obey God's commandments (Lev. 18:28, 20:22).

[22] Cf. Mishnah *kelim* 1:6.

TABLE 8.1

|  | DISCRETIONARY רשות | COMMANDED מצוה | OBLIGATORY חובה |
|---|---|---|---|
| Mishnah |  |  |  |
| Rabbis | Deferments | No deferments |  |
| Yehudah |  | Deferments | No deferments |
| P. Talmud |  |  |  |
| Hisda |  |  |  |
| Rabbis |  | David's wars | Joshua's wars |
| Yehudah | Israel initiates |  | Defensive wars |
| B. Talmud |  |  |  |
| Rava |  |  |  |
| All agree | David's wars of expansion |  | Joshua's wars of conquest |
| Yehudah |  | Preemptive strike |  |
| Rabbis | Preemptive strike |  |  |
| Maimonides (Mishneh Torah) | Other nations, to extend borders for prestige | 7 (Canaanite) nations, Amalek, defence |  |
| Nahmanides |  | Settling and living in the Land of Israel |  |

After Nahmanides and until the modern period there is hardly anything added to the terse Talmudic discussion and puzzling medieval dispute between Maimonides and Nahmanides. References occasionally appear among late medieval/early modern Jewish commentators and scholars, and these have inevitably been picked up by modern thinkers who treat aspects of war in the modern Israeli context. But only a commentary called the *Megillat Esther* enters the narrow canon of medieval discussion.

## Megillat Esther

Literally facing Nahmanides' critique of Maimonides' *Book of Commandments* in the standard traditional edition of this work[23] is a commentary known as the *Megillat Esther* or "Scroll of Esther,"[24] by Rabbi Yitzhaq Leon ben Eliezer, a Jew of Spanish heritage who lived in Ancona,

---

[23] *Mitzvot `aseh leda`at haramban*, 42a, right column.
[24] First printed in Venice in 1592.

Italy during the early to mid-sixteenth century.[25] This work defends Maimonides' position against Nahmanides, based primarily on the Three Vows (see chapter 5).

It is my opinion that the Rabbi [Maimonides] considered the commandment of dispossessing the Land and settling it to be in force only during the days of Moses and Joshua, David, and the period during which we were not exiled from our Land. However, after we were exiled from our Land, the commandment is no longer valid throughout the generations until the coming of the messiah. On the contrary, we are commanded, according to what the [sages] said at the end of Tractate Ketubot [110a], not to rebel against the nations in order to go and conquer the Land by force. They proved this with the verse (Song 2:7): *I make you swear, o daughters of Jerusalem...*, which they interpreted to mean that Israel is not to go up [to the Land] in a wall.[26] When Nahmanides claims the sages teach that the conquest of the Land is a Commanded War, this refers to when we will no longer be enslaved to the nations [i.e., in the future]. And when he also said that the sages praised living in the Land of Israel to the point of hyperbole, this was during the period that the Temple was still standing [i.e., in the past]. But now it is not a commandment. This is according to what the [sages] said there [in Ketubot 110a], that anyone who ascends from Babylonia to the Land of Israel transgresses a positive commandment, as it is said (Jer.27:22), *They shall be brought to Babylon and there they shall remain.* If it were a commandment for all ages to live in the Land of Israel, how could a prophet[27] come after Moses and contradict his words,[28] for a prophet is not at all free to innovate, let alone to contradict! Regarding the citation [Nahmanides] brings from Midrash Sifrei in which the [sages] cried and recited the verse (in Sifrei 17:14), "You will dispossess it and settle it" (Deut. 26:1), it appears to me that they wept because it was impossible for them to carry out this verse ['s instructions] because the Temple had been destroyed. The proof of this is that [those sages] tore their clothes because they were mourning the Destruction, for if the commandment were still in force after the Destruction, why did they weep and tear their clothes, for they would have

---

[25] On the uncertainty over his exact identity, see Yitzhak Englard, "The Halakhic Problem of Giving Back Territories from the Land of Israel: Law and Ideology" (Hebrew) *HaPeraklit* 41 (1993): 18, note 24.

[26] See chapter 5, above.

[27] He is referring to Jeremiah in the verse just cited.

[28] That is, if God's command to conquer given through Moses were eternal, then Jeremiah's words would contradict the divine message. God's command through Moses must have therefore been time-bound and not eternal.

been able to carry it out even then? It is therefore said that this commandment is clearly not in force after the Destruction of the Temple, may it be quickly rebuilt, amen![29]

The *Megillat Esther* articulates Maimonides' position explicitly, against Nahmanides, that the commandment to conquer and settle the Land of Israel is not operative in the present time, meaning the time of Exile after the destruction of the Jerusalem Temple. It was indeed in effect in the past when the Temple was still standing, and it will be in force again in a future time with the arrival of the messiah. Because the commandment to conquer the land was valid for a limited time rather than binding throughout the generations, Maimonides did not include it in his enumeration of the commandments.[30]

*Megillat Esther* was one of the first to take up the challenge of treating the dispute between Maimonides and Nahmanides. Its author is virtually unknown aside from this work, which itself is not of great interest beyond this particular paragraph. It may have been included in the standard printed editions of Maimonides' *Book of Commandments* because it countered Nahmanides and articulated concisely the argument between them. In any case, because it was printed opposite Nahmanides in the standard editions, its response to and defense of Maimonides became part of what would become the classic dispute over the validity of Commanded War after the destruction of the Second Temple. Maimonides and Nahmanides, along with *Megillat Esther*, were studied and argued in the academies and yeshivas in many parts of the Jewish world. New comments were added occasionally, although they did not command much attention until the beginning of the Zionist movement in the late nineteenth century (see chapter 9).

In addition to clarifying the positions of Maimonides and Nahmanides, *Megillat Esther* brought the Three Vows into direct relation to the issue of Commanded War. As noted in chapter five, the construct of the Three Vows had emerged much earlier as a preventive to militant Jewish political activism. In the Middle Ages it became a rebuttal to the claim that the divine command for conquest remains in force, even through settlement rather than military conquest of the land. Aviezer Ravitzky shows that the Three Vows did not find its way into discussions over the suitability

---

[29] Rabbi Yitzhaq ben Eliezer de Leon, The *Megillat Esther*, commandment 4.
[30] Recall that Maimonides read the command regarding the destruction of the Canaanite nations as an eternal command to promote monotheism rather than conquer the Land of Israel. It was thus eternal, but it was not a command for conquest.

or correctness of ascension to the Land of Israel until after Nahmanides' ruling to obligate relocating and settling in the Land for all generations. Use of the Three Vows became a counterpoint to the powerful position of Nahmanides. Those who opposed the Nahmanidean position considered the Land of Israel a messianic category beyond the reach of human yearning, while those who favored immigration attempted to dissociate the Land from any messianic context.[31] Justification for immigration tended to be based, rather, on the piety argument. Because piety required carrying out as many of God's commandments as possible, and because many of the biblical commandments were possible only within the borders of the Land of Israel, immigration could be justified for individuals and their families for the purpose of fulfilling the commandments.

The foundational source for all future discussion about Commanded War would henceforth be the famous dispute between Maimonides and Nahmanides, along with the accompanying clarification and support for the former by *Megillat Esther*. Maimonides did not consider conquest of the Land to be one of the core commandments of the Torah. Nahmanides claimed that he should have. *Megillat Esther* brought the Three Vows into the discussion in support of Maimonides. As Ravitzky has demonstrated, the Three Vows became both symbolic of and a tool for restraining mass migration to the Land of Israel during the medieval period. Until the coming of modernity and the emergence of modern national movements, Jewish life in Diaspora simply made the notion of conquest, whether militarily or in the form of mass settlement, bizarre and unimaginable, reserved only for the rare individual.

Students of the tradition in subsequent generations puzzled occasionally over Maimonides' omission of the command for conquest in his enumeration of the commandments, despite the repeated divine command in the Torah to conquer the Land of Israel. But interest in the subject was only theoretical. Any human conquest of the Land of Israel was both impossible and forbidden, according to the Three Vows: *do not wake or rouse love until it is wished*. Despite the Jewish Expulsion from Spain in 1492, the publication of Judaism's most authoritative work of Jewish Law (called the *Shulchan Arukh*) in the following century, and a few millenarian movements (including the most profound messianic movement led by Sabbatai Zevi in the seventeenth century), nothing significant was added to the discussion.

This would change only with the emergence of nationalism and national movements in modern Europe. For those modern Jews who still

[31] Ravitzky, Messianism..., 220–221.

believed that Commanded War did not apply in what seemed to be the endless present between the destruction of the Temple and the coming of the messiah, Maimonides was read according to the plain meaning of his writings. To those who could not agree with this position, a number of theories were presented to try to explain such an odd omission by "the great eagle," one of the many sobriquets applied to the greatest medieval Jewish thinker.[32]

---

[32] These will be examined in some detail in the following chapter. For an overview, see J. David Bleich, *Contemporary Halakhic Problems* vol. II (New York: Ktav, 1983), pp. 196–198, notes 7–9.

# PART III | The Emergence of Jewish Modernity

*Holy War on Hold*

# CHAPTER 9 | The Crisis of Modernity and Jewish Responses

*We were alone, as was Joseph the dreamer, alone among his brothers who mocked him.*

RABBI JOSEPH SOLOVEITCHIK

Scattered across five continents, Jews emerged into modernity at varying times and speeds in different places. Our story unfolds from this point in Europe where the great changes occurred that would produce a period of history defined as modern. Europe never really achieved true political unity despite attempts from the early Middle Ages to the present, because it always lacked a sufficient uniformity of culture or worldview. The forces that would produce what we today call "modernity" emerged first in the Western and Central parts of Europe and then entered Eastern Europe only subsequently. It should not be surprising, therefore, to observe that the Jews of Western Europe modernized before most of those in the eastern parts of the continent.

Modernity represented a crisis for Jewish continuity, since it effectively challenged the authority of the tradition that had served as the glue holding most of the Jewish people together for nearly two millennia. The history of Jewish emancipation and the Jewish responses to modernity are well known and need not be rehearsed here aside from the way it affected Jewish thinking on war.[1]

---

[1] A large literature exists on the Jewish emergence into modernity; see Lois C. Dubin, "Enlightenment and Emancipation," in Nicholas de Lange and Miri Freud-Kandel (eds.), *Modern Judaism: An Oxford Guide* (Oxford: Oxford University Press, 2005), 29–41, Paul Mendes-Flohr and Jehuda Reinharz (eds.), *The Jew in the Modern World*, second Ed. (Oxford, 1995); David Sorkin, *The Berlin Haskalah and German Religious Thought: Orphans of Knowledge* (Portland, OR: Valentine Mitchel, 2000); idem, *Moses Mendelssohn and the*

Early modern Jewish thinkers took little interest in either biblical or rabbinic teachings on war. Modernizing Jews were far more interested in integrating into the existing national structures than in recreating their own. The early religious reformers were intent on emphasizing aspects of Judaism that found the closest cultural parallels with their new non-Jewish neighbors. As opportunities for integrating into the new national cultures increased, many began to jettison what was identified as cultural or national aspects of traditional Jewish identity and practice, choosing to focus instead on what they considered the spiritual or theological aspects that found parallels among their Christian compatriots.[2] The most radical result was a vision of Jewish identity that was purely spiritual. This trend toward religious reform was a Western European phenomenon because that was where Jews were first emancipated from their degraded status and welcomed into the common weal. The much larger Jewish population in Eastern Europe did not share that experience. By the time modernizing movements became popular in Eastern Europe, the nature of nationalism had changed and the Jews felt less welcome to participate in the growing national movements there. Jewish emancipation in the east was never as significant nor complete.

Throughout Europe the modern nation-state assumed responsibility for the civic, political, and military duties that had previously been under the purview of the medieval Church or nobility. Individual Jews in the liberal west were largely willing, whether or not they sympathized with Jewish religious reform, to grant the nation-state most of the civic and political responsibilities that were previously regulated by Jewish law and tradition. The communal religious trends that became Reform and Conservative Judaism also deferred such responsibility to the state. So did the modernist neo-Orthodox Jews associated with Rabbi Samson Raphael Hirsch (d. 1888), who also distinguished between civic issues and religion.[3]

Not all emancipated Jews identified with the new religious movements of Judaism. Many assimilated as best they could out of Jewish identity

---

*Religious Enlightenment* (London: Peter Halban, 2004); Michael Stanislawski, *Zionism and the Fin de Siècle: Cosmopolitanism and Nationalism from Nordau to Jabotinsky* (Berkeley and Los Angeles: University of California, 2001); Shmuel Feiner, *New Perspectives on the Haskalah* (Oxford: Littman Library, 2004).

[2] David Ellenson, *After Emancipation: Jewish Religious Responses to Modernity* (Cincinnati: Hebrew Union College Press, 2004); Michael Meyer, *Response to Modernity a History of The Reform Movement in Judaism* (New York: Oxford, 1988); Gunther Plaut, *The Rise of Reform Judaism: A Sourcebook of its European Origins* (New York: Wold Union for Progressive Judaism, 1963); Joseph Blau, *Reform Judaism: A Historical Perspective* (New York: Ktav, 1973).

[3] Miri Freud-Kandel, "Modernist Movements," in Nicholas de Lange and Miri Freud-Kandel (eds.), *Modern Judaism*, 81–92. Jacob Katz, *Out of the Ghetto: The Social Background of Jewish Emancipation 1770–1870* (New York: Schocken, 1973).

entirely and into European national or international culture and politics. Others associated with Jewish social and political movements identifying with Jewish history and culture but not with religion. These movements—which included the secularist *Haskalah* (Enlightenment)[4] that spawned the Jewish labor and socialist movements, communists, and Jewish nationalists, including Zionists—were more interested in new ideas in social philosophy and economics than in Jewish religious teachings. Some certainly resonated with biblical images of heroism, including heroism in war, but those who would find interest in religious views on matters such as war were limited almost entirely to the traditionalists, those Jews who attempted to resist the temptations of modernity by retrenching into what would become a range of positions that are now generally lumped together as Jewish Orthodoxy.

Jewish Orthodoxy, by definition, attempted to remain unmoved, to stay true to the singular demands of what they considered an authentic and unchanging tradition. They claimed that, unlike the modernizing groups mentioned above, they would never distort or manipulate the ancient tradition in order to come to terms with the powerful forces of modernity. Indeed, with no stimuli imposed from outside, the tradition may have had little reason to adapt or evolve. But Europe was in the throes of rapid and often radical change. The historical context within which all European forms of Jewish identity existed demanded social, political, and religious responses from all of its inhabitants. No Jews, including even those with the most earnest intentions, could resist. All responded to the need to come to grips with the steamroller of modernity, and none, including those who would be known as Orthodox and even Ultra-Orthodox, could avoid adjustment and change.[5]

We observed in Part 1 that political, cultural and military stimuli forced Jewish tradition to adapt radically to the destruction of Jewish national

---

[4] Usually translated as "enlightenment," *Haskalah* refers to a movement of European Jews to actively pursue modernization. The *Haskalah* was more of a phenomenon than a movement, since its character and goals varied between the urban centers and the different periods of its existence. At the extremes, radical *maskilim* encouraged full European assimilation while others were "secret *maskilim*" who were deeply attracted to Jewish enlightenment ideas but remained traditionally observant Jews; most *maskilim* found themselves between these edges of the spectrum, although the *Haskalah* was essentially antireligious in its stress on modernization (Azriel Shochat, Judith Baskin, and Yehudah Slutzky, "Haskalah" in EJ2, 8:434–444; Israel Bartal, "Responses to Modernity: Haskalah, Orthodoxy, and Nationalism in Eastern Europe," in Shmuel Almog, Jehuda Reinharz, and Anita Shapira [eds.], *Zionism and Religion* [Hanover, NH: Brandeis University Press, 1998], 13–24; Azriel Shochat, 444).

[5] Eliezer Don-Yehiya, "Traditionalist Strands," in de Lange and Freud-Kandel (eds.), *Modern Judaism*, 93–105, Gerald Cromer, "Withdrawal and Conquest: Two Aspects of Haredi Response to Modernity," in Laurence Silberstein (ed.), *Jewish Fundamentalism in Comparative Perspective* (New York: New York University Press, 1993), 164–165.

institutions associated with the Jerusalem Temple and self-government. The once innovative positions of the Talmud in the face of this crisis had become well established by the time of the emergence of modernity; they were considered as old and established as those of the Bible itself. The positions of Maimonides and Nahmanides concerning the commandments to conquer and settle the Land of Israel were well within the acceptable parameters of post-Biblical Jewish thinking. Maimonides could universalize. Nahmanides could particularize. Their dispute was academic, for premodern Jews could hardly conceive of a situation in real and not imagined time, when the People of Israel would have the opportunity to go up to the Land of Israel "in a wall." It was simply impossible to imagine short of the arrival of the messiah.

This would all change with the emergence of modernity and its most powerful political product of nationalism, including Jewish nationalism. The only Jewish expression of nationalism to endure would be Zionism. Zionism had emerged as one of a number of Jewish responses to the challenges brought by modernity in the context of Eastern Europe: the lack of Jewish emancipation there, the failure of Western liberal nationalism to penetrate effectively, the rise of conservative expressions of romantic nationalism that rejected Jewish participation, the continued material hopelessness of Eastern European Jewish life in the Pale of Settlement, violent pogroms directed periodically against Jews in much of the area, and rejection of Jews from full involvement in internationalist movements.[6]

Although the earliest Zionist thinkers were religiously observant Jews, the Zionist movement soon became overwhelmingly secular, led and galvanized by activists of the Jewish "Enlightenment" (*Haskalah*) known as *maskilim*. These were modernizing Jews who felt themselves emancipated intellectually but found that they remained in universal social and political bondage to the Gentiles. Many also felt that they remained in bondage to the traditional Jewish establishment that was retrenching against the forces of modernity. They organized secularizing and often anti-religious groups to seek out a means of release from the misery of Eastern European Jewish life. Zionists were, as they are today, anything but monolithic. While Zionism represented a shared trajectory of Jewish nationalism, the variety of expression within the movement was surprisingly diverse, and its members tended to be extremely ideological. It has been suggested

[6] Bartal, "Responses to Modernity: Haskalah, Orthodoxy, and Nationalism in Eastern Europe," in *Zionism and Religion* (Hanover, NH: Brandeis University Press, 1998), 13–24; Walter Laquer, *A History of Zionism* (New York: Schocken, 1976), 3–135, Howard M. Sachar, *A History of Israel*, third edition revised and updated (New York: Knopf, 2007), 3–17.

that Herzl's greatest achievement may have been constructing a Zionist Congress that would fit them all under one tent.[7] The birth of Zionism was neither quick nor easy. It was a difficult labor and the newborn offspring of mother Judaism and father nationalism was a weak baby indeed, weak in both numbers and influence in relation to the other modernizing Jewish options of the late nineteenth century.

## The Emergence of Zionism: A Movement to Save Jews or a Movement to Redefine Jewishness?

We must keep in mind that many of the core tenets of Zionism were not new. The notion of immigrating to the Land of Israel to establish Jewish settlements there was by no means novel. The Bible, the Talmud, and traditional Jewish liturgy and ritual extol the sacred Land and its fruits, and express longing for the day when Jewish exiles throughout the dispersion will return to their land.[8] And Jewish thinkers of all periods and places did not hesitate to praise the merits of Jerusalem and the Land of Israel, citing the extraordinary nature of the place: its exceptional produce, water, air—a land flowing with milk and honey. This exaltation of the Land of Israel was mostly custom, however, and did not suggest that the writers of these words believed the Jews should establish an independent Jewish polity there.[9]

The great Jacob Emden, for example, known as the *Yabetz* (d. 1776), was one of the outstanding scholars of his generation in the German lands of Ashkenaz. A legal authority and powerful anti-Sabbatean polemicist who condemned active messianism, he yet chastises the Jews for living in the polluted lands of exile (*aratzot teme'ot*) while leaving the Land of Israel

---

[7] Jehuda Reinharz, "Zionism and Orthodoxy: A Marriage of Convenience," in *Zionism and Religion*, 124 (for the diversity of Zionist expressions, see idem, 116–139).

[8] Dov Schwartz, *The Land of Israel in Religious Zionist Thought* (Hebrew) (Tel Aviv: Am Oved, 1997), 219 and notes there.

[9] On Jewish, Christian and Muslim travelers and pilgrims and their perceptions, see J. D. Eisenstein (Ed.), *Otzar Massa'ot* (New York: Eisenstein, 1926); Michael Ish-Shalom, *Christian Travels to the Land of Israel* (Hebrew, Tel Aviv: Am Oved, 1979), Thomas Wright, *Early Travels in Palestine* (New York: Ktav, 1968), Robert Wilken, *The Land Called Holy: Palestine in Christian History and Thought* (New Haven: Yale, 1992), Menahem Mor, and Brian Le Beau (eds.) *Pilgrims and Travelers to the Holy Land* (Omaha: Creighton University Press, 1996); Nathan Schur, *Twenty Centuries of Christian Pilgrimage to the Holy Land* (Tel Aviv: Dvir, 1992). See also, Michael Signer, "The Land of Israel in Medieval Jewish Exegetical and Polemical Literature," in Hoffman (ed.), *The Land of Israel*, 220–233; Isaac Hasson (ed.), *Fada'il al-Bayt al-Muqaddas* (of Abu Bakr Muhammad b. Ahmad al-Wasiti), Jerusalem: Magnes, 1979; Mujir al-Din al-'Ulaymi al-Hanbali, *Al-Uns al-Jalil bitarikh al-Quds wal-Khalil* 2 vols. (Amman: Maktabat Dandis, 1999).

desolate. In his *Ladder of Beth El*,[10] after providing a purely historical explanation for the sorry physical state of the Land of Israel in his time, he writes, "And truly is there great astonishment over holy Israel [the people]. In every place they are stringent in the details of the commandments that they keep, they treat everything in great detail and spend lots of money and work very hard to observe them in the fullest way possible. But why are they scornful and lazy about this beloved commandment [of living in the Land of Israel], the post upon which the entire Torah hangs?"

Emden lived shortly before the stirrings that would produce Jewish nationalist movements. The true Zionist precursors began to write in the following century. Sometimes referred to as proto-Zionists or "harbingers of Zionism,"[11] traditional Jews such as Rabbis Yehuda Alkalai (d. 1878) and Tzvi Hirsch Kalischer (d. 1874) were profoundly influenced by modernity and the growth of modern European nationalism.[12] Alkalai, for example, was responding to the growth of nationalism and what he saw as its negative impact on the Jews when he wrote in language that would be familiar to readers of Nahmanides: "This commandment [of living in the Land of Israel] was emphasized by our rabbis to the extent that they considered leaving the Land of Israel akin to practicing idolatry. Moreover, they emphasized that we are commanded to inherit the Land and settle it, and that this is an eternal commandment that is in force even during the time of Exile."[13] The precursors were of course familiar with the restrictions set forth by the Three Vows, but they interpreted their meaning in a manner that allowed settlement in the Land of Israel. Alkalai, for example, insisted that the Three Vows did not require Jews to be passive about their collective future but rather allowed agricultural settlement in the Land of Israel with permission of those who ruled over it.[14] He noted a counter-position from the same Midrash collection containing the Three Vows: "Had Israel

---

[10] Excerpted from *Amudei Shamayim Sulam Beit El lehaga'on hechasid Yavetz z'l* and printed in *Hama`ayan* 7 (1967), 1–3.

[11] Jacob Katz, "On Elucidating the Conception of the Harbingers of Zionism," (Hebrew), in *Shivat Tziyon* 1 (1950), 91–105.

[12] Josef Salmon, "Tradition and Modernity in the Beginning of Religious Zionist Thought (Hebrew)," in (no ed.), *Zionist Ideology and Policy: Collected Essays*. Jerusalem: The Zalman Shazar Center, 1978 21–37; Jody Myers, *Seeking Zion: Modernity and Messianic Activism in the Writings of Tsevi Hirsch Kalischer* (Oxford: Littman Library, 2003). The exception to this model was the secular socialist Moses Hess (d. 1875); Hertzberg, *Zionist Idea*, 116–138; Laquer, *History of Zionism*, 46–54.

[13] G. Kressel (ed.), *Rabbi Yehuda Alkalai and Rabbi Tzvi Hirsch Kalischer: Selected Writings* (Hebrew) (Tel Aviv: Mitzpeh, n.d.), p. 45.

[14] Eli Holzer, "The Evolving Meaning of the Three Oaths Within Religious Zionism" (Hebrew), *Daat: Journal of Jewish Philosophy and Kabbalah*, 47 (Summer, 2001), 130.

ascended like a wall from Babylonia, the Temple would not have been destroyed a second time."[15]

Throughout the earliest stage of Zionist organizing during the period of the "Love of Zion" (*Hibbat tziyyon*) movement in the 1880s, traditional and secular Jews worked together despite their many differences and the tensions that they produced.[16] By the turn of the century, however, the leadership was shifting into the hands of secularizing Jews who were feeling alienated from Jewish tradition and anxious to find a way out of the morass of Eastern European Jewish life. Zionism would become a largely secular movement, and while its general history and growth cannot occupy us here, the dynamic between the secular majority and the small religiously observant minority is of particular importance to our chronicle of the holy war revival.[17]

The first stirrings of the movement that would become Zionism began in the 1860s and 1870s, a time when secular Jews were seeking a solution to the European Jewish predicament through integration and assimilation into their countries of residence. That response was abhorrent to traditional Jews; consequently, some began to consider a solution through settlement in the Holy Land.[18] Like all traditional Jews, however, they were confronted with the prohibition against "going up in a wall," that is, mounting an organized movement of Jews to resettle the ancient land.

Calling for the purchase of land in Palestine and the resettlement of large numbers of Jews there was also reminiscent of the forbidden and disastrous messianic actualizing movements of past centuries. Such movements in the recent past, such as those of Shabbtai Zevi in the seventeenth century and Jacob Frank in the eighteenth century, had ended in tragedy for large numbers of Jews.[19] The calamitous failures of those movements were perceived in retrospect as divine punishment for attempting to force God to bring the final and ultimate redemption of the Jewish People.

---

[15] Song of Songs Rabba 8:11 cited also by Ravitzky 1996, 240 note 58. Cf. Yoma 9b.

[16] Ehud Luz, "The Limits of Toleration: The Challenge of Cooperation between the Observant and the Nonobservant during the Hibbat Zion Period, 1882–1895," in *Zionism and Religion*, 48; idem, *Parallels Meet* (Philadelphia: Jewish Publication Society, 1988), 44–54.

[17] See Ehud Luz, "The Limits of Toleration," 66–67.

[18] Yosef Salmon, "Zionism and Anti-Zionism in Traditional Judaism in Eastern Europe," in Shmuel Almog, Jehuda Reinharz, and Anita Shapira (eds.), *Zionism and Religion* (Hanover, NH: Brandeis University Press, 1998), 25–43.

[19] On these and other Jewish "messianic movements," see Abba Hillel Silver, *A History of Messianic Speculation in Israel: From the First Through the Seventeenth Centuries* (Boston: Beacon, 1927); Aharon Zeev Aescoly, *Jewish Messianic Movements, Sources & Documents on Messianism in Jewish History: From the Bar Kokhba Revolt until Recent Times,* 2 vols. (Hebrew, Jerusalem: Bialik Inst. 1956).

Jews were therefore restrained from joining acts of "rebellion against the Gentiles" by "ascending in a wall." They were cautioned not *to wake or rouse love until it is wished.*[20] On the contrary, Jews must wait. The day for the inevitable mass return to the Land of Israel must remain God's secret until it is miraculously revealed to his people. Any independent Jewish initiative would only endanger Jews and delay the final, definitive act of divine deliverance.

Rabbis Kalischer and Alkalai sought a middle ground by claiming that, while the final redemption would be a miraculous act of God, individual Jews could contribute to a "natural" (as opposed to miraculous) redemption that was actually a precondition for the final act of divine salvation. For Kalischer, the process consists of two stages, the first being a human undertaking that would go so far as to include rebuilding the Jerusalem Temple. This human act would demonstrate to God the necessary depth of human commitment that would then trigger the final, miraculous redemption of God.[21]

According to Alkalai and Kalischer, their programs would not defy the demands of the Three Oaths. They were not attempting to "force the end," which would come to pass only when God willed. They did not call for a forcible Jewish conquest of the Land of Israel, nor did they attempt to go against the will of the nations. Yet these proto-Zionist rabbis were proposing a solution to the "Jewish Problem" that was considered a blurring of the lines between acceptable and forbidden behavior, which elicited the criticism of other, traditional Jews.[22]

From Kalischer onward, those Zionists who were religiously observant tried to show that Zionism does not contradict the edict of the Three Vows. One source that has informed virtually all argument in this regard is Nahmanides' position on "settling the Land," even though it represented a minority opinion and remains controversial to this day.[23] In typical Jewish fashion, attempts were made to reconcile seemingly conflicting positions. A proto-Zionist colleague of Kalischer named Rabbi Eliyahu Guttmacher of Graditz, for example, penned the following: "Many err by thinking that

---

[20] Song of Songs 2:7 and repeated in that book (see chapter 5).

[21] Jody Myers, *Seeking Zion,* 63–73, Luz, *Parallels Meet,* 42–44.

[22] Shmuel Almog confirms that messianism challenged secular Zionism from its earliest days (he cites a letter from Peretz Smolenskin raising the threat that messianism represented for the movement in 1881), though it seems obvious that Zionism succeeded in large part because of its ability to harness the tremendous power of messianic speculation and longing among Jews, including secular Jews ("Messianism as a Challenge to Zionism," in Tzvi Baras [ed.] *Zionism and Eschatology* [Jerusalem: Zalman Shazar Centre, 1983], 433–438).

[23] Myers, *Seeking Zion,* 202–205.

they will be sitting comfortably, every person in his own way and in his own house, and suddenly the gates of heaven will open and make miracles in heaven and on earth, and all the promises of the prophets will be fulfilled and they will be called from their dwelling places. But this is not the way it is. ... I say that what is required is settling the holy land (*yishuv eretz haqedoshah*), to begin to take the soil from its slumber under the hand of the Arabs and to observe the commandments that are possible at this time, so that it will give its fruit to the people of Israel, who will make God happy in the process, and compassion and mercy will be awakened."[24]

Jewish nationalism emerged as emancipation and assimilation through the aegis of the Eastern European secular Haskalah movement of the 1860s–1870s was failing, coupled with the devastating pogroms that followed the assassination of Tsar Alexander II in 1881. The "Love of Zion" movement came into being immediately afterward and was led mostly by prior advocates of the Haskalah, but it was not merely an attempt to solve the physical problems of the Jewish masses of Eastern Europe. It was also an endeavor to create a future for Eastern European Jewish modernists who had failed up to that point to find an existential solution to their Jewish marginality. For many "lovers of Zion," as the members of this movement were called, attempts at assimilation in the East were an utter failure.[25] The shocking reality of the pogroms stimulated many who had previously sought assimilation to seek a solution in emigration to the Land of Israel, where they believed Jews could establish self-reliant communities.

Some religious Jews interpreted this turn toward a Jewish solution among secular Jews as grasping at straws. Others, however, were moved by their brethren's abandonment of assimilation and return to Jewish life, noting how the physical act of "return" in Hebrew *(shivah)* derives from the same root as the official religious term for repentance, *teshuvah*. Some considered the secularists' interest in a movement to settle Palestine to be a form of religious repentance *(teshuvah)* and return to Judaism. Could this momentous change signal the beginnings of the messianic era, a sign of its imminent arrival? Other religious Jews considered the Love of Zion movement simply a practical means for uniting a Jewish community that was increasingly divided in response to the stresses and temptations of

---

[24] The awaked compassion and mercy referred to here is God's when he will bring the messiah. Y.L. Hacohen Maimon (Fishman) in *Hatziyyonut Hadatit Vehitpatchutah*, p.262 (רס"ב), and first printed in a collection memorializing Rabbi Abraham Isaac Kook, vol. 3 (Jerusalem: Mossad Harav Kook, תצ"ז). The pagination is according to the special printing that year by the Zionist Agency.

[25] Luz, *Parallels Meet*, 13–15, Laqueur, *History of Zionism*, 74–83.

modernity. There was a growing realization among all traditionalists that modernity was threatening to rend the fabric of Jewish life and endanger Judaism as a whole. Some therefore saw the movement to settle Zion as a means of restoring the unity of the Jewish People.[26] The rabbis who joined the "Lovers of Zion" did not consider the Three Vows as a restriction to simple agricultural settlements in the Land of Israel, but rather only a restriction to creating an independent Jewish society there.[27]

The latter assessment, practical and nonmessianic, would become the official position articulated by the religious leadership that supported resettlement in Palestine. They believed in traditional messianism, that God would determine when the time was right to bring the messiah. They were opposed to ascension to the Land of Israel "in a wall;" the work of the Zionists, therefore, must not result in a movement that would attempt to "force the hand" of God. Their public support for Zionism was based on the twin practical benefits of relieving Jewish suffering and keeping modernizing Jews Jewish. Identifying Zionism as a movement to aid Jewish suffering was of particular importance because of the danger of associating Zionism with messianism, a perception that would mean little to secularists but that could spell the end of the movement for traditionalists who had assimilated the importance of the Three Vows.

The founder of the religious Orthodox Zionist organization known as Mizrachi, Rabbi Isaac Jacob Reines, wrote in 1899, "There is nothing in this ideology that relates to the idea of messianic Redemption.... In none of the acts or aspirations of the Zionists is there the slightest allusion to future Redemption. Their only intention is to improve the conditions of life of Israel, to uplift their honor and to accustom them to a life of happiness...how then can one compare this idea with the [traditional] idea of Redemption?"[28]

---

[26] Luz, *Parallels Meet*, 46–47.

[27] Elie Holzer, "The Evolving Meaning of the Three Oaths," 132–134.

[28] Jacob Reines, *Sha`arey Orah Vesimchah* (Vilna, 1899), pp. 12–13, as cited by Ravitzky, "Religious Radicalism and Political Messianism in Israel," in Emmanuel Sivan and Menachem Friedman, *Religious Radicalism and Politics in the Middle East* (Albany, NY: State University of New York Press, 1990), p. 11. Dov Schwartz considers Reines to be more open about the divinely redemptive nature of Zionism, but I do not see this in his public discourse. Schwartz admits that Reines was conflicted, with apologetic public statements meant to appease his Orthodox religious opponents, and his own personal "theological response" (Schwartz, *Religious Zionism: History and Ideology* [Boston: Academic Studies Press, 2009], 3, 10–14. As I will show in the following chapters, Reines and others in Mizrachi did in fact believe or at least hope that the Zionist movement would trigger divine Redemption, but they could hardly make that view public. Because of the sensitivity of the issue, most would not admit it even to themselves. Only after the appearance of what they believed to be signs of impending Redemption did they dare to get in touch with their feelings about it, and when that occurred

Despite the declarations of Reines and other leaders in the religious Zionist camp, they could not keep Zionism separate from messianism. The tension between Zionism as a modern, activist national movement and the traditional requirement to await divine redemption was never resolved. In 1891, Rabbi Abraham Yakov Slutzki, one of the prominent rabbinic supporters of the Lovers of Zion, edited a collection of essays by rabbinic authorities called *Shivat tziyyon* ("Return to Zion"),[29] which supported nascent Zionism. But as Jody Myers points out, "In the first forty pages... virtually all letters are by men who espouse messianic interpretations of current events and regard the agricultural development of the [Jewish community of Palestine] as preliminary to the messianic age."[30]

It is clear in retrospect that most observant religious figures supporting Zionism considered or at least hoped that the movement in some way corresponded to the beginning of divine Redemption. The views of Kalischer and Alkalai have already been cited. Other rabbinic leaders supporting the early Zionists held similar positions. Rabbi Zevulun Leib Britt considered Zionism to be a secular movement that would pave the way for a later, associated, divinely caused redemption. Rabbi Meir Berlin (Bar-Ilan) believed the sudden change in secular Jews' interest in Zionism to be the result of God's will. Rabbi Samuel Mohilever believed from the beginning that the engagement of secular Jews in Zionism after having first abandoned Judaism was a sign of Zionism's redemptive nature. These are all "neo-messianic" views that reflect a hope, barely articulated openly, that Jewish self-realization in the Land of Israel would be redemptive and stimulate the time for the final messianic coming. Even in Rabbi Reines, who criticized the neo-messianic outlook of Kalischer and Alkalai and claimed to found Mizrachi on the need for practical activism to save Jews from pogroms and economic deprivation, one may find a messianic angle. He suggested, for example, that it could not have been their own free-thinking volition that led the secularists to Zionism, but rather a greater reason that was hidden even from them.[31]

---

they sometimes read their assessment back to earlier times (see Joseph Wanefsky, *Rabbi Isaac Jacob Reines: His Life and Thought* [New York: Philosophical Library, 1970], 138–140). As ironic as it may appear at first glance, the tendency toward neo-messianism among Zionists was much more pronounced and obvious among the secularists than the religiously observant (Israel Kolet, "Zionism and Messianism" [Hebrew], in Baras [ed.] *Zionism and Eschatology*, 419–431). On Reines, see Joseph Wanefsky, *Rabbi Jacob Reines; His Life and Thought* (New York: Philosophical Library, 1970).

[29] Warsaw, 1891–92.

[30] Myers, *Seeking Zion*, 221, note 1.

[31] Ravitzky 1996, 33, 38, and see Shimoni, *The Zionist Ideology*, 143, 149–151, Myers, *Seeking Zion*, 221 and note 2.

The very act of engaging with staunchly secular Jews in the Zionist project was another problem that Reines and the other Zionist rabbis had to face. Most traditional Jews could not believe that redemption in Palestine, whether human or divinely planned, could possibly succeed at the hands of Jewish renegades who had abandoned Jewish religious observance and commitment. Working and even associating with them suggested to many a kind of de facto sanction, which they would not condone. The traditional Jews who opposed Zionism were divided into two camps separated by geography and ideology. In the West and particularly Germany, the "neo-orthodox" followers of Samson Raphael Hirsch (d. 1888) consciously allowed themselves to be influenced by modern mores, while remaining punctilious observers of Jewish Law.[32] In the East and particularly centered around Pressburg, the "ultra-orthodox" who followed the position of Rabbi Moses Sofer (the *Hatam Sofer*, d. 1839) attempted to seal themselves off from modernity through self-seclusion and rigid observance. They differed over many issues, but both communities agreed in their condemnation of Zionism. They eventually came together to form an organization called Agudat Yisrael (the Unification of Israel) in 1912 in order to oppose the attempts of religiously observant Zionists to represent all of Jewry in the international forum.

Notwithstanding the eventual, overwhelmingly negative reaction of the traditional Jewish religious leadership to emerging Zionism, most of the earliest Zionists were, in fact, practicing traditional Jews. The leadership, however, tended to be secular, and the rank-and-file became increasingly so quite rapidly. The secularism of many, such as among the cultural Zionists who followed the lead of Ahad Ha'Am, was almost a mission.[33] Their quest included a redefinition of Jewish identity that would remove Jews from what they considered the dark obscurantism of the tradition into the light of modernity.

The secular trend became undeniable with the arrival of Theodor Herzl onto the stage of the Zionist movement in the mid-1890s. Tensions mounted between the religiously inclined and the secularists as the leadership began increasingly to consider their project an existential as well as practical solution to the "Jewish Problem." It was becoming ever more apparent that Zionism was developing into something more than a movement to rescue fellow-Jews from the physical plight of Eastern European life. A militant and

---

[32] Yaakov Zur, "German Jewish Orthodoxy's Attitude toward Zionism, in Shmuel Almog, Jehuda Reinharz, and Anita Shapira (eds.), *Zionism and Religion* (Hanover, NH: Brandeis University Press, 1998), 107–115.

[33] Hertzberg, 1966, 249–288.

energetic group began to articulate a program of Zionist activism that would radically redefine Jewish identity in modern, secular nationalist terms.

Hence a critical gap formed between the traditionalists, who hoped that Zionism would bring wayward secularists back into the fold of the tradition, and the secularists themselves, who aspired to a new Jewish identity that would bring obscurantist traditionalists to identify with a new and "normalizing" modern Jewish spirit. It was the cultural program of Zionism in particular, so closely associated with Ahad Ha'Am, that threatened the early neutrality if not support of the religious traditionalists.[34] "Culture" in the context of Cultural Zionism meant developing a new and modern expression of Jewishness through the creation of a fresh—and by definition, nonreligious—national culture. Such an enterprise posed a direct challenge to the status quo of traditional Jewish religious culture based on living out the divine commandments.

The goal to create a new kind of Jewish character through the development of a modern national culture represented a radical revolutionary change in Jewish identity. In itself a kind of neo-messianism, the new, secular Jewish identity was expected by its advocates to solve the existential problem of Jews by providing those who could no longer live contained by religious tradition with a modern, worldly yet Jewish character. This objective posed a grave challenge to the principles of traditional Judaism and threatened to slide into its own anti-Jewish (or anti-religiously Jewish) "false messianism," or so it seemed to traditional religious Jews. During the last two years of the nineteenth century the rift between the secularists and the religious Zionists began to grow to such an extent that it seemed impossible to bridge.[35]

Traditionalist reservations about Zionism grew exponentially after the leadership of the movement was secured by secular Jews who denigrated the commandments of traditional Judaism. While all traditionalists objected to the secularization of the movement, some continued to support its goals of Jewish unity and improving the miserable situation of Eastern European Jewry through settlement.

By the turn of the century, some key Orthodox leaders opposed to the Zionists collected the views of prominent contemporary anti-Zionist rabbis throughout Eastern Europe and published them in a devastating and highly effective critique of Zionism under the title, *Light for the Righteous*.[36]

---

[34] Shlomo Avineri, *The Making of Modern Zionism* (New York: Basic, 1981), 112–124, Hertzberg, *Zionist Idea*, 51–72, 247–277.

[35] David Vital, *Zionism: The Formative Years* (Oxford: Clarendon Press, 1982), 41–42, 189–229.

[36] *Or Layesharim*, edited by S.Z. Landa & J. Rabinowitz, Warsaw, 1900; Salmon, "Zionism and Anti-Zionism," 32.

The chief objection to Zionism presented in this work was its dangerous secularizing force—considered even more dangerous than its predecessor, the Haskalah. Only one contribution suggested that the essential goal of Zionism, settling the Land of Israel through natural (that is, secular) means, conflicted with traditional messianic concepts. By the early years of the twentieth century, however, when the powerful culturalist factions claimed that they held the key to the future of the Jewish people, religious traditionalists began not only to condemn the movement but also its values, including the centrality of Jewish nationalism, the use of the Hebrew language, and even its emphasis on the "commandment" to settle the Land of Israel.[37]

It was only at this point that Orthodox anti-Zionists began to refer to the movement consistently as a form of false messianism. Zionism, they pointed out, was a movement that intended to redeem the Jewish people by secular means rather than patiently observing the Torah commandments and waiting for the supernatural redemption that would come by the hand of God. To bring messiah the Jewish people must return en masse to the Torah. Moving to the Land of Israel with the Zionists would accomplish the opposite because it would lead to apostasy among Jews who would throw off the yoke of the commandments while attempting their own false, secular redemption. The result would be a major disaster because of the arrogant attempt to "force the hand of God."

This is evident from a second collection of anti-Zionist essays published two years after *Light for the Righteous*. The critical theme of this second collection, entitled *Position of the Rabbis*,[38] changed from a critique of the secularism of Zionism to its messianic nature. And its contributors were mostly from Hasidic thinkers, in contrast to the non-Hasidic or anti-Hasidic contributors to *Light for the Righteous*. It naturally followed the Hasidic tendency to stress theological issues that transcend the formal sphere of Jewish law. The messianic argument against Zionism became central. Because of the increased concern for what was considered the messianic nature of Zionism, this period also marked the beginning of the consistent use of the Three Vows by Orthodox anti-Zionists in order to discredit Zionism as an attempt to force God's hand. Previous to the emergence of Zionism, there was little need to cite the Three Vows. It would become a major argument against Zionism from that time onward.

---

[37] Luz, *Parallels Meet*, 211–212.

[38] *Da`at Harabbanim,* Warsaw, 1902.

# Zionism *and* Judaism: The Mizrachi Movement

Despite the overwhelming rejection of Zionism among Orthodox Jews by the turn of the century, a small minority continued to support it. But they were in a quandary over how to justify their support in the face of growing criticism from the Orthodox camps. They found themselves on the defensive and exhibited a noticeably apologetic element in their arguments.[39]

The earlier, proto-Zionist precursors such as Alkalai and Kalischer were not burdened by such a situation, since in their time a generation and a half earlier, nearly all Jews in Eastern Europe were traditional and punctilious in their religious observance. The call of the precursors was to move to the Holy Land and establish colonies of Jews who were fully observant in carrying out the divine commandments. The first modern settlements were indeed quite traditional, some requiring full religious observance among all Jewish residents in their bylaws. However, in light of the demographic and political reality toward the end of the century when the colonies were becoming increasingly secular, religiously observant Zionists found it problematic to remain with the movement and still differentiate themselves from the larger and growing numbers of secularists. It was unthinkable, however, for religious Zionists to separate from the movement because of the frequently articulated commitment by all parties to Jewish unity.

Their opportunity came, or perhaps was forced upon them, in 1900–1902 when the highly secular Democratic Faction, a radical group that demanded immediate expansion of secular cultural activities within the Zionist Organization, formed its own distinct group that remained within the organization but with a separate headquarters.[40] It appeared as an organized block in the Fifth Zionist Congress of 1901, and demanded, in addition to enhanced cultural activities, a separation of Zionism from religion. This galvanized some of the more religiously observant Zionists to organize their own faction in 1902, called Mizrachi, a name coined from some of the letters of the term, *merkaz ruchani*, meaning "spiritual center."[41]

---

[39] Ravitzky 1996, 36. See also Yehuda Reinharz, "Zionism and Orthodoxy: A Marriage of Convenience," in Shmuel Almog, Jehuda Reinharz, and Anita Shapira, Anita (eds.), *Zionism and Religion*. Hanover, NH: Brandeis University Press, 1998, 116–139.

[40] Stanislawsky, 108–109.

[41] Vital 1982, 216–224. Some earlier local Zionist organizations in Eastern Europe had already gone by that name. It was in 1902 that it was appropriated for a separate block within the larger Zionist movement. For an English translation of the Mizrachi manifesto, distributed in leaflet form at the sixth Zionist Congress of 1902, see Mendes-Flohr and Reinharz, *The Jew in the Modern World*, 546.

Mizrachi intended to settle the Land of Israel according to traditional religious law and practice, and it worked hard publicly to combat the Zionist Organization's quest for a "new culture" of Judaism, though as we shall observe presently, in fact its leadership was profoundly influenced by its involvement with secular Jews who were dedicated to creating a new Jewish ethos.[42] As articulated in its statement of principles, Mizrachi took upon itself special responsibility "to strengthen and broaden the feeling of religion within Zionism...to guide our children in the spirit of Torah, morals and ethics, and to cause a pure spirit to take hold among our brethren through religious commandments...."[43] Its policy statement included mention of its commitment to raise funds and carry out the business of the Zionist movement "...as God-fearing Zionists [taking on responsibility] as basic Zionists; but even more so as God-fearers who know that settling the Land of Israel and strengthening it is a commandment from the Torah."[44]

Those who formed Mizrachi soon found their numbers and influence shrinking as the movements comprising what would become Labor Zionism grew to become the leading stream within the organization. They persevered nevertheless, and many found inspiration in the commitment and dedication among their secular partners. Some, such as the founder of Mizrachi, Rabbi Reines, noted that the drive of many among the secularists was almost religious in character. He attested in his public discourse that the Zionist idea "carries no note whatever of the idea of redemption...In all the actions and endeavors of the Zionists, there is no hint of the future redemption, and their entire aim is simply to improve the Jewish condition and raise the people's dignity and standing, and bring them to a happy life...."[45] However, Reines attributed the neo-messianic zeal of so many secular activists to something more powerful than simple nationalism: "There is no greater sacrilege than to allege that Zionism is part and parcel of secularism...for the truth is that it is precisely the holiness of the land that induces the secularists to participate in the movement."[46]

---

[42] Dov Schwarts, *Religious Zionism*, 13.

[43] Yosef Bramson, *The Last Days: The End is Hastening* (Hebrew) (Jerusalem: 2nd Ed. Daf-Chen, 1987), p. 68.

[44] Bramson, *The Last Days*, p. 68.

[45] *Sha`arey Orah Vesimchah* (Vilna 1909), 12–13, cited in Michael Zvi Nehorai, "Rav Reines and Rav Kook: Two Approaches to Zionism," in (no ed. listed), *The World of Rav Kook's Thought* (s.n.: Avi Chai, 1991), 256.

[46] Zalman Abramov, *Perpetual Dilemma: Jewish Religion in the Jewish State* (Jerusalem and New York: World Union for Progressive Judaism, 1976), 71. A decade or so after Reines' death, Rabbi Shmuel Chayyim Landau (d.1928) referred to the Zionist Movement as a whole as a kind of "neo-messianism," though without using our contemporary terminology. And nearly a

The official position of Mizrachi would lead to a logical but never-theless shocking result during the Sixth Zionist Congress in 1903, when the Zionist Organization was confronted with the "Uganda Scheme." The British government had proposed the establishment of an autonomous Jewish colony in East Africa within what is now the state of Kenya, and this proposal was strongly backed by Herzl. Consistent with its official a-messianic position of rescuing Jews from the distress of Eastern Europe, Mizrachi voted overwhelmingly in favor of accepting the offer for imme-diate settlement in East Africa.[47] Such a decision would, of course, neces-sitate draining virtually all settlement resources away from developing the Land of Israel.

Witnesses to the debates of the Congress were appalled at the readiness of Orthodox Jews to give up the Holy Land so quickly. In fact, it was the deep and romantic ties to the Land of Israel among the *secular* Zionists that defeated the program, and Mizrachi's support for the Uganda Scheme ultimately resulted in a reduction of its stature within the Congress. The Sixth Congress voted in favor of the proposal, but a large and emotional opposition among secular Zionists managed to reverse it within the year. It became unmistakable that the emotional, neo-messianic attachment to the Land of Israel among the secularists would allow no alternative. The Uganda proposal demonstrated that, despite secularism and the fading influence of religion, even the secular streams would remain deeply—and perhaps mystically but most certainly nostalgically—attached to Zionism's historic roots and national past in the Land of Israel.[48]

Reines and the Mizrachi faction as a whole continued to justify Zionism to traditional Jews in order to increase their support for the movement. In fact, however, the opposite occurred. While Mizrachi under Reines' leadership denied that it represented any kind of innovation, it actually produced a new and original synthesis of traditional Judaism and mod-ern nationalism. It would eventually produce a unique theology that has

half century before Arthur Hertzberg popularized the term, he wrote, "There is disagreement about the nature of Zionism, but if one examines it deeply and penetrates into the essence of the notion, we find that it is a continuation of the messianic idea in Israel *(hara`ayon a meshichi beyisra'el)*" (Bramson, *The Last Days*), 105.

[47] Reines wrote to Herzl after the Congress, "[W]e have acceded to the African proposal, because we are attentive to the needs of the people, which we love more than the land; and the needs of the people, whose situation is deteriorating materially and spiritually, dictate a safe refuge, wherever it may be…" (Moshe Heiman [ed.], *Minutes of the Zionist General Council. The Uganda Controversy*, vol. 1 [Jerusalem, 1970], as cited by Elie Holzer, "Attitudes Towards the Use of Military Force in Ideological Currents of Religious Zionism," in Schiffman and Wolowelsky, *War and Peace in the Jewish Tradition*, 377–378.

[48] On the Uganda Scheme, see Laqueur, 122–129.

only recently been examined as such.[49] By eschewing the cultural element of secular Zionism while attempting to preserve its political character, Mizrachi essentially abdicated from working to influence the emerging culture of Zionism in its own Jewish image, thereby giving free reign to the secularists to set the agenda for the movement. The formation of Mizrachi in 1902 established the principle that Zionism would consist of two streams with equal rights, the traditional or religious, and the progressive or secular. This divide has remained largely in place to this day.

More crises faced Mizrachi over the years, including the resolution at the Tenth Zionist Congress in 1911 that called for the establishment of the Hebrew University and other cultural institutions. Mizrachi fought against them and lost, but continued to remain within the Zionist Organization. A number of traditionalists seceded from Mizrachi in response to its failure to prevent the creation of new Zionist cultural institutions. Religious Zionists thus became increasingly isolated by the Orthodox community, and their rejection among many was absolute. The sentiment of one member of Mizrachi is articulated by Rabbi Joseph Soloveitchik.

When the Mizrachi was founded in 1902, the founders of our movement fulfilled the commandment "Get thee out of thy country, and from thy kindred, and from thy father's house," because whoever joined the Mizrachi was almost evicted from his homeland and from the home of his spiritual father. We were alone, as was Joseph the dreamer, alone among his brothers who mocked him.[50]

Mizrachi lost the battle against the new, secular nationalist definition of Jewishness, but it refused to leave the Zionist Organization. Henceforth it would find itself preoccupied with a constant holding action against the overwhelming impact of secularity on the Zionist project. Mizrachi's decision to divide into a separate stream within the larger movement, along with its cultural defeats and its sinking numbers in relation to the secularists, caused religiously observant Zionists to look inward and place their energies increasingly in their own developing institutions and inner life. They remained ideologically on the defensive, always required to justify what would be called "Religious Zionism" as a legitimate expression of religious Orthodoxy.

---

[49] Dov Schwartz, *Meshichiut: Faith at the Crossroads; a Theological Profile of Religious Zionism* (trans. Batya Stein). Leiden: Brill, 2002.
[50] *Five Expositions* (Hebrew), pp. 19–20, cited in Dov Schwartz, *Faith at the Crossroads*, 138.

We should not neglect to mention here that small groups of religiously Orthodox Jews were active in most of the major Zionist political groups, including overwhelmingly secularist groups such as some of the socialist movements and parties. There were also Jews in the Zionist movement who defined themselves as religious but not Orthodox, whether religiously liberal Western European Jews or more religiously observant Jews from the Middle East and North Africa who did not fit into the streams of Judaism defined by the European experience. The formal divide between "religious" and "secular" has become blurred somewhat in recent years as Conservative *(masorti)* and Reform (or "Progressive" = *mitqadem*) religious Zionist groups today define themselves by using the same language as the Orthodox, declaring that they, too, are Zionist *(tziyyoni)* and religious *(dati),* though independent of the Orthodox religious establishment.

At any rate, official "Religious Zionism" represented by Mizrachi was obliged to remain a minor though loyal player in the Zionist movement, tagging along with the larger movement rather than serving as a competitive and influential force within it. Thus Mizrachi and religiously Orthodox Zionism in general took on a kind of second-class ideological status and identity within a movement that was extremely ideological. The second-tier status of Religious Zionism remained in the general national consensus of the larger Zionist community until well after the establishment of the state. Its loyal but inferior status and institutional persona would have a profound impact on the generation that followed.

## Conquest Through Settlement: Hapoel Hamizrachi

The Mizrachi was made up mostly of the middle class, and people of such background were not inclined to face the physical hardship of labor in an undeveloped Palestine. While Mizrachi leadership was working with the secular political Zionists in Europe to establish frameworks for a Jewish sanctuary or shelter in the Land of Israel, an activist group of labor-oriented religious Zionists emerged that would put the political efforts of Mizrachi to work on the ground. They created Hapoel Hamizrachi, meaning "The Mizrachi Worker," in Palestine in 1922. It took on the platform of synthesizing religion with an ideology of labor and applied it immediately to activist settlement, founding its first agricultural settlement, Sedeh Yaaqov, in the Jezreel Valley in 1927.

As mentioned previously, the earliest settlements founded by Jews at the beginning of the Zionist movement were religious and required that members pledge to live religiously observant lives. But as the movement secularized and divided into political movements that represented contemporary theories of interest, new settlements were established by close-knit groups representing these political and social ideas. Hapoel Hamizrachi followed this trend by creating agricultural settlements that reflected its own social and religious notions base on the Nahmanidean principle of "settling of the land." Settling the Land was an active and core element of the Hapoel Hamizrachi's Zionist religious philosophy, and it was intimately tied into its other core idea of material and spiritual productivity through labor.

Hapoel Hamizrachi actualized the Nahmanidean position that settling the Land of Israel was a commandment from the Torah and took it as a theological dogma.[51] Although not always explicit, the activist ideology of Hapoel Hamizrachi was based on an association between settling the Land and the impending arrival of the messiah at "the revealed End" *(haqetz hameguleh)*.[52] The emotional support of belonging to a larger Zionist movement provided encouragement for their program of settlement even in the face of religious Orthodox anti-Zionist critique. Mizrachi activists exuded an optimism that reflected their expectation of an impending messianic arrival. And like their secular comrades, they considered themselves no longer passive and no longer mere victims of history. They engaged in a natural, human-initiated redemption that would bring on, at a time when God would choose, the supernatural and ultimate divine Redemption.

While this expectation conforms with the messianism of religiously Orthodox ultra-nationalists in today's activist "Settler Movement" (see Part 4), Hapoel Hamizrachi activists differed from current Settler Movement activists by taking great care to refrain from acts of political terror or revenge. The first testing ground for their ideals was the "Arab Revolt" of 1936–1939, during which time the Jewish community of Palestine suffered greatly from Arab acts of violence and terror directed against it. Eliezer Don-Yehiya has shown that whereas the Mizrachi movement (as well as many other sectors of the Jewish community) remained ambivalent about engaging in Jewish acts of counter-terrorism against Arab civilians, Hapoel Hamizrachi was adamantly opposed.[53]

---

[51] "Hapoel Hamizrachi," in Yitzhak Refa'el and Shelomo Zalman Shragai (eds.) *The Book of Religious Zionism* (Hebrew) (Jerusalem: Mosad Harav Kook, 1977), 55–181; Dov Schwartz, *Faith at the Crossroads,* 138–140.

[52] See Rabbi Uzi Kalcheim, "The Vision of the 'Revealed End' in the Perspective of the Generations," (Hebrew) in *Sefer Hatzionut Hadatit* 2 vols. (Jerusalem: Mosad Harav Kook, 1977), I, 96–110.

[53] Eliezer Don-Yehiya, "Religion and Political Terrorism: Orthodox Jews and Retaliation during the 1936–39 'Arab Revolt' " (Hebrew), *Zionism* 17 (1993), 155–190.

Hapoel Hamizrachi activists preached political activism and even military activism if necessary, but were strongly influenced also by modern socialist-democratic and universalist values. Both political-military activism and socialist-democratic values were modern ideas that entered their worldview from outside the strict traditional Judaism that they claimed to live by, but they found sources for their ideas in the Jewish moral tradition and, especially with regard to the universal values of moral justice, the biblical prophets. It was thus a combination of religious and secular values, rather than the pragmatic political justification for restraint *(havlagah)* in the face of Arab violence, that drove the activists in Hapoel Hamizrachi during the late 1930s. It is ironic, based on our current understanding of the term, that some Poel Mizrachi activists called their combined activism in settlement and physical restraint in the face of Arab violence a "holy war" *(milchamah qedushah)*.[54]

A second major difference between Hapoel Hamizrachi and the activist Settler Movement that would emerge some five decades later may be found in their position regarding political control over the lands defined biblically as the Land of Israel. The issue of political control was first introduced by the British Peel Commission of 1937, which raised the prospect of the partition of Mandate Palestine into two separate states, one Arab and one Jewish. Theoretically, at least, all expressions of Religious Zionism agreed that the entire Land of Israel was promised by God to the Jewish People and is therefore ultimately theirs to possess. There was nevertheless a difference of opinion over whether acceptance of the partition proposal represented a waiver of that right. Most agreed that it would and refused to accept the proposal. However, a substantial minority, mainly from Hapoel Hamizrachi, felt that the question of partition was a political (meaning practical) issue and not one of religious law. Opting for partition therefore was considered to be the best political decision at the time and did not relinquish the Jews' divinely endowed right to all of the Land of Israel.[55]

Although dynamic at both institutional and activist levels, the religious Zionists of Mizrachi and Hapoel Hamizrachi remained second-class citizens within the larger Zionist Organization. Like other factions within the movement, they built a cadre of followers and created settlements, youth groups, summer camps, and training camps for establishing new settlements. This would sustain them, as it did the other groups within the larger

[54] Don-Yehiya 1993, p.172.
[55] Shimoni, *The Zionist Ideology*, 339–340.

Zionist Organization. But unlike other Zionist factions, two critical aspects of this activist, religiously Orthodox Zionism would enable it to thrive decades after the successful establishment of the State of Israel—exactly at a time when the others found themselves floundering for lack of a relevant political ideology. These are the combination of theological dogma in association with settling the land, and the deep and confident, even if not publicly articulated, association between settlement and the anticipated messianic coming.

CHAPTER 10 | From Practicality to a New
Messianism

> When there is a great war in the world, the power of messiah is
> awakened.

ABRAHAM ISAAC KOOK

The controversy over the Uganda Scheme in 1903 proved that even secular
Zionists could not divorce themselves from the nostalgic and metahistorical association with the Land of Israel. Labor Zionism, which was heir to
the two antireligious and universalist perspectives of the Haskalah and
socialist movements, dominated the Zionist Organization by the 1930s.
It was called *tziyyonut sotzialistit* in Hebrew, and saw itself as part of a
universal socialist movement whose goal was to establish a just collectivist
society in Mandate Palestine that would parallel the activities of its sister
factions throughout the world. Part of a universal movement, it sought to
realize its universal goals within the particular context of Palestine. This
established a natural tension between its universal and particular aspirations, which was not so different from some other socialist movements in
other parts of the world.

The mix of universalism and particularism was expressed in interesting ways. Ironically perhaps, given the ubiquitousness of its secular universal motifs, secular Labor Zionist ideology and writings were saturated
with religious motifs and symbols of traditional Judaism, though interpreted and articulated in ways that supported its own agendas.[1] In fact,
secular Zionism, even among the most radical atheists, exhibited, to use

---

[1] Anita Shapira, "Religious Motifs of the Labor Movement," in Almog, Reinharz and Shapira
(eds.), *Zionism and Religion*, 250.

Arthur Hertzberg's term, an active, paradoxical neomessianism.[2] Religious (or metareligious) mystical ideas of redemption, the return to the ancestral home, and the realization of a messianic kingdom on earth remained at the core of secular, labor ideologies.[3] Even Ber Borochov, the leading Marxist Zionist theoretician, could not, in the final analysis, adequately explain his deep spiritual association with the Land of Israel that required his classless society to be created only there. And Herzl himself (though by no means a socialist) alluded to his messianic image on a few occasions, such as when he contrasted himself with the infamous false messiah, Shabbtai Zevi: "The difference between myself and Shabbetai Zvi (the way I imagine him), apart from the difference in the technical means inherent in the times, is that Shabbetai Zvi made himself great so as to be the equal of the great of the earth. I, however, find the great small, as small as myself."[4]

The very language of ancient Hebrew, which was inherited and revived into a modern language by secular Zionists, was full of romantic, evocative religious biblical terminology and imagery that, partly by necessity and partly by choice, was re-used in near mystical fashion for secular contexts associated with the settlement program and the development of a modern, national Jewish identity.[5] The word used to identify the agricultural pioneers was *chalutzim,* which, in the Torah, referred to the armed tribal warriors who fought under Joshua to conquer the Land of Israel.[6] Agricultural labor in the settlements was `avodah, the biblical term for sacrificial offerings to God in the Jerusalem Temple. And the entire project of settlement was sometimes called *kibbush,* meaning conquest, though in the early Zionist sense it was removed of its military association. Thus even the revived language of Hebrew, as it served the Zionist project, remained mystically biblical at its core as it recalled both the history of a divinely guided age and the redemption of the People of Israel through activism in acquisition of the Land of Israel. New settlements were given biblical

[2] Hertzberg, *The Zionist Idea,* 74–76. See also David Ohana, *Political Theologies in the Holy Land: Israeli Messianism and its Critics* (New York: Routledge, 2010), 1–16.

[3] Shapira, "Religious Motifs," 254.

[4] Shmuel Almog, *Zionism and History: The Rise of a New Jewish Consciousness* (Jerusalem: Magnes Press, 1987), 61.

[5] Fred Halliday, *Religion and Nation in the Middle East* (Boulder, CO: Lynne Reinner, 2000), 42–43

[6] The word means "girded with strength" or "equipped for war," and while the term dropped out of use during the Middle Ages, it was revived as part of the Zionist project to convey the meaning of pioneering (Ilan Troen, "Frontier Myths and their Applications in American and Israel: A Transnational Perspective," in *Israel Studies* 5.1 [Spring, 2000], 304; Henry Near, *The Image of the Pioneer in North America and Pre-State Jewish Palestine* [Haifa: Institute for Study and Research of the Kibbutz and the Cooperative Idea at the University of Haifa Discussion Paper No. 69, January 1987,] 2–4, note 3 [pages specific to notes 1–2]).

names, and whenever possible, nonbiblical place names were changed to those reflecting either biblical places or Zionist activism.[7] The pioneers removed the direct biblical associations with violent armed conquest and bloody sacrifice from the revived terminology, so *kibbush* by *chalutzim* through `avodah* was understood to mean that the success of the activist pioneers would take place through physical labor. But the parallel classical meaning always remained embedded in the language, particularly for those familiar with biblical stories (which included everyone), so that the subtext to the same phrase was "the conquest by the warriors would be through sacrifice to God."

The deep meaning of this kind of language, so unmistakably associated with the glorious days of biblical conquest and Temple sacrifice, was about redemption on the one hand, and militancy on the other. Always lurking behind the modernist, universal veneer was the language's native, particularist core.

In parallel with the general tension between universalism and particularism inherent in the Zionist project, religious Zionists naturally associated their practical activities on the ground with a deeply ingrained metahistorical hope. Even if not fully articulated, religious Zionists could not help but observe what seemed to be the messianic nature of the Zionist successes in settling the Land of Israel, bringing the land to flower and returning the Jewish exiles to the Promised Land.[8] Familiarity with and belief in the theologies of traditional Judaism reinforced the time-honored religious endeavor to find deep and transcendent meaning in history. Yet there was little public articulation of these feelings and observations among religious Zionists because of the constant pressure from their secular Zionist comrades on the one hand and their non-Zionist Orthodox brethren on the other. While the secularists disparaged them for clinging to religion in what the secularists were certain would become a secular age, the non-Zionist Orthodox accused both communities of attempting to force God's hand, of "going up to the Land of Israel in a wall." This would begin to change with the publication of a small book by Rabbi Abraham Isaac Kook.

## Abraham Isaac Kook

Abraham Isaac Kook (1865–1935) was born in Griva in today's Latvia and received the standard, rigorous traditional Orthodox yeshiva education of

---

[7] Troen, *Imagining Zion*, 149–159.
[8] Ravitzky 1996, 37–39.

the non-Hasidic Eastern European Jews, eventually reaching the renowned yeshiva of Volozhin.[9] A curious and independent thinker, he became profoundly influenced by the spirit of certain modernist movements that existed entirely outside of Jewish religious tradition. This would place him ultimately on a path that would lead him away from typical East European ultra-Orthodox thinking. In the spirit of the Haskalah he studied philosophy as well as Bible and Hebrew language, and he also studied Jewish mysticism. Unlike most *maskilim,* however, Kook always remained fully within the traditional community of Jewish Orthodoxy.

The nationalist movements that he observed rising around him, including the emerging Zionism that he personally witnessed, had a profound impact on his thinking. He wrote his first publication treating Jewish nationalism in 1901, three years prior to his emigration to the Land of Israel.[10] When he arrived in Ottoman Palestine in 1904, he served as rabbi of the small Jewish community in Jaffa. He cultivated close ties with Jews of all backgrounds and opinions and immediately identified with the Zionist movement, yet he joined neither secularist nor religious Zionist organizations. He remained independent, engaging in argument with secularists over theology and observance, and with religious anti-Zionists over his open connections and association with secular Zionists.

After the First World War and the designation of the British Mandatory Government over Palestine, Kook was appointed by the Mandate Authority to become the first Ashkenazi Chief Rabbi of Mandate Palestine in 1921. A truly independent, humanist thinker, Rabbi Kook remained fully interested in general human affairs from the perspective of religiously Orthodox Zionism. He seemed always to communicate his deep respect and love for all the Jews of Palestine, though he was constantly at odds with secular Zionists, religious Zionists, and Orthodox anti-Zionists alike.

In consonance with the larger modernist intellectual movements of his age, Kook believed that humanity was progressing toward a higher stage of development. To him, the secular Zionists had only abandoned religion

---

[9] For English language works on Abraham Isaac Kook, see Jacob Agus, *Banner of Jerusalem: The Life, Times and Thought of Abraham Isaac Kuk* (New York: Bloch, 1946); Isadore Epstein, *Abraham Yitzhak Hacohen Kook: His Life and Works* (Torah Ve'Avodah Library: 1951); Zvi Yaron, *The Philosophy of Rabbi Kook,* translated by Avner Tomaschoff (Jerusalem: World Zionist Organization, 1991); Benjamin Ish-Shalom, *Rav Avraham Itzhak Hacohen Kook: Between Rationalism and Mysticism,* translated by Ora Wiskind Elper (Albany, NY: SUNY Press, 1993); Bezalel Naor (translator), *Orot* (Northvale, NJ: Jason Aaronson, 1993); Lawrence Kaplan and David Shatz (eds.), *Rabbi Abraham Isaac Kook and Jewish Spirituality* (New York: New York University, 1995); Simcha Raz, *An Angel Among Men: Impressions from the life of Rav Avraham Yitzchak Hakohen Kook*, trans. Moshe Lichtman (Jerusalem: Kol Mevaser, 2003).
[10] Yaron, *The Philosophy of Rabbi Kook,* 1.

temporarily in their vital striving to improve society and heal the world. He believed that a divine spark lay at the heart of their social passion and that it would eventually burst forth to infuse not only their own endeavor, but also all human endeavor with selfless devotion and even heightened spiritual enthusiasm.[11] His was a messianism of universal proportions in which not only Israel, but also the entire world would benefit from God's final Redemption. His Zionism, accordingly, was not of the practical type of Rabbi Reines and the Mizrachi. It was a full-blown and unabashed religious messianic Zionism that directly equated the Zionist enterprise with the beginning of the ultimate Redemption. This put him constantly at odds not only with the Orthodox non-Zionists and anti-Zionists, but also with the religious Zionists of Mizrachi.

Rabbi Kook wrote his most influential work, *Orot*, during World War I and far from Palestine. He had traveled out of Ottoman Palestine in 1914 to attend a conference of the Agudat Yisrael in Europe and became stuck there at the outbreak of the war, unable to return. He first lived in Switzerland and then London during the war years, where he wrote this seminal work. It was immediately criticized, not only for its support of secular Jews who were settling the Land of Israel, but also for its obscurity. One reviewer wrote, "It would be very good if the author, the Rav, the *gaon* (brilliant intellect), would clarify more explicitly his deep thoughts, lest he present an opportunity for opponents. Especially now, when our new enlightened Jews of the type of the 'Zaddik' Martin Buber, are striving with all their strength to create a new species of mystery religion, it is very dangerous to write things which are misunderstood by the people, and which the new 'mystics' can easily find—because the ideas are not sufficiently explained—proofs and endorsements."[12]

Kook wrote in an obscure style, at least in part, because of the intensity of his thinking and feeling, but also because he felt that he was privy to a wisdom for which clarity was simply limited by language:[13] "The most difficult problem in the constitution of my message was how far to lower

---

[11] Zvi Yaron, "Kook, Abraham Isaac" (*Encyclopedia Judaica*, first edition, 10:1182–1187); Zvi Zinger and Benjamin Ish-Shalom, "Kook (Kuk), Abraham Isaac," EI2 12:289–293; Ella Belfer, "The Land of Israel and Historical Dialectics in the Thought of Rav Kook: Zionism and Messianism," in Lawrence Kaplan and David Shatz (eds.), *Rabbi Abraham Isaac Kook and Jewish Spirituality* (New York: New York University, 1995), 257–275.

[12] In *Haderekh*, the official Hebrew organ of *Agudat Yisrael* published in Vienna, Nos. 11–12 (1920), pp. 126–127, in Naor, translator, *Orot*, Introduction p. 37–38.

[13] Kook seemed to have considered himself privy to understanding mysteries of the divine will, and a number of his students considered him to be a prophet (Dov Schwartz, *Challenge and Crisis in Rabbi Kook's Circle* [Hebrew] [Tel Aviv, 2001], 8 and n. 2, and throughout).

the mysteries of the universe."[14] In a revealing letter to his parents in 1920, the year of *Orot*'s publication, he noted that he simply reads the traditional sources differently than most and in an innovative manner. "To explain the sources would be of no avail. Most of the time, the sources do not state explicitly my thought. Only after contemplation and deep feeling do they reveal this."[15]

The obscurity of language and allusions in Kook's writings make analysis a difficult task, and a range of varied interpretations have been derived from them. We will have occasion later to examine some vectors of interpretation of his writings, particularly through his son and most influential disciple, Rabbi Tzvi Yehuda Kook. Kook the father was not a systematic theologian or ideologue. He would jot down his thoughts as they came to mind and he denied any talent for organization.[16] His published writings were edited by his son Tzvi Yehuda both during his lifetime and after his death, so the son's organizational program had a significant impact on the meaning of his father's *oeuvre*. A range of commentaries have been written to attempt to make explicit what is not obvious in his original work.[17]

The first part of the book, *Orot*, is made up of three sections: "The Land of Israel," "The War," and "The People of Israel." It is quite exceptional for a Jewish religious work to even take up the topic of war, let alone place it in such a prominent position between the Land of Israel and People of Israel, and it is to this that we immediately turn.

The section on war treats the meaning of the Great War, the First World War, which Rabbi Kook experienced in a state of temporary exile outside Palestine. It is made up of ten paragraphs that, typical to his writing style, contain dozens of citations and allusions to traditional Jewish writings from the Hebrew Bible through rabbinic and medieval religious texts. Consonant with the reaction of many to the horrific brutality and immense destruction and loss of life caused by the war, Kook believed that it marked a turning point in human history. His conclusion differed from that of many secular humanists, however. It was not a "war to end all wars" but, rather, something of such immense scope that it signaled a divinely wrought cosmic change in history. His opening sentence of the section entitled "The War" reads "When there is a great war in the world,

---

[14] *Igrot Hara'aya* 2:36, cited in Yaron 1991, 17.

[15] Naor, 58.

[16] Yaron 1991, 9.

[17] At least two translations with commentary and references of his citations and allusions have been written to date on the section that follows, that of Naor, and that of David Samson and Tzi Fishman, *Harav Avraham Yitzhak Hacohen Kook: War and Peace* (Jerusalem: Torah Eretz Yisrael Publications, 1997).

the power of messiah is awakened,"[18] alluding to the traditional Jewish concept of the "birth pangs" of messiah—terrible and horrific events that will accompany the beginning of the messianic end.[19]

As with all wars and all events of history, God is the ultimate first cause, and such a massive war as the one he witnessed could only spell a cosmic change in history that results, ultimately (even if difficult for us to comprehend), in a better world. "Evil is destroyed and the world made better (literally: 'the wicked are destroyed from the world and the world is perfumed').... And afterwards, at war's end, the world is renewed in a new spirit and the footsteps of the messiah are especially revealed."[20] Of course there are innocent deaths as well, but the massive numbers of innocent deaths in such an enormous war as World War I brings a kind of cosmic expiation, since tradition teaches that the death of the righteous brings atonement. The collective will of humankind then becomes more positive, paving the way for the beginning of the End. That expected End is intimately associated with "the settlement of the Land of Israel."

In his second paragraph, Kook notes how the great heroes of the Bible, who are cherished for their holiness, all engaged in war. He uses the singular form as if the many wars depicted in Hebrew Scriptures were one long war that he describes as necessary in cosmic terms. "The world situation that had developed then, and of which war was so necessary, caused those souls whose inner sensitivity was so complete to come to be. A war for their survival, survival of the nation, a war of God was in their inner consciousness." It was war that brought out the inner spark of holiness in the biblical heroes. By emulating them in his day, he wrote, we essentially revive them and their combination of spiritualism and heroism in ourselves.

Referring to the end of Jewish political independence under the Romans, he wrote, "We left world politics by coercion, within which was a [certain] inner desire, until a propitious time when it will be possible to govern

---

[18] Abraham Isaac Kook, *Orot* (Hebrew). Jerusalem: Mosad Harav Kook, 1993 (13th printing), p. 13. All translations are mine.

[19] BT Megilla 17b: "War is the beginning of Redemption (*milchamah nahme atchalta dege 'ulah hi*)," and Sanhedrin 97a–98b, Sota 49b (and see Yaron, *Philosophy*, 267–268). Jewish tradition is not monolithic on this or on most other details of messianic thinking, and a wide range of views may be found about the messianic "birth pangs," as the Sanhedrin pages cited here testify. Kook's association of the War with Israel's impending redemption was certainly influenced by his presence in London at the granting of the Balfour Declaration on November 2, 1917. At a London rally following the Declaration, he said, "I have not come to thank the British but to congratulate them for being privileged to be the source of this Declaration to the People of Israel." (Yaron, 318, n. 12). There remains some difference of opinion whether *Orot* was written while Kook was in Switzerland during the first two years of the War, or while he was in London for the remainder.

[20] *Orot* p. 13.

without evil and barbarity.... The delay was necessary ... But now the time has arrived, very soon, the world is stabilizing and we can already prepare ourselves, for we will be enabled to conduct our government on the basis of goodness, wisdom, integrity and the clear divine illumination."[21] Kook states, moreover, that it can be learned from the Bible itself how God established only the foundation of the nation of Israel in ancient days, for God knew that the world was not yet ready for its leadership.

The fourth paragraph takes a different approach to the problem, stating that, were it not for the sin of Israel worshiping the golden calf, Israel would have occupied the Land of Canaan without war.[22] The inhabitants of the Land of Israel would have surrendered to Israel "because the name of God would have awakened in them the awe of [divine] majesty, and no form of warring would have occurred." The sin of the golden calf, however, postponed the process by thousands of years, when at one time the world will finally be perfected in a peaceful manner and its inhabitants recognize the special nature of Israel.

The following short paragraph finds the cause of the World War in the moral repression of a profane, secular society,[23] causing the pressure of anger and emotional sickness to build to the point of explosion. However, in paragraph six, Kook suggests that engagement in war has a deep national purpose. While all nations develop uniquely through natural processes, "wars deepen the special value of every people," by forcing the nation at war to articulate its inner character more forcefully than in peacetime. "Every time that nations fight one another, [their] special characteristics are activated that bring them closer to their own [unique] perfection."[24] This, in turn, activates the perfection of Israel because Israel is affected cosmically by the developing perfections of the world's nations: "Israel is the general speculum of the entire world." The World War thus activates the processes of national development among the world's nations, which in turn brings closer the ultimate Redemption.

---

[21] Paragraph 3 (p. 14).

[22] Cf. Midrash Exodus Rabba 32:1. According to a position cited in BT Sanhedrin 102a, all evil that ever befell Israel was a result of worshipping the golden calf. As a result of Israel's suffering, however, they would merit the coming of the messiah (Midrash Seder Eliyahu Zuta 4).

[23] *Hatarbut hachilonit*, which carries with it a sense of the profane in foreign culture outside of the range of the holy. See the traditional Aramaic biblical translations called *targum*s of Yonatan on Deut. 23:3 (`amaya cholona'ei) and Onkelos on Ex. 29:33 (*chillonai*) which are constructed from the Hebrew root *ch.l.l.* meaning "profane," the same root for the modern Hebrew word for secular: *chiloni*.

[24] That is, the characteristics' own perfection.

In paragraph seven, Kook observes that the national essence of Israel is developing greatly in the modern period and that its special nature derives, in part, from its history of adversity dispersed among the nations of the world. It has grown and progressed wherever it has been by internalizing its experience. Even the pain and suffering it experienced has brought it growth. "From the countless waves of trouble that pass over her from the nations, from all the diasporas, [Israel] derives great wealth of knowledge and farsighted vision, adding the pure aspects from without to her own possessions." As a result of modern history, "[Israel] has come to understand that she has a land, she has a language, a literature, that she has an army, [which] she has begun to recognize in this very World War.[25] But above all, she knows that she has a light of a unique life that crowns her and crowns the entire world through her." Thus Israel's developing national essence is grounded in its position as the central figure in world history. Its special role is bringing it, and along with it the entire world, to Redemption.

The last three paragraphs are far longer than the previous seven. In paragraph eight, Kook lambastes his contemporary Western world for the evil it produced and prophesies its absolute destruction in apocalyptic terms.[26] "...and the atonement will surely come: the complete cancellation of all the apparatuses of contemporary culture with all their lies and deception, with all their evil filth and poison venom. All of that civilization that boasts to the tune of lies must be effaced from the world and in its place will arise a kingdom of lofty holy ones.... The dissipation of the power of the nations drunk with the cup of poison shall certainly come. God has opened His arsenal and brings forth the weapons of his anger.... The present civilization with all of its foundations will be demolished, its libraries, theaters and institutions, and all the laws that at base are vain and wickedness, and all the evil niceties of [its] lifestyle and sins will pass in their entirety.... Therefore, all of present day civilization will be utterly destroyed and on its desolate ruins a world order will be established in truth and the knowledge of God."

In the penultimate paragraph, Kook explains that the end of European civilization and European order requires the reconstruction of Jewish civilization. "The world order that is now collapsing as a result of the raging storms of bloodied swords requires the building up of the Israelite nation. The building of the nation and the revelation of its spirit are one and the

---

[25] The British established a Jewish "Zion Mule Corps" that served in the British army during WWI. See J. H. Patterson, *With the Zionists in Gallipoli* (New York: George H. Doran, 1916); Sachar, *History of Israel*, 91–92.

[26] Reminiscent of the apocalypse of Daniel 7, including some parallel phraseology.

same, all integrated with the world order that is crumbling and seeking a power filled with unity and superiority, all of which exists in the soul of the entirety of Israel.... The hour has come, the light of eternity,[27] the light of the God of Truth, the light of the God of Israel revealed through His people, a wondrous people, must be revealed through recognition and the recognition must become internalized by the nation, to recognize the unity of its own powers, to recognize God who dwells within it." That recognition will produce a contribution from the depths of its own resources of prayer, Torah, faith, intellect, spirit and bravery, with the result that "all the civilizations of the world will be renewed through the renewal of our spirit." The act of revitalizing the nation of Israel will remove the evils and errors of the world's civilizations. "The present destruction is a preparation for a new revival that is deep and unique. The light of exalted kindness sparkles. The name of God, *I will be that I will be* (Ex.3:114) is revealed. *Give praise to our God*." (Deut. 32:3).

The final paragraph of this section is not a conclusion; Kook was not a linear thinker. Yet it begins with a statement about a world at its maturity. "When the world has grown up, when the lofty splendor of the sanctity of Israel has appeared, there is no support for any harlots, for all those who stand on the outside, to establish any basis to counter the light of Israel, to fortify some mystic illumination, [or] base of faith that will be able to stand outside the reality of the [Israelite] nation, its honor and the outpouring of its cherished holiness." The Endtime that will mark a truly mature world is entirely dependent upon Israel and its special nature as God's chosen people. No other religious system will dominate Israel, which will emerge spiritually triumphant. But the paragraph then continues by returning to the present state of the world's disgrace and ends with a simple cry for repentance. The current degradation of the world has brought low the soul of Israel as well, and this in turn has rent the fabric of cosmic unity. But the community of Israel will cry out. The wise among Israel will lead the call, for they recognize the true state of the world and of the Israelite nation. They also understand the cosmic rift and the profound sadness of God at the state of affairs in the world below; and they therefore call for repentance.

Kook's language is forceful and confident, though allusive and often obscure. The ten paragraphs of "The War" do not hang together as one coherent essay, but rather appear as moments of inspiration in response to the overwhelming and shocking nature of the First World War. They

---

[27] Or "light of the world" (*or `olam*).

repeat themes and ideas in a way that is not readily apparent from the few selections provided here, and they begin and end in a style that seems more a description than an argument. Yet his conclusion is clear. The war demonstrates, despite its horrors and the deaths of many innocents—indeed *because* of this sinful reality on such a massive scale—that God is moving history in the direction of its inexorable climax. The Great War proves the failure of secularism and the lesser forms of more recent expressions of monotheism that brought the world to its terrible present,[28] yet it is also a turning point toward Redemption.

The Jewish People has suffered in exile but has grown profoundly from the experience. Despite its past and current suffering, it must now reach into its own heart and reactivate its national and spiritual core to reestablish its place as God's own spiritual leaders for the world. Redemption will come, and that redemptive process will include the reestablishment and universal recognition of the Jewish nation's position as God's chosen people. Although he hardly mentions the Land of Israel in these paragraphs, elsewhere he forcefully articulates the spiritual and material importance of the Land. In fact, the section on war is sandwiched between the opening section of the book on the Land of Israel *(Eretz Yisrael),* and the following section on the revival or renaissance of the People of Israel *(Yisrael Utechiyato).*

Although Kook may seem to exhibit a certain audacity by finding universal Jewish significance in a war, even as overwhelming as World War I fought between gentile nations, he does not stray from Jewish tradition when he finds deep meaning in the world's wars. Parallel to apocalyptic literature beginning with the Book of Daniel, Rabbinic literature is rife with content that assigns meaning to the wars of the great powers of ancient days because God is the mover of human history. We have noted in Part 1 how the Babylonian and Roman wars that destroyed the Jerusalem Temples were envisioned to be God's design rather than that of empires. Yet Kook is bold in his willingness to assign divine significance to wars in which Israel is not directly involved. His response to the War represents an attempt by a deeply spiritual and committed religious leader to find meaning and consolation in a world that appears to have been turned on its head—a situation that he understood to fit scenarios suggested in rabbinic sources as signs of an impending Endtime. He is profoundly influenced by vectors of modern thinking such as nationalism, humanism, positivism,

---

[28] Kook's writings, including the book under discussion here, contain numerous rejoinders to and critiques of Christianity, such as in *Orot* 21–22, where Christianity is termed heresy *(haminut).*

and Darwinism, and he applies certain versions of these trajectories to his observation of the position of world Jewry in his own time, concluding thereby that Jewish nationalism associated with God's own Holy Land represents a divinely ordained leap forward in the path toward Jewish and universal Redemption.

Kook's bold thinking about war here serves as a kind of breakthrough in public Jewish discourse. While it had always been known in traditional Jewish thought that wars, as all historical occurrences, derive from the divine will, Kook's analysis of World War I re-activated Jewish thinking about war and brought it into public discourse. Perhaps war is no longer something to avoid at all costs, as had exilic Jews for nearly two thousand years. Perhaps, as Josef Trumpeldor and Vladimir (Ze'ev) Jabotinsky concluded, the nominal Jewish involvement as an independent unit in the British army in the Great War signaled a future for Jewish military activism.[29] In any case, Kook's writings here brought the topic and meaning of historical wars into the realm of public discussion in the Jewish world. But this is not the only barrier he broke.

One of the most enigmatic sections of *Orot* is chapter 34 in which Kook, surprisingly, extols the benefits of physical exercise *(hit'amlut)*, an activity absolutely foreign to the tradition of yeshiva learning. "Exercise, which the Israelite youths in the Land of Israel engage in to strengthen their bodies in order to be powerful sons of the nation, increases the spiritual power of the superior righteous who engage in the unification of the holy names to increase the dissemination of the divine light in the world. One revealing light cannot exist without its partner." He then alludes to the fatal gladiatorial contests of 2 Sam. 2:14: *Let the youths arise and sport before us*, meaning in that context, "let the youths get up and fight one another to the death." Referring to the Midrash called Leviticus Rabbah (26.2), Kook claims that David's general, Avner, was punished only because he made sport of the blood of youths—not because he trained them to fight. In fact, according to Kook, "The youths should engage in this sport in order to strengthen their power and spirit for the strength of the nation in general. This sacred act of worship raises up the divine presence ever higher, just

---

[29] Elie Holzer sees Kook as a quietist who eschewed force as a means of furthering the messianic goal (Holzer, "Attitudes Towards the Use of Military Force in Ideological Currents of Religious Zionism," in Lawrence Schiffman and Joel Wolowelsky, eds., *War and Peace in the Jewish Tradition*. New York: Yeshivah University, 2007, 347–348). But his powerful writings, which were so heavily influenced by his experience of World War I, brought war firmly into the religious discourse of divine Redemption. The obscurity of his writing then opened up this topic to a range of interpretation and accompanying contention over the true meaning of what was deemed Kook's precient thought.

as it is raised up by songs and praises uttered by David, king of Israel, in the Book of Psalms."[30]

Kook's interest in building strong bodies as well as strong minds was part of the *Zeitgeist*, and other Jews such as Zishe Breitbart in Europe and Henry Houdini in America personally acted out this modernizing element.[31] It also found its way into Zionist ideology and was strongly articulated in Revisionist Zionism. Vladimir Jabotinsky concretized such ideals as physical strength and power in his vision of a national movement that would be an "iron wall" in relation to its opponents, whether the Arabs or the British. Abba Achimeir, one of the great intellectuals and educators of Revisionism, considered militarism and aggressiveness to be a healthy manifestation of national vitality, using the adjective "healthy" as the antithesis to delicate and fragile "vegetarians," who represent the weakness and inhibitions that have no place in the strong new Hebrew nation.[32] Yehoshua Heschel Yeivin called for the "creation of the race of Jewish ruffians *(biyronim)*."[33]

Jabotinsky, Achimeir, Yeivin, and the other Revisionist ideologues were secularist Jews who were deeply infused with the social and political ideas of modern nationalisms and their activist movements. Rabbi Kook, on the other hand, was an ultra-Orthodox Jew, whose ethos traditionally abhorred physical prowess as a manifestation of pagan ways. Some religious Jews have therefore been confounded by Kook's reference to the importance of exercise and his association of exercise with martial arts. One recent, but unlikely, explanation is that the term *hit`amlut* was a code word in the early Jewish secret defense organizations for underground military training. Thus Kook would not have been praising physical exercise per se, but rather the need to train for military defense or perhaps even conquest of the homeland. This would also clarify his otherwise odd reference to 2 Sam. 2:14. In a letter dated June 21, 1926, Kook wrote, "Touching on the general striving, on the part of some of our youth in the Land of Israel, toward exercise, to strengthen physical power—if its goal should be that the nation, upon its return to the Land, should also be armed with physical strength—this has no practical bearing, due to our many sins, in the

[30] Kook, *Orot*, 80.

[31] Sharon Gillerman, "Samson in Vienna: The Politics of Jewish Masculinity," *Jewish Social Studies*, Vol. 9, No.v2 (2003), 65–97.

[32] Anita Shapira, *Land and Power: The Zionist Resort to Force* 1881–1948. Oxford: Oxford University Press, 1992, 194–195.

[33] Shapira, *Land and Power,* 198. Use of the term, *biryonim,* meaning "hooligans" or "ruffians" was quite conscious; the far more nuanced *qana'im* ("zealots") would have been expected. This particular choice of words was meant as a rebellion against the normative post-Bar Kokhba Jewish approach to war (Shapira, *Land and Power,* 32).

state of holiness of our generation. The matter is but a looking to salvation, that God grant a new spirit in the heart of the generation, to understand the ways of God and to look to the true salvation which will come about through steps of redemption that God arranges for Israel's return to the Holy Land, as a sprouting forth of salvation. These matters are connected to mysteries of Torah and very holy thoughts, which I was forced to reveal a bit for the correction of the generation...."[34]

But Kook was indeed influenced by the intellectual currents of modernity, and that influence had a profound impact on his thought in general. Kook would go even further toward reviving the sanction of divinely authorized war in his book, *Vision of Redemption*, where he would refer to a *conquest* of the Land of Israel. "Accordingly, the Jewish National Fund's land purchase and transfer from gentile to Jewish hands implements the Divinely ordained 'Conquest of the Land of Israel,' whose weight equals that of all the Biblical precepts, seeing that it entails war and loss of life which preservation 'and he shall live by them' overrides all the other commandments. Although no military conquest is here involved, we must concentrate on land acquisition with the religious fervor that inspires the pious worship of God."[35] We can discern in these words how biblical terminology is recycled in a radically different modern context. "Conquest" in this reference means acquisition, but Kook associates this with related language of war, such as the loss of life, which would not be expected in relation to mundane land purchase.

Kook's deep attachment to the Land of Israel and its importance in the process of impending Redemption has already been mentioned. And we recall from chapter 8 that his reference to conquest is informed by Nahmanides and the Midrash Sifrei. But Kook is willing to go even further. "[A]t the foundation of the law the Torah obligates us to be engaged in this (the conquest of the Land of Israel) even if it means going to war. And in the natural course of war, there is always the danger of dying. And regarding all of the commandments of the Torah it is written, 'To live by them.' But this is not the case with the conquering of the Land of Israel...."[36]

---

[34] Naor, 42.

[35] Tomaschoff's translation in Yaron 1991, 212.

[36] Cited in Samson and Fishman, 63 note 4 (parenthesis in original). The position that defensive fighting or fighting for the Land of Israel (that is, Commanded War) does not transgress the commandment " 'and live by them' (Lev.18:5), but you should not die by them" (BT Sanhedrin 74a) is accepted in current Jewish legal thinking (Shlomo Goren, *Law of the State* (*Mishnat Hamedinah*, Jerusalem: Ha`idra Rabba, 1999, Hebrew), 124, *idem*, "Army and War in the Light of the Halakhah," *Mahanayim* 121 [1969], 8 (Hebrew); Aryeh Benosovsky, "The Law of War and the Participation of Women in War" (Hebrew), *Hatorah Vehamedinah* 5 [1953], 62), etc.

Rabbi Kook could not be described as a militarist, although his passionate messianism certainly contained militant elements. But the nature of his messianism, so deeply influenced by the contemporary *Zeitgeist*, forced him to break through some of the most basic patterns of traditional Jewish thinking that were often described negatively by secular Zionists as exilic. Kook was a staunchly Orthodox Jew, but he was profoundly influenced by the intellectual currents of his day. These include not only the modern idea of nationalism, but also an interest in developing the physical as well as intellectual and spiritual sides of the human person, something profoundly new in Jewish culture but which in some Jewish circles had already begun to gain real significance.[37]

Kook's willingness to employ the idioms he does is an expression of his modern, messianic nationalism. The purpose of Kook's Zionism was not merely to save the lives of Jews living in physical distress as was the articulated position of the religious Zionist organization, Mizrachi. In fact, some students of Abraham Isaac Kook maintain that he never even mentioned the concepts of refuge and political asylum that were the mantra of both political and religious Zionists of his day.[38] His goal was much more ambitious. Indeed it was cosmic, for the enormous disruptions that he experienced in the World War were among the many signs pointing to the immanent and divinely initiated Redemption of the Jewish People. And the redemption of Israel would, in his view, result in the redemption of the entire world.

## Kook's Legacy in Religious Zionism

Rabbi Abraham Isaac Kook was a powerful figure and intellect, mystic, and activist, who directly motivated hundreds and perhaps thousands of Jews involved in the Zionist project. There is no doubt among scholars that he left an extraordinarily powerful mark on Zionism in general and Religious Zionism in particular. Of particular importance is his open embrace of the messianic nature of Zionism, a position that was quite contrary to the pragmatic position articulated by Jacob Reines and the official position of Mizrachi. Kook's unguarded and powerful sanctification of

---

[37] The social critic and philosopher, and one of Herzl's most ardent followers, Max Nordau (d. 1923) used the term "muscular Judaism" in 1903 when addressing a Jewish athletic club in Berlin. Nordau was a forceful proponent of *Muskeljudentum* (Mendes-Flohr and Reinharz, *The Jew in the Modern World*, 547–548).

[38] Samson and Fishman, p. 249.

Zionism moved Mizrachi and Religious Zionism in general toward a more messianic stance, even if historians disagree over its extent and timing.

There can be no doubt that Kook's legacy includes a powerful articulation of the "messianization" of Religious Zionism. But it is also apparent that religious Zionists felt a level of discomfort with messianism because of the powerful critique of their non-Zionist and anti-Zionist Orthodox brethren and the constraint of the traditional Three Vows. For many, as we shall observe later in reference to the 1967 War, the messianic nature of their involvement was unconscious and left unacknowledged. But it was never abandoned. Abraham Isaac Kook's legacy would become extremely significant only a generation later through his son, Rabbi Tzvi Yehudah Kook, who succeeded only late in his own life in popularizing his father's difficult messianic metaphysics.[39]

---

[39] Dov Schwartz, "A Theological Rationale for National-Messianic Thought: Rabbi Tzvi Yehudah Kook" (Hebrew), *Hatziyyonut* 22 (2000), 61–81.

# CHAPTER 11 | The New Jew

In blood and fire Judea fell, and in blood and fire shall
Judea rise again.

YAKOV CAHAN, *HABIRYONIM*

## Defense and Militancy in Zionist Palestine

Arthur Herzberg was perhaps the first to point out that what is generally
regarded as "secular Zionism," defined as such because of its negative stance
toward religious observance and behaviors, is actually a far more complex
phenomenon. Various subgroups within the larger mass of nonobservant
Jewish Zionists have been shown to have more or less transcendent, even
mystical, foundations to their ideologies. One person who came to epitomize
the secular but mystical connection with the land and with physical labor
was Aaron David Gordon (d. 1922). Born in Russia in 1856, Gordon came to
Palestine in 1904 as an agricultural laborer, where he first lived in Petah Tik-
vah and finally made his home in Degania, the first Jewish collective farm.
Gordon had been a white-collar worker all his life and had no experience
with agricultural labor, but he believed that physical labor on the land would
bring about both personal redemption and the collective redemption of the
Jewish people. Ascribing to labor pioneering a neomystical status and arguing that it created an organic balance between the Jew, the Land, and Jewish
culture, Gordon became the inspiration for a generation and more of Labor
Zionists who saw in his example a path to personal and national fulfillment.
He founded the Hapoel Hatzair Labor Zionist movement, and his pragmatic
socialism dominated the ideology of the Israel Labor Party for many years.[1]

---

[1] Hertzberg, *The Zionist Idea*, 368–386.

Gordon became a legend in his own time and came to epitomize that neomystical association of land and labor, of bringing about personal and national redemption through personal commitment in working the land. For some such as him, it was the experience of labor that linked the individual to the hidden aspects of nature and being, which, in turn were the source of the spiritual life. But according to Gordon, for Jews it was labor in their own land that was necessary. "What are we seeking in Palestine? Is it not that which we can never find elsewhere—the fresh milk of a healthy people's culture?"[2] The overwhelming rejection of the Uganda Proposal the year before Gordon's immigration shows how the mystic-romantic notions of fatherland that emerged in mid to late nineteenth-century European nationalist revival movements penetrated deeply into Jewish nationalism as well.[3] While not a religious aspiration, per se, the mystical meaning of land for Zionism comes close to transcending any clear demarcation that might be imagined between the physics of secularism and metaphysics of religion.

Chaim Weizmann's proclamation before the 1937 Peel Commission on Palestine was certainly a political statement but—perhaps in an attempt to appeal to British Christian believers—it also contains a powerful metaphysical element. As Weizmann reported at the twentieth Zionist Conference in 1937: "I told the commission: God has promised Eretz Yisrael to the Jews. This is our charter."[4] And in a famous gesture, David Ben Gurion held up a Bible before the United States President Truman when articulating the Zionist right to Jewish control of the Land of Israel and declared "this is our mandate."[5]

We have noted in the previous chapter how this mystic romanticism was reflected in the language of the Zionist pioneers, who described themselves as *chalutzim*, a biblical term that denotes both a person in the vanguard of a cause and one who is armed and ready for war.[6] Anita Shapira has shown how the pioneering terminology reflects the romantic association with the ancient Israelite conquest of the Land of Canaan.[7]

---

[2] Hertzberg, *the Zionist Idea,* 374.

[3] Laquer, *History of Zionism,* 279.

[4] Barnet Litvinoff, *The Letters and Papers of Chaim Weizman,* 2 Vols. (New Brunswick, N.J.: Rutgers University Press, 1984), Vol. 2, p. 286.

[5] David Ben-Gurion and Thomas Bransten, *Recollections of David Ben-Gurion* (London: Mac-Donald, 1970), 120; Mordechai Nisan, "Gush Emunim: A Rational Perspective," *Forum* 36 (Fall-winter, 1979), 16. See also David Ohana, *Political Theologies in the Holy Land,* 120.

[6] See Numbers 32:21–32, Deuteronomy 3:18. *Hechalutz* ("The Pioneer") was the name of an organization of Jewish pioneers that became a mass movement in the 1930s for training workers to emigrate to Palestine (Laquer, *History of Zionism*), 326–328.

[7] Anita Shapira, *Land and Power: The Zionist Resort to Force, 1881–1948* (New York: Oxford University Press, 1992).

"Conquest" (*kibbush*) was one of many slogans used by all the Zionist groups in their settlement of the Land of Israel, whether religious or secular, even in the early periods. They did not have in mind the military connotation of the term, though it certainly expressed an aggressive, even militant approach to claiming and settling the land that was, according to their reading of the Bible, the Jewish national patrimony. Conquest was a familiar term in the literature of the period, but in its early Zionist context it meant the hard labor of settlement rather than military action.

The militant language employed by the earliest Zionist pioneers of the labor camp derived from the contemporary rhetoric of socialist revolutionary movements generally. In the Palestinian Zionist context its meaning was less militant than among many of the international vanguards of socialism. Micha Josef Berdichevsky, one of the great proponents of early Labor Zionism and known as a militant nationalist, wrote, "The war for which we are being prepared is very simple, not dangerous in the least. What we desire is to engage in patient labor, work devoid of any bloodshed, work that is only civilized colonization. Diligent labor is our sword and bow."[8]

Zionist pioneers freely employed traditional Jewish terminology in their articulation of the new concepts and activities engendered by their engagement in the modernizing life of the farms and villages of Palestine. This tendency to "Judaize" modern and sometimes foreign notions through the use of traditional Jewish terminology has been a Jewish activity from ancient days and continues in modern Israel to this day. As has been shown in earlier chapters, the phrase, "conquest of the Land" (*kibbush ha'aretz*) derives from a combination of biblical imagery and terminology from rabbinic and medieval Jewish literatures; it was often used by the socialist Zionist pioneers to refer to peaceful, though assertive, Jewish colonization of the Land of Israel. During the wave of Jewish immigration to Palestine known as the Second Aliyah (1904–1914), young pioneers used the term "conquest of labor" *(kibbush ha`avodah)* as a slogan to articulate their desire to work the land and to supplant local Arabs in the agricultural sector.[9] Other well-known and well-used idioms were also constructed out of the term, *kibbush,*[10] such as "conquest of the deserts

---

[8] Cited in Shapira, *Land and Power,* 41.

[9] Even earlier, "conquest of the [Jewish] communities" was used by Herzl to convey the need for Zionism to take the lead in Jewish public discourse, especially in Western Europe (Almog, *Zionism and History,* 188–193), but biblical or traditional Jewish imagery seems unlikely to be at play in this case.

[10] Decades later, after the 1967 War and the establishment of Jewish control over the West Bank (the Judea and Samaria of the Bible), some objected passionately to the use of the term

(*kibbush hashemashot*), found in a discussion about the future of pioneer-ing among religious Zionist youth shortly after the establishment of the State,[11] and "conquest of the sea" (*kibbush hayam*) in relation to building the port of Tel Aviv in the 1930s.[12]

The use of such symbolic language of conquest was not limited to secular Zionists. As the source for the last example demonstrates, activists in the religious Zionist B'nai Akiba youth movement also used the term freely in the nonviolent sense of activist settlement. The very first issue of the B'nai Akiba newsletter *Zera`im*[13] refers to the settlement achievements in Palestine as "a great conquest."[14] And in an installment issued in 1936, a poem appears enti-tled "I Hear Your Song, Conquerors of the Third [Conquest of] Canaan."[15]

Terminology is important. The nuances and implications that derive from a term's long literary history can convey important subtle shades of meaning, particularly among a highly literate population that continues to read, study, and discuss all layers of its long-lived and extensive national literature. Certain ancient terms that become modernized in the revival of the Hebrew language thus retain at least nuances of their old meanings, especially with regard to key symbolic language such as "conquest." Like many such expressions, Conquest of the Land became a motto, a slogan that carried with it a special meaning that was particular to the historical context in the early period of Zionist colonization. As with other slogans and mythic images, however, their sense and significance sometimes take on new meaning as the historical and political contexts change. This has been the case with the idiom, Conquest of the Land.

---

"conquest" because of its common association with what was then unpopular Western colonial-ism and imperialism: "We relate with all contempt to the portrayal of our returning home as if we are 'conquerors' and identified according to the international legal definition of conquerors of foreign lands...We are not 'conquerors' of foreign soil, alien lands, we who come here as returnees to the inheritance of our ancestors, but rather, returnees home to the lands of the tribes of Israel..." (Rabbi Tzvi Yehudah Kook, in response to a 1980 ruling of the Israeli Supreme Court that denied the right of a group to create a settlement called Elon Moreh on the West Bank [Bramson, *The Last Days*, p. 240 (parentheses in original).]). But the negative association with colonialism was not an issue in the early part of the century.

[11] "About Our Pioneering Path (`al darkeynu hechalutzit)" *Zera`im* 104 (Feb., 1949), 4.

[12] Troen, *Imagining Zion*, 154. Posters with such slogans were printed and distributed in Jewish communities in Europe and the US in order to garner material support from the Jewish commu-nity for building up Palestine. A display of these classic posters with slogans such as "conquest of labor" and "conquest of the deserts" was featured prominently in the long and grandiose approach to the departure lounges in Ben Gurion Airport in 2011.

[13] The name, *Zera`im*, which means "seeds," was chosen by the founding editor to convey the com-bined importance of Torah learning and labor (Yonatan Shalem, "Thus did *Seeds* Sprout" [*kakh navtu zera`im*], *Zera`im* 400 [Tevet/January, 1974], 10.)

[14] *Zera`im* 1 (Sept. 1935), p. 6

[15] *Zera`im* 5 (Feb. 1936), p. 5. Many more examples could be cited.

The ideologues and early pioneers who settled and built up the New Yishuv in Palestine[16] naturally carried with them the worldviews that they had acquired in their countries and communities of origin. These worldviews were constructed out of the internal world of Jewish tradition and culture, along with various outside intellectual and social vectors of influence that had been internalized by those who found themselves engaged in the Zionist program. There was no single ethos or ideology that typified the Zionist pioneers who settled the Land of Israel, as the many parties and movements among the small community of the Yishuv easily attest. Yet certain trends may be identified that typified the various subcommunities there. A range of groups and organizations could be identified as communist, socialist, social democrat, liberal, even fascist, and each generated its own worldview. But however individual was the worldview of each party or movement, they also had much in common within the Zionist world of the New Yishuv.

By 1920, the leadership and overwhelming majority of the Yishuv identified with one or another of the parties and groups in the socialist or Labor camp. The largest and leading party in this camp was usually the *Mapai* or "Workers' Party of the Land of Israel"[17] (or its predecessor, *Achdut ha`avodah,* the "Unity of Labor" party), though the names and factions were somewhat fluid. The socialist camp dominated the Zionist enterprise from that early period through the first few decades after independence, and it set the ideological and behavioral tone for the majority population. Although some other ideological camps such as the Revisionists under Vladimir Jabotinsky and then Menachem Begin also had a powerful impact, certain aspects of the socialist-Zionist ethos became so universally internalized by the population that they could be considered typical of Zionism as a whole. Anita Shapira has chronicled the increased militancy of Zionism from its romantic European dreams of a peaceful settlement in the Land of Israel to the harsh reality of Ottoman and Mandate Palestine.[18] The growing ethos of power among the majority secular Zionist community during the prestate period would also influence the attitude of religious Zionists toward the meaning and significance of Israel's wars.

---

[16] The "Old Yishuv," meaning the old settlement of Jews in the Land of Israel, included all the communities of traditional Jews before the arrival of the Zionists and those within that group who did not join or support the Zionist program. The "New Yishuv" refers to the modernizing pre-State Jewish community that included both secular and religious Jews, most but not all of whom were Zionists. This group is often referred to in Zionist writings simply as "The Yishuv."

[17] An acronym from the Hebrew *mifleget po `alei eretz yisra'el.*

[18] Shapira, Anita. *Struggle and Disappointment* (Tel Aviv: Hakibbutz Hame'uchad, 1977, Hebrew); idem, *Land and Power: The Zionist Resort to Force* 1881–1948. Oxford: Oxford University Press, 1992.

The idea of a military force for the creation of a Jewish state did cross Theodor Herzl's mind,[19] but he rejected that option. A product of liberal Central Europe, Herzl believed that the creation of a Jewish state would solve the problems of the Jews while it simultaneously relieved the world of the burden of the "Jewish Problem." He believed that the Arabs living in the land of the future state would benefit so greatly from the economic and social improvement brought by the Jewish colonists that they would happily acquiesce to Jewish sovereignty there.[20]

The overwhelming majority of Zionists who settled the Land of Israel and lived among the Arabs of Palestine arrived at a similar conclusion, though for a different set of reasons. These were the adherents of socialist Zionism who represented both the primary leadership and largest body of Zionists from the end of the First World War onward. As a whole, socialist Zionists believed that friction between themselves and the local Arab inhabitants of the land was not a product of any genuine conflict of interests between the two peoples. Rather (and according to a variation of classic socialist analysis), the tensions were a result of agitation and incitement by reactionary elements among the Arabs themselves who feared the change and resultant loss of their own power represented by the progressive values of Zionist colonization. Thus the Arab effendis feared the inevitable moment when Jewish and Arab workers would unite and remove the yoke of bondage imposed upon them by their wealthy Arab capitalist masters. The British rulers, likewise, according to this analysis, engaged in a policy of "divide and rule" between the Jewish and Arab populations of Palestine in order to further their imperialist interests. Eventually, however, the Arabs would realize that socialism—as represented by Jewish socialist-Zionist ideologies—was the solution to their economic and social problems. In due course they would acquiesce even to the establishment of a Jewish government in Palestine, because it would honestly and ethically represent the interests of all the inhabitants of the state. There are no class or national interests that stand between Arabs and Jews. On the contrary, the problems with the Arabs would recede as society progressed and advanced.[21]

Ironically, and despite the frequent use of "conquest" and such slogans as "In blood and fire Judea fell, and in blood and fire shall Judea rise

[19] Shmuel Almog, *Zionism and History*, 116.
[20] Theodor Herzl, *Old-New Land* (New York: Bloch, 1960, first published in 1902 as a utopian novel in German as *Altneuland*), 124–130, Shapira 1992, 9–10.
[21] Shapira 1992, 117, 121.

again,"[22] socialist Zionists believed that their project was one of settlement and not militant conquest. They believed, despite the fact that they were generally disinterested in the Arabs culturally or socially, that their enterprise was one of peace and brotherhood in which they held out a helping hand of friendship to their Arab neighbors. Had they realized that their project was inherently in contradiction to the national aspirations of the local Arab inhabitants of Palestine, their socialist ideological system would probably have collapsed. This, according to Shapira, is one of the reasons that the leaders of the Labor movements were so slow in identifying the conflict with the Arabs as one of competing nationalisms.[23]

The early Zionists were deeply affected by the modern intellectual and social trends of their day, and showed an interest in developing a new kind of Jew who was more in tune with the social and philosophical trends of modernity. Long before Kook wrote of the need for physical exercise, Nordau had raised the need to create a "muscular Jewry" *(Muskeljudentum)* to a committee of the Zionist Congress of 1898.[24] Jews were typically identified by non-Jews through the stereotypes of intellectual ability but physical inferiority, he said. This encouraged anti-Semites to deride the Jews, and the Jews themselves came to internalize the negative perception of their neighbors.[25] By becoming strong of body and will, Jews would rise in the esteem of their neighbors, thereby heightening their self-esteem as well. The perceived need for physical exercise to develop strong nations was part of several discourses, often associated with state-building, in nineteenth to twentieth century Europe and America. It is hardly surprising that such a discourse would emerge among contemporary Jewish nation-builders as well. Nordau, of traditional Orthodox Jewish parents but highly modernized and secular himself, was one of the early leaders of Zionism. When he learned that the Jewish athletic association in Berlin called itself, perhaps not surprisingly, Bar Kokhba, he proclaimed, "Whoever embraces

---

[22] The slogan was adopted by *Hashomer*, the organization and defense force established in 1909. The line originates in *"Habiryonim,"* a poem by Yakov Cahan that extols those who fight and struggle physically with strength and vitality to redeem the Land of Israel (*Kitvei Ya'qov Kahan* [2 vols.] [Tel Aviv, 1948], Vol. 2, pp. 13–17), and it became the slogan of the Revisionist Movement (Menachem Begin, *The Revolt* [New York: Nash, 1977], pp. xi–xii).

[23] Shapira 1992, 122–123.

[24] Earlier, in 1893 though of less impact, the German Zionist, Fabius Schach, addressed the Young Israel Society in Berlin with the following words: "We national Jews must never be bookish people. Instead we must be men who relish life, who are worldly and armed to struggle for survival, to fight for their honor and for their aims." (Almog, *Zionism and History*, 109).

[25] For a careful examination and deconstruction of these images, see Daniel Boyarin, *Unheroic Conduct: The Rise of Heterosexuality and the Invention of the Jewish Man* (Berkeley and Los Angeles: University of California, 1997).

the slogan of 'Bar Kokhba' signifies that there is a latent aspiration for honor in his heart."[26]

Given the generally negative image of Bar Kokhba that prevailed in traditional Jewish literature after the failure of the Bar Kokhba Rebellion, it is of interest to note his revival in the late nineteenth and early twentieth centuries. Yael Zerubavel has chronicled the growth of the heroic image of Bar Kokhba among modernizing Jews who were struggling to redefine Jewish identity in ways that were consonant with their newly developing aspirations.[27] The trend toward remythologizing Bar Kokhba into a great military hero along with the final epic defense of Masada by the zealots was particularly pronounced in Zionist circles and became formalized in Israeli public education.[28]

The notion of normalizing the Jewish condition by restoring the body to its proper stature was a recurrent theme in Zionist writings. Such restoration and normalization tended to be associated with the "honest" work of farming the Land and also of self-defense. Military expressions of the *Muskeljude*, however, were not entertained by the Zionist Organization and the overwhelming majority of its European membership, at least not in the early period. Max Bodenheimer (d. 1940), one of the founders of the World Zionist Organization and among Herzl's first assistants, proposed to Herzl in 1903 to forge the Zionist Organization into a military type of movement based on hierarchy and discipline, similar to what he was familiar with in his Wilhelmine Germany. Some four months before Herzl's death, Bodenheimer urged him in a memo to build the nucleus of an armed force that would occupy Palestine militarily in order to protect the colonists from the "fanaticism" of the local majority population. Although Herzl promised to discuss the memo, he never did.[29]

But the situation in Palestine was different from Europe, and the pioneering settlers there immediately identified with the need for the new, more physical Jew in image and reality.[30] Honor, dignity, and self-respect

---

[26] Shapira 1992, 13.

[27] Yael Zerubavel, *Recovered Roots: Collective Memory and the Making of Israeli National Tradition* (Chicago: University of Chicago, 1995), 48–59, 96–113, 178–191; idem, *Bar Kokhba's Image*, in Schäfer, *The Bar Kokhba War Reconsidered*, 279–297.

[28] Zerubavel, "The Death of Memory and the Memory of Death: Masada and the Holocaust as Historical Metaphors," *Representations* 45 (Winter, 1994), 72–100.

[29] Almog, *Zionism and History,* 116–117.

[30] Ahad Ha-Am retained a more traditional view that stressed the need to retain and emphasize the moral and intellectual genius of the Jews over physical normalization (Hertzberg, 51–66), but the one Zionist ideologue that maintained a truly pacifist orientation was A. D. Gordon, an exceptional person on many accounts (Laquer, 285–286, Avineri, *The Making of Modern Zionism*, 151–158). On the conflict over self-image in Palestine, see also Israel Kolatt, "Religion,

were traits of great importance to the early Zionists deployed as workers in Palestine. They strove to create a new type of Jew who, unlike the exilic Jews who passively suffered pogroms and anti-Semitism in the Diaspora, would stand up and defend himself with honor in the Land of Israel. This aspiration was often couched in anti-religious rhetoric. From the *maskil*, Yehudah Leib Gordon (d. 1892), through Micah Joseph Berdichevsky (d. 1921) and onward, the blame was often placed by secularists on the attitude of Judaism and its leaders. It was the sin of passivity inculcated by the Jewish religion and its proponents that caused that Jews be uprooted from their land.[31] This passive state was spread throughout the Jewish communities through the experience of exile *(galut)*. The result was a negative and self-defeating communal "exilic condition" (or mentality) that is referred to disapprovingly as "exilism" *(galutiyut)*. The physical and psychic weaknesses, lack of dignity and self-respect, and victim mentality that arose in exile created a kind of collective quisling personality that invited attack from the gentiles. All would be rectified upon return to the Land and the re-creation of the ancient, proud personality that is so apparent from the narratives of the Bible.[32]

In the earliest period in Palestine, some young men adopted symbols of power from the local Bedouin, since they had few such symbols from their own recent tradition. Most illustrated histories of Zionism include classic photographs of Jewish guardsmen from the earliest waves of Zionist immigration to Palestine on horseback, wearing the Bedouin *kefiyya* (headdress) or high Tcherkessian wool hat, armed with weapons and ammunition belts slung over their shoulders. From the outset, and especially with the second wave of Zionist immigrants who began entering Palestine in 1904, the pioneers refused to be meek in the face of violence directed against them. They desperately tried to dissociate themselves from the image of the weak and helpless Diaspora Jew who would not or could not defend himself from attacks of the gentiles. This was the first stage in the evolution of an activist and eventually militant ethos among Jews who would establish a Jewish state through force of arms.

Because the inevitable conflict with the local Arabs had to be understood by the socialist Zionists in terms of classic socialist ideology rather

---

Society, and State during the Period of the National Home," in Shmuel Almog, Jehuda Reinharz, and Anita Shapira (eds.), *Zionism and Religion* (Hanover, NH: Brandeis University Press, 1998), 273–301.

[31] Luz, *Wrestling with an Angel*, 43–44; Almog, "The Role of Religious Values in the Second Aliyah," in *Zionism and Religion*, 244.

[32] Luz *Wrestling with an Angel*, 50–56.

than one of competing ethnic or national aspirations, it took a long time for them to imagine the possibility of an all-out military confrontation. Their naiveté was influenced also by their own experience as having been excluded from full participation in European culture and society, and many felt a certain solidarity and even excitement associating with "fellow-Semites" whom they admired as having been so deeply associated with the Land through agriculture and pastoralism. They believed that the class solidarity and unity of interests between Jewish and Arab workers would eventually transcend any enmity between them. Arabs, they believed, were not conscious of this fact only because they were being manipulated by the Arab ruling classes to view the Jews as exploiters. Optimistic almost to the end, they anticipated that the Arab majority would eventually see the error of their opposition to Zionist settlement and join the progressive forces. They therefore developed what Shapira terms a "defensive ethos" that would only protect against occasional Arab violence. Initiating violence was considered both immoral and unhelpful. They assumed that eventually, even defense would no longer be necessary.

This defensive ethos was revolutionary but not violent, militant but not vengeful or vicious. It taught not to hate the Arabs, but neither did it attempt to understand them. Above all, it taught that the Zionist project could be realized without real military violence. It was a settlement movement calling for the peaceful and incremental colonization of the Land. Although the language included the term, *kibbush*, it was not a military conquest. In the vocabulary of the socialists who upheld the defensive ethos, the term, "power," meant a "critical mass" of Jewish settlers who would tip the balance of leadership and influence to the modern Jews of Palestine, even if they were not yet the majority population.[33] It was inevitable, they believed, that the Jewish national home of Palestine would eventually become an independent nation-state.

In hindsight, with the perspective of time and detached analysis, the majority secular socialist concern for universal justice within a colonization movement that uprooted local populations seems bizarre. How could such a combination of opposing social forces and ideas make sense? The central leadership and majority of the Jewish population that internalized the "defensive ethos" usually discouraged overtly violent acting out among their members. The goal was highly aggressive activism but without violent political or settlement activities. The defensive ethos allowed

---

[33] The Zionists were not only fighting for influence against the local Arabs, but also against the entrenched power of the Old Yishuv, the long-established communities of Orthodox religious Jews who did not support their efforts.

its adherents to consider themselves part of the international movement of socialist revolutionaries in solidarity with oppressed peoples throughout the world, even including the local Arab inhabitants of Palestine that it was displacing.

The problem with this ideology was, of course, that it did not really fit the historical reality of Ottoman and Mandate Palestine. Palestinian Arabs were not in real labor solidarity with the Jews. They were rarely offered inclusion into the various worker cooperatives and unions that were established by the Jewish emigrants, and the Arab and Jewish economies grew into basically separate systems.[34] Most of all, although Arab antipathy to the Jewish settlers did include an economic component, the conflict between the two peoples was at base a conflict of nationalist aspirations.[35] The Zionist leadership of the Yishuv began to comprehend this fully only during the course of the Arab Revolt of 1936–1939.

## Who Is the Enemy? The Arab Revolt and Jewish Responses to Terror (1936–1939)

The Arab Revolt was not the first act of Arab violence against Jewish settlers. As early as 1908, when Palestine was still under the control of the Ottoman Empire, a brawl with no deaths erupted between Arabs and Jews in Jaffa, and was probably remembered because the Jews fought back against their attackers. The secret defense group called *Bar Giora*[36] was established about this time, which soon developed into a civil guard organization called *Hashomer* ("The Guard"). Several farmers and guardsmen of Hashomer were killed during the Ottoman period. In March of 1920, six settlers were killed by Arabs in the northern settlement of Tel Hai, including the famous and mythic farmer-fighter, Joseph Trumpeldor. In April of the same year, an angry crowd of Arabs during the Nebi Musa celebrations attacked Jews in Jerusalem. In May of 1921, more than a dozen Jews were killed in Jaffa, and in August of 1929, a series of riots throughout the

---

[34] Ilan Troen, *Imagining Zion: Dreams, Designs, and Realities in a Century of Jewish Settlement* (New Haven: Yale University Press, 2003), 47–59.

[35] I use the term "nationalist" in a general sense. That is, before the local Arabs considered themselves a Palestinian nation, the conflict was nevertheless one between two different peoples that could be defined ethnically, nationally or tribally. What it *wasn't* was a simple class issue.

[36] Simeon Bar Giora was a Jewish military leader in the Great Revolt against Rome (Josephus, *Wars* 9:3–12, in *Josephus: Complete Works* [Grand Rapids: Kregel, 1981], 540–543; Uriel Rappaport, "Bar Giora," in *EJ2* 3: 150–151).

length and breadth of Palestine killed many dozens of Jews, especially in the mixed Arab-Jewish cities of Hebron and Safed.

In 1920–21, a countrywide defense organization called the *Haganah* (meaning "defense") was formed. It was not always effective, such as during the Arab riots of 1921, and it was again caught largely off guard during the riots of 1929. The Haganah was an overwhelmingly secular Zionist phenomenon, but the question of religious Orthodox participation in the military defense organization arose, at least within some yeshivas, in response to the 1929 riots. Among the Orthodox communities willing to consider organizing into the Haganah, the overwhelming issue under discussion was not whether defense of Jewish communities in Palestine constituted Commanded War or some kind of legal definition that would condone fighting. The issues under discussion, rather, were whether it is permissible for religiously observant Jews to work together with nonreligious Jews, or whether certain activities such as military training or actions would occur on the Sabbath and religious holidays.

The commander of the Jerusalem region of the Haganah, Yakov Pat, tells of his meeting with Rabbi Abraham Isaac Kook about forming a defense unit of observant Jews in 1933.

> I went to [see] him, and he began by stating that he requires the idea of defense, and that in his view, defense takes precedence over Sabbath [restrictions]. However, he wanted to know whether it was possible to avoid training on the Sabbath. I tried to explain that the lack of time is a major hardship, and because of that it is necessary to take advantage of every free hour and train on the Sabbath. And for the sake of secrecy, it was more secure to train on the Sabbath because it was customary for our youth to practice on the Sabbath, which could be used as an effective screen [to hide the training] from the [Mandatory] Power. The rabbi listened to my words and finally said that of all things, he asks of me to allow separate training for the religious during weekdays. All of my suggestions for training without weapons and the like were rejected by him.... (when I tried to be clever by saying that perhaps it is best for the yeshiva students to be integrated with the "heretics" *(apikorsim)* so that they influence them positively... the rabbi answered that it seems to him that it could work the opposite way...).[37]

The Arab Revolt that began in 1936 was different from previous violence. It began as a spontaneous response to killings and counter-killings between

---

[37] Bramson, *The Last Days*, p. 123.

Arabs and Jews in April of that year, and it mobilized thousands of Arabs from every stratum of society.[38] Preparations were soon made to organize a general Arab strike, which resulted in tremendous grassroots support from broad segments of the Arab population. Arab leaders responded by forming the Arab Higher Committee, which turned what had begun as a violent protest into an organized rebellion that continued in one form or another for some three years. There was no denying the nationalist sentiment of this rebellion. It was an organized political action under a central command. Most of the Arab population of Palestine was disciplined in their support of the actions, leaving the Jews with little doubt of the national nature of the revolt.

Although most Jews were unwilling to give up the old ideology of settlement and the socialist hope of brotherhood with the Arab working class, they began to understand the conflict in terms that would require rethinking the use of force. It was during this period that the meaning of *power* began to shift from the sense of a "critical mass" to the more familiar physical-military sense. The initial response of the Labor leadership to the Revolt was typical of the defensive ethos. The statement of the Mapai Central Committee on May Day, only a little over a week after the outbreak read, "We come with true aspirations for peace, dignity, and mutual assistance. We do not come as conquerors but as builders. Yet we shall not retreat in the face of bloody attacks."[39]

Many socialists dismissed the Arab use of terror as "fascist" and denied the nationalist roots of the uprising. The Jewish communal response included the policy of self-restraint *(havlagah),* both because of the ethical principles of the established ethos and because of the pragmatic assessment that self-restraint would turn the British Mandate authorities in favor of the Jews. This decision accentuated the internal tension within the Zionist self-image, because the position of restraint pitted the deeply held self-image of the Zionist activist as brave, bold, and uncompromising against that of the cowardly, helpless, and submissive Diaspora Jew that they were so desperately trying to discard.

While the majority was struggling with how to respond to the ongoing violence of the Arab Revolt, a group of militant activists formed an organization dedicated to violent retaliation called *Etzel*, an acronym for *Irgun Tzeva'i Le'umi* (National Military Organization), often shortened to

---

[38] Baruch Kimmerling and Joel Migdal, *Palestinians: The Making of a People* (New York: Free Press, 1993), 96–123; Tom Segev, *One Palestine, Complete: Jews and Arabs under the British Mandate* transl. Haim Watzman (New York: Metropolitan, 2000), 366–374, 382–392.

[39] Shapira 1992, 223.

"the Irgun."[40] The kinds of retaliatory acts they committed would be classified today as terrorism and were indeed classified as such by the British mandate authorities.[41] Others outside the Labor camp such as the influential poet, Uri Zvi Greenberg, wrote in support of violent reprisals and other militant acts in response to the violence of the Arab Revolt. Not only were such acts of terror considered by the Etzel to be an effective means of dealing with Arab violence, they were also considered deeds of glory that gave the Etzel activists an exalted role in the leadership of Zionism.

Of particular importance for this book is the influence of the radical periphery's spirited military activism and ongoing violence on the Zionist center. The meaning of self-restraint (and hence the response that it engendered) changed in the Labor camp during the three-year period of the Revolt, from pure defense of Jewish settlements and neighborhoods, to defense in conjunction with military actions that today would be called "anti-terror tactics." Small, well-trained mobile units called FOSH (for field squads) would be sent out to lie in wait for Arab squads and gangs before they made contact with Jewish areas. This, in turn, helped further erode the old defensive ethos and replace it with a far more proactive stance.

The evolving forceful nature of Jewish attack included certain tactical and ideological restraints to excessive violence. These tend to be categorized under the term, "purity of arms" *(tohar hanneshek),* wherein fighters make use of their weaponry and power only for the fulfillment of the mission, and innocent bystanders may not be injured. But this ideology emerged as a reaction to the terrorism that was practiced by Etzel and the general change among more mainstream groups in the direction of violent reprisal. Benny Morris has documented how the Haganah, as well as Etzel and Lechi,[42] engaged in both retaliatory and preemptive actions that would be considered acts of terror today.[43]

---

[40] For a recent study, see Judith Tydor Baumer, *The "Bergson Boys" and the Origins of Contemporary Zionist Militancy*, transl. Dena Ordan (Syracuse, NY: Syracuse University, 2005).

[41] One of the first to attempt such acts was Shlomo Ben Yosef, who tried to attack an Arab bus on the Rosh Pina-Safed road in 1938 as an act of violent revenge for the Arab murder of Jews on the Golan Heights. No one was hurt in his attempt, but he was caught by the British Mandate authorities and hanged. Ben Yosef was remembered in 2005 when a group of ultra-rightist Jews held a *pulsa dinura* ceremony at his grave, in which they attempted through magic to bring about the death of Prime Minister Ariel Sharon for pushing through the disengagement process from the Gaza Strip, just as they did thirty-one days before the murder of Yitzak Rabin in 1995 *(Yedi`ot Acharonot)* July 27, 2005, p. A-2.

[42] A radical break-off from *Etzel*, organized by Avraham (Ya'ir) Stern and called the "Stern Gang" by the British Mandate authorities, functioned as a purely terrorist group (Robert John and Sami Hadawi, *The Palestine Diary* 2 vols. [New York: New World Press, 1970] Vol. 1, 344). *Lechi* is an acronym for "Fighters for the Liberty of Israel" *(lochamei cherut yisrael).*

[43] Benny Morris, *Israel's Border Wars* (Oxford: Oxford University Press, 1993), 185–187.

The Orthodox religious community of Palestine was divided, of course, between Zionists and non-Zionists (which included anti-Zionists), and each of these camps was further divided into a number of different groups and organizations. The religious non-Zionists repeatedly opposed any Jewish violent reprisals, while the religious Zionists were divided over the issue. Eliezer Don-Yehiya chronicles the inclination among some religious Zionists toward violent retaliation that directly paralleled the position of secularists who advocated acts of terror.[44]

The religious Zionist camp was divided between the Mizrachi and Hapoel Hamizrachi. The Mizrachi inclined toward a combination of traditional Jewish and Political Zionist ideas, including the aspiration for "greater Israel" *(eretz yisra'el hashelemah)* that would include all of the biblical lands. Although Hapoel Hamizrachi would not object to such an objective, it leaned toward the more universalistic values of the socialist movements and was inclined to be more experimental with religious ideas such as promoting a more egalitarian role for women. Although religiously observant, Hapoel Hamizrachi tried to become part of the secularist Workers Federation called the Histradrut[45] in the 1920s, but was rejected. Thereafter it functioned as part of the world Mizrachi movement. There were frequent conflicts between Hapoel Hamizrachi and Mizrachi because of the socialist trends of the former, but there was also a certain amount of crossover between the memberships of the two groups. Hapoel Hamizrachi came out strongly and consistently in favor of restraint *(havlagah)*, and strongly condemned indiscriminate acts of violence against Arabs.

When the newspaper *Hatzofeh*, the mouthpiece of the International Mizrachi Movement, started publication in the midst of the Arab Uprising in September, 1937, most of its articles condemned acts of retaliation. *Hatzofeh* represented both Mizrachi and Hapoel Hamizrachi, and its arguments regarding retaliation were based on both moral issues and on pragmatic ones, so it is not always possible to determine which stream is represented in its editorials. On the question of whether violent reprisals would be helpful to the Zionist cause in the long run, the newspaper declared, "The conclusion is: 'We shall show restraint therefore, on moral grounds and also from the [perspective] of the national accounting.' "[46]

---

[44] Eliezer Don-Yehiya, "Religion and Political Terrorism: Orthodox Jews and Retaliation during the 1936–39 'Arab Revolt' " (Hebrew), *Hatziyyonut* 17 (1993), 155–190.

[45] *Histadrut ha`ovdim be'eretz yisra'el*: the Federation of Workers in the Land of Israel, the overall Jewish labor organization in Palestine and later in the State of Israel.

[46] Don-Yehiya, 169.

The Chief Rabbis of Mandate Palestine, both Ashkenazi (Isaac Herzog) and Sepharadi (Yakov Meir), wrote stridently and consistently against engaging in any kind of violent responses to Arab terror. Their reasoning followed Jewish religious tradition closely and warned openly against harming innocent people. Most of the Yishuv agreed that restraint was called for, both for moral reasons and based on the belief that the British favor the side taking the moral high ground.

They were shocked when the British produced the White Paper of May 17, 1939 severely limiting Jewish immigration to Mandate Palestine.[47] *Hatzofeh* reacted by condemning the British for de facto encouraging violence and punishing restraint by rewarding Arab violence with the White Paper. "This is the lesson we learn," it said, but it nevertheless insisted on a policy of restraint.[48]

*Hatzofeh* was criticized severely for this position by Rabbi Bloi, a representative of the (non-Zionist to anti-Zionist) Agudah, because its position suggested that there might be a political usefulness in terror even though it must be banned for religious and moral reasons. To Bloi there should not have even been a discussion of its possible usefulness. Rabbi Isaiah Shapira of Hapoel Hamizrachi also condemned terror and cited God's words to David in the Bible: "You shall not build a House in My name because you are a man of war and spilled blood."[49] David was punished, he said, even though the blood he spilled was actually legitimate because his victims were not innocent. How much worse is the spilling of the blood of innocent victims of acts of reprisal against civilians. *Hapoel Hamizrachi* wrote:

> "This is a holy war *(milchamah qedoshah).* Let us not profane it by spilling the blood of the innocent and let us not walk in the way of the nations around us. We refuse to ruin [50] our holy war through murdering innocent people, and we will not defile the land by polluting it with [innocent] blood.... Let us not spoil the moral purity of our war. The Rock of Israel will appear for our counsel and will send His holy help."[51]

---

[47] On the 1939 White Paper, see John and Hadawi, Vol. 1, 315–320, 357–359; Tom Segev, *One Palestine*, 440–443, Sachar, *History of Israel*, 204–226.

[48] June 19, 1939, lead article entitled, "Whither?" *(le 'an)*, cited in Don-Yehiya, 170–171.

[49] 1 Chron. 22:8.

[50] Literally, "We will not fail *(lo nakhshil)* our holy war."

[51] Don-Yehiya, 172. Hapoel Hamizrachi was consistent in its opposition to indiscriminate anti-Arab violence, with leaders such as Yeshayahu Bernstein and Moshe Shapira speaking actively against it. Mizrachi was less so (Elie Holzer, "Attitudes Towards the Use of Military Force in

Note that the term here is "holy war" *(milchamah qedoshah)* but not Commanded War *(milchemet mitzvah),* the operative term in Rabbinic Literature for divinely authorized warring. The meaning of *milchamah qedoshah* in this document is more akin to "holy struggle." Unlike the Hapoel Hamizrachi and non-Zionist Agudat Yisrael Workers' Party *(Poalei Agudat Yisrael),* Mizrachi did not present a single unified position condemning the terror because, aside from the fact that engaging in terror compromised the unity of the Zionist leadership that they all supported, some of its leadership at least half-heartedly supported it.

Rabbi Yehudah Leib Maimon (Fishman), one of the most important leaders of Mizrachi and their representative on the directorate of the Jewish Agency, publicly condemned the initiation of retaliatory violence. However, he felt that "...we are guilty for the deaths [of five Jews by Arab terrorists in 1937] because of our unceasing sermonizing on behalf of restraint." He warned that the Jews of the Yishuv were teaching their children to be cowards, and that if he were young, he himself would "go out and take revenge for the blood of Jews that was spilt."[52] Maimon tried to base his reasoning on Jewish sources, saying: "Our religion opposes murder and the spilling of blood, but in these days, according to Maimonides, one must consider every individual of the community from which the criminals came as if he himself were [also] a criminal."[53] Maimon did not claim to speak for his movement, though he carried tremendous weight within Mizrachi. His words cited here were recorded in the minutes of meetings of the directorate of the Jewish Agency, not printed in a public forum.

Rabbi Meir Bar-Ilan (Berlin), the president of Mizrachi, did not fully support the position of restraint. According to those who knew him at the time of the Arab Revolt, Bar-Ilan was unhappy with the policy of restraint, which allowed "...the Arabs to shoot at us...as if we were birds." Menachem Ussishkin, a secularist and one of the most influential leaders of the Zionist Movement, said in a meeting of the Zionist Workers' Committee that Jewish morality forbids the killing of innocents even if doing so would bring great progress to the national standing, saying "If we were told...today to kill innocent Arabs so that tomorrow the White Paper would be withdrawn, I would not agree to do it." In response to Ussishkin when he cited "Do not commit murder" from the Ten Commandments, Berlin said, "We also have the verse, 'do not let a single person [of the

---

Ideological Currents of Religious Zionism," in Schiffman and Wolowelsky, eds., *War and Peace in the Jewish Tradition,* 379–384).

[52] Don-Yehiya, 173.
[53] Don-Yehiya, 174–175.

enemy] live' "[54] Berlin did not explain exactly what he meant by quoting the verse, and he was verbally taken to task for it by other members at the meeting. When he was asked directly, "Do you agree with terror?" He answered: "Terror—no, response—yes."[55]

These views of the two principal rabbinic leaders of Mizrachi were expressed in closed meetings. The official organs of Mizrachi consistently condemned acts of terror by Jews. Only rarely was there an exception. In November, 1938, an article in *Hatzofeh* claimed that although Jewish morality condemned hurting others for personal gain, it required everything for the good of the national whole. The Revisionists out of which Etzel sprang, however, claimed that the "Jewish morality" cited among those who counseled restraint was not really Jewish morality at all, but rather Christian morality, and that the Jewish God is a "zealous God," the "Lord of Armies."[56]

Newspapers and other organs of both Zionist and non-Zionist Orthodox Jews expressed near-disbelief that Jews would be involved in acts of terrorist violence against Arabs during this period. They denied it initially, some suggesting even that Arab communists committed the violence in order to stimulate a reaction. When it became evident that Jews and even Orthodox Jews were involved in these acts, they tended to explain them as a result of non-Jewish influence. The Jewish perpetrators were influenced by the mores of foreign nations or had abandoned Jewish tradition. They called for "healing from this sickness" of violence by "a complete return to the Source of Israel by abandoning the broken sources of the strangers that have taken over our souls, and an absolute return to the God of Israel."[57]

Agudat Yisrael tended to take the most strident and consistent anti-terrorist stance among the religious parties. Don-Yehiya considers this to be a result of their being more deeply influenced by traditional Jewish exilic thinking, culture, and history. The Agudah tended to avoid supporting their views with traditional Jewish textual sources, however, because they did not want to assign religious significance to modern political and national issues by treating them according to Jewish law and tradition.

The Zionist Orthodox parties, in contrast, tended to justify their positions through citation of traditional sources. Their openness to modernizing ideas in fact influenced them to take innovative positions that differed

---

[54] Don-Yehiya cites him as saying in the Hebrew, *lo techayeh kol nefesh*, but the reference must be to Deut. 20:16: *lo techayeh kol neshamah.*

[55] Don-Yehiyeh, 175.

[56] Usually translated as "Lord of Hosts."

[57] Don-Yehiyeh, 178–185.

from those of their more traditional compatriots, yet they used traditional styles of interpretation to justify the modernizing positions. Although some were deeply influenced by modern socialist-democratic and universalist values, they tended to present support for their ideas through the Jewish moral tradition, and especially the biblical prophets, in order to ground them religiously and thus demonstrate their consistency with Judaism.[58]

Overall, therefore, the Orthodox religious establishment of the Yishuv was ambivalent toward Jewish acts of terror against Arabs during the Arab Revolt. Most denounced the acts of their Jewish compatriots publicly, but although no polls were taken at the time, their tremendous frustration over lack of Jewish success in responding to the violence generated an inclination toward acts of terror in return. These counterterrorism attacks were called "acts of reprisal" *(pe'ulot tagmul)*. They were not defined as terrorism by the Jewish community, of course, and the idea of engaging in these actions was inspired by the Arabs themselves. The result, however, was violence perpetrated against civilian as well as irregular military targets. Jewish acts of terror during the Arab Revolt parallel what we will observe was carried out two generations later by Jewish radicals engaged in what they defined as Commanded War. The Orthodox Jews of the 1930s, however, would never have considered that such a definition could apply to them because the notion of Commanded War had not yet been revived. It would take two major miracles before the dormant notion of Jewish holy war would be reawakened.

## After the Revolt: The Road to War

By burning fields, orchards, and forests planted by Jewish settlers as part of their dream of making the desert bloom, the Arab Revolt not only targeted individual Jews and their settlements, but also the entire colonization enterprise. These acts hurt the pioneers spiritually as well as physically and were rightly interpreted as attempts to destroy the entire Zionist program. They were also a huge jolt to the self-image of the altruistic, moral pioneer. Meanwhile, the voices of fascism had grown powerful in much of the world outside Palestine during the period of the Arab Revolt (1936–1939). Fascist regimes in Spain, Germany, and Italy were established and on the rise while the "progressive forces" of the Soviet Union and the international progressive movements were in retreat. The propaganda of

---

[58] Don-Yehiyeh, 189–190.

both fascism and its detractors glorified heroes who exhibited great physical courage and militancy.

As is well known, the British attempt to quell Arab unrest with the White Paper severely limited further Jewish immigration to Palestine, exactly at the time that Diaspora Jews were feeling more endangered than they had been in decades. These external developments further encouraged a surge of activism in the Labor Zionist camp. Such factors, including the evolution in military method from pure defense to defense in conjunction with preemptive and offensive actions, did not immediately change the overall worldview of the Zionist majority, but they moved it toward a more militant position that would eventually come to see war as the only possible means to resolve the situation.[59]

The feeling was augmented during the early 1940s by a number of other factors. The Arabs continued to warn that they would never share government equally with the Jews in Palestine; indeed, they freely stated their intention to uproot the Jews from the area. With the outbreak of the Second World War and the growing reports about the evil fate of the Jews of Europe, the Zionist leadership concluded that it had to be prepared for military solutions to political problems. Moreover, with Field Marshal Rommel's penetration of Egypt and near-conquest of Palestine, Palestinian Jews were suddenly confronted with the possibility that they would someday be required to survive in Palestine without the buffer of the Mandate authorities and their forces. During this period as well, a new generation of native Jews in Palestine was reaching adulthood. Educated to be proud, confident, physically strong, and to love the biblical Land of Israel as their own possession, this generation was ready and eager to demonstrate its native connection to the Land through physical means. "The qualities of the warrior distinguished this generation from the preceding one, and endowed it with a special standing. The life-style of the fighter became the key formative experience for its members.... The issue of confronting a competing national movement, which had been a considerable worry for their fathers, was unimportant for them."[60]

Despite the movement from a defensive to a proactive ethos within the majority Zionist population of Palestine prior to 1948, there remained a palpable ambivalence with regard to the use, and certainly the veneration, of military force. This is quite evident in the recurring phrase, "there is no choice" *(eyn bererah)* in reference to fighting both the Arabs and

---

[59] Shapira 1992, 242–257.
[60] Shapira 1992, 360–363.

the British. The young Jewish fighters referred to themselves as warriors rather than soldiers, meaning that they both valued and considered themselves to be citizen fighters rather than part of a professional army. There perhaps remained in the psyches of even the native-born Palestinian Jews, born of many centuries of exile at the mercy of great armies, a wariness or fear of the professional soldier. Although tempered over the years, the socialist credo with its sense of universal moral commitment also tended to keep extreme nationalist zeal in check. These factors did not prevent the commanders of Jewish forces in the period leading up to and during the War of Independence in 1948 from making hard and even brutal decisions. It also did not prevent certain atrocities from being perpetrated by Jews during this period.

No attempt is being made here to portray Jewish fighters as more or as less humane or moral than other fighters engaged in similar struggles. It is difficult to imagine any military struggle without some factions captivated by the thrill of war and others opposed to violence as a means of resolving conflict. My intent here is to indicate how a "national ethos" of the majority Zionist community of pre-state Palestine, including the religious Zionists, was formed out of the historical timidity of their Diaspora existence and fashioned into one of proud defender of their native Land of Israel. It evolved into an ethos that first accepted and then advocated proactive aggression in order to ensure the success of the Zionist project. This process was largely complete by the end of World War II, and certainly so by the year of the establishment of the State of Israel in 1947–48.

It should be noted here that despite the increase in militancy of the Yishuv toward both the British and the Arabs, and despite the increase in British and Arab violence directed against the Jews of Palestine, there was surprisingly little expression of hatred directed by Jews toward the Palestinian Arabs. This was partly a result of the humanitarian socialist ethos of brotherhood among all peoples, but it was also a basic part of the "defensive ethos" specific to the mainstream Yishuv that taught a philosophy of tolerance toward the Other. When this attitude became difficult in the face of the real experience of Arab violence and terror, a careful distinction was made between "good Arabs" and "bad Arabs." As a result, anger and hatred were not intended to be directed against the Arabs as a whole.

Yet there was no great love of Arabs, either. The agenda of the Zionists was to create Jewish "normalcy." With some exceptions, there was little appreciation for or even curiosity about Arab culture. To most Zionists, Arabs lived in the Land of Israel more in the abstract than in any concrete sense, and their image was governed by typical stereotypes as backward, premodern or unmodern, and violent. As the tensions increased during and after the Arab Revolt, Jews and Arabs became increasingly alienated from one another. This allowed for increased mythologizing on both sides and a kind of dehumanizing that tolerated the increased use of violent force. Especially among the second generation of Palestinian-born Jews, the feeling was neither love nor hatred toward Arabs, but rather, apathy.[61] Yet throughout the prestate period and even to this day, the official message of the Zionist leadership has been that Jews must take up arms to defend themselves and their legitimate rights to live and prosper on the Land, but they must not hate even the enemy that tries to destroy them.[62]

[61] Shapira 1992, 130, 180–181, 362.

[62] Statement by Israeli President Moshe Katzav during the violent period of the *Intifadat al-Aqsa* at the annual commemoration of soldiers of Israel who died in defense of the state, April 24, 2001 and broadcast by national television.

CHAPTER 12 | From Holocaust to Holy War
*Israel's War of Independence*

There is no ruling [*halakhah*] that forbids us from establishing a
Jewish state with the permission of the nations before the coming of
the redeemer.

RABBI ISAAC HALEVI HERZOG, FIRST ASHKENAZI CHIEF RABBI
OF THE STATE OF ISRAEL

## The Holocaust

It is known to many observers how profound and overwhelming has been
the impact of the Holocaust on world Jewry. Not as many are aware of how
the Holocaust has affected Jews in sometimes radically different ways.
I sketch out here two polar responses, each exemplifying one end of a complex spectrum.

For some Jews, the Holocaust has taught that they must never avoid caring for the welfare of all peoples, for as victims of the most horrific case of
genocide, Jews must always shoulder their awesome and unique collective
responsibility to ensure that such a horror never occurs to people of any
religion, race, nationality, or other defining characteristic anywhere or any
time again. Others have drawn a quite different conclusion, namely, that
the blindness and indifference of the world to the unimaginable suffering
of the Jews abdicates the eternal victims from responsibility for attending
to the needs of the world, requiring only that they engage in any and all
means to ensure their own survival. Henceforth, and in light of its own
profound wickedness in either engaging in or turning a blind eye to the
genocide of the Jews, the world has no moral right to judge the morality of
Jewish behavior.

During that period of unspeakable horror, the Jews of Europe were not organized to defend themselves physically, since they were scattered among the nations of Europe and had no independent political body or military force for defense and rescue. The situation of Exile, of being "scattered among the nations," to use a biblical term (Ezek. 36:19), was accepted at the time by virtually the entire Orthodox Jewish world as normative. Jews had lived for many centuries according to the restrictions of the Three Vows by refraining from actions that could be understood as "rebelling against the nations of the world."[1] It is important to note, however, that Jews engaged in armed resistance against the Nazis in many areas, from urban ghettos to villages and the forests of Eastern Europe, and as individual members of organized resistance and allied armies. Toward the end of the war, the British allowed the formation of a "Jewish Brigade" made up mostly of Jews living in Mandate Palestine who fought the German army, especially in Northern Italy. Jewish fighters in these groups included the religiously observant. Formal justification for this fighting was unnecessary, since it was so obviously a matter of survival.[2]

A vast literature has developed over the past fifty years that treats the Holocaust and its complex and multifaceted effects on the Jewish self-image. This chapter is limited to the rare reference by Orthodox thinkers at the time who invoked its overwhelming effect on Jewish history in their view on war. The one brief entry with this angle into the maze of Holocaust writings was written by a rabbi from Budapest who died in a cattle car of a Nazi transport from Auschwitz.

## The Holocaust and Its Impact on Rabbi Yisakhar Taikhtel

Yisakhar Shlomo Taikhtel was born in 1885 in Hungary and raised in an ultra-Orthodox, anti-Zionist community. An exceptional student, he soon had the opportunity to lead a community and became a leader of Hungarian Jewry. Like the overwhelming majority of the ultra-Orthodox *(Haredi)* community, he opposed Zionism and even wrote against it in the *Yiddische Zeitung* in Munkatsh in 1936.[3] However, as he personally witnessed the destruction of European Jewry at the hand of the Nazis during the Second World War, he changed his view of Zionism entirely. He came to the

---

[1] See chapter four.

[2] Saving lives *(pikuach nefesh)* overrules all commandments in Judaism aside from the prohibitions against idolatry, illegal sexual relations, and murder (BT Yoma 82a).

[3] When Munkatch (Mukachevo) was under Czechoslovakian rule.

conclusion that all Jewry, including Haredi Jewry, was obligated to join even with secular Zionists in immigrating to the Land of Israel and building it up. This position was spelled out in his book, *The Joyful Mother of Children*,[4] which has achieved a significant level of popularity in Israel, especially among the religious Zionist community.[5]

The book presents a powerful argument against the anti-Zionist Orthodox position forbidding immigration to the Land of Israel and building up the land. According to Taikhtel, his personal experience of the Holocaust caused him to understand that the exile was intended only to be a temporary punishment for the sins of Israel. Unfortunately, however, Jews had become accustomed to living apart from the Land and have therefore mistakenly considered exile a "second home" to their authentic home in the land of the Bible. Their banishment had become easy during certain periods, but God always reminded his people not to become accustomed to exile by bringing calamities upon them. Jews have nevertheless persisted, mistakenly; they "rejected the desirable land and put no faith in God's promise" (Ps. 106:24–25) because building up the Land was so difficult. The cycle of calamities then became a normal state of affairs and was accepted as such, so that Jews failed to understand that their suffering in exile was actually caused by their refusal to take the initiative to resettle the Land of Israel. The Holocaust was the final and unmistakable sign that Jews must reestablish sovereignty over their ancient land. Taikhtel suffocated to death in a sealed cattle car that shipped survivors of Auschwitz ahead of the conquering Soviet army in 1945. His manuscript survived.

Taikhtel counters all the well-known anti-Zionist arguments of ultra-Orthodox Jewry, from the claim that moving en masse to Palestine will bring disaster as an attempt to "force the hand of God" to the argument that good Jews are forbidden to join forces with the ungodly and anti-religious sinners who call themselves secular Zionists. The arguments that concern us here are those treating war and the conquest of the Land.

Taikhtel wrote that the conquest of the Land of Israel by Joshua occurred through natural means *(derekh hateva`)* rather than through a divine miracle. If Joshua's generation had been worthy, God would have caused Israel

---

[4] Hebrew: *Em habanim semechah*. The title is a direct citation of the last line of Psalm 113, which is found in the Jewish liturgical section called "Praise" *(Hallel)* sung during festivals and certain other joyful occasions.

[5] First published in Budapest by Salomon Katzburg in 1943 two years before Taikhtel's death, reprinted in New York by H. S. Taikhtel in 1969, reprinted again in Jerusalem in 1983 by Machon Pri Ha'Aretz and subsequently released with the same printing by Kol Mevasser in 1998. The work has been translated by Pesach Schindler under the title, *Restoration of Zion as a Response During the Holocaust* (NY: Ktav, 1999). Citations are from the Kol Mevasser edition.

to control the Land of Israel through direct divine intervention.[6] God was not entirely absent, of course, but divine intervention occurred in the form of a "natural miracle" *(nes tiv`i)* rather than a divine miracle. This is why God commands Joshua to be strong and courageous, and uses similar language in relation to the keeping of the commandments. Because Joshua and the Israelites of his generation were indeed strong and courageous, not only in war but also in the study of Torah and observance of commandments, they succeeded in the Conquest.[7] Similarly, Ezra succeed in bringing masses of Jews back to the land centuries later because he studied Torah and taught precepts and commandments to Israel.[8] Therefore, if Israel will be strong and courageous in the two tasks of keeping the commandments and actively engaging in settlement, it can again "conquer" the Land of Israel even in this day.

Conquest in and of itself is not adequate to justify sovereignty over a land, for a conquest can be nullified by a subsequent conquest. God therefore clarified in the Bible that Israel *inherited* the Land of Israel.[9] The Land is a divine inheritance that passes throughout the generations, giving Israel the authority to reclaim the land, even through conquest, though the conquest will be successful only if it is combined with Torah study and observance of God's commandments.

During the years of devastation during World War II and the Holocaust, European Jewish energies were devoted to survival. Little was written on Jewish thought and practice during this period, and little of what managed to be written survived to be published. Taikhtel's book is an example of the few contemporary writings that were published in Europe during that difficult time. The conditions of Europe and the Jews' simple need to survive inhibited the writing—though not the thinking—about such issues as war. The broadest spectrum of the Jewish community never ceased debating the issues of dignity, power, and survival in relation to Judaism and Jewish identity during the war years, even though little was published.

During the war the Jews of Palestine were occupied with their own survival and were confronted with three major sources of fear and distraction: the increasingly active competition and antagonism between them and local Palestinian Arabs; constant friction and jockeying for position with

---

[6] Recall the position of Kook cited in chapter 10 and based on traditional sources, that were it not for the sin of Israel in worshiping the golden calf, Israel would have occupied the Land of Canaan without war.

[7] Taikhtel, 57.

[8] See Ezra 7:10 (Taikhtel, 59).

[9] Taikhtel, 53–54.

the British Mandatory Government; and the distinct possibility of an eventual German invasion. After the War, the third distraction was replaced with the huge problem of European Jewish refugees, while the intensity of the other two was ratcheted up to an increasingly high level until the 1947–48 war. This is the situation that brings us to the final period leading to the establishment of the State of Israel.

## Who Broke Which Vow?

The establishment of the State of Israel marked an absolute about-face for Jewish history. Never since the destruction of the Jerusalem Temple had there been a sovereign Jewish state, a polity wherein Jews would establish their own political and military leadership. Jews had been conditioned toward quietism for many centuries. Active political and military engagement marked a revolutionary change in the Jewish self-concept, and it had a profound impact on all Zionist factions, including the religious.[10] This radical development was viewed with favor and tremendous enthusiasm by most Jews throughout the world.[11] It also required some very serious innovation in thinking among all segments of world Jewry. One important series of adjustments had to be made with regard to Jews serving in a Jewish army.

With the end of the Mandate looming and hostilities between Jews and Arabs escalating, the Jewish community of Palestine was required in very short time to create a system of public governance and organized armed forces. Its Jewish citizens would naturally be drafted to join the armed forces and to fight its wars. For the Orthodox, joining a Jewish army raised a number of immediate issues, such as the observance of Jewish dietary laws and the Sabbath in the army and in battle, treatment of enemy soldiers on the battlefield or as captives, and the induction of women into the armed forces.

One of the most pressing questions for religious Zionists was whether a Jewish army in the Land of Israel represents "going up as a wall" against

---

[10] Samuel Heilman, "Quiescent and Active Fundamentalisms: The Jewish Cases," in Martin Marty and R. Scott Appleby, *Accounting for Fundamentalisms*, vol. 4 Chicago: U. of Chicago Press, 1994, 173–196.

[11] There were exceptions to this enthusiasm, of course, such as among the ultra-Orthodox anti-Zionist Satmar Hasidim and Neturei Karta, and a few other groups such as the American Counsel for Judaism that was founded by a group of Reform rabbis who opposed the rising nationalist sentiment associated with Zionism and the establishment of the State of Israel (Thomas Kolsky, *Jews Against Zionism: The American Council for Judaism 1942–1948* [Philadelphia: Temple University, 1990]).

the will of God.[12] If the Jews are required by God to live in a state of exile, a Jewish army must be forbidden and Orthodox Jews must refrain from joining. But with the Holocaust and the end of the Mandate, perhaps this time is different. Could these be signs of something greater than human history? Could this upheaval be a sign that God has willed the beginning of the messianic age and these the birth pangs of the messiah? Then perhaps Jews are obligated as a community to indeed "go up as a wall" to the Land of Israel and fight to establish a Jewish political state. But if this is the case, then who has the authority to send a Jewish army out to war if there is no king and no Sanhedrin? Is fighting in the new Jewish armed forces an act of defense because of the state's position of being surrounded by belligerent nations? Should fighting therefore be considered a Commanded War? Would victory in a war of independence be equivalent to the conquest of Joshua? If so, does it render war for political control a Commanded War? If conquest is a divine command, then what is the geographical limit beyond which Commanded War becomes Discretionary War, since the biblical references to the boundaries of the Land of Israel are not uniform? How does one determine which of the several different biblical representations of the borders of the Land apply? How should a religiously observant Jew react to a commanding officer, the parliament, or head of state who commands engaging in an action that might be defined as a Discretionary War? Must he fight, or can he return home to marry his beloved or simply opt out if he is disheartened (Deut. 20:7–9)? Are preemptive attacks allowed as a legitimate component of Commanded War (BT Sotah 44b)? Under what conditions would they be considered so? Can or should women be drafted? Must they be, based on the requirement that "everyone must go forth, even a bridegroom from his chamber and a bride from her bridal pavilion" (Mishnah Sota 8:7)? May women join the armed forces voluntarily? Should there be a difference in the rules of engagement against nearby enemies as opposed to enemies far from the borders of the Land of Israel (Deut. 20:10–18)?

These and dozens more questions about the problem of observing stringent Jewish ritual and moral-ethical commandments under the difficult conditions of army life, on the Sabbath, or in situations of battle have occupied religious thinkers and jurisprudents from the establishment of the State of Israel to this day. One category of discussion in the Orthodox world is the existential meaning of making war under the flag of a sovereign Jewish nation. The notion of Commanded War had to reenter the

---

[12] This issue as well as the others raised in this paragraph are treated in chapters 4–6.

conversation among religious Zionists, and that conversation influenced the discourse and opinions about war and about the enemy in the larger Jewish world as well.

## The 1947–48 War of Independence and a Sovereign Jewish Army

Like all wars that mark the emergence of a new national entity, Israel's War of Independence had a profound impact on the state's national mythologies and collective self-concept. Israel's Jewish citizenry found tremendous comfort and relief in its success, particularly in light of the overwhelming disaster of the Holocaust that had ended only two and a half years earlier. Of particular interest here are the ways in which religious Zionist communities defined—and therefore, constructed meaning out of—Israel's modern wars.

The few years between World War II/the Holocaust and the declaration of the State of Israel passed as a frenzy of frantic activity. The Jewish community of Palestine was fighting the British mandatory government, struggling against an increasingly aggressive Arab population, and expending great energy and resources to smuggle European refugees through a British blockade against Jewish immigration. It was a period of tremendous stress and activism, not a period for deep reflection and calm study on the topic of war. As one rabbi articulated it many years later, "During the days when the blood of our young brothers was spilled like water and the young men of Israel were plundered by ravenous wolves like sheep brought to slaughter, the questions of war and armies could not be brought to the light of Torah and ethics of Torah by way of the princes of learning."[13]

Today's many Jewish journals and publications treating issues of religious law in relation to reconstituted Jewish life in the Land of Israel did not exist prior to the establishment of the state. The topic that would force a major reordering of Jewish thinking was the state itself. But the very day that the Jews of Palestine proclaimed an independent Jewish State of Israel, armies from five Arab states attacked it. The engagement of observant Jews in the 1948 War, therefore, could be justified at the time as a war of defense, a justification that is supported explicitly in the Palestinian Talmud and the Code of Maimonides.[14]

---

[13] Rabbi Gedalia Felder, "War and Army in the Light of the *Halakhah*," (Hebrew) *Torah shebe`al-peh* 1982, 117.

[14] PT Sota 8:1, Mishneh Torah, *melakhim* 5:1. See chapters 5 and 7.

Yet there still remained the question of how to justify religiously observant Jews' participation in an organized Jewish army. A story is told in the Talmud (BT Mo'ed Qatan 26a) about the great Talmudic sage, Samuel, originator of the famous Jewish dictum, *dina demalkhuta dina*—"the law of the [non-Jewish] government is the law."[15] His saying was codified to mean that Jews are obligated to obey the civil laws of the nations in which they live. Religious laws are another matter, of course. Jews are obligated to observe religious law and custom even under outside pressure, but they must allow the civil sphere to be governed by the power of the land. As the story is told, Samuel, who lived in Babylonia,[16] was informed that the Persian King, Shapur, had massacred twelve thousand Jews in Mezigat-Kasrey.[17] Despite the religious requirement that Jews rend their clothes as a sign of mourning upon hearing terrible news, Samuel did not tear his clothes. Given the enormity of the disaster and the unmistakable ruling that one's garment must be rent upon hearing such bad news, it was astonishing that Samuel did not rend. A number of reasons are suggested until a conclusion is finally reached: the Jews brought the massacre on themselves by rebelling against the Persians. How do we know that there was a rebellion, asks the text? The evidence was the tremendous sound of the blasts that were played by the rebels, so great according to Rabbi Ammi that it broke down the walls of neighboring Ludkiya.[18]

Whether or not this story is historically accurate makes little difference for our purposes. Its importance lies in its role of informing the traditional behavior of exilic Jewry: live fully observant Jewish religious life within the legal framework of a foreign power. Do not rebel against the ruling authority. Rebellion will bring disaster because it is breaking the oath exacted by God. God will not allow success until the arrival of the messiah. A natural question raised during the violent period just prior to the declaration of the State of Israel was whether the contemporary battles against the British and Arab *fedayeen* (irregulars), and the impending war with neighboring Arab states that seemed inevitable, were cases of Jewish rebellion and a breaking of the oath.

---

[15] BT Gittin 10b, Nedarim 27b-28a, etc.

[16] Babylonia (*bavel*) is a Jewish term for the lands of Mesopotamia. The Babylonian Empire, which destroyed the First Temple and took many Judeans into exile to Babylon, was conquered by the Persians in 543 B.C.E. and never recovered. Despite the fact that there has been no entity called Babylonia for millennia, Jews have always referred to their compatriots living in Mesopotamia as Babylonians and the area as *bavel*.

[17] Perhaps Caesarea-Mazaca, the capital of Cappadocia.

[18] Perhaps Laodicea? Rashi on *leqol yetire*: "The noise of the musical instruments of those who rebelled."

Rabbi She'ar Yashuv Cohen, at that time an exceptional young yeshiva student in Jerusalem and later the chief rabbi of Haifa, weighed in early on the issue of Orthodox participation in the armed forces of the new Jewish state. He was confronted with the perspective that it is preferable for religious Jews to engage entirely in the study of sacred texts than to put on a uniform, because the merit of traditional Torah study would awaken the mercy of God on behalf of the Jews in general. He countered this position with the well-known dictum that saving Jewish lives[19] takes precedence over all the commandments of the Torah, including the commandment of Torah study, save the three commandments that forbid idolatry, illegal sexual relations, and murder: "It is therefore a commandment to transgress all the other prohibitions in favor of the possibility of saving life, and those who are quick to do so are praised..."[20]

But She'ar Yashuv Cohen then added that justification for joining the new Israeli army transcends the simple requirement of saving life. It is also based on the commandment of settling the land as articulated by Nahmanides.[21] Nahmanides himself based his position on a rabbinic source, the midrash called Sifrei (re'eh). Some of Cohen's interlocutors therefore argued that the commandment was only a "rabbinic commandment" (mitzvah derabbanan), which would render it secondary to a "Torah commandment" (mitzvah de'orayta). Cohen responded that the commandment of settling the land had to be a Torah commandment because it was equated by the Sifrei to all the other commandments in the Torah. Because so few commandments are cited with such charged language,[22] settling the land fits into a special category. As for the problem of the Three Vows and immigrating to the Land of Israel "as a wall," "The wall of exile of the nations' regimes that surrounded our land since [the time] we were exiled and distanced from it through the vows against us not to ascend to it was brought down by the word of God. God annulled His vow through the public declarations of the kings of the lands and the ministers of the nations, acknowledging our divine right to our land."[23]

---

[19] Usually referred to as *pikuach nefesh* in Jewish sources, though Cohen uses a more active reference: *hatzalat nefesh* (Cf. Hatam Sofer on *Ketubot* 61b).

[20] Bramson, *The Last Days*, 173.

[21] See chapter 8.

[22] These include Sabbath observance (PT Berakhot 1:1), circumcision (BT Nedarim 32a), required alms giving (BT Bava Batra 9a), and the commandment of putting special tassels on the corners of one's garments (BT Nedarim 25a).

[23] Bramson, 175. We shall address the impact of the Balfour Declaration and decisions of the League of Nations in later chapters.

## Can Orthodox Jews Serve in Israel's Armed Forces?

It is this uncertain historical and religious environment in which Rabbi Isaac Halevi Herzog (1888–1959), the first Ashkenazi Chief Rabbi of the State of Israel, wrote his responsa on war.[24] The responsa are not dated in any of the three available editions, but it is evident that the historical context is the period just prior to and during the beginning of Israel's War of Independence. The driving force behind Herzog's views is the commandment of saving lives *(pikuach nefesh)* in the wake of the Holocaust and the tremendous fear of Palestinian Arab irregulars and neighboring national armies on the eve of independence. He expresses a palpable fear that if the Jews would fail to establish a sovereign Jewish state, the likelihood of violent acts of revenge by the Arabs would lead to massacres and, he hints, perhaps even something like another Holocaust: "It is also clear that if we surrender and live under them, they will massacre and exile us, the inhabitants of the Land of Israel. In order to prevent that, it is clear that we are commanded to make war and trust in God."[25]

Herzog concluded that Israel needed a universal military mobilization, but such a mobilization required a draft, meaning forced induction into the armed forces. Required induction is possible for Orthodox Jews only for the purpose of Commanded War, which had been virtually removed from application to real history by the rabbis of the Talmud. The only way to reverse that was for Herzog to argue the applicability of Commanded War in his contemporary situation.

Most wars of state are international expressions of politics and are initiated by nations for political purposes. Such wars would generally be considered Discretionary Wars, which require the authority of a king and the great Sanhedrin to prosecute. Neither a king nor the Sanhedrin existed in mid-twentieth century Palestine, and in any case, compulsory general mobilization was not allowed for Discretionary Wars. Herzog's goal, therefore, was to understand his current situation as one in which participation of Orthodox Jews in war was not merely acceptable, but

---

[24] *Collected Writings of Rabbi Yitzhaq Isaac Halevi Herzog, Chief Rabbi of Israel* (Hebrew), "Legislation for Israel According to the Torah, Vol. 1: Laws of Government and Justice in the Jewish State, Appendix A: On the Establishment of a State Prior to the Coming of the Messiah." Jerusalem: Mosad Harav Kook/Rabbi Herzog Memorial, n.d. Reprinted with some differences in *Sefer Hatzionut Hadatit* (2 vols.) (Jerusalem: Mosad Harav Kook, 1977), 1:60–71, and in *Techumin* 4 (1983), 13–24.

[25] Collected Writings 130.

actually mandatory. This was possible only through the designation of the contemporary fighting as Commanded War. Given the perspective of the Jews of Palestine immediately after the Holocaust and during the violent and uncertain period prior to Israel's declaration of independence, it was quite natural to consider Jewish fighting to be purely defensive. To use the language of Maimonides, it was "aid to [deliver] Israel from an attacking enemy."[26]

Herzog's responsa begin as answers to questions that were posed to him regarding the contemporary situation. One question asks whether the prohibition of the Three Vows forbidding Jews from ascending to the Land of Israel en masse was still in force given the pressing need for Holocaust survivors to immigrate to the new state and the pressing need of the new state for a larger Jewish population. He answered:

> I do not understand the nature of the question. There is no ruling *(halakhah)* that forbids us from establishing a Jewish state with the permission of the nations before the coming of the redeemer. Without this permission we run into [the issue of] the Three Vows at the end of [BT] *Ketubot* (111a) and *Midrash Song of Songs* on the verse *I have made you swear....* However, the Three Vows have validity, in my opinion, only in relation to the nations that rule over the Land of Israel. This is quite clear, that [the prohibition] not to rebel against the nations of the world has no validity in relation to the nations that do not rule, for this is not their business.
>
> The question has validity in the case where the nations in power over the Land of Israel give permission while other nations do not agree, and in which case a war occurs between the powers and it becomes incumbent upon us to join in the war with the nations in power over the Land of Israel against the opposing nations. But that too, in my opinion, is not within the meaning of the vow—that is, in relation to the Jews who live outside the Land of Israel, for they would be considered rebellious, and we find in [BT] *Mo`ed Qatan* 26a that Samuel did not rend [his garment] over 12,000 Jews who rebelled against the King of Persia [who had jurisdiction over them]; for Samuel, according to his view, a view that was accepted without exception, [this] is *dina demalkhuta dina* ("the law of the [non-Jewish] government is the law"). Therefore, when they rebelled against the king of Persia they transgressed a Torah command. But in relation to the nations that do not have power over Israel,

---

[26] Maimonides, *Kings* 5:1 (see chapter 7).

it is not rebellion but rather, war, and it is not said [written] that God made Israel swear not to make war[27] against the nations of the world.[28]

In other words, the British Mandate government was the ruling power over Mandate Palestine, and it acquieced to the United Nations Partition Plan that included the establishment of a Jewish state. Neither the Arab irregulars nor the armies of neighboring states represented the ruling power over Palestine, so any fighting against *them* would not represent rebellion. His reference "to join in the war with the nations in power over the Land of Israel against the opposing nations" appears to refer to the British struggle against the Axis powers during the Second World War.

## The Mitzvah of Settling the Land According to Maimonides

Like many Jewish religious scholars, Rabbi Herzog was baffled by the omission of settling the Land from Maimonides' *Book of Commandments*. He notes that the commentator supporting Maimonides in the face of Nahmanides' critique (the *"Megillat Esther"*) claimed that Maimonides intended that settling the Land should be excluded from the list of the commandments only until the days of the messiah. Other scholars argued that settling the Land of Israel is not a commandment even after the coming of the messiah, since when that occurs God himself will bring the people of Israel back to its land. Herzog counters that position with Maimonides' statement that the messiah will make wars, and it would then be obvious that such wars would be for the sake of conquering the Land of Israel. Herzog then asks, "why would [the messiah] make wars if it is not even incumbent upon us to go up to the Land and settle it?" He answers with another question: "how would he make wars if the majority of the inhabitants of the land are foreigners (*nokhrim*)?" But since it is said that the messiah will initiate war when Israel is in the majority, how can Jews become the majority if it is not a commandment to immigrate to the Land? That, detractors say, will come from heaven.[29] But if that is the case, then why have a war at all if there is a heavenly promise! "The deduction is invalid from the outset."[30]

---

[27] Meaning that the prohibition was specifically against a war of rebellion, but not against any and every possible kind of war.

[28] *Collected Writings*, 121. Cf. Kalman Neuman, "The Law of Obligatory War and Israeli Reality," in Levin and Shapira, *War and Peace in Jewish Tradition*, 187–191.

[29] *Shezeh yavo al-yedei ruach mimarom.*

[30] *Me`iqra dedina pirkha.*

In other words, Herzog understands the prohibition forbidding rebellion against the nations of the world to mean that Jews must not try to rebel against the powers ruling over them wherever they may be in the diaspora, even if the powers are oppressive. But that does not prevent Jews from leaving those oppressive environments to immigrate to the Land of Israel. The conclusion of the "Three Vows" text that Israel may not go up "as a wall," therefore, means that Israel may not go to war against the nation that is in control of the Land of Israel. Furthermore, Israel may not try to force its way into the Land of Israel if the power ruling the Land of Israel allows immigration while the powers outside do not allow Jews to emigrate. But if Jews have permission both to immigrate to the Land of Israel *and* to leave the countries in which they currently live, then there is no way to relieve them of the commandment of settling the Land of Israel.[31]

But if this seems so obvious, what is the reason for Maimonides' puzzling omission of Settling the Land of Israel from his counting of the commandments? "It occurs to me that the omission of Maimonides is for another reason: his book, *Sefer Hamitzvot*, was written in Arabic, and he was fearful of the nations and in particular the Muslim nations of his day, that they not destroy the Jews in their midst, heaven forbid, when they read in a book of the greatest legalist among Israel that it is a commandment upon Israel to conquer the Land. Therefore, he omitted this commandment. However, because the commandment is missing he had to hint that his counting [of the commandments] is not complete.... Although he speaks a great deal about the commandment to dwell in the Land of Israel and not to leave it, he does not explicitly say that it is a commandment to immigrate to the Land of Israel (*hilkhot ishut* 13:19). There it is explained that this is only a Rabbinic commandment and not a positive commandment from the Torah, and he relies on *hilkhot melakhim* (chapter 5) on that which he had already passed judgment, that everyone is obligated to ascend to Land of Israel."[32]

On the following page Herzog suggests that Maimonides "... refrained, from fear of the danger, to explain openly that Israel is commanded to conquer the Land of Israel that was then in the hands of the Muslims, so [he wrote] the commandment to conquer the seven nations, and people would understand the intention...." Furthermore, says Herzog, the three promises mentioned in the Three Vows narrative are interdependent. Israel is required to promise that it will not rebel against the nations or go up

---

[31] *Collected Writings* 123–124.
[32] *Collected Writings*, 124 (parentheses in original).

"as a wall," but the nations are also required to promise that they would not oppress Israel too much. "Because the nations already transgressed this vow and oppressed more than the amount allowed when they engaged in massacres, etc., we have been released from all of our vows."[33]

"The result of all the above is that when there is a chance for success, the vow does not constitute an obstacle because its validity has already expired, as explained above. There is no fear [of transgression] of the vow, so that when the nations of the world give us a Jewish state, this is not a case of rebellion or going up as a wall for the following reasons: (1) The Mandate government did not conquer the land for itself, but rather, for us, and did not establish a formal government but only representative status for the League of Nations.... The authority of the League of Nations passed to the United Nations.... and although Britain betrayed us... it did not forbid our engaging in war; (2) The Arab inhabitants of the Land of Israel lost sovereignty over the land [to the Turks] long ago, and the land was conquered in WWI not from them, because they no longer had rule over it, but from Turkey, and we have no dispute with them.... This can in no way be considered 'rebellion.' "[34]

## The Command of Conquering the Land

"The command of conquering the Land is a positive Torah command according to Nahmanides, and this is Commanded War. But it appears that Maimonides disagrees." Rabbi Herzog again struggles with the problem of the absence from Mamonides' *Book of Commandments*, not only of settling the Land, but of conquering the Land *(kibbush ha'aretz)*. "[Maimonides] says that Commanded War consists of war against the seven nations, war against Amalek, and helping Israel from an enemy attack, etc. It looks as if Maimonides does not consider war of conquest of the Land to be in that category. But the seven nations have already perished from the world, and this is not a law for messianic days [only] and without present application *(hilkheta lemeshicha)*, so why did Maimonides mention this war in his code...? And why did he mention war against Amalek?...."[35] In other words, Maimonides' listing these two cases of Commanded War seems odd because both would appear no longer to be possible, since the Canaanite nations have died out or assimilated to other cultures and the Amalekites are no longer identifiable.

---

[33] *Collected Writings* 126, and again on 127.
[34] *Collected Writings* 127. CF *Techumin* 4 (1983), 19.
[35] *Collected Writings* 128.

"But if you say that if [Commanded War has no more meaning in history] then there is no reality anymore to Commanded War, [Maimonides] adds, 'and helping Israel against enemies that attack it.' [Therefore,] even if we accept all the above [that the two Torah commandments that comprise Commanded War are no longer possible], I say that this war of ours is helping Israel against enemies that attack us.... These Arabs who live in the Land and their associates, the kings of Arabia, are attacking us though we have been satisfied with [only] a portion [of the entire Land of Israel]. We have not attacked them to conquer all of the Land from them. But their goal is not to give us [even] a tiny portion of the Land. Their goal is actually to force us out or destroy us, and this has been their goal for as long as we have been a large minority in the Land. This war, therefore, must be considered legally a war of "helping Israel against enemies that attack us." This is Commanded War, and with Commanded War there is need only for the command of the king."[36]

## The Authority of the King in Our Day

As we learned in chapter 6, even in the case of Commanded War which does not require a rabbinical court of seventy-one (also called the Sanhedrin), there needs to be a responsible authority to call up troops for war. Political authority in the biblical and rabbinic periods, when Jewish law was theorized and established, was based on kingship. Two other authorities during biblical times could be theoretically acceptable, those being prophet and priest, but the priesthood had long ago lost its authority with the last destruction of the Jerusalem Temple, and prophecy had ended.[37] Without a king, therefore, Commanded War would seem to be impossible. But the dynastic line of the the legitimate Davidic kings had been lost for many centuries by the generation of Rabbi Herzog. No legitimate Israelite king could be identified.

Herzog solves the problem in the following way: "I say that as long as there is no eternal kingdom, the king need not be from the house of David, and such a king does not require anointing. So his authority comes from the people because he is chosen by the people, and we need to say that the people in its entirety, and particularly the People of Israel that are settling in the Land of Israel...has the authority of the king regarding issues

---

[36] And not also the Sanhedrin in order to call up an army with a compulsory draft and send it to war. *Collected Writings* 129

[37] Tosefta Sota 13:3, BT Yoma 9b, Sota 48b, PT Sota 9, etc.

of state, so when a clear majority declares war, it has the authority of the king who has it in his power to compel."[38]

If the justification for taking up arms is simply that of saving lives, then the legal category for Jewish engagement in military activities in Palestine could be that of "saving lives" *(pikuach nefesh)*. This notion, which is much discussed in rabbinic sources, was certainly operative when Jews were living in diaspora communities around the world under the rule of foreign peoples. Rabbi Herzog wants to clarify, however, that saving lives is not the authoritative principle for Jewish involvement in the armed forces in Palestine/Israel. "Know that we are not discussing [this topic] according to the principle of saving lives, [i.e.] that all are required to save the lives of Israel, because if there were a situation in which enemies attack us and announce that if we surrender to their rule they would not harm us, that would be a case of saving lives. But this is not the case here. Rather, when they attack us in the Land of Israel and we already have the right to establish our own state, this is a case of Commanded War. However, if they do not attack us, but we attack them to expand the border of Israel, then this is a case of Discretionary War."[39]

## Initiating Battles to Prevent Foreign Conquest

In chapter 2 we considered a situation that took place during the Maccabean wars against the Greeks. A Jewish community refused to violate the Sabbath by defending itself during an attack, a refusal that resulted in its massacre and destruction. The Babylonian Talmud (Eruvin 45a) discusses Jews taking up arms on the Sabbath to fight enemies who attack them or, in some cases, intend to attack them. Traditional Jewish commentators extended the discussion considerably. Some suggested that if Jews hear of the possibility of an enemy assault, they are allowed to initiate attack on Shabbat in a preemtive strike. From this Rabbi Herzog derives the following: "Therefore, help against an enemy who comes against [Jews], not necessarily with regard to those who have already come, but also to those planning to come, is Commanded War, not necessarily to wait until they will actually come, but rather, going out immediately to war."[40] He then

---

[38] *Collected Writings* 129. Herzog cites here the equivalent earlier ruling of Abraham Isaac Kook in his *Mishpat Cohen* (#144, paragraph 22). Cf. *Mishpat Cohen* (Jerusalem: Mosad Harav Kook, 1985), 337–338.

[39] *Collected Writings* 130.

[40] *Collected Writings* 131, he cites *Shulchan Arukh* Orach Chayyim 329:6, which codifies a reading of BT Eruvin 45a, including the permissibility of a preemptive strike against an enemy that is

extends this further to mean that preventing any foreign people from conquering the Land of Israel is a Commanded War: "Therefore, helping Israel from the hand of an enemy includes even saving Israel from the conquest of its Land by any gentile [nation], and this is within the category of Commanded War."[41]

Rabbi Herzog is evidently influenced by the Holocaust, for he continues: "This [ruling] does not apply only to the Land of Israel when there is an Israelite government. It also applied even outside the Land. Any area in which Jews live as a majority has status like the Land of Israel in relation to this issue, and it is forbidden to give to gentiles an opportunity to conquer it, even if they do not have their own self-government, for in Bavel [where the rabbis of the Talmud formulated the policy] they did not [have self-government], but rather a kind of internal autonomy. How much the more so with the Jewish community of the Land of Israel, which has a recognized internal governance now; it is forbidden to allow the nations to take control of [Jewish-owned] land. Preventing this is Commanded War."[42] The Chief Rabbi arrives at the following conclusion: "I believe that there is agreement that this is Commanded War, and that the power of the Jewish community of Palestine to require mobilization in conjunction with the majority of Israel outside the Land is comparable to [the authority] of a king."[43]

The highest religious authority of the fledgeling State of Israel thus justifies a universal draft on the grounds that wars fought by the Jewish State are, by definition, defensive, hence Commanded War. Because the enemy was identified as desiring nothing less than the destruction of the Jewish State and its inhabitants, even preemptive attacks are in the category of defense, hence Commanded War. The recent and very real experience of the Holocaust helped Rabbi Herzog establish this position, as he articulates plainly in his writing. Commanded War requires a universal draft, without the proviso of deferments that were established in the Hebrew Bible and confirmed and extended by the Talmud.[44] "Every one must go out [to fight] in commanded wars, even a bridegroom from his chamber and a bride from her wedding canopy."

We can observe no obvious messianism in his writing here, though perhaps with some imagination one could uncover some latent messianism,

---

judged to be intending to attack.

[41] *Collected Writings* 132.

[42] *Collected Writings* 132.

[43] *Collected Writings* 132, *Techumin* 4 (1983), 24.

[44] Deuteronomy 20 and BT and PT Tractate Sotah, chapter 8.

since the entire Zionist project, like other national and international movements of the period, exuded a kind of chiliastic emotion. But the issues articulated by Rabbi Herzog are quite straightforward. The Jews of the Yishuv are under attack and are required to defend themselves in this Commanded War, a clear and unmistakable case of defense "to deliver Israel from an attacking enemy."[45]

Such a ruling by the official rabbinic authority representing the Jewish State was necessary in order to allow the minority religious Zionist community to join with their much more numerous secular comrades in defending their cities, towns, and agricultural settlements—indeed, to defend the new nation-state as a whole. Yet even the authority of the Chief Rabbinate of the State of Israel, which held much more religious and political prestige in the early years of the state than today, was not accepted by all religiously observant Jews. Accommodation had to be made for a large population of ultra-Orthodox Jews that refused to join the armed forces and refused to accept its authority.

Religious Zionist participation in military units had been informal up to this point. Any ad hoc reasoning supporting it during the prestate period needed to be revised and authorized formally according to Jewish legal thinking in order to defend against critics in the Orthodox world who condemned it as a transgression against religious law. The problem was exacerbated by the fact that Orthodox Jews were fighting in a Jewish army run by secular Jews. The decision by the Chief Rabbi was necessary in order to keep the Orthodox in the Zionist camp—and to keep them in the Orthodox community as well, since many traditional Jews were abandoning their religious practices in favor of secular Zionist Jewish identity during that period. After the Holocaust, participation in a Jewish army that would defend the lives, rights, and honor of Israel became in and of itself a kind of holy act to secular Israelis.[46] It required no religious justification. Religious Zionists, however, needed an official, authentic traditional means of authorization. It did not happen overnight, but the process was public enough that Israel's wars would eventually take on a deep sense of sanctity for religious and secular Jews alike, particularly in light of the near-successful genocide of the Jews that had taken place only a few short years previously.

---

[45] To use Maimonides' taxonomy (Mishneh Torah, *Hilkhot Melakhim* 5:1 [Cf. PT Sotah 8:1]).

[46] While "Israel" refers to the Jewish collective in traditional Jewish literatures, "Israeli" refers to citizens of the State of Israel, some 20 percent of which are not Jews. As we move into the period of Israeli statehood, I use "Israeli" to refer specifically to Jewish Israelis, since the discussion is centered only on that community.

PART IV | The Jewish State

*Holy War Revived*

# CHAPTER 13 | 1948 to 1967

*From Defensive War to Preemptive War*

Bless the State of Israel, the beginning of the flowering of our
Redemption

FROM THE "PRAYER FOR THE STATE OF ISRAEL"

The establishment of the State of Israel marked a huge paradigm shift for the Jewish people. Not since the destruction of the Jerusalem Temple had Jews been in control of a sovereign state wherein they would be governed by their own leaders. This revolutionary change was viewed with tremendous enthusiasm and favor by Jews throughout the world. It also encouraged serious innovation in thinking about Jewish identity and behavior. Important adjustments had to be made with regard to Jews serving in a Jewish army.

With the declaration of the Jewish State of Israel and the subsequent victory in a war for independence, the Jewish community of Palestine was required in very short order to create a system of public governance and organize its armed forces out of unofficial institutions that had been developing for decades previously. All of its state institutions were henceforth to become official and their legal and political status defined and standardized. The citizens of the new state would naturally be drafted to join the newly organized armed forces, now called the Israel Defense Forces (IDF), and to fight its wars.

We have observed how joining an official Jewish army raised a number of difficult ritual, moral-ethical, and existential issues for Orthodox Jews. Many of those issues hinged on defining the nature of war in contemporary history. A core category of discussion in the Orthodox world, therefore, became the existential meaning of making war under the flag of a sovereign Jewish polity in the modern period. We will observe how the idea of Commanded War entered into the conversation of Religious Zionism and how that phenomenon influenced the discourse and, therefore, opinions about war and about the enemy in the larger Jewish world.

## After the Revolution

After 1948, the semantic significance of "conquest" *(kibbush)* began to change. It first started to lose its revolutionary meaning, but then took on a different sense after 1967 and into the 1980s. Especially after 1967, "conquest" moved beyond the traditional meanings assigned to it by the Talmud and Nachmanides. Likewise, it came to transcend the early socialist-Zionist pioneer sense of the 1920s and 1930s. "Conquest" would evolve into a far more aggressive military act. Several factors contributed to this development, including the decline of secular Zionist ideologies, the rise in yeshiva education among religious Zionists, and the great personal investment and sacrifice of religiously observant Israelis in establishing settlements and building communities in the territories conquered in 1967.

It is a commonplace of history that the ideological fervor driving revolutionaries to expend tremendous energies and make extraordinary personal sacrifices tends to fade "after the revolution." This was certainly the case with Zionism. After the establishment of the State of Israel many of the old slogans, including those of "conquest of the land," "conquest of the deserts," and the "conquest of labor," lost their attraction along with their pioneering ideological significance. These conquests were complete, at least symbolically, as Israel became an officially recognized state and a partner among the nations. For the first time it could—and was desperately in need of—creating or expanding its national institutions with little outside interference.[1] Tremendous energies continued to be devoted to land development, agriculture, the general economy, and the military. But after 1948 these forces quickly matured. The state was established but there was no time to sit back and enjoy the extraordinary success. An Arab boycott, the need to secure borders, the absorption of unprecedented numbers of Jewish refugees from both post-Holocaust Europe and the Middle East and North Africa, and other urgent social, economic, and political and military needs moved the general ethos from one of ideology to pragmatism.[2]

---

[1] David Ben Gurion, the founding leader of the new State of Israel, attempted to continue the revolution by directing it toward settling and developing the desert regions. He set a personal example by moving to the desert kibbutz outpost called Sde Boker, but despite his efforts, the revolution faded.

[2] Charles Leibman and Eliezer, Don-Yehiya, *Civil Religion in Israel: Traditional Judaism and Political Culture in the Jewish State* (Berkeley and Los Angeles: UC Press, 1983).

The old slogans began to lose their resonance during the period of normalization in the 1950s and 1960s, even among those who were suckled on the milk of the socialist-Zionist parties and youth groups. Although all the prestate political parties and factions espoused positive visions, some virtually utopian, of the new Jewish society that would be built in a Jewish state, most secular Zionists, including the neomessianists discussed in earlier chapters, were preoccupied with the great initial stresses of survival after independence. And in fact, the simple fact of the state's existence did serve to realize many of the prestate aspirations. Citizenship in the Jewish State provided those previously degraded Jewish inhabitants of foreign nations with physical safety and a legal status with full civil rights and freedoms. And there were plenty of immediate problems that needed serious attention, ranging from the absorption of masses of new immigrants to establishing an acceptable system of governance and setting up virtually every other aspect and institution necessary for a successful nation-state.

Some of the core ideals of Zionism remained strong. One was settlement, which remained crucially important for three major reasons. First, it was necessary for *kibbutz galuyot*—"ingathering of exiles," in order to provide housing and a livelihood for the hundreds of thousands of Jewish refugees from post-Holocaust Europe and from Arab nations.[3] It would also establish Jewish demographic dominance in areas of the state with large Arab populations, and it would create settlements along border areas that would serve as a deterrent to population infiltration and military incursions from neighboring Arab countries. "Ingathering of exiles," along with certain other ideological standards, continued to resonate with the realities of the state for pragmatic reasons, but the general ideology of pioneering settlement weakened as the reality of statehood sunk in to the mindset of the average Israeli citizen. New challenges to the state's viability and success emerged, such as economic and scientific development, increased military capability, diplomacy, and so forth, but for the Zionist establishment, the revolution was over. It had succeeded.

This trend was evident also among religious Zionists, most of whom followed the general path of the secularist agenda. Despite the establishment of a national legal and governmental system that was secular and did not meet the requirements of Jewish tradition, most religious Zionists felt satisfied that they were free to devote their energies to building up the

---

[3] The "ingathering of exiles" is the name of one of the petitionary prayers at the core of thrice-daily worship in traditional Judaism, established in the Talmud (BT Megillah 17b) and based on Isaiah 11:12 and 27:13. The entreaty is clearly messianic. That such an activity was actually occurring with the establishment of the state was not missed by those who recite it.

Land within the political borders of the new state, strengthen and expand the religious communities and their religious education system, and try to influence the majority secular citizens of the state through establishment channels. Many were satisfied to work toward the messianic Endtime by "Judaizing" the state and improving its institutions.

Despite the normalizing of many religious Zionists through statism, the revolution of statehood was nevertheless understood by most, including many who were engaged in the postrevolutionary normalization, as a stage in a process that would end only with the arrival of the messianic Redemption. At a deep level, the establishment of the Jewish State, only a few short years after the near destruction of the Jewish People in the Holocaust, held a powerful, even supremely transcendent and apocalyptic significance.[4] This extraordinary period of history could not be random. It must signal the beginnings of messianic fulfillment. The state was thus accorded a certain sanctified status, and despite the natural antagonism between the religious and secular communities of the new nation-state, they both went out of their way to cooperate in establishing and refining the institutions necessary for governance and development.

But the country that emerged after the revolution was a secular state, even if Jewish, and it was governed by legislative and legal systems based on secular European and American models. This fact provided concrete symbolism for religious Zionists to the reality that the revolution was both a success and a failure. Gideon Aran articulated this tension well. "Political sovereignty, concretized in a network of governing institutions resting on a modern, secular basis, spelled the end of any illusion that Jewish secularism could be dismissed as a passing phenomenon."[5] Religious Zionists never succeeded in stemming the secularization of the movement, which will be recalled was one of the justifications for their engaging in Zionism that they argued against their non-Zionist and anti-Zionist Orthodox brethren. In fact, as I noted previously, their decision to separate into the semi-independent organization of Mizrachi resulted in their marginalization within the Zionist Organization and movement. That marginalization continued after the establishment of the state when the religious Zionist camp insisted on establishing its own separate state-run religious school system. Other institutional expressions of withdrawal from the mainstream of the new state with its emphasis on a modern secular Jewish national identity occurred as well.

---

[4] Dov Schwartz, *The Land of Israel*, 215.
[5] Gideon Aran, "From Religious Zionism to Zionist Religion," in *Social Foundations of Judaism* ed. C. Goldscheider and J. Neusner (Englewood Cliffs, NJ: Prentice Hall, 1990), 261.

To most religious Zionists, the ultimate objective of Zionism is none other than the Great and Awesome Day.[6] Some, such as normalizers within the religious Zionist camp, were satisfied to yearn for it in the traditional manner that refrained from attempting to determine the time of its coming. Others considered it imminent but were content to live and work as fellow-citizens in a Jewish but secular state to help in its realization. The irresolvable tension between the achievement of the secular state and aspiration to a messianic fulfillment eventually led to a silent crisis in the following generation that would help spawn a new and activist religious Zionist movement called *Gush Emunim* a few decades later.[7]

In the meantime, many religious Zionists, who normalized to a greater or lesser extent in parallel with their secular fellow-citizens, continued to hold and teach the Zionist principles of settlement and attachment to the Land of Israel. But unlike their secular comrades who viewed these ideals as a political and social solution to the existential "Jewish problem," religious Zionists considered them as necessary steps on the journey to the final and ultimate Redemption. In the religious context they were not limited to the territories gained through the United Nations Partition Agreement and the additional areas captured in the War of Independence. They applied, rather, to the larger, biblically defined Land of Israel that included territories extending beyond the formal borders of the new State. As the ideologies of secular Zionism waned during the first two decades after the establishment of the state, the passion of Orthodox religious Zionists remained strong, even if not particularly evident. After 1967, and especially after 1973, however, the passions would be activated, and one could hear religious Zionists referring to themselves and their allies as the "true Zionists" *(tziyyonim amittiyim)* in relation to their secular political opponents, not infrequently even the government of Israel.[8]

---

[6] See Malachi 3, and especially 3:23. This yearning for redemption is a traditional Jewish aspiration in general and is ubiquitous outside of the Zionist context. Although a redemptive messianism is quite evident in the Zionism of the rabbis Kook, it was not until after 1967 that it became evident to most in the religious Zionist community as a whole, as will be demonstrated below.

[7] Gush Emunim will be examined in some detail below.

[8] See, for example, the description by Rabbis Isser Kalonsky and Chayim Shteiner of the removal of the last residents of the town of Yamit in Sinai (and outside the biblical borders of the Land of Israel), when it was returned to Egypt in 1982: "There were those who thought that perhaps it was possible to annul the governmental decision to expel [the residents] of the Yamit area and transfer it to strangers.... There was hope that a large settlement movement would be formed from all parts of the Land of Israel so that the government would withdraw from the struggle against thousands of true Zionists" (Bramson, *The Last Days*, 237–238). Many other examples could be cited.

In the intervening period immediately after the establishment of the state and into the 1950s, a kind of uncomfortable stasis set in within Mizrachi, which had been the official organ of Religious Zionism, and the National Religious Party that emerged and formed out of it in the new Israeli parliament called the Knesset.[9] Achieving their educational goals and ensuring the state support necessary for their institutions required working within the secular governmental system, and partnering with government represented a tacit acceptance of the new, secular culture of Zionism that was represented by the state. It will be recalled that religious Zionists justified their initial engagement in Zionism partly in order to *combat* the Zionist majority's quest for a new culture—meaning modern and secular—of Judaism. The fact that religious law would not become state norm, aside from a small part of family law that applied to the Jewish inhabitants of the state, was another expression of the failure of Religious Zionism to realize its original goals.

Considerable energy was thus expended to function within a system that was, on the one hand, considered unacceptable. On the other hand, the very establishment of the state after nearly two thousand years of collective suffering in exile was considered a marvel that bordered on divine sanctification. At the very least it offered a safe haven for persecuted Jews, which had been an important justification for Orthodox Jews to engage in the Zionist Movement in the first place. And Jewish political control over part of the biblical Land of Israel allowed for the observance for the first time in many centuries of certain "Commandments Tied to the Land" *(hamitzvot hateluyot ba'aretz),* thereby providing the ability to carry out more of the divine will in the form of obedience to the commandments of God.

Toward the end of the 1950s and into the 1960s, some of the emerging new generation of religious Zionists began to criticize their parents' generation for becoming too complacent about the character of the new Jewish State. This is evident from the pages of the religious B'nai Akiba Youth Movement newsletter, *Zera`im,*[10] in which they criticize their parents' generation for its neglect of yeshiva learning in its inclination toward physical pioneering and its acceptance of the general Labor Zionist ethos,

---

[9] On the National Religious Party, see Abramov, *Perpetual Dilemma,* 163–167; Stewart Reiser, *The Politics of Leverage: The National Religious Party of Israel and Its Influence on Foreign Policy* (Cambridge, MA: Harvard University Press, 1984); Susan Hattis Rolef, "National Religious Party," in *EJ2,* 15: 27–28.

[10] First issued in 1936 and continuous to the present, *Zera`im* is a useful tool for examining the developing and changing positions of Religious Zionism as conveyed to the youth with an eye for the future.

including the aspect that assigned religious Zionists a kind of "second-class status."[11]

As a rule, during this period, religious Zionists who were more closely associated with socialist-communalist principles epitomized by Hapoel Hamizrachi shared more of the neomessianic ethos of Labor Zionism and expressed that in their establishment of many agricultural settlements. They tended to be less messianic in the traditional Jewish sense. Those who associated Zionism more directly with traditional views of messianic redemption tended to be more critical of the normalizing policy of government. This trend became more obvious after the 1967 and 1973 Wars. Put differently, those religious Zionists who were less inclined to associate the State of Israel with messianic Redemption tended to be more willing to compromise on issues of territory and settlement. Those who considered the settling of the Land of Israel to be an indispensable and essential step in the final Redemption were far more unyielding with regard to policy that might eventually cede any part of the Land of Israel.[12] Wherever they might sit on the scale of messianic expectation, however, Rabbinic Judaism has always placed tremendous emphasis on the time when messianic redemption will indeed occur, and since the earliest days there have been attempts to recognize signs that the age may indeed be imminent. The possible transcendent significance of the first Jewish independent self-government since the time of the ancient Jerusalem Temple, therefore, simply could not be ignored.

## *Reshit Tzemichat Ge'ulateynu*—The Beginning of the Flowering of Our Redemption

It has been customary for centuries for Jews to include a prayer for the civil authorities and governments in which they reside, perhaps based on the biblical books of Jeremiah 29:7 and Ezra 6:10.[13] On September 21, 1948, only four short months after independence and while the country was still at war, the Orthodox Zionist press *(Hatzofeh)* and the secular newspaper,

---

[11] Yair Sheleg, *The New Religious Jews* (Jerusalem: Keter, 2000), 29–31, and see chapter 9.

[12] Shimoni, *The Zionist Ideology*, 335.

[13] Ismar Elbogen, *Jewish Liturgy*, transl. Raymond Scheindlin (Philadelphia: Jewish Publication Society, 1993), 162; David Golinkin, "Prayers for the Government and the State of Israel," in David Golinkin, *Insight Israel: The View from Schechter* (Jerusalem, Schechter Institute, 2006), pp. 114–125 (http://www.schechter.edu/insightIsrael.aspx?ID=35); Joseph Tabory, "The piety of politics: Jewish prayers for the State of Israel," *Liturgy in the Life of the Synagogue: Studies in the History of Jewish Prayer* ed. Ruth Langer and Steven Fine (Winona Lake: Eisenbrauns, 2005), 225–246.

*Ha`aretz*, reported that the two chief rabbis of Israel were composing a prayer for the new Jewish state. The prayer itself was cited along with endorsements from prominent rabbis.[14] Its language invests the new State of Israel with transcendent, symbolic meaning that is decidedly messianic: "Our Father in heaven, Rock of Israel and its Redeemer, bless the State of Israel, the beginning of the flowering of our Redemption..." *(reshit tze-michat ge'ulateynu)*. The prayer was immediately denounced by the non-Zionist and anti-Zionist Orthodox communities for recognizing the state as part of the divine plan.

The newspapers were right that the text of the prayer was formulated through the office of the Chief Rabbinate, but the authorship of the line associating the Jewish state with the flowering of divine Redemption is shrouded in legend. The words are reminiscent of a reference to the Balfour Declaration by Rabbi Abraham Isaac Kook, who referred to the declaration as "the beginning of the flowering of our salvation *(reshit tze-michat yeshu`ateynu)*,"[15] and others have attributed to Rabbi Kook a similar phrase, "the beginning of the sprouting up of the Redemption *(reshit tzemichat hage'ulah)*,"[16] both almost identical to the current text found in virtually all but the anti-Zionist Orthodox prayer books in use today. According to the personal secretary of Chief Rabbi Herzog, the actual phrase that was established in the liturgy originated with the Israeli Nobel Laureate, S. Y. Agnon who, after having been shown a draft of the prayer, suggested it to the Chief Rabbi.

In the following year (1949) in the run-up to the elections for the first Israeli Parliament *(Knesset)*, some two hundred leading rabbis issued a public manifesto that opened with the following words, "Let us give thanks unto the Lord for having, in his abundant mercy and kindness, granted us to see the first shoots of the beginning of the Redemption *(atchalta dige'ulah)* through the establishment of the State of Israel."[17]

Thus, while Rabbi Abraham Isaac Kook was criticized by religiously observant Zionists and non-Zionists alike (though for different reasons) for openly declaring the messianic nature of modern Zionism, the

---

[14] Tabory, "Piety of Politics," 233.

[15] Kook's letter of 1933 was reprinted in the first issue of *Zera`im* (1936), in which he refers to his own time as "now, at the time of the flowering of Redemption" *(akhshav bizman tzemichat hayeshu`ah)*.

[16] Bernard M. Casper, "Reshit Zemichat Geulatenu," in *Religious Zionism after Forty Years of Statehood* ed. S. Spero and Y. Pessin (Jerusalem: Mesilot, 1989), 70 n. 4; On the various versions before standardization and attempts at emendation, and calls by some religious Zionists to refrain from reciting the prayer, see Tabory.

[17] Casper, "Reshit...," 61.

religious Zionist camp took hold of the idea and instituted it formally in the standard liturgy after independence. This was a complete reversal of the public position of Rabbi Reines and the other early leaders of Mizrachi that Zionism was not messianic but merely a movement to relieve the suffering of Jews.[18] The new messianic prayer for the state was soon recited in nearly all synagogues, which demonstrated unmistakably that whatever the pronouncements of the early Mizrachi leaders, the emergence of the Jewish state out of the ashes of the Holocaust was interpreted by most religious Zionists to be at least a signpost on the road to the final Redemption. "And so during the first years after the establishment of the State, a sense of 'hearing the footsteps of the Messiah' *('iqveta dimeshicha)* reigned among the public, and especially among national religious Jewish circles."[19]

This sentiment died down as the natural process of normalization set in after independence. We have noted above how the religious Zionist factions went along with normalization, even if grudgingly. In public forums, religious Zionists tended to avoid referring to the messianic or religiously redemptive nature of the state as expressed by Kook and articulated in the early pronouncements after independence. Messianic and redemptive associations continued to exist, to be sure, and they were acknowledged daily in prayer. They made up an important part of the religious Zionist world view but were not often voiced loudly because those holding them felt that they were a small stream within a powerful river that was moving in a different direction.

And there was, of course, the immediate task of absorbing hundreds of thousands of Jewish refugees into the new state immediately after the war. This "ingathering of exiles" required tremendous effort and sacrifice on the part of the entire community. During these years, therefore, the Reinesian theme of relieving Jewish suffering resurfaced among religious Zionists, because the most pressing immediate need was for refuge and shelter for homeless Jews. The transcendent role of the state was not to be recalled in any deeply significant way until after 1967. As one representative of Hapoel Hamizrachi Kibbutz Movement put it even in 1966, "Let us, therefore, be realistic and logical and accept the state as *rescue* and not as *redemption* of the Last Days."[20]

---

[18] See chapter 9.

[19] Avraham Halperin, "The State of Israel in Religious Thought and the Education of our Generation" (Hebrew) *Amudim* 242 (April, 1966), 256.

[20] Halperin, "The State of Israel in Religious Thought and the Education..." 257 (emphasis in original).

# The Qibya Affair

The 1948 War established the reality of a Jewish State, but it did not guarantee its security or even determine its political borders. The frontiers drawn up by the Rhodes Armistice Agreements in early 1949 had not been intended to be permanent, and they made no real concession to civilian needs. The boundaries were not clearly marked, and they often cut off Arab villages or homeless refugees on the Arab side of the border from their fields and wells on the Israeli side. A significant number of Arabs who had fled into Jordan during the fighting returned subsequently to reclaim their possessions or to join their families that had remained in what became Israel. Some villagers living outside the unofficial borders even crossed the frontier on a regular basis to till their land on the Israeli side, either because they wished to retain possession of the lands by working them or because it was not clear to them (or to others) exactly where the borders were actually located.

Israel, in the meantime, was settling newly arrived Jewish refugees from Europe and the Arab world along these border areas in small settlements, and these settlements were sometimes located where abandoned or destroyed Arab villages had existed only shortly before.[21] Israeli authorities were therefore quite concerned with Arab infiltration across the vague borders. The IDF engaged and killed hundreds of infiltrators during the first few years after independence.[22] By the early 1950s, Arab infiltrators and militia groups known as *fedayeen* were engaging in thievery, smuggling, and retaliation against Jews who had settled in the border areas, sometimes in what had once been their own native villages. Some settlers were killed and their settlements set on fire. Israel, in turn, engaged in reprisal raids against the perpetrators, against the Arab police or army units in the area, or simply against nearby Arab villages as a kind of collective punishment, in the hope of discouraging more incursions.[23]

Sachar notes how "[t]he violence reached a crescendo of sorts in 1953" when a cell of Arab irregulars crossed the Jordanian border and threw a grenade into a house in the Jewish village of Tirat Yehudah, well inside the Israeli side of the border, killing a mother and her two children.[24] That violence was committed on October 12. An overwhelming Israeli military reprisal was carried out within days in which sixty-nine Jordanians, at

---

[21] Troen, 208–219.

[22] Sachar, *History of Israel*, 443–444.

[23] Benny Morris, *Israel's Border Wars: 1949–1956* (Oxford: Oxford University Press, 1993).

[24] Sachar, *History of Israel*, 444.

least half of them women and children, were killed in the Jordanian village of Qibya.[25]

As is often the case in such incidents, Israeli sources and Arab sources differ over whether the large number of people killed was intentional. In any case, Prime Minister Ben-Gurion was embarrassed by the revelation and dissembled by insisting that the action was not a planned military operation but rather, a spontaneous act of revenge by the Jewish villagers of Tirat Yehudah. The truth of the military's responsibility eventually became known, but it was before this revelation that Rabbi Shaul Yisraeli (d. 1995), one of the most venerable early thinkers in the post-independence activist religious Zionist camp, wrote his rabbinic responsum *(teshuvah)* on the massacre.[26] Born in Belarus, Rabbi Yisraeli came to Palestine at age twenty-four and became a student of Rabbi Abraham Isaac Kook, after which he served in many authoritative halakhic and administrative capacities in the religious Zionist community in Israel. He begins his extremely dense halakhic/ethical discussion with a brief introduction, in which it appears that he accepted Ben-Gurion's pretext that the military operation was actually a civilian act of revenge.[27]

Since the end of the "formal" war of the Arab states against Israel by the armistice, acts of infiltration by armed Arab gangs for the purpose of thievery and robbery have not ceased. On the contrary, in the past year these infiltrations have become increasingly daring and loaded with murder cells simply for the sake of murder. During the month of *cheshvan* [late fall in the Jewish calendar] this year, criminal gangs carried out a brutal act of murder of an entire family in a Jewish village. It appears that the gangs are organized and encouraged with the support of the Arab population in the [Jordanian] areas near the border. And because they were not punished but on the contrary, they received encouragement through the monitoring apparatus of the United Nations, it was decided to instill fear on the border inhabitants for their acts of horror.

---

[25] Morris, *Border Wars*, 240–276.

[26] I focus on Yisraeli because of his profound influence on the thinking of Religious Zionism in the early post-independence period. But another Orthodox thinker, Yeshayahu Leibowitz, also wrote an influential article in response to the Qibya affair entitled, "After Qibya" (*Beterem*, 1953/1954, 168–173). Leibowitz, however, was not a leader of the religious Zionist camp, and his views had little influence on that community.

[27] Shaul Yisraeli, "The Qibya Affair in the Light of Halakhah *(taqrit qibiya le'or hahalakhah)*," *Hatora vehamedina* 5 (1953), 71–113; reprinted with some expansions in his *Amud Hayemini* (Jerusalem, 1966), chapter 16: "Military Actions for the Protection of the State." I refer here to his original publication.

The village that was victimized decided that it is forbidden to sit with arms folded until the arrival of more killings, heaven forbid, so one night it vigorously attacked the Arab village of Qibya, which was proven to be the place of the murderous gangs and which received the support of its population. The Arab village of Qibya suffered material and human losses. Women and children were included among the killed. The "greater" world that had stood by indifferently to repeated acts of murder of people in Israel, was "shocked" to its foundation at the act [against] Qibya, which was in effect only an act of vengeance that flowed from the collective fury of the inhabitants of the border and the Israeli community in general. The enemies of Israel carried out this scheme because the State of Israel did not work through the Security Council of the United Nations.

We know well the "righteousness" that distinguishes the line of diplomacy of the protecting nations. We do not live according to their commands, and we shall not learn righteousness and justice from them. However, we are obligated to clarify the path of our response and its glory according to the Torah, whose paths are the paths of pleasantness and all of its ways, peace.[28] This article is thus dedicated to clarifying the Torah perspective on this topic.[29]

Yisraeli's article is a highly technical argument intended to justify the validity of the reprisal operation in halakhic terms.[30] His argument rests on defining as perpetrators not only those who actually engaged in the physical act of murder, but also those who conspired with the actors to carry it out. Both are defined by Yisraeli as "the pursuer" (harodef), a well-known category in Jewish law. Yisraeli bases his inclusion of the conspirators in this category on the writings of Rabbi Meir Simchah Hacohen of Dvinsk, who reached the legal decision that, because the intent of Jewish law is to save the intended victim, both the one who commits the act and the conspirator must be considered guilty of "pursuit" for the purpose of murder.[31]

---

[28] Proverbs 3:17.

[29] Yisraeli, "The Qibya Affair," 71 (quotes in original). Kalman Neuman claims that Yisraeli was aware that the brutal reprisal was an "authorized military operation" despite the tone of innocence in his essay ("The Law of Obligatory War and Israeli Reality," in Levin and Shapira, *War and Peace in Jewish Tradition*, 197 n. 33.

[30] For a cogent analysis of the issues that are raised by Yisraeli, and the important moral-ethical issues that Yisraeli does not address, see Gerald (Yakov) Blidstein, "The Treatment of Hostile Civilian Populations: The Contemporary Halakhic Discussion in Israel," *Israel Studies*, 1:2 (Fall, 1996), 27–44. My reading of Yisraeli is influenced by Blidstein.

[31] Yisraeli, "Qibya," 92.

But Yisraeli then extends the category further, from those responsible through the direct act of instigation to the larger population that supports the actors but does not take an active conspiratorial part in the deed itself (or necessarily even knows about it).[32] Gerald Blidstein considers Yisraeli's extension to be a foundational case of a modern religious authority working with traditional sources in a way that is motivated to promote a particular point of view.[33] Blidstein is careful to note how tendentious readings have been used by modern religious decisors, not only to justify radical acts or social-political sentiments, but also to counter them. His point, made from the perspective of a scholar of philosophy and ethics, is that the sources and the halakhic process that are assumed to be politically neutral and uninfluenced by personal bias are nevertheless used by scholarly leaders in creative and sometimes tendentious ways that can be demonstrated to support predisposed moral-ethical or political positions.[34]

From the perspective of the historian of religion, however, such creativity in the reading and "management" of authoritative sources is a given. Reading is never neutral. The reader is always invested in the reading process and is affected by an abundance of factors. This is simply part of human nature. New readings, unexpected realizations, and previously undetected messages turn up under certain conditions that allow or promote a new understanding of an old text. We have observed how Talmudic sages in the aftermath of the Bar Kokhba Rebellion discovered the Three Vows, which radically altered thinking about political activism in Jewish history (chapters 4–5). And we have seen how the pressing need of a universal military draft after the establishment of the state influenced thinking about previous assumptive readings of traditional sources (chapter 12).

Yisraeli's inclusion of the general Arab hinterland within the category of "pursuer" has had a significant influence on the activist religious Zionist community. Although it has not been accepted by all religious decisors,[35] it has become influential in raising the bar of acceptability in relation to the killing and injuring of noncombatants in "collateral damage" during military operations and in vigilante violence directed against

---

[32] Yisraeli, "Qibya," 92ff.

[33] It should be mentioned here that Leibowitz is profoundly aware of this phenomenon as well: "We uproot the category of sacred from its place and transfer it to things for which it was not intended, with all the danger bound up in such a distorted use" ("After Kibya," 173).

[34] Blidstein, "The Treatment of Hostile Civilian Populations...," 29ff.

[35] Rabbi Chaim David Halevi (former Chief Rabbi of Tel-Aviv), for example, refuses to apply the status of "pursuer" to the population that is not directly involved in the act ("The Rule of 'He Who Comes to Kill You, Kill Him First' in our Public Life," *Techumin* 1 [1980], 62–75 [Hebrew]).

Arab communities that are perceived as aiding and abetting those bent on committing violence against Jews.

Rabbi Sha'ul Yisraeli was one of the first to write seriously and openly about both the halakhic and transcendent meaning of the Jewish State, and he did so long before the 1967 War.[36] Like many if not most religious Zionists, he considered certain international events leading to the establishment of the State of Israel to be God-given signs and markers along the path to messianic deliverance. Decisions of the League of Nations, the United Nations and even individual governments were read as signs of impending Redemption. "The essence of the return of [the people] Israel to the Land of Israel is not through an overt divine visitation *(peqidah geluyah)*, for then the Vow would have been removed, but rather, through ascension with the permission and authority of the political powers."[37]

In a complex examination of the positions of earlier authorities, Yisraeli sought to show how the commandment of conquest of the land through settlement remained in force and would eventuate in this epoch with the divinely wrought redemption of the people of Israel. Mass immigration to Palestine and, later, the State of Israel was part of the divine plan. As noted previously, the prohibition against ascending in a wall was defined by the authoritative medieval Ashkenazi commentator, Rashi, as ascending "together by force" *(yachad beyad chazaqah)*. According to Yisraeli, such an act was neither the intent nor the modus operandi of the Zionist Movement. But in any case, the United Nations authorized the Jews to establish a Jewish state and declare national independence that would open the gates of the state to mass Jewish immigration. This act of an international body representing the community of nations caused the authority of the vow "not to ascend in a wall" to expire. Upon this expiration, all of Israel is required to engage in "conquest of the Land." The warning not to rebel against the nations of the world thus applied only in the lands of the Exile and only before the official world political organizations approved of the establishment of a Jewish homeland or state in the Land of Israel. After the United Nations declaration, fighting for a Jewish state in the Land of Israel could no longer be considered rebellion against God's command. "The establishment of the State in our days, which occurred according to the declaration of the nations to give the right to Israel, is the stage of which it is stated, 'until [God] pleases,'[38] and it is the first stage in the way of [divine] Redemption,

---

[36] *Sefer Eretz Chemdah* (Jerusalem: Mossad Harav Kook, Fourth Printing: 1999. First published in 1957).

[37] Yisraeli, *Eretz Chemdah*, 31.

[38] Translated above in chapter four as "until it is wished" (*Song of Songs* 2:7, 3:5, 8:4).

through which a strong public and independent rule in the Land of Israel is the establishment of the kingdom of the King Messiah."[39]

## The Slide to War: 1956*

The Qibya Affair was exceptional only in the magnitude of death and destruction and the considerable political repercussions that it generated within Israel as well as in the international arena. In retrospect, Qibya may not appear so surprising. The success of the fighting in 1947–48 brought Israel its independence, but it did not result in secure borders, and it uprooted hundreds of thousands of Palestinian Arabs. Subsequently, Israel suffered many casualties from the large numbers of incursions of Palestinians and Arabs from neighboring states, and it responded with anti-infiltration measures that often included retaliatory strikes initiated as a strategy of deterrence.[40] Benny Morris has shown how the overwhelming majority of Arab infiltration was economically or socially, rather than politically, motivated.[41] Whatever the motivation, the movement of Arabs crossing the borders raised the specter of a destabilizing increase in Israel's Arab population, and government leaders feared losing much needed land and strategic depth in the border areas that might be reclaimed by returnees. Some of the infiltration also included thievery and violent acts of vengeance, so Israel had reason to fear any escalation of incursions. Residents in the border settlements, many of whom were new immigrants from Arab countries, suffered persistently and often grievously from the infiltrators.

During most of the period between 1948 and the 1956 Suez War, Israel engaged in a "free fire" policy toward infiltrators along the border.[42] This, according to Morris, encouraged infiltrators to arm themselves and subsequently, to engage in more shoot-outs with Israelis that further escalated the violence. The Qibya Affair was the result of a strategy "... of hitting the offenders' village or district... with the aim of both frightening the locals into reining in the infiltrators and forcing the relevant Arab government to curb infiltration. This involved knowingly killing innocent civilians."[43]

---

* The heading "The Slide to War: 1956" is taken from Benny Morris, Israel's Border Wars: 1949–1956 (Oxford: Oxford University Press, 1993).

[39] Yisraeli, *Eretz Chemdah*, 35.

[40] E.L.M. Burns, "The Israeli Policy of Retaliation," in E.L.M. Burns, *Between Arab and Israeli* (London: George G. Harrap, 1962), 58–68.

[41] Benny Morris, *Border Wars*, 428.

[42] Morris, 126–141.

[43] Morris, 435.

That particular strategy was ended with Qibya because the political cost of such collective, indiscriminate punishment of civilians was too great.[44]

Soldiers serving in the Israeli Defense Forces at this time included religiously observant Jews who looked to their rabbis and tradition for guidance on such issues as these, yet aside from the writing of Shaul Yisraeli and the very different response of Yeshayahu Leibowitz, there was very little public discussion of the issues in the religious community. In fact, Leibowitz, Yisraeli, and Rabbi Shlomo Goren, who was the Chief Rabbi of the Israel Defense Forces, were practically the only public voices in the Orthodox community to treat the issues of religion, war, and state at the time. The latter two wrote prolifically on these topics and had a powerful impact on the emergence of the Settler Movement in the next decades.

Violence between Israel and its neighboring states continued to escalate as Israel's tactics changed with its effort to press the Arab governments to rein in the infiltrators. Arab civilian casualties came at a steep political cost after Qibya because of British and American criticism, so Israel tried to limit its reprisals to Arab military targets. These actions required larger fighting units, which ultimately increased the violence, damage, and loss of lives on both sides. Focusing on military targets contributed to an escalation in the size and number of attacks and counterattacks, which reached a certain peak with the reprisal raid on the Egyptian military headquarters at Gaza in February, 1955.[45] Egypt was not in a secure enough military position to respond directly, so Nasser began to activate the *fedayeen*,[46] irregular fighters who derived largely from Palestinian refugee populations. They were trained by Egypt to infiltrate Israel from Gaza with the specific purpose of engaging in guerrilla warfare against Jewish targets. *Fedayeen* units were also activated in Syria, Lebanon, and Jordan. Although Israel enjoyed some short-term success in its goal of stopping incursions and violence against Jews through its retaliatory tactics, it did not succeed in the long run, and its continuing strategy of reprisal raids was hindering receipt of the political and military assistance that it felt it needed from Britain and the United States.

Throughout this period, Israel felt politically as well as militarily isolated and under siege, and especially after the Gaza attack in 1955. The escalating Israeli military response to the *fedayeen* netted for Nasser an arms deal of unprecedented proportion with the Soviet Union, delivered

---

[44] Morris, 436.

[45] Sachar, *History of Israel*, 481–482, Morris, 86–93.

[46] Burns, 85–122. The term means, literally, "men who sacrifice themselves," in this case commandos, or to soldiers who are willing to risk their lives recklessly for the cause.

by Czechoslovakia.[47] It was this arms deal that pushed Moshe Dayan, and then Ben Gurion, to orchestrate a reason for a preemptive assault on Egypt that would destroy its army before the weaponry could be absorbed and used against Israel.[48] A series of Israeli incursions into Egyptian territory, however, did not provoke an adequate Egyptian military response to justify a preemptive strike. But the escalating Arab propaganda, political warfare (including the refusal to recognize Israel's right to exist), the blockade of Israeli shipping at the Straits of Tiran, the closure of the Suez Canal to Israeli ships and other vessels bringing goods to the port of Eilat, and the tremendous tension derived from the constant infiltration and border skirmishes all exerted pressure on Israel to break out of the cycle.

It was during this difficult time for Israel in the mid 1950s that Nasser, craving to rid Egypt of all Western political control, began to remove British citizens from Egyptian territory. As Egypt was tilting toward the Soviet Union, France approached Israel in the spring of 1956 with a plan to topple Nasser with British help. The plan was for Israel to prosecute a land campaign later that year with combined British and French air support, eventuating in the conquest of Sinai and the capture of the Suez Canal. With the world distracted by the Hungarian Uprising on October 23, Israel began its preemptive "Sinai Campaign" on October 29. By the evening of November 4, the Sinai Peninsula was in Israeli hands.[49]

The religious Zionist community hardly engaged in public discussion over the nature of the war or its justification. It could have been defined as a case of defensive war, as was the 1948 War, but this would have been difficult to support since the actual engagement between Israeli and Egyptian militaries was so obviously initiated by the Israel Defense Forces. From the perspective of Jewish religious tradition, a case could have been made to justify a preemptive attack that, according to the Babylonian Talmud, was intended to "weaken [a belligerent enemy] so that they would not march against them."[50] Chief Rabbi Shlomo Goren of the Israel Defense forces rejects this position in his foundational article on this war. He takes a different tack entirely by considering whether the religious status of the captured areas established by the Bible and Talmud justified their conquest.[51] He is careful not to employ language that might suggest divine

---

[47] Sachar, *History of Israel*, 473–474, 481–483.

[48] Morris, 288–296.

[49] Burns, 177–185.

[50] Sotah 44b, literally, "weakening idol worshippers so that they would not march against them" (see chapter 5).

[51] Shlomo Goren, "The Sanctity of the Land of Israel According to its Borders in the Torah," (Hebrew) *Machanayim* 31 (*Erev Chanukkah*/December) 1957, 5–11.

guidance in the success of the Sinai campaign of 1956, even though earlier he was one of the foremost religious leaders to call upon Jews to recognize the religious significance of the state.[52] "With the splendid success of the IDF in expanding the borders of the State of Israel and the conquest of the Sinai Peninsula, the issue of the sanctity of the conquered area has been awakened, whether all or part of it."[53]

## Sanctity of the Land of Israel *(Kedushat ha'aretz)*

In order to understand Goren's line of thinking it is necessary to clarify the notion of sanctity afforded to the Land of Israel in Jewish tradition, and the difference between the levels of sanctity known as "primary sanctity" and "secondary sanctity" *(kedushah rishonah and kedushah sheniyah).* The importance of the sanctity of the Land is connected to the issue of divine commandments because certain commandments may be observed only within areas sanctified by its borders. These commandments include such requirements as donating portions of the agricultural harvest or setting them aside for the poor *(leqet, shikhechah, pe`ah, terumot and ma`asrot),* the sabbatical year during which farmlands are required to lie fallow, rules of the jubilee years, certain observances associated with religious festivals, and so forth. These particular commandments cannot be observed outside of the Land of Israel. In fact, a majority of the positive commandments listed in the Torah are associated with life within the borders of the Land of Israel. Since it is always preferable to observe more of the divine precepts,[54] it is better (all other things being equal), to live within the Land of Israel where Jews are obligated to fulfill more of them.[55]

---

[52] Tabory, "Piety…," 16.

[53] Goren, "The Sanctity" 5.

[54] Baba Kama 38a, Avodah Zara 3a.

[55] This remains such an important position that pamphlets and even entire books such as the anonymous *The Mitzvah to Live in Eretz Israel* are given away in diaspora Jewish schools to convince diaspora Jews to move to Israel (Anonymous, *The Mitzvah to Live in Eretz Israel* [Beer Sheva: Beit Yosef Institute, 2005]). According to some sources, however, the inherent holiness of the Land is itself sufficient to generate merit even without fulfilling commandments (J. David Bleich, "Judea and Samaria: Settlement and Return." *Tradition* 18 [summer, 1979], 203). There exists a counter-tradition, however, which takes the opposite position, namely, that because of the "frightening holiness and dangerous uniqueness of the Land of Israel, and…the prodigious religious demands that the land makes upon its inhabitants…" the punishments for not living up to the requirements of the commandments dependent on the Land are so frightening that nobody should move there (Ravitzky, *Messianism*, 46–51). This view is held by some of the staunchest anti-Zionist Orthodox groups such as the Hasidic communities of Satmar and Munkacs. I am grateful to Aryeh Cohen for bringing this position to my attention.

This appears simple enough, but the special commandments observable only within the Land of Israel remain in force only in areas that have remained "sanctified." Not every part of the biblical Land of Israel has retained its original sanctity with regard to fulfilling commandments. The situation is complicated by the inconsistency between the various biblical delineations of the borders of the Land of Israel. In sum, not only are the biblical depictions of the borders of the Land of Israel inconsistent and therefore open to dispute, not all of the areas within those borders are considered to have retained their original sanctity thereby requiring Jews living in them to observe the special "commandments dependent upon the Land" *(hamitzvot hateluyot ba'aretz)*.

One must keep in mind that in the religious system of rabbinic Judaism, it is always meritorious to observe the commandments. The more commandments one observes, the greater the merit. Most of the positive commandments[56] are associated with living in the sanctified areas of the land of Israel, but if the land is no longer sanctified, the commandments dependent upon the Land are no longer required and, therefore, one loses the obligation (and even the option) to carry them out. The logical question then follows: From what (and where) does the sanctity of the Land derive? Is not the Land of Israel by definition entirely sacred?

According to the sages, the original sanctity of the Land of Israel derived from the Israelite conquest under the leadership of Joshua. This is the "primary sanctity," associated with the Israelites who entered the land after the Exodus from Egypt. A "secondary sanctity" derives from the resettlement of the Land by the Judean exiles who returned under Persian auspices from Babylonian captivity under the leadership of Ezra and Nehemiah. The first group consists of the immigrants from Egypt (`olei mitzrayim)* and the second, the immigrants from Babylon (`olei bavel)*. Whenever the land was in a state of sanctity *(kedushah)*, observance of all commandments dependent upon the Land was required and the merit derived from them was efficacious. If the Land were to lose its sanctified status, then not only would those commandments no longer be required, they would be forbidden.

The earliest layer of rabbinic discourse on the subject considers the original (or primary) sanctification of the Land to be eternal: "The primary sanctification rendered it sacred for its own time and sanctified it

---

[56] Positive commandments are those that one is obligated to observe (the "thou shalt..." commandments). Negative commandments are those activities that one is obligated to avoid (the "thou shalt not..." commandments).

for the future (i.e., forever)."[57] Later authorities, however, did not all agree. Some claimed that the primary sanctification rendered it sacred for its own time, but not for the future.[58] Maimonides resolved the situation in the following language: "All [the land] that was under the control of the immigrants from Egypt and that was sanctified by the first sanctification had its sanctification annulled when they were exiled, for the first sanctity existed only because of the conquest, which sanctified for its own time but not for the future. When the exiles ascended [from Bavel] and took control of a small part of the Land, they sanctified it by the second sanctification, which remains in force forever, for its own time and for the future."[59]

This relationship between sanctity and conquest is complicated by another statement of Maimonides that is referred to by Goren, one that has less support in the canonical texts of rabbinic literature but has had a significant impact on the religious Zionist community.

> The "Land of Israel" refers to any place among the lands that an Israelite king or prophet has conquered on behalf of most of Israel. This is called "conquest [on behalf] of many" *(kibbush rabim).* But an individual Israelite or a family or tribe that has gone and conquered a place for itself, even from the land that was given [by God] to Abraham, is not considered the Land of Israel until all of the commandments are practiced there. This is why Joshua and his court *(bet dino)* divided all of the Land of Israel into tribes even though not [all of it] had been conquered: so that there would not be "conquest [only on behalf] of an individual" *(kibbush yachid)* when each and every individual tribe would go up and conquer its own holding.[60]

Goren observes from these sources that the sanctity of the Land derived from military conquest is not eternal, but is valid and in force only as

---

[57] Mishnah `Eduyot 8:6: *"sheqedusha rishonah qideshah lesha`tah veqideshah le`atid lavo."*

[58] *Qideshah lesha`tah velo qideshah le`atid lavo* (BT., Megillah 10a, Chagigah 3b, Yevamot 16a, Makkot 19a), etc.

[59] Mishneh Torah, Terumot 1:5.

[60] Mishneh Torah, Terumot 1:2. "Conquest [on behalf] of the many" *(kibbush rabim)* does not appear, to my knowledge earlier than Maimonides. He seems to establish it by analogy from the term, unusual in rabbinic literature, "commandment on behalf of the many" *(mitzvah derabim),* found in the Talmud only in BT Berakhot 47b and absent entirely from early halakhic Midrash. The conclusion is drawn in more recent argument that, just as an individual may not conquer parts of the Land of Israel for one's own benefit, an individual (including even the Prime Minister of the State of Israel) may not give up parts of the Land of Israel for one's own benefit, but only with the consent of the entire community through a referendum, an argument that was made repeatedly in the fall of 2005 with regard to the Israeli withdrawal from Gaza.

long as Jews remain in power. When that period—Goren uses the term, "conquest"—is ended, so too is the sanctity ended. This is what happened in the case of Joshua's conquest with the immigrants from Egypt. The sanctity ended with the destruction of the First Temple. But sanctity established through civilian settlement is eternal, so the sanctity established in the areas settled by the immigrants from Babylonia at the time of Ezra and Nehemia is eternal. These areas, however, are much smaller than the areas conquered by Joshua, so the eternally sanctified areas of the Land of Israel are much smaller than those that might have been expected simply because they lie within the broader biblical borders of the Land of Israel associated with the conquest of Joshua.

Goren continues by noting that the sanctity of the Land was established in the Torah during the earliest days of Israelite settlement. This was the only period when all of the People of Israel lived within the borders of the Land of Israel. The sages concluded by this that after the destruction of the First Temple and the dispersion of Israel, the Land's sanctified status requiring observance of all the laws dependant upon the Land was lost because not all of the People of Israel continued to live there. With a reconquest or resettlement, therefore, even on behalf of the many, some kind of sanctifying act is necessary in order to reestablish the sanctity that requires observance of the commandments dependent upon the Land. Goren derives from this that even those areas lying outside the biblical borders of the Land of Israel, as long as they have been conquered by an Israelite king or prophet with the consent of the majority of Israel, can be considered to be like the Land of Israel, with the caveat that their sanctity (kedushah) applies only with an act of sanctification.[61]

Maimonides ruled, however,[62] that any areas conquered outside of the Land of Israel before all of the Land of Israel is conquered cannot achieve the sanctified status of the Land of Israel. Even the great King David was chastized by rabbinic tradition for conquering Aram Zobah (in today's Syria) before all of the areas within the biblical borders of the Land of Israel had been conquered.[63] According to Goren, therefore, those areas conqured by David with the approval of the Sanhedrin, the high court representing all of Israel, still could not attain the status of the Land of

---

[61] Accordingly, it is therefore possible also to prevent sanctification of the area despite conquest with the consent of the majority of Israel (Goren, "Sanctity," 6–7). The reader should keep in mind that these arguments are all supported through the citation of biblical and rabbinic sources, most of which are not reproduced here.

[62] Mishneh Torah, Terumot 1:3.

[63] Sifrei, `Eqev 51 (see chapter 8).

Israel. He derives from this that there are therefore three levels of status with regard to the question of sanctity of the Land: the Land of Israel that does or can have full sanctity, unconquered lands lying outside of the borders that can have no sanctity, and those outside the borders that have been conquered by an Israelite king or prophet with the approval of a religious court but have not yet achieved the level of sanctity of the Land of Israel.[64]

The issue looming behind this discussion is that of settlement. We observed in Part 2 that despite the rabbinic construct of the Three Vows intended to avoid the dangers of violent gentile reaction to Jewish rebellions and mass immigration to the Land of Israel, rabbinic sources place great emphasis on living within the borders of the Land of Israel.[65] According to Goren, the merit lies in living within the sanctified areas of the Land of Israel where so many more commandments may be observed. The same talmudic passage in which the Three Vows is introduced forbids Jews from moving away from the Land of Israel.[66] The Sinai Peninsula captured by Israel in 1956 is considered to be outside of the Land of Israel. How then, according to Goren, could Jews move from where the sanctity of the Land obtains within the borders of the State of Israel, into areas of mundane status conquered in 1956, particularly when certain particularly important and sacred areas within the biblical borders have not yet been brought under Israeli control?

"It has been asked, therefore, how can the conquered area [in the 1956 War] be sanctified when our own palace has not been conquered[67] and the footstool of the feet of our God is in the hand of strangers?"[68] Goren is referring to the rabbinic condemnation of King David, who is assumed to have been able militarily and politically to conquer all of the Land of Israel but chose not to do so.[69] At the time that Goren wrote his article, Israel had not yet conquered all of Jerusalem and the other parts of the biblical Land of Israel that came under Israeli control in June 1967, and it seemed impossible for it to do so. According to Goren, therefore, "This does not prevent inaugurating the sanctification of the Land for other conquered areas."[70]

---

[64] Goren, "Sanctity," 8.

[65] BT Ketubot 110b–111a.

[66] BT Ketubot 110b–111a.

[67] Goren's word for palace, *palterin*, is from Sifrei Devarim 51, a Midrash that chastises King David for conquering neighboring lands when idolatry is found within his own palace (a reference to Jerusalem) by the Jebusites.

[68] Goren, *Sanctity*, 9. The "footstool of the feet of our God" is a reference to Jerusalem (Aramaic Targum and rabbinic commentaries to Psalm 99:5, 132:8, and Lamentations 2:1).

[69] Sifrei Devarim 51.

[70] Goren, *Sanctity*, 10.

Maimonides is unambiguous in his law code[71] that an Israelite king cannot conquer in a discretionary war without the approval of the Sanhedrin, the great law court of seventy-one. This creates a problem for Goren, for the Sanhedrin no longer exists and the political impossibility of creating a universal religious law court for the Jewish people was quite evident to him. He solves this problem by noting that elsewhere, "Maimonides wrote, 'The Land of Israel' refers to any place among the lands that an Israelite king or prophet has conquered on behalf of most of Israel. This is called 'conquest [on behalf] of the many.' Therefore, an Israelite king or prophet, on behalf of most of Israel, is sufficient and does not require the Sanhedrin."[72]

It will be recalled from chapter 12 that Rabbi Isaac Halevi Herzog had already taught that because the power of an Israelite king derives from the people, support of a majority of the population of Israel gives a democratically elected political ruler the power to declare war. Rabbi Goren argued the same position, but supported his view by citing Rabbi Abraham Isaac Kook,[73] and argued, therefore, that areas conquered by the State of Israel beyond the borders established by the armistice agreements of the late 1940s can be sanctified according to Jewish law, even without the authority of the Sanhedrin. He derives from this, although not as plainly as stated here, that it is therefore not problematic for Jews, including Orthodox Jews, to move from within the recognized borders of the state to conquered territories outside those borders in order to settle those newly conquered territories.

Goren does not define the 1956 War as a preemptive war, despite the apparent acceptability of such an assessment. Instead, he refers to the Israeli invasion of the Sinai Peninsula in the Sinai Campaign as a war of defense, hence Commanded War. "War to save Israel from an attacking enemy (`ezrat yisra'el miyad tzar) is not associated only with the Land of Israel, but includes every place where saving Israel from the hand of an enemy occurs, and by means of war and conquest it is possible to save them and help them; the ruling is that this kind of war is Commanded War."[74] "Our war, therefore, was really to help Israel from the hand of an attacking enemy that was coming against us, and certainly this is Commanded War regarding everything relating to conquest outside the boundary of the borders of the Land according to the Torah... Therefore, the ruling

[71] Hilkhot Melakhim 5:6.
[72] Goren, *Sanctity*, 10, citing Maimonides, *Terumot* 1:2 (the full text is provided earlier).
[73] Goren, *Sanctity*, 11, citing Kook's *Mishpat Cohen* (no page number is cited).
[74] Goren, *Sanctity*, 10.

regarding this war is that of Commanded War in every way. Such conquest is conquest on behalf of the many *(kibbush rabim)* according to all Torah rulings, as long as it was the will of the people."[75]

Although Rabbi Goren never uses the term, "settlement" or "settling the land of Israel" in his essay, he raises most of the questions that will occupy the religious Zionist community with regard to settlement for many decades to come. May one move outside the borders of the Land of Israel in order to settle areas that might not appear to require the same observance of the commandments? Is conquest by the Israel Defense Forces under the authority of the elected government of the State of Israel equivalent to the conquest of an Israelite king or prophet with the authority of the Sanhedrin? Once such a conquest occurs, can conquered territories be returned? Throughout his discussion, not only does Goren refrain from mentioning settlement, he never raises the issue of pending Redemption or the messianic nature of the state, its armed forces, or the territories conquered during the war. These questions would only arise with the extraordinary events of 1967.

## A Decade of Development Toward a War to End Wars

The period from 1956 to 1967 was one of brisk economic development and continuing demographic growth. The population of Israel grew rapidly, deserts were cultivated, universities enlarged and extended, shipping expanded, a national water carrier constructed, and the military developed. This period also saw increased inflation and difficulties managing the economy, uncertainty over how to treat the Arab minority, and a demographic shift within the Jewish population of the state in favor of those originating from the Middle East and North Africa.[76]

It was in the middle of this period that an extraordinary trove of treasures directly related to the Bar Kokhba Rebellion was discovered in the Judean Desert in 1960–1961 by a team of archaeologists headed by Yigal Yadin.[77] This reawakened the question among Jews of the nature of the Bar Kokhba Revolt and its meaning for a Jewish state that perceived the hostile Arab countries surrounding it, like the Roman Empire of the second

---

[75] Goren, *Sanctity*, 11.

[76] Sachar, *History of Israel*, 515–614.

[77] Discoveries of artifacts relating to the Bar Kokhba rebellion had begun as early as 1952, but the most remarkable occurred in 1960–1961 (Yigal Yadin, *Bar Kokhba: The rediscovery of the legendary hero of the Second Jewish Revolt against Rome* [New York: Random House, 1971]; Zerubavel, *Death of Memory*, 83–86; idem, *Recovered Roots*, 56–59, 63–68, 129–133).

century, bent on its destruction. It is in this context that Rabbi Shlomo Goren considers the nature of the modern State of Israel and asks whether the Jewish people could have succeeded in conquering the Land and establishing Jewish rule there without a Torah or prophetic command and without messianic influence.[78] "There was a great argument among the sages of Israel regarding the status of Bar Kokhba.... Some of the sages of Israel and heads of the Sanhedrin, or the majority, did not recognize him as the messianic king, nor his period as a messianic period and destiny according to the prophets. Rather, they saw in him and his military successes in conquering the Land an intermediate stage of freeing the Land from the hands of strangers without any connection to the predictions of the prophets and the redemption of Israel."[79]

However, says Goren, if there were not some feeling among the Jews that the Bar Kokhba rebellion was in some way messianic, many (or perhaps most) would probably not have joined in the fighting. Goren cites the uncensored version of Maimonides' Code of Jewish Law (*Melakhim* 11:4),[80] which states that if Bar Kokhba had succeeded in rebuilding the Temple and returning the exiles to their land, then he would certainly have been the messiah. But if he was not entirely able to accomplish these things and it became clear that he was not the messiah, he could nevertheless "'...be like all the other acceptable and fit *(kasher)* Davidic kings...'" From these words it is clear that it is possible [to view] the establishment of an independent Jewish state as a midpoint between the destruction of the Second Temple and the messianic revival.... [T]he result is that there is authority for the possibility, according to the Torah and prophecy, to establish an independent [Jewish] state in the Land of Israel in an intermediate time between the Second Temple and the messianic period, with no direct link with the realization of the messianic vision. Rather, any such state can ultimately, by virtue of development according to the Torah, be a first and determinant stage in the realization of the messianic vision of the prophets of Israel in the messianic age."[81]

Rabbi Goren's position here is cautious. He is writing in 1960 when the state was small and beleaguered by the surrounding Arab countries. Yet it was expanding economically and was finding a certain military security

[78] Shlomo Goren, "The State of Israel as a Stage in the Vision of the Prophets of Israel," (Hebrew) *Mahanayim* 45 (1960), 8–11.

[79] Goren, "Stage in the Vision," 10.

[80] Cf. Yemenite version of *Melakhim* 11:8–9 according to http://www.mechon-mamre.org/e/index.htm (checked 10/7/08).

[81] Goren, "Stage in the Vision," 11.

in its position among the protagonists of the Cold War. Goren was careful not to imply that the establishment of the state and the success of its wars were signs of an impending divinely wrought Redemption, and he did not admit to any direct association between the state and the messianic process. But he argued, contrary to the non-Zionist and anti-Zionist Orthodox, that an independent Jewish state is acceptable on the authority of Jewish tradition ("according to the Torah and prophecy"). And he allowed for the possibility that such a state could be a "... stage in the realization of the messianic vision."

Shortly after the Bar Kokhba discoveries, during the years 1963–1965, archaeologists under the direction of Yadin made astounding discoveries at Masada, the hilltop fortress and "last stand" of the Jews in the first century rebellion against Rome.[82] Bear in mind that Masada was famous for the famous mass suicide of its fighters and their families rather than submission to the might of Rome. The Israeli press was notified of the discoveries as they were uncovered and identified, which stirred up tremendous emotion in this country that identified closely with the fortitude and sense of desperation associated with the Masada fighters.[83]

In 1964, and in response to these ongoing discoveries, Shlomo Goren wrote an article in *Machanayim*, the official organ of the IDF, entitled, "The Heroism of Masada in the Light of Halakhah."[84] He begins, "The heroic and bold behavior of the fighters of Masada when they saw the end of the war and realized the impending consequence, deciding each to fall at the hands of his comrade as free people and not to become enslaved to

---

[82] Yigal Yadin, *Masada: Herod's Fortress and the Zealots' Last Stand* (Jerusalem: Steimatzky's, 1966.

[83] This was not the first time that Masada was used as a symbol of Jewish heroism. Zionists identified with the site as early as 1912 with the first documented excursion to it. The use of Masada in Zionist discourse grew after the translation of Josephus' *Jewish War* into Hebrew in 1923 and the subsequent publication of an epic poem by Yitzhak Lamdan, "Masada," with the resulting Zionist slogan, "Never again shall Masada fall" (Jacob Lassner and S. Ilan Troen, *Jews and Muslims in the Arab World: Haunted by Pasts Real and Imagined* [New York: Rowman and Littlefield, 2007], 271–274).

[84] *Mahanayim* 87 (1964), 7–12. The journal's name is the dual form of the word for "camp," a term used in modern Hebrew as a military camp, and references the "two camps" *(machanayim)* of Jacob in Genesis 32. It has appeared as a weekly, monthly, and annual publication intended for the Israeli soldier public. Edited by Rabbi Menachem Hacohen, it began as "Pages for the Religious Soldier" during the War of Independence. In 1953 it became a weekly called *Machanayim*. By 1960, *Machanayim* became, among other things, a platform for the writings and opinions of Rabbi Shlomo Goren, the first Chief Rabbi of the Israel Defense Forces and subsequently the Ashkenazi Chief Rabbi of the State of Israel. It ceased publication before the 1967 War for reasons that were unrelated to that war, but was renewed a half-year later (Akiba Zimmerman, " 'Machanayim' The Story of a Religious-Military Periodical" [Hebrew], *Gesher* 12 [Nov. 1992], 108–115).

the enemy, raises the weighty Jewish legal problem: was their behavior acceptable or not." It is remarkable that he never uses the modern Hebrew word for suicide, *hit'abdut*, but rather "self-death" *(lamut mitat-`atzmo)*,[85] a term that does not have the same absolutely negative association in modern Hebrew. He concludes with five examples for which self-death in wartime is acceptable to Jewish law despite Jewish condemnation of suicide.

Not long afterward the militant heroism and self-sacrificial profile associated with Masada and so admired by Rabbi Goren was challenged, beginning as a response to the emotional frenzy that was heightened by the press coverage and government response to the finds. This became known as the critique of the "Masada complex."[86] Even in 1964 and no doubt in reaction to the inclination toward the heroic ethos that was accelerated by the Bar Kokhba finds, Israel Ta-Shma wrote an article in the same edition of *Machanayim* in which Shlomo Goren's article appeared, arguing that Jewish tradition had, overall, not considered heroism to be a Jewish cultural norm.[87] But the heroism and valor associated with war, even war that might result in suicide, had by that time percolated deeply into Israeli society. As usual in such situations, it was the social and historical context that so deeply informed the ethos of the society, and this shall be observed more closely as our examination of divinely authorized war moves into the late 1960s and 1970s.

---

[85] Also, *lamut biyedey `atzmo, lehamit et `atzmo*, etc.

[86] Robert Alter, "The Masada Complex," *Commentary* 56:1 (July 1973); Nachman Ben-Yehuda, *The Masada Myth: Collective Memory and Mythmaking in Israel* (Madison, Wisconsin: Univ. Wisconsin: 1995).

[87] Israel Ta-Shema, "Aspects of Heroism in the Halakhah," *Machanayim* 87 (1964), 72–75. A third article on the topic is found in the same issue, by David Flusser, "Heroism and Martyrdom," 76–79.

CHAPTER 14 | 1967 to 1973

*The Miracle of Conquest and the*
*Test of Yom Kippur*

The Eternal One of Israel will not deceive and will not change
His mind.

I SAMUEL 15:29

## 1967: The Messiah Is on His Way

Menachem Friedman observed that "If Israel's 1948 War of Independence
is viewed as a Zionist war for the establishment of an emergent secular
Jewish state, the Six-Day War can be defined as a Jewish war that reflected
a substantive historical change in dialectic between Exile and Redemption.... [I]t marked the point at which a substantially different religious
reality came into existence."[1] The June war of 1967 sparked a revival
of secular as well as religious ideologies to justify the establishment of
Jewish sovereignty over the captured lands,[2] but particularly among religious Zionists it opened a floodgate of emotions that had been pent up and
hidden, often even from those who held them.

The emotionality of the war's extraordinary military success needs
to be placed in context. The state of Israel had experienced tremendous

---

[1] Menahem Friedman, "Jewish Zealots: Conservative versus Innovative," in *Jewish
Fundamentalism in Comparative Perspective*, ed. Laurence Silberstein (New York: New York
University Press, 1993), 159. On the 1967 War, see Michael Oren, *Six Days of War: June 1967
and the Making of the Modern Middle East* (Oxford: Oxford University, 2002); Tom Segev,
*1967: Israel, the War, and the Year that Transformed the Middle East* transl. Jessica Cohen
(New York: Macmillan, 2007).

[2] David Weisburd, *Jewish Settler Violence: Deviance and Social Reaction* (Philadelphia:
University of Pennsylvania Press, 1989), 20.

economic and demographic growth between the 1956 and 1967 wars, and it enjoyed a sense of confidence that was remarkable given the destruction of millions of European Jews twenty years earlier. The "years of hardship" *(shenot hatzena')* that followed the establishment of the state had passed and the intolerable infiltrations of Arabs across the borders had been reduced, though not stopped. Despite the anxiety of existence surrounded by hostile Arab states, there was a growing sense of comfort among the Jewish population. But some marginalized political and religious groups continued to aspire to a Jewish state that would comprise all of the biblical Land of Israel.

On the eve of Independence Day on May 12 at Yeshivat Mercaz Harav ("The Rabbi's Center Yeshivah") named after Rabbi Abraham Isaac Kook,[3] occurring exactly one day before the beginning of the crisis leading up to the 1967 War, Rabbi Kook's only son, Rabbi Tzvi Yehudah Kook, "delivered a festive sermon, in the midst of which his quiet voice suddenly rose and he bewailed the partition of historic Eretz Yisrael and the inability of the Jews to return to the holy cities of Hebron and Nablus."[4] Three weeks later, his students would consider his words truly, not merely metaphorically, prophetic.

Part of the reason for their prophetic assessment of his message lies in the astonishing events of the following weeks leading up to the outbreak of war on June 5. Israel found itself surrounded by millions of Arabs who were being exhorted to destroy it. Egypt's President Gamal Abdul Nasser had received and absorbed massive Soviet military armament during the previous decade. With the blessing of the USSR, he expelled the United Nations' Expeditionary Force (UNEF) that had been established in the Sinai Peninsula after the 1956 War, concentrated over a hundred thousand troops in the Sinai Peninsula, and closed the Straits of Tiran to Israeli shipping. He persuaded Syria and Jordan to join the preparations for war, and even Iraq, Morocco, Tunisia, and Saudi Arabia offered at least token use of their armies and communications.[5]

It appeared to the Israeli public that the United Nations cared little about the military buildup and what appeared to be an impending invasion, while Europe seemed to express little interest in the military pressure

---

[3] To be called by one's students "The Rabbi" *(harav)* is an exceptional epithet. This yeshivah was and remains the intellectual center for a redemptive form of Religious Zionism that considers the establishment of the State of Israel to be a step in the inexorable journey leading to divinely authored Redemption.

[4] Ehud Sprinzak, *The Ascendance of Israel's Radical Right*, 44. A significant portion of that sermon is translated in the following chapter.

[5] Sachar, *History of Israel*, 622–635; Oren, 136–137.

swelling up in the region. 1967 was only twenty-two years after World War II. More than one quarter of the Israeli population at that time had either survived the horrors of the Holocaust as refugees or had lost close relatives to the systematic Nazi genocide. There was palpable fear that another Holocaust was in the making. As part of the war preparations in Tel Aviv, mass graves were dug in the main football stadium.[6]

Nasser gave speech after speech exhorting his people and soldiers to be ready for the onslaught. The Jews would be destroyed. Tel Aviv would be emptied of its inhabitants. The Zionist entity would exist no more.[7] Whether Nasser had the actual intention to invade or was simply attempting to gain political stature through an act of military bravado, he gave every impression to Israel that he was serious. And Israel took him seriously. The Israeli chief of staff, Yitzhak Rabin broke down temporarily over the stress, and the entire Jewish world held its breath, with terrible fear and apprehension over the future of Israel.[8]

The alarm and dread throughout the Jewish world was almost overwhelming, but in one day the war was essentially over. Arab and Israeli perspectives on the buildup and commencement of the war differ considerably.[9] But whether the Israeli military decided to take advantage of a situation well in its favor or launched its preemptive attack as a means of softening what it considered to be an inevitable and overwhelming blow, it managed to destroy the air forces of all the neighboring Arab nations within hours. With Israeli control of the skies, the war was won. It ended formally six days later.

To the Jews of Israel and the world, who were terrified at what seemed to them to be an impending massacre, the quick and relatively painless victory was miraculous. To many in the religious Zionist world, miraculous was not merely a metaphor. It was reasonable for them to consider the astonishingly swift and nearly painless victory to be a sign of the approaching Redemption, a signpost along the inexorable journey to a final divine

---

[6] Michael Bar Zohar, *The Longest Month* (Hebrew) (Tel Aviv: Levin Epstein, 1968), 153–154.

[7] The rhetoric was serious and the verbiage was articulated from a number of quarters in the Arab world. On the question as to whether or not Nasser actually threatened to throw the Jews into the sea, see Moshe Shemesh, "Did Shuqayri Call for 'Throwing the Jews into the Sea'?" *Israel Studies* 8.2 (2003) 70–81.

[8] For the period leading up to the 1967 War, see Oren, Segev, and Walter Lacqueur, *The Road to War 1967: The Origins of the Arab-Israeli Conflict* (London: Weidenfeld and Nicolson, 1969), Nadav Safran, *From War to War: The Arab Israeli Confrontation 1948–1967* (New York: Pegasus, 1967).

[9] See Hisham Sharabi, "Prelude to War: The Crisis of May-June 1967," in Ibrahim Abu-Lughod (ed.), *the Arab-Israeli Confrontation of June 1967: An Arab Perspective* (Evanston, IL: Northwestern University, 1970), 49–65.

deliverance that began with Zionism. Even staunchly secular Jews found themselves drawn toward their religious roots.[10]

Before the "miracle," while the new state was normalizing after independence and prior to the buildup of tension in May of 1967, Religious Zionism had become stuck in a kind of religious and ideological doldrums. As will be examined in greater detail, the lack of inspirational ideological movement leadership would soon be challenged by a new generation of religious Zionist activists. But before the 1967 war people in the activist religious Zionist community were troubled about the direction of the State of Israel and wondered out loud about the existential nature of a mostly secular Jewish state and the insignificant role of religious Jews within it. Was the community of Israel abandoning hope in God's redemption, and would that cynicism result in failure or perhaps even another great disaster for the Jewish people? The following reflection, for example, was published in the Religious Kibbutz Movement newsletter in late spring of 1966: "The central question is this: Is it permissible for the people of Israel from the religious standpoint, or might it be required, to engage in a great and definitive act based on human reason and analysis of history, or is the people obligated to wait for a sign from divine providence in order to know which way to go?"[11] The astonishing victory of the 1967 War became "the sign from divine providence" to which this writer was referring—and for which so many people seem to have been waiting.

It was only after this extraordinary event that most religious Zionists acknowledged (or perhaps began to recognize) what they considered to be the truly messianic, redemptive nature of Zionism. In previous chapters we have observed the neomessianic spirit of Zionism as articulated in word and deed among secular Zionists, but that was a different phenomenon. It was a kind of social utopianism in Jewish form that was not anchored nearly as deeply by the powerful energy of scriptural textual affirmation as was Religious Zionism. This is not to suggest that secular Zionist activists did not frequently cite scriptural references and traditional symbols in their ideological messages, their poems, and their art. But this was part of their program to contextualize, indeed to Judaize culturally, through symbols and language, what was at its core a modern European-style nationalist movement.

---

[10] Sachar, *History of Israel*, 614. "[Moshe Dayan] would even refer to the Six-Day War of 1967 as an expression of the nation's yearning for the land of its forefathers, rather than as a war of survival." (ibid p. 479).

[11] Aharon Nahlon, "The Religious Significance of the State of Israel," *Amudim* 242 April 1966, 256.

We have previously noted how Zionism began in Europe as a modern European nationalist movement, and like most such movements it contained within it utopian, redemptive, and neomessianic elements. But while modern nationalism was Judaized *culturally* among the secularists who desired to re-imagine their Jewish identity differently than through the traditional rabbinic model,[12] it was Judaized *religiously* among religious Zionists to create in significant ways a very different result. A large part of nationalism's Judaization among religious Zionists was messianic and redemptive according to traditional Jewish patterns, much more than the early religious Zionist leaders would acknowledge, even to themselves. The obvious religious messianism of Rabbi Abraham Isaac Kook and his students represented only a small minority of religious Zionists that had little impact on the larger community until after the 1967 war. It is of course evident that the composition of the Prayer for the State of Israel was an expression of messianic aspiration that burst forth immediately after the success of independence. But Mizrachi, the National Religious Party, and the intellectual organs that publicly represented the political and religious worldview of Religious Zionism only rarely hinted that the establishment of the State of Israel was part of the divine plan that would culminate in the messianic coming. All that changed after the victory in 1967. It seemed as if a dam had burst and everyone in the religious Zionist camp was writing about the beginning of the messianic Redemption.

Most of the articles in the June 1967 issue of the Religious Kibbutz Movement newsletter, *Amudim*,[13] thanked and extolled God for the miracle of salvation.[14] Verses from Psalms and the daily liturgy were cited, as well as ecstatic expressions of relief and joy: "Salvation is the Lord's!! (Prov. 21:31)…, Anyone today who reads the press, anyone today who listens to the radio…is a witness to the explosion of faith in the Rock of Israel and its Salvation,[15] for whoever saw the miracle face to face—has been swept

---

[12] Benedict Anderston, *Imagined Communities:Reflections on the Origin and Spread of Nationalism* (London: Verso, 1991).

[13] The newsletter of the Religious Kibbutz Movement (*hakibbutz hadati*), established in 1938 as *Alonim*, meaning simply, "bulletin." Its first editorial board consisted of three kibbutz members: David Interiligtor, Aharon Nusbach (Nachalon), and Dov Konwahl. Thirty-nine issues of *Alonim* were printed in various formats. The last issue came out in December, 1949, and after a hiatus of slightly more than a year, was reissued as "Religious Kibbutz News" (*yedi`ot hakibbutz hadati*). It became *Amudim* (meaning "pages" or "columns") from October, 1957. Because of the previous formats, the first issue of *Amudim* appeared as number 114 (1957), and has appeared monthly without interruption to the time of this writing.

[14] The following citations are all drawn from this issue, number 256 (volume 15:10 [June 1967]).

[15] A liturgical reference to God built out of biblical phraseology.

along the powerful current..., Rabbi Shlomo Goren is the [priest] anointed for war... [16] And so we have merited unintentionally to be at the next level on the way to our redemption. *On the way to real redemption*—and no longer merely *the beginnings of redemption* (italics in original).... Not only the Israel Defense Forces (IDF) established the State, and not only the conquerors of Canaan paved the way.[17] Not only the readiness and dedication of the People of Israel won this war. Heaven forbid, lest the expression of this great victory be articulated only by the victorious march of the IDF that demonstrates its strength, *'for it is You who gave us the power for fighting...'*[18] The flowering of our Redemption...."

The sense of redemption was so powerful that calls were made to transform the traditional daily Orthodox liturgy much more significantly than the addition of the "flowering of redemption" prayer mentioned in the previous chapter. Rabbi Moshe Levinger, who would become one of the most controversial early activists in the Settlement Movement, claimed that it was forbidden to return even one inch of land that was given to Israel by God. Israel has the moral right and responsibility to realize its destiny and to recover and never return "what was stolen from Israel 1897 years ago."[19] In the following issue of *Amudim* (July-August), Tzuriel Admonit of Kibbutz Yavneh called on the Chief Rabbinate to eliminate the traditional mourning sections *(tachanun)* from the daily liturgy.[20] Rabbi Menachem

---

[16] Rabbi Goren was the chief rabbi of the Israeli Defense Forces in 1967, and is likened to the priest divinely authorized to sanctify Israel's soldiers for battle, referenced in the Babylonian Talmud (see chapter 5).

[17] The clearly acknowledged association between the 1967 War and the divinely ordained conquest of Canaan under Joshua's leadership is remarkable.

[18] This last line, in italics, is constructed from Deut. 8:18. In the Deuteronomy context, the meaning of the Hebrew *chayl* is something closer to sustenance or wealth, though the root can also mean "strength" and even "army" (from this word is constructed the modern Hebrew word for soldier). Here is another and quite normal example of playing with the range of meaning in the Hebrew to derive appropriate meaning.

[19] His words are entitled, "The Flowering of Our Redemption," a play on the liturgical phrase that considered the State of Israel to be the *"beginning* of the flowering of our Redemption" (*Amudim* 256 [June 1967], 304). After the 1967 War, his teacher, the influential Rabbi Tzvi Yehudah Kook, wrote, "People speak of 'the dawn of Redemption.' In my opinion we are in the midst of Redemption. The dawn took place a hundred years ago. We are in the parlor, not the hallway" (Charles Leibman and Asher Cohen, "A Case of Fundamentalism in Contemporary Israel," in *Religion, Democracy, and Israeli Society* ed. Charles Liebman [Amsterdam: Harwood, 1997], 68).

[20] He also called for the elimination in the daily morning blessings *(birchot hashahar)* of the sections, *shelo asani eved, shelo asani ishah*, and to rely, both men and women alike, on *she`asani yisrael*; to eliminate the mourning of the counting of the *omer*, to do away with the minor fasts and other acts of mourning aside from *tisha be'av*, and to celebrate the day of capturing Jerusalem (Tzuriel Admonit, "From Tzuriel's Correspondence," *Amudim* #257–258 [July–August 1967], 257–258, 334–335).

Hartom called for other liturgical changes in order to acknowledge publicly the miracle of redemption actually in progress.[21]

Surprisingly, and despite the cover photograph of a unit of soldiers holding their company flag at a gate to the Old City of Jerusalem, the tone conveyed by the B'nai Akiba Youth Movement newsletter, *Zera`im*, was less ebullient than that of the kibbutz movement newsletter.[22] It expressed more of a sense of shock at the surprising positive military turnaround. In fact, the editors appeared to be less confident in God's hand in the victory of the 1967 War than in the 1956 War, when they headlined their column with "Salvation is the Lord's" and ended with "The IDF came out strengthened by this battle and ready for the next to come. Therefore, this was the great hand of God in Egypt!"[23] But movement ideologues soon began to write in those pages with a different tone. The following issue of *Zara`im* featured Rabbi Yakov Ariel (Stieglitz) and Moshe Tzvi Neriya, who ascribed deep and transcendent meaning to the war and the Israeli conquest of biblical lands.[24]

These and other leaders in the youth movement were engaged during this critical time in stimulating the natural inclinations of religious Zionist youth toward activism, Torah study, and pioneering that were activated by the sudden acquisition of virtually all of the biblical Land of Israel. Whether or not it was evident to most, the ideological leadership purposefully encouraged the larger secular and non-Zionist Orthodox community to understand the brilliant victory as yet another divine sign that Israel was on the road to Redemption. This surge in millenarian aspiration was different from the short and limited public eruptions after independence and the quick victory of 1956. The unleashing of messianic hope and determination after the 1967 War simply would not die down.

The victory in 1967 radically changed the political, military, and religious landscape, though the religious changes were less immediately

---

[21] His suggestions include significant changes as in the liturgical core of the thrice-daily prayer service known as the "Eighteen Benedictions." These include changing the benediction called *boneh yerushalayim*, to "And to Jerusalem Your city You have returned with compassion! (*veliyrushalayim `irkha berachamim shavta*)." And he would change the benediction called *birkat ha'avodah* to "And may the worship of Your people Israel always be acceptable, just as our eyes have seen Your merciful return to Zion" ("Suggestions of Rabbi Hartom," *Amudim* 257–258 (July–August), 335–338.

[22] *Zera`im* 322 (June-August/SivanTammuz, 1967).

[23] *Zera`im* 186 (November-December/Kislev-Tevet, 1956), 2.

[24] Neriya, "Upon Your Ramparts, Jerusalem," *Zera`im* 324 (Av/August–September, 1967), 3 and see chapter 13. Neriya had been editor of *Zera`im* for years previously, but based on the tone of the editorial comments in relation to that of his article, it appears that he was no longer editor at the time of the war.

apparent than the political and military changes. Some of the many issues that the 1967 war raised for religious and nonreligious Zionists alike included questions about the nature of the Zionist enterprise as articulated by the role of the state, the significance of the newly acquired territories and their settlement by Jews, and the significance of the Israeli army. The first issue following the war of the halakhic journal, *Shanah Beshanah,*[25] contained five articles dedicated to these issues from a relatively broad religious Zionist perspective, focusing in particular on the religious or sacred nature and legal status of the territories conquered in the war that were defined biblically as the Land of Israel.[26]

Another halakhic journal, *Torah Shebe'al Peh,* published by Mosad Harav Kook,[27] contained no articles treating war or the religious nature of the Land of Israel until after the victory in 1967. The first issue after the war included three articles on war and territory, and one on the problem of Jews treading upon the sacred ground of the Temple Mount.[28] The IDF

---

[25] 1968 (no volume numbers are provided for this annual publication). *Shanah Beshanah* ("Year by Year") began immediately after independence under the name "Torah and State" *(Hatorah Vehamedinah)* as an organ of the "Association of Rabbis of Hapoel Hamizrachi" *(Hever Harabbanim shel Hapoel Hamizrachi).* It represents the activist theological/intellectual arm of Mizrachi, which produced thirteen issues between 1949 and 1962. It came under the auspices of the Chief Rabbinate of the State of Israel in 1960–1962 and its name changed to *Shanah Beshanah.* Both formats were edited by Rabbi Shaul Yisraeli (d. 1995). The original name of the journal is an expression of the inseparable relationship between the new nation-state and Jewish religious law and tradition. Yisraeli dedicated his life, through teaching and writing, to his belief that a modern Jewish state can and must be administered in complete accordance with halakhah.

[26] The titles of these articles: "The Question of the Territories Liberated by the IDF" (public forum), Chief Rabbi of the State of Israel Isser Unterman: "The Acquisition *(qinyan)* of the Nation is not Open for Trading," Rabbi Shaul Yisraeli, "To Hold On to the Liberated Territories with all our Might," Tzvi Kaplan, "The Western Wall in Halakhah," Chayyim Rivlin, "The Law of the Land of Israel in the Teaching of Nahmanides (700 years since his *aliyah*)," Yona Cohen, "The Six Day War." This compares with only four articles on topics of war in the previous fourteen years, and a total of twelve articles on the topic in general since the inception of the journal and its predecessor during their first twenty years of existence. Five articles treating war were published in 1949–1950 in response to the establishment of the state. Very little was written on the topic between 1950 and the 1967 War. The Orthodox community in the United States also responded to the war through publication. These were mostly in the popular Jewish press, but a small growth in scholarly religious responses can also be discerned, beginning with Aryeh Newman, "The Centrality of Eretz Yisrael in Nachmanides," *Tradition* 10 (summer, 1968), 21–30.

[27] *Torah Shebe'al Peh* ("The Oral Torah") was first edited by Rabbi Yehuda Leib Hacohen Maimon (d. 1962) and represented the proceedings of an annual conference at Mosad Harav Kook, beginning in the summer of 1958. Specific topics are chosen each year and examined in detail with the purpose "...of spreading the Oral Torah here in popular lectures aimed at the larger diverse public in all of its various subgroups and levels" (anonymous introductory pages, presumably from the editor, J. L. Maimon, *Torah Shebe`al Peh* 1959, 5).

[28] Chief Rabbi of the State of Israel Ovadia Yosef, "On the Rule of Entering into the Area of the Temple in This Era," Rabbi Shaul Yisraeli, "Commanded War and Discretionary War," Rabbi

magazine *Machanayim* ceased publication shortly before the 1967 War, but began publishing again in 1968. The first two issues after the 1967 War (issues 116 and 117) treat the conquered places that are holy to Jews and Judaism. Issue 117 also treats the war and those conquered areas with little or no Jewish religious significance such as Gaza.[29]

One might expect that religious journals treating issues of state would naturally take an interest in questions regarding war in the aftermath of a major military conflict. But this did not occur after the 1956 War, which, as in the 1967 War, resulted in the speedy conquest of large territories. Three factors may have determined the radically different perception of these two victories. First, the territories conquered in 1956 were outside the biblical borders of the Land of Israel. Second, although the 1956 War also brought a swift victory, Israel was aided militarily by two of the world's great military powers, France and Britain. And third, as will be observed in more detail, the nearly eleven years between 1956 and 1967 marked a large change in the existential position of the state of Israel and in the particular yearnings and self-concept of the religious Zionist community.

The triumph in 1967 was Israel's alone, or Israel's with the help of the Almighty. In fact, the victory was often articulated in religious Zionist publications through such imagery as the "hand of God." If it was God's design, then was it not a holy war? Would it not be confirmation, finally, that the Jews have been given divine authority for the establishment of the Jewish State? What, then, of the Three Vows?

Until 1967, one recurring and unanswered question found in the literature was whether what was recognized by some as the breaking of the two vows made incumbent upon Israel was justified by the establishment of the state. The two vows, it is recalled, are pledges God required of Israel that it would not engage in mass immigration to the Land of Israel ("ascension in a wall") and that Jews would not attempt to rebel against their degraded position among the Gentiles ("rebellion against the nations"). According to the schema, the third was God's requirement that the Gentiles pledge not to oppress the Jews too much in return for the Jews remaining true to their pledges.[30] The religious critics of Zionism had claimed that the mass immigration to the Land of Israel and then the State of Israel through

Mordekhai Ilan, "Whether Sanctified for Its Own Time [or] Sanctified Forever," Rabbi Moshe Tzvi Neriya, "Jerusalem the Sacred City and the Temple," all in *Torah Shebe'al Peh* 10 (1968).

[29] Issue 121 (1969) is devoted to issues of peace and is entitled, "On Peace in Jewish Sources," and the following year, issue 124 is devoted to articles on the messianic idea *(hara`yon hameshichi)*.

[30] See chapter 5.

the Zionist Movement, and the determination of the state to set its own independent political course even sometimes against the will of the United Nations, were violations of this agreement. This criticism was occasionally countered by religious Zionists by the claim that Zionist activism and the establishment of the State were justified cosmically by the Gentiles' breaking of *their* vow not to persecute the Jews too much during the modern period, first by the Russian pogroms of the late nineteenth century and then particularly by the Holocaust.

This is not a trivial question for religious Jewry. For many, the stakes are extremely high. What is at stake is the possible Redemption of the Jewish people—or possibly another catastrophe along the lines of the destructions of the two Jerusalem Temples and the disaster of the Bar Kokhba Rebellion. Perhaps the best way to imagine the possible negative outcome of the wrong interpretation is another Holocaust, however one might imagine such a forbidden thought.

In other words, does Gentile persecution of Jews in the late nineteenth and twentieth centuries justify the breach of the Jewish promise to God for self-restraint symbolized by the Three Vows, therefore permitting or even encouraging Orthodox religious engagement in Zionism, building up the State of Israel and the acquisition of territory defined by the Bible as belonging to the People of Israel? Might such an end to Jewish self-restraint even represent engagement in the messianic process leading to the final Redemption?

Or does the meaning of modern European persecution of Jews lie elsewhere? Could the persecution of Jews in the modern period represent, say, a divine warning to the Jewish people to cease breaking away from religious tradition by forming liberal religious or secular movements or, simply, to refrain from modernizing in any manner? If so, then perhaps Zionism is only another forbidden attempt to "force God's hand," which already resulted, according to this view, in the horror of the Holocaust and may well cause something like it again.

To most Orthodox Jews, the 1967 War put to rest any doubt about the Zionist enterprise. After 1967, the question about Jewish responsibility for redemption or destruction would be asked differently by many, and especially those who would become activists in the movements to settle the Biblical Lands conquered (or to use the language of many in these movements, liberated) in the war. The miraculous victory of the war was a clear sign that God intends for Israel to conquer and settle all of the Biblical Land of Israel, including those lands extending beyond the borders established by the United Nations Partition Plan of 1947 or armistice agreements established through the 1948 War. God's national messianic design was made manifest by the great victory accomplished in a mere six days. Would it not be a great failure of the Jewish people if they were to defy the command explicit in the miracle of this victory? Failure to carry out the divine will could be disastrous, based on the traditional Jewish historiography of obedience = success/disobedience = failure.

*Shanah Beshanah*, the annual publication of the Chief Rabbinate of Israel, published a transcript of a celebration at Mosad Harav Kook after the 1967 War.

> In celebration, they repeated the oath of the Babylonian exiles: "*If I forget thee O Jerusalem, let my right hand be forgotten....*"[31] Then Rabbi Tzvi Yehudah said: "The Torah prohibits giving up even one inch of our liberated land. This is not a conquest and we are not conquerors of foreign lands.[32] We are returning to our home, to the inheritance of our ancestors. This is not an Arab land. This is the inheritance of God, and the entire world must become accustomed to this thought. It will thus be better for all of us."...Rabbi Tzvi Yehudah Kook refused to end his words until the entire assembly accepted the yoke of heaven and repeated after him: "*Hear O Israel, The Lord our God is One*," and promised that they would never forget the vow regarding Jerusalem.[33]

The intensity and volume of writing by those who would become engaged in the settlement movements as ideologues or as activists increased dramatically after the 1967 War. Particularly among the ultra-nationalist Orthodox engaged personally in the "conquest" (both peaceful and military) of settling all of the Land of Israel,[34] the "Six-Day War" represents a major paradigm shift.[35] Such religious militancy was simply inconceivable prior to that watershed event.

---

[31] Psalm 137:5.

[32] This is also the position of Rabbi Shaul Yisraeli on the question of the territories "liberated by the IDF:" "To Hold on to the Liberated Territories with All Our Might." (*Shanah Beshanah* 1968), 106. This view is in reference to the legality of acquiring and keeping the territories. Because they belong to Israel on the basis of biblical authority, Israel did not forcibly take land belonging to someone else, but rather simply took control over what it had always owned. Such a position does not denigrate militancy or military conquest.

[33] Rabbi Tzvi Yehudah Kook, "On Questions of the Territories Liberated by the IDF," (Hebrew) *Shanah Beshanah* 1968, 108–109.

[34] On Nahmanides' position that settling the land is equivalent to conquering the land, see chapter 8. Maimonides also uses the term *kibbush* in the sense of acquiring land through legal contract (*Hilkhot Terumot* 1:1).

[35] Don-Yehiyeh, Eliezer, "The Book and the Sword: The Nationalist Yeshivot and Political Radicalism in Israel," in Martin Marty and R. Scott Appleby, *Accounting for*

In addition to the radical shift in existential value that the 1967 War wrought for the State of Israel, it also put Israel in the center of the world media map where it has remained ever since.[36] It stimulated the development of Israeli television, and all Israel's news organs grew exponentially. The raised profile and increased world interest in that tiny state (of some two and a half million Jewish inhabitants in 1967) lent it a status far greater than similarly placed nation-states, thus adding support for the view of Israel's transcendent nature. As a result of the messianic suggestion associated with the military conquest of the 1967 war, Orthodox religious scholars, and particularly religious Zionist activists and thinkers, became deeply invested in legitimating the right for Israel to control those territories and in justifying Jewish militancy in general.

The increase in traditional religious scholarship over this issue reflects a trend that had remained quiet for years, a yearning that was too dangerous and frightening to articulate publicly. Watershed events such as the 1967 War do not cause paradigm shifts as much as they mark a change that had begun earlier and accelerated afterward. It is now evident that many Orthodox thinkers began, only after 1967, to cite in public a range of arguments by premodern rabbinic thinkers that support the messianic nature of the State of Israel. They were not ignorant of these arguments previously. After 1967 they cited traditional sources to buttress the position that not all Jews are required to return to traditional Jewish religious practice in order for the messianic Redemption to occur, and that the great agricultural successes of the modern Jewish state are signs of the immanent Salvation.[37] Rabbi Haim Druckman, one of the activist leaders of Gush Emunim and the Settler Movement that would emerge in the decade after the 1967 War, said,

> I could come up with... plenty of quotations from authoritative sources, according to which we are living in an era of redemption, but I prefer to observe reality. After two thousand years Jews return to their homeland;

*Fundamentalisms*, vol. 4 Chicago: U. of Chicago Press, 1994, 264–265.

[36] Uri Urbach and Chagai Segal, *And Today They Use It to Wrap Up Fish: Prophecy about Destruction and Miracles: 1967–1992* (Hebrew) (Beit El: Sifriat Beit El, 1992), 9–11.

[37] Shlomo Aviner, *A People [Rising Up] like a Lion'* (Hebrew, Jerusalem, 1983), 2:114–115, 119–120. See also Rabbi Meir Blumenfeld, "On the Vow Not to Go Up As a Wall," (Hebrew) *Shanah Beshanah* 1974, 151–155, Rabbi Menachem M. Kasher, "Torah Position on the Vow that Israel Not Go Up as a Wall to the Land of Israel," (Hebrew) *Shanah Beshanah* 1977, 213–228, Rabbi Moshe Tzvi Neriya, "Our Right to the Land of Israel," (Hebrew) *Torah Shebe`al Peh* 1974, 149–180, etc. Abraham Isaac Kook was of course the exception, who wrote about the messianic implications of the new Jewish settlements' agricultural attainments even before the Balfour Declaration (Zvi Yaron, *The Philosophy of Rabbi Kook* [Jerusalem: World Zionist Organization, 1991], 234–235).

the desolate land is being continuously built; there is a unique process of the ingathering of the exiles; we have won independence and sovereignty which we did not have even during the era of the Second Temple. What would you call this reality if not a reality of redemption?[38]

Nevertheless, and despite the increased messianic feeling associated with the conquests and successes of Israel's armed forces, establishment rabbis remained careful in their deconstruction of the Three Vows. The chief rabbi of the Israel Defense Forces and later chief Ashkenazi rabbi of Israel, Shlomo Goren, provides three reasons for the cancellation of the force of the Three Vows, two of which rely on earlier authorities.[39]

For the first, Goren cites Chayim Vital (d. 1620), the student of Moses Alshekh and the chief disciple and amanuensis of the great mystic, Isaac Luria, who placed a time limit of one thousand years on the vow, after which it was no longer operational. Goren cites Meir Simchah Hacohen of Dvinsk (d. 1926) for the second reason that the Three Vows were no longer in force. According to Meir Simchah, the Allied Powers' 1920 confirmation in San Remo of the British Balfour Declaration concerning the establishment of a Jewish national home in Palestine was a public affirmation that henceforth mass immigration to Palestine could no longer be considered rebellion against the nations.[40] The third reason is based on the requirement for the Jewish people to defend themselves from attack, which, as we have observed, Maimonides and the Palestinian Talmud consider a form of commanded war that requires all the able-bodied to fight. The 1967 War was

> ...an act of defense of the rights of the State of Israel to sail freely in the Red Sea Straits [which are] within the borders of the holy Land of Israel.... [T]he war over Judah and Samaria was forced upon us by Jordan, which attacked us.... For the Vow was only against a war of conquest [initiated] by us from outside, and not a defensive war, which is considered a commanded war to which all [must] go out to fight, even a bridegroom from his chamber and a bride from her wedding canopy. The Vow does not apply in any way to a war of survival such as this.[41]

---

[38] Sprinzak, *The Ascendance...*, 111.

[39] *Torat Hamedinah* (Hebrew, Jerusalem: Chemed, 1996), 36–42.

[40] Meir Simchah writes, "When the fear of The Vows passed with the permission of the kings [at San Remo], the commandment of settling the Land of Israel, which is equal to all of the commandments in the Torah (*Sifrei, re'eh*), arose to its [former] status. It is incumbent upon every individual to help with all one's might to carry out this commandment." (Bramson, *The Last Days*, p. 92. Parentheses in original).

[41] *Torat Hamedinah*, 42.

Rabbi Goren cites Chayim Vital further in order to provide support for the Zionist project. Most traditional commentators consider the vow articulated in the repeated Song of Songs verse, *I make you swear, o daughters of Jerusalem... do not wake or rouse love until it is wished*, to be operational indefinitely. They believed that the end to its validity is an inscrutable decision of God, into which humanity has absolutely no input. Any human attempt to discern the divine will as to the time of the messianic Redemption is doomed to failure and catastrophe. Vital, however, suggested that God will be willing to bring Redemption only after the Jewish people communicates its intense desire for it: *"do not wake or rouse love until it is wished*, for the sparks of the (divine) redemption need to be awakened by the spiritual will of the people, as it is written there, it is for this reason that *I make you swear o daughters of Jerusalem."* Goren understood Vital's comment to caution Israel not to attempt to awaken the Redemption until they are able to achieve the necessary spiritual will and desire. The necessary spiritual will and desire is the meaning of *love* in the biblical verse. The conclusion therefore is that when Israel is truly ready and its desire is great enough, then it will actually awaken the desire of God to bring divine redemption.[42] What does not need to be said by Rabbi Goren is that the Zionist project and the very existence of a vibrant Jewish state are demonstrations of Israel's readiness and desire, and that it has reached a point where it is indeed entering the final process of Redemption.

## The Remilitarization of Conquest

Shortly after the 1967 War, Rabbi Shelomo Zalman Shragai (d. 1995)[43] gave a speech before representatives of the World Congress of [Orthodox] Synagogues at Heichal Shelomo, the Jerusalem headquarters of the Chief Rabbinate of the State of Israel. In that speech he said, "At this time when we have seen such miracles and wonders, the vow, or what is called the "Three Vows," has fallen and is annulled." He exclaimed that the strength of

---

[42] Shlomo Goren, *Mishnat Hamedinah* (Hebrew, Jerusalem: Ha'idra Rabba, 1999), 23.

[43] Shragai was a stalwart activist and rather radical in Hapoel Hamizrachi from the 1920s through his brief stint as mayor of Jerusalem in 1950–1952 and then as head of the Immigration Department of the Jewish Agency until 1968. While it is not always possible to distinguish between rhetoric and deeply felt belief in traditional religious discourse, Shragai wrote in neomessianic terms when he used such expressions as "the revelation of the divine presence in the establishment (or "revival"—*tequmah*) of the State of Israel" (*Immediacy and Eternity* [*sha'ah venetzach*], Jerusalem: Mosad Harav Kook, 1960, 387), and note the similar reference in his words cited here (Cf. Dov Schwartz, *Land of Israel*, 133–139; idem, *Challenge and Crisis*, 283–291).

Israel in the 1967 War "... shows that the Three Vows no longer exist.... We were witnesses in the Six Day War that God heard our prayers on Hoshana Rabba:[44] 'Hoshana of Three Hours,' for in the first three hours of the war we merited to get the better of our enemies, who said (Ps. 83:5) *Come let us wipe them out as a nation*, but after the war the people were awakened and said (Ps.118:23) *This was from God*[45].... We must know that the continuation of the full redemption and the establishment of the divine presence *(shekhinah)* in the State of Israel is dependent on us, to the extent that we emigrate to the Land and fill it with Torah and commandments and add to its holiness the holiness of our lives in Torah and commandments.... The second thing we need to remember is that we must know that the divine presence will return to its place only with the *aliyah* of Jews as a wall *(kechomah)*." [46]

This reference to ascending "as a wall" requires closer examination. Recall that the Talmud section treating the Three Vows had the Hebrew rendering "in a wall" *(bechomah)*. Shragai's rendering is "as a wall" *(kechomah)*. The different prepositions might appear to have little significance, but each rendering actually refers to a different Talmudic subtext. The subtext to "in a wall" has been examined in chapter five, above. The subtext to "as a wall" is a different Talmudic passage, but one that treats the same subject of ascension to the Land of Israel.

> Resh Lakish was swimming in the Jordan. Rabbah Bar Bar-Hana gave him a hand. He [Resh Lakish] said to him. "By God! I hate you![47] It is written (Song of Songs 8:9): *If she be a wall (im chomah hi), we will build upon her a turret of silver; if she be a door, we will enclose her with boards of cedar.* If you had made yourselves *as a wall (kechomah)* and had gone up altogether in the days of Ezra, you would be like silver that does not rot. But since you went up like doors, you are like a cedar that rots!"[48]

Resh Lakish was a third-century Palestinian sage who was known to excoriate the Jews of Babylon in his day for not having returned to the

---

[44] "The Great Hosanna." This specific term usually refers to the seventh day of the fall festival called "Tabernacles" *(Sukkot)*, during which a long series of poetic hymns are recited that include the words, "O Save!" *(hosha`na, hoshi`ah na)*.

[45] This Psalm is recited in the special Thanksgiving service in the synagogue *(Hallel)* in great joy and song, and his use of the phrase recalls the full recitation of thanksgiving.

[46] Sh. Z. Shragai, "*Aliyah* to the Land: Eternal Command," *Shanah Beshanah* (Hebrew) 1969, 275–278.

[47] Or, "We hate you" (plural "you"). Resh Lakish was referring to Bar Bar-Hana and the Babylonian Jewish population he represents.

[48] BT *Yoma* 9b. The visual difference in the orthography between the letter, "*kaf*," of "as a wall" and the letter, "*beit*," of "in a wall" is extremely slight.

Land of Israel when allowed by the Persian Empire at the time of Ezra and Nehemiah in the fifth century B.C.E. According to his thinking, had enough Jews remained in or returned to Judea by the time of the Roman occupation, the Jews would have succeeded in their rebellion and remained an independent polity in their land. But according to Resh Lakish, the lack of numbers contributed decisively to the final destruction of the Jerusalem Temple.[49] Rabbah bar Bar-Hana, a contemporary of Resh Lakish, was a Babylonian sage who went to the Land of Israel to study but then returned to Persian Mesopotamia (Jewish "Bavel"), where he reportedly suffered personally from persecutions by the ruling Sassanian Empire.

"*In* a wall" thus refers to the prohibition against ascending to the Land of Israel en masse. "*As* a wall," according to Shragai's citation, refers to a missed opportunity. Shragai's use of the latter suggests that he considered the missed opportunity of previous eras to be correctable in the current situation by a mass movement of Jews to the Jewish State. "As a wall" thus evokes a sense of Jewish power.[50]

Although the impediment of the Three Vows was radically reduced among religious Zionists after 1967, it remained a polemical tool for the diminished pool of Orthodox anti-Zionists. Anti-Zionist rabbis continued to write and republish pamphlets and tracts condemning Zionism, and the Three Vows was an important weapon in the anti-Zionist arsenal.[51] The Three Vows continued, therefore, to have some force, and yeshiva students continued to raise the question of whether they applied to the contemporary situation.

Rabbi Tzvi Yehudah Kook (d. 1982), the only child of Rabbi Abraham Isaac Kook, had become the symbolic leader of the activist camp of religious Zionist youth by the 1960s. Rabbi Tzvi Yehudah, as he is often called, was the head of Mercaz Harav, which had become the intellectual center of activist Religious Zionism not long before the 1967 War.[52] When

---

[49] See BT Kiddushin 39b, JT Berachot 2:5(3) etc. Resh Lakish was known as a robust and physically imposing man who had been a gladiator or robber prior to having returned to his religious roots in order to become a Talmudic sage.

[50] There are other attempts to understand the difference. Rabbi Ya`qov Ariel, for example, understands "in a wall" to mean "forcibly," and "as a wall" to mean "en masse" (Ya`qov Ariel, *In the Canopy of Torah: Responsa* [Hebrew]. Kefar Darom: Institute for Torah and Land, 2003, 17, note 1).

[51] See, for example, Rabbi Yoel Teitelbaum (d. 1979), *On the Redemption and the Recompense,* (Hebrew) Brooklyn: Jerusalem Publishing, 1967 (5th printing, Jerusalem 1982). Teitelbaum is the head of the Satmar Hasidim, a community that is adamantly opposed to Zionism and the establishment of a Jewish polity for the traditional reasons cited earlier.

[52] Gideon Aran, "From Religious Zionism to Zionist Religion," in *Social Foundations of Judaism,* ed. Calvin Goldschneider and Jacob Neusner (Englewood Cliffs, NJ: Prentice Hall, 1990), 259–281; Menahem Friedman, "Jewish Zealots: Conservative versus Innovative," in,

asked about the Three Vows shortly before the October War of 1973, he gave the following answer.[53]

> With regard to the rebellion against the nations of the world, when we were forced to expel English rule from here it was not rebellion against them, for they were not the legal rulers over our land. Rather [they were] temporary mandatory authorities [who were here] in order to prepare the rule of the People of Israel in its land as per the decision of the League of Nations, according to the word of God in the Bible. So when they abused that role, their time had arrived to depart from here. Lastly, ascension in a wall, about which we have been warned: this wall is nothing but the rule of the nations over our land and the place of our Temple. As long as that wall stands, [it does so] through the divine decree of exile. But in the course of the results of the revealed End [of history *(haqetz hameguleh)*], [the divine decree] was annulled and this wall fell, for "the mouth that forbids is the mouth that permits."[54] The Master of the Universe who set up this wall like "an iron partition that divides Israel from its Father in Heaven,"[55] is the one who annulled and took down that wall. And since there is no wall, there is no delay. The issue of ascension in a wall is like the one who vows not to enter a house. When the house falls down, he does not need an [official] annulment of his vow.[56]

Kook equates the proverbial wall of the Three Vows with foreign rule over the Land of Israel. God ordained this foreign rule in the past, but like Shaul Yisraeli, Kook claims that God has since annulled the authority of foreign rule over the Land of Israel. This, according to both Yisraeli and Kook, can be proven from the very establishment of the State of Israel as a Jewish polity. His use of the term, "iron partition" *(mechitzah shel barzel)* evokes another image in the mind of a person familiar with traditional

---

*Jewish Fundamentalism in Comparative Perspective* ed. Laurence Silberstein (New York: New York University Press, 1983), 148–163; Myron Aronoff, "The Institutionalisation and Cooptation of a Charismatic, Messianic, Religious-Political Revitalisation Movement," in *The Impact of Gush Emunim: Politics and Settlement in the West Bank* ed. David Newman (New York: St Martin's Press, 1985), 46–69. On Rabbi Tzvi Yehudah Kook, see chapter 15.

[53] Rabbi Tzvi Yehudah Kook, "Clarification About the Claim of the Three Vows" (Hebrew) in *Linetivot Yisrael*, 3 vols. (Jerusalem: s.n., 1997), 2:217–218. This brief statement was originally published in *Hatzofeh*, the daily Hebrew newspaper of the Israeli National Religious Party, September 15, 1973, one month before the War.

[54] A reference to God (this is a citation from the Palestinian Talmud, *Terumot* chapter 9).

[55] A slight variation from BT *Pesachim* 85b and Sota 38a.

[56] Cf. *Shulchan Arukh, Yoreh De'ah,* 216:6.

Jewish learning. The "iron partition" found in the Talmud[57] is symbolic of a powerful barrier that nevertheless cannot obstruct the relationship between God and the Jews: "...even an iron partition cannot divide between Israel and its Father in Heaven." The iron partition of foreign rule or even contemporary foreign interference, therefore, cannot keep the Jews back from their divinely ordained birthright, the Land of Israel.

Tzvi Yehudah Kook was not an original thinker, but he was considered to have been the person most intimately familiar with the words and writings of his famous and influential father, and he was successful in popularizing his ideas. His intimate association with his father along with a powerful charisma often attested to by his students led him to become greatly influential himself. Tzvi Yehudah came to symbolize a messianic, activist approach to Zionism that, following Nahmanides,[58] considered settlement of the land to be an eternal command and an activist expression of "conquest." His yeshiva students strove to live deeply religious lives while carrying out the activist program of Nahmanides, thereby fulfilling the timeless divine command to conquer the Land of Israel and liberate it from the Gentiles.

Although Tzvi Yehudah claimed the mantle of his father, not all of students of Abraham Isaac Kook accepted his representation. Elie Holzer articulates the distinction between father and son most distinctly.

> While for the elder R. Kook the achievement of national revival without force was a hallmark of redemption, his son and the latter's pupils interpreted Israel's renewed involvement in miliatry affairs and war as yet another sign of ongoing, visible redemption. In their view, miliary activism had also become an expression of the "Manifest Redemption" (*ha-ketz ha-megulleh*) and the renaissance of the "Uniqueness of Israel" (*segullat Yisrael*)....One can therefore point to a gradual but unmistakable process of radicalization, a progress from the interpretation of military renaissance and wars as having spiritual meaning to a call for purposeful military activity.[59]

Like all Zionists, the students at Mercaz Harav were influenced by the ethos of earlier generations of secular neomessianic Zionist pioneers who

---

[57] See *Shulchan Arukh, Yoreh De'ah*, 216:6.

[58] *Addenda* to Maimonides' *Book of Commandments*, positive commandments 4 (printed with traditional editions of Maimonides' *Book of Commandments*). See chapter 8.

[59] Elie Holzer, "Attitudes Towards the Use of Military Force in Ideological Currents of Religious Zionism," in Schiffman and Wolowelsky, *War and Peace in the Jewish Tradition*, 343–344.

settled the land by building villages and collective farms even in the face of the physical opposition of Arabs and the British Mandate Authority. Mercaz Harav blended the Zionist pioneering ethos with Torah learning. Rabbi Tzvi Yehudah and his yeshiva thus taught and represented a confident synthesis between the optimistic pioneering of secular Zionism and the deep trust in divine redemption of religious Orthodoxy. Here was conquest revisited, conquest in a new garb. It combined the spiritual fervor and religiosity of religious Orthodoxy with the militant activism and land-centeredness of classic socialist Zionism. It was a return to the Land in both a Nahmanidean and Gordonean sense.[60]

During the early period of the vitalization of Religious Zionism in Kook's yeshiva and in the yeshivas that were established by its graduates prior to the 1967 War, this invigorated sense of Nahmanidean-Gordonean conquest was self-confident and activist, but nonviolent. It was associated with the agricultural settlements of the religious kibbutz and moshav movements and with a revitalization of Jewish learning. After the 1967 War it became increasingly energized and aggressive, and an organized political-religious movement would emerge from its ideological mixture of religious orthodoxy and militant activism. But as we shall observe in more detail, the movement was actualized only in the aftermath of the 1973 War and the sudden surge of discussion in Israel about returning the territories captured in the 1967 War. This threat of returning land, and particularly the biblical patrimony of Biblical Judea and Samaria (the West Bank), caused tremendous consternation within the community organized around Tzvi Yehudah and Yeshivat Mercaz Harav.

Prior to the 1973 War, very few new civilian settlements were founded in the territories acquired in 1967, and those that had been established in the territories were located in areas of heavy Jewish settlement prior to 1948 that had been lost in the fighting during or before the War of Independence. These new settlements held great symbolic value, not only for religious Zionists but for most Israelis, because they proved the resolve and the ability of Jews to return to the villages from which they had been forcibly exiled by war, and because they demonstrated physically and publicly the right of Jews to live anywhere in the Land of Israel.

But the heavy losses of the 1973 war suddenly raised doubt about the new confidence brought about by the 1967 victory. Voices within the Israeli public began calling into question the assumption of Israel's overwhelming military superiority in the Middle East taken for granted after

---

[60] On A. D. Gordon, see chapter 11.

the 1967 war. In the wake of the triumph of 1967, the Labor Government publicly affirmed its willingness to trade land for peace but at the same time insisted on resettling areas that had been settled before 1948 by Jews but lost in the 1948 war.[61] The response in the Arab world was so negative that there soon developed an Israeli mantra articulated by government and believed firmly by the public that there was nobody among the Arabs who was willing to consider the offer. In the wake of the near catastrophe of 1973, influential voices raised anew the possibility of returning land for a peace treaty with neighboring Arab countries. This public conversation caused great consternation among a group of activist religious Zionists.

Only a few months after the October 1973 War, and after several small meetings, a few hundred people came together in the settlement of Kfar Etzion, a famous and symbolic religious Zionist settlement that had been lost with great casualties and heroism in the 1948 War but reestablished with great acclaim after the 1967 War. It was there, in February of 1974, that an activist movement was born under the leadership of such well-known personalities as Beni Katzover, Menachem Felix, Hanan Porat, and Rabbis Moshe Levinger, Eliezer Waldman, Yochanan Fried, and Haim Druck-man.[62] The government of Israel had been giving mixed messages for years over whether they endorsed the growth of settlements in these territories. When talk of returning territories increased in the aftermath of the 1973 War, activists in the movement quickly accelerated the pace of settlement activity in the West Bank, even without government permission.

This settlement movement, which generated a number of related organizations, became known as *Gush Emunim*, the "Block of Faithful."[63] That name has been discarded, but it still typifies what is now called the Settler Movement. The history of this important development cannot be treated here, but much has been written on it elsewhere.[64] We must keep in mind

---

[61] Sachar, *History of Israel*, 673–674.

[62] David Weisburd, *Jewish Settler Violence: Deviance as Social Reaction* (University Park, PA: Penn. State University Press, 1989), 25.

[63] The full name, originally, was *gush emunim bamafdal*, "The Block of the Faithful in the National Religious Party." As the name suggests, its members considered themselves true to the genuine principles of Religious Zionism, which they claimed the party leaders had abandoned in their move toward post-independence normalization.

[64] Only a few of the great many studies can be cited here: Janet O'Dea, "Gush Emunim: Roots and Ambiguities: The Perspective of the Sociology of Religion," *Forum on the Jewish People, Zionism and Israel* 2 (25) (1976), 39–50; Kevin Avruch, "Traditionalizing Israeli Nationalism: The Development of Gush Emunim," *Political Psychology* 1:1 (spring, 1979), 47–57; Janet Aviad, "The Contemporary Israeli Pursuit of the Millennium," *Religion* 14 (1984), 199–222; David Newman, "Gush Emunim Between Fundamentalism and Pragmatism," *The Jerusalem Quarterly* 39 (1986), 33–43. The following article by Don-Yehiya serves as a bibliographic essay of the major studies prior to 1987: Eliezer Don-Yehiya, "Jewish Messianism, Religious

that both parts of the Nahmanidean-Gordonean synthesis—religiously Orthodox Zionism and secular socialist pioneering Zionism—began as modern neomessianic national movements. Combined through the energy of war and the expectation of an imminent, divinely wrought Redemption, traditional religion and modern nationalism created a powerful, activist, postmodern messianism.

One result of the emergence of Gush Emunim after 1973 (and the Settler Movement that perpetuated the Gush's ideals) was that the Three Vows basically have been annulled. Some in the Orthodox world such as the Satmar community of Hasidim continue to follow them, but aside from these and a much smaller group called the Neturei Karta ("Guardians of the City" [of Jerusalem]), the Orthodox Jewish world has been largely overwhelmed by the fervor that began with the victory of 1967 and took on a frantic zealousness in the wake of the near-disaster of 1973.[65]

## 1973: Further Proof of the Sanctity of Our Wars

The 1973 War is known in Israel as the "Yom Kippur War" because it was initiated by Egypt and Syria on Yom Kippur (the Day of Atonement), the most sacred day of the Jewish religious calendar and a day of intense fasting and penitence. Unlike the long buildup to the 1948 war and the lighting strikes initiated by Israel in 1956 and 1967, the 1973 War came as a complete surprise and caused great loss of lives and significant initial loss of territory. Large areas of the Sinai Peninsula and Golan Heights were taken by Egypt and Syria, and Israeli casualties were very high. As in 1967, the 1973 War caused great astonishment throughout Israel and the Jewish world, but the shock this time ended with dismay rather than exultation. Israel's sense of power and invincibility inspired by the extraordinary success of 1967 was broken by 1973.

---

Zionism, and Israeli Politics: The Impact and Origins of Gush Emunim," *Middle Eastern Studies* 23.2 (1987), 215–234. See also Roger Friedland and Richard D. Hecht, "The Politics of Sacred Place: Jerusalem's Temple Mount/*al-haram al-sharif*," in *Sacred Places and Profane Spaces* ed. Jamie Scott and Pauls Simpson-Houseley (New York: Greenwood Press, 1991), 21–61.

[65] The Three Vows continue to cause a certain low level of anxiety among some religious Zionists, however, and it never dropped out of the discussion entirely, even after 1973. See, for example, Rabbi Aharon Soloveitchik, "On *Milchemet Mitzvah* in the Land of Israel at this Time," *Shanah Beshanah* 1974, 136–146; Rabbi Meir Blumenfeld, "On the Vow Forbidding Ascension in a Wall," *Shanah Beshanah* 1974, 151–155; Rabbi Menachem Kasher, "A Legal Opinion on the Vow that Israel not Ascend in a Wall to the Land of Israel," *Shanah Beshanah* 1977, 213–228; etc.

Most of the territory lost at the beginning of the war was regained by its end, and parts of Israel's armed forces had even advanced beyond the Suez Canal toward Cairo to encircle Egypt's Third Army. But Egypt and Syria had great initial successes, and they broke the image of Israel's military unassailability. Israeli military positions were overrun and civilian settlements evacuated, and thousands of Israelis lost their lives.[66] The failures and resultant deaths caused deep distress in Israel and a great deal of soul-searching. This war could have been interpreted to mean that the successes of the 1967 War did not represent a divinely wrought miracle for Israel after all but was simply another mundane war. The signs could have been interpreted to mean that establishing the state was not part of the divine plan. The failures of 1973 could have been understood as a warning that Israel was not spiritually ready to retain the Bible Lands captured in 1967 but should trade them for peace in a Jewish "rump state."

Surprisingly, the 1973 War did not prove to be a major setback to the growth of messianism and the Nahmanidean-Gordonean sense of conquest that had begun to blossom in the wake of the 1967 victory. A number of fundamental compositions were penned to make sense of the setback and to come to terms with the disappointment. Janet Aviad notes how "rationalization of the war demonstrates the strength of the messianic motif and is an example of the capacity of religious Zionist thinkers to overcome historical reversals."[67] She refers specifically to Rabbi Yehuda Amital's short collection of essays, *From out of the Depths*,[68] which refers to the reversal of the war as a form of purification: "Why has this war come about? What is there to conquer? Why has the war of Gog and Magog occurred? For what reasons are the unknown and faraway lands of the north brought to conquer the Land? After the establishment of the state of Israel, there can be only one significance of the war: the purification and refinement of the community of Israel."[69]

When Rabbi Tzvi Yehudah Kook was asked the reason for such apparent reversals on the path of Redemption, he answered, "This is only a temporary delay. One must not be childish about this, but see the global revolutions, recognize—through great insight—the divine plan of 'God's

---

[66] For the 1973 War, see Lester Sobel (ed.), *Israel and the Arabs: The October 1973 War* (New York: Facts on File, 1974); P. R. Kumaraswamy (ed.), *Revisiting the Yom Kippur War* (London: Frank Cass, 2000).

[67] Aviad, "Contemporary Israeli Pursuit of the Millennium," in *Religion* 14 (1984), 204.

[68] *Mima'amaqim*, which derives from Psalm 130:1 "From out of the depths I call to you, Lord," (on the significance of this title, see the following chapter).

[69] Yehuda Amital, *From Out of the Depths*, written in 1974 (Hebrew) (Jerusalem Alon-Shevut: Har Etzion Association, 1986) 28. His work is often cited by students of modern Israeli messianism and the radicalization of Religious Zionism. On Rabbi Amital and his change in perspective, see chapter 13.

returning the captivity of Zion'[70] that passes through many twists and turns. The greater a thing, the more complicated it is. The process of our Redemption is a historic fact of gigantic proportions. What appears contrary to this process is only a temporary delay."[71] Many other rationalizing writings could be cited.[72] In fact, the threat represented by the failures of the 1973 War actually caused an increase in rationalization and a resurgence of messianic, militant activism that will be examined in some detail in the next chapter. Fear that the war would result in concessions of territories during negotiations between Israel and Egypt energized for many the need to hold onto them.

The negotiations following the war raised the possibility for the first time since 1948 of real peace with an Arab neighbor. One question on the minds of many was whether decision making should be based exclusively on the new political and military reality resulting from the war, or whether there exists a higher consideration based on a divine imperative that transcends the give-and-take of ordinary politics. The fear that peace negotiations might result in the loss of Bible lands generated a movement to provide a concrete expression of protest against returning territories. Giving up land was equated with giving up God's one and only offer to fulfill the messianic-Zionist ideal of Jewish settlement in all of the Land of Israel. Among many, giving away land was tantamount to giving away Redemption.

The 1973 War thus initiated a great boost in activism, especially but not entirely on the political right and among religious Jews. Their enthusiasm energized many who had not been politically active, and even enthused

---

[70] Psalm 126:1.

[71] Tzvi Yehudah Kook, "Between a People and Its Land" (Hebrew), excerpted from *Conversations of Rabbi Tzvi Yehudah* in *Artzi* 2 (1982), 21.

[72] See, for example, Rabbi Shlomo Aviner, *A People [Rising up] Like a Lion* (Hebrew) (Jerusalem, 1983), 2: 176–190. In response to the war, Sephardic Chief Rabbi of Tel Aviv Chaim David Halevi wrote: "Actually, nothing happened in the Yom Kippur War for which we should be particularly worried. True, there was a famous failure to notice, because of which the IDF was not prepared to retaliate when it occurred...But actually, the IDF succeeded within only a few days to move to attack, which drove away the enemy....Actually, one could say that the ease of victory of the IDF in the Yom Kippur War was much greater than all the victories of the past....An additional problem troubles the religious Jew who believes that the establishment of the State of Israel is part of the concretization of the messianic vision. On the face of it, reason forces [one to think that] the development of redemption would have to be expressed in advancement and improvement, which was the way it was until the 6 Day War. The retreat that came as a result of the first blow of the Yom Kippur War was not a territorial retreat alone in the eyes of the religious believer, but rather, a retreat from the path of going up to the complete redemption, for he is not able to understand why [the war] was necessary....It was most certainly one of the secrets of the highest providence which flesh and blood will never understand until after the act [of redemption] and its fulfillment. Nevertheless, it is possible to understand with the help of our prophets and rabbis." ("The Meaning of the 'Yom Kippur' War among the Battles for the Redemption of Israel," *Torah Shebe`al Peh* 1975, 63).

some on the center-left who were raised on the Zionist ideology of set-tlement and building up the Land of Israel. The goal of the new activism was an intensive settlement program in those territories that were under negotiation for possible return to the nations that had controlled them prior to 1967. That program, a combination of symbolic protest and active set-tlement, purposefully incorporated within it some of the most powerful and heroic symbols of pre-state Zionist pioneering. The significance of this renewal of Zionist symbolism was not lost on the media, as is unmistak-able from the article written for the large Hebrew daily, *Ma`ariv* about the illegal establishment of a settlement in 1974 at a location in the territories called by the settlers, Elon Moreh.[73]

At their head stood the leader of "Yeshivat Hamercaz,"[74] Rabbi Tzvi Yehudah Kook, and the Knesset members, Ariel Sharon and Geula Cohen. They engaged in a scheme reminiscent of the Stockade and Tower [settlements]:[75] an area of about two dunams set off and walled by a fence, some sixteen tents set up with an Israeli flag. Soon after-ward, Rabbi Kook and the Knesset members Sharon and Cohen planted trees... After the [negative] position of the [Israeli] government was made clear, the settlers gathered two days before the [designated date for establishing the] settlement in the hamlet of Mechulah in the Jordan Valley. Yesterday they inaugurated a new version of a "Burma Road"[76] in order to distract the security forces that had known about the settle-ment [plans already] for a while...[77]

The aggressive, militant pioneering symbolism of the Stockade and Tower settlements and the "Burma Road" could not be lost on the Israeli

---

[73] A location near Nablus (Shekhem) where, according to Genesis 12:6–7, God appeared to Abraham and promised that he would give the land to his seed.

[74] Mercaz Harav Kook.

[75] The tactic of creating the "Stockade and Tower" settlements *(chomah umigdal)* overnight was a powerful and successful tactic in overcoming violent Arab opposition and the British Mandate Authority prohibition against erecting new Jewish settlements in prestate Palestine. The first Stockade and Tower settlement, Tel Amal, was raised in one day on December 10, 1936, and subsequently became the model for fifty-seven settlements established between 1936 and 1939.

[76] The original Burma Road is a thousand mile roadway linking Burma (now Myanmar) and China, built under Japanese fire while battling disease and monsoons during World War II in order to supply Allied forces in China. During the 1948 Arab-Israel War, an American military officer named Mickey Marcus oversaw the heroic and dangerous building of a secret road through the rough Judean Hills to bring supplies to the besieged Jewish sector of Jerusalem. Construction of this route, nicknamed Israel's "Burma Road," succeeded in breaking an Arab blockade that was starving Jerusalem's Jewish inhabitants.

[77] *Ma`ariv*, June 5, 1974, in Bramson, *The Last Days*, p. 204.

public. Even the name of the new settlement carried powerful biblical images of God promising the lands upon which Abraham walked to the patriarch's descendents. Calling up these symbols along with the planting of trees and showing the Israeli flag lent a powerful heroic Zionist legitimacy (and to some, religious transcendence) to activities that had been officially outlawed by the government. Such an assertive Zionist action in the face of an obstinate ruling power was not new to Zionist history, for it marked the standard operating procedure during the British Mandate period. But that was before the establishment of the State of Israel. Now, the same pioneering Zionist approach was invoked against what was portrayed as the anti-Zionist policies of the Israeli government in its attempt to block Jewish settlement in the conquered/liberated territories, thus likening the nonsupportive government of Israel with what was considered an illegitimate British mandated government over prestate Palestine.

The 1973 War marked another watershed in Israeli history: the fall of Labor Zionism from ideological dominance in the Jewish State, for it was the Labor Government of Golda Meir that took the major blame for the failures of 1973. As with most watershed events, the event only made apparent an ongoing trend and pushed it to its ultimate conclusion. After the fall of the Labor government secular Revisionist expressions of Zionism filled the vacuum, but the greatest change was in the rise of what might accurately be termed "Judaized" Zionism.[78]

All expressions of Zionism are of course Jewish. Zionism is, by definition, a Jewish national movement. But the secular ideological forces of socialist Labor Zionism and its "loyal opposition" in Revisionist Zionism were, at least theoretically, purely economic, social, and political in nature. Conversely, the fluid coalition of ideological forces driving the various expressions of "Judaized" Zionism of the Settler Movement emerged out of a Jewish religious or neoreligious base, even among many Jews who would not define themselves as religiously observant.

The humanist-universalist outlook behind the socialist vision lost favor at the same time that international pressure on the country increased after 1973 to return territories captured in the 1967 War. This combination increased an inward-looking perspective, which activated a religious vision that would become instrumental in forming a new range of expression among Jewish nationalist ideologies. The most conspicuous expression of

---

[78] An expression of this trend can be found in Moti Karpel, *The Revolution of Belief: The Decline of Zionism and the Rise of the Alternative of Belief* (Hebrew) (Alon Shevut: Lekhatchila, 2003).

this newly vitalized spiritual national vision was found among the communities that made up Gush Emunim. There were and continue to be secular Jews on the political right, such as Ariel Sharon and Geula Cohen, previously mentioned in relation to Elon Moreh, who have been an essential part of Gush Emunim and the Settler Movement, but as the movement became more closely associated with religious values the religious activists rose up to become its ideological leaders. Those activists also succeeded in seizing the ideological leadership of Religious Zionism in general, which has come to exemplify through their influence a deep and traditional messianism—as opposed to the secular or neomessianism of Labor—that lay embedded but largely dormant in the movement.[79]

There can be no doubt that the intense drive to establish Jewish settlements in the territories conquered in 1967 did not originate simply from greed associated with being forced to return valuable real estate in the wake of the 1973 War. Neither was it the euphoric victory in 1967 and sense of divine providence associated it. Gideon Aran has been particularly persuasive in demonstrating how the roots that flowered into Gush Emunim were established much earlier and in the fertile soil of modern, Jewish religious nationalism.[80]

## The Revitalization of Zionist Ideals Through Religion

In order to make sense of the revolutionary nature of the Settler Movement we need to detail a portion of Zionist history presented in previous chapters. We observed how Religious Zionism was formed around a synthesis of seemingly disparate ideals. "Torah and labor" *(torah va`avodah),* for example, combined the religious ideal of traditional religious learning with the socialist labor ideal of working the land. And recall that `avodah was an ancient and common Jewish term for worship. Working the land thus came to epitomize a form of religiosity in and of itself. *Avodat ha'adama,*

---

[79] Dov Schwartz attributes this fundamental change almost single-handedly to the deep, charismatic nature of Rabbi Tzvi Yehudah Kook, who succeeded in popularizing and institutionalizing the powerful messianism that his father was unable to convey to the masses (Schwartz, "A Theological Rationale...," 77–81). But Tzvi Yehudah's charisma had little impact until late in his life and only after the political, social, and demographic situation was right in the late 1950s and 1960s culminating in the "miracle" of the victory in 1967. Tzvi Yehudah became the symbolic catalyst for the surge and open articulation of messianism within Religious Zionism that was ready to burst forth due to the combination of social, historical, and religious factors mentioned above.

[80] Gideon Aran, "From Religious Zionism to Zionist Religion," in *Social Foundations of Judaism* ed. Calvin Goldscheider, and Jacob Neusner (Englewood Cliffs, NJ: Prentice Hall, 1990), 259–281.

therefore, while meaning "working the land" in modern Hebrew, retained a sense of its literal meaning of "worshiping the land," particularly among some trends of Labor Zionism such as those influenced by A. D. Gordon.[81] But traditional European Jewish life out of which Zionism emerged distinguished hierarchically between the ideal life of Torah learning and the unenviable occupation of farming or other labors. The synthesis between the two thus epitomized a certain tension between these values.

Another example of this tension can be seen in the willingness of religious Zionists, unlike their non-Zionist or anti-Zionist Orthodox brethren, to work closely with secular activists. That meant working with secular Jews who scorned traditional religion, including a general disdain for the religious Zionists who represented it. Of course there were plenty of personal friendships between the two Zionist communities, but I am discussing ideological trends, and Zionism was at its core an ideological movement to reenvision Jewish identity from its complex traditional combination of religious faith and peoplehood to one defined largely by the categories of modern European nationalism.[82]

These tensions reveal an essential paradox in classical Religious Zionism. On the one hand, religious Zionists represented a modernist response to contemporary European social and political movements by joining with secular Jews in a Jewish project from which the obviously religious aspects had been removed. Zionism was defined by the secular leadership of the Zionist Movement as a new form of Jewishness, an authentic and modern, nonreligious expression of Jewish identity that made Jews equal to all the other nations of the modern world. Yet religious Zionists were not secular in their personal practice, nor ultimately, in their outlook. They refused to reject Orthodox Judaism, and they defined themselves as observant, religious Jews.

As religious Jews, they were not fully accepted in the Zionist Movement, which held a basically anti-religious ethos. They were therefore associated with a subcategory of Zionism—"Religious" Zionism. Unofficially, the "religious" part denoted something less than full acknowledgment. Although not fully accepted and integrated into the movement, they were nevertheless condemned by fellow-Orthodox Jews for joining with the secularist free-thinkers who had no respect for God and religious life. *Nicht aheen; nicht aherr* is the Yiddish phrase, which describes their position as "neither here nor there," "neither fish nor foul." On the one hand,

---

[81] For parallel biblical linguistic forms in relation to the worship of God, see Exodus 36:1ff, 10:8, 11, 24; Numbers 7:9; Joshua 24:14; Psalms 2:11, 100:2, etc.

[82] Shlomo Avineri, "Zionism and the Jewish Religious Tradition," in *Zionism and Religion*, 1–9.

they were not secular enough but too religious; and on the other they were not religious enough but too secular.

Religious Zionists had argued against the critique of their Orthodox colleagues by claiming that their involvement with secularists would serve as a kind of brake on the secularization of Jews and would eventually reverse the trend, bringing wayward Jews back into the fold of religion. At the same time they claimed that they were not messianists who were rebelling against the Three Vows but merely working to create a safe haven for Jews who were being persecuted and killed by the Gentiles. Yet when they joined the Zionist Movement they were joining a secular neomessianic movement to bring Jews en masse to the Land of Israel in order to settle the Promised Land. And the excitement and purpose of this neomessianism stimulated their own deeply felt, even if not often articulated, sense of religious messianism that was so much a part of traditional Jewish life and always closely associated with return to the Land of Israel and its settlement.

Religious Zionists persisted in their Zionism throughout the prestate period in the face of severe criticism from most of Orthodox Jewry. They remained in a quandary. *Nich ahin; nicht aherr.* On the one hand, they were marginalized by the non-Zionist and anti-Zionist Orthodox. On the other, their own nonreligious Zionist colleagues rebuffed them because they continued to represent an oppressive Orthodox religious establishment rejected by the secularists. They were pushed out of the leadership of the Zionist Movement long before the establishment of the state, and were compensated with symbolic positions that had little power or influence. Their secondary status persisted after independence. They found themselves marginal on both counts—as observant Jews and as Zionists.

Religious Zionists were burdened with an additional problem. By joining the highly demanding program of Zionist pioneering, and particularly the arduous program of establishing and maintaining agricultural settlements in often hostile conditions, they were obligated to forgo the traditional practice of Torah study, along with the status that accrued for such learning in traditional Jewish culture. The religious Zionist pioneers were willing to make such compromises, but by doing so they lost status that in traditional Jewish culture was so deeply associated with Torah learning. Their decision to dedicate themselves to building up the land removed them from the world of yeshivah learning and a high level of religious culture and practice associated with that learning. To religious Jews who remained within the traditional yeshivah world that was dominated by non-Zionists and anti-Zionists, these pioneers were seen as farmers ignorant of Torah, as `amey ha'aretz—literally, "people of the land," a term that had taken on a sense of ignorance and even stupidity in traditional Jewish culture. There is the *am ha'aretz lemitzvot* shamed for not meticulously observing the commandments, and `am ha'aretz latorah* stigmatized as ignoramuses for not studying Torah. Religious Zionists were disparaged for both. A leading Israeli academic who grew up in the activist religious Zionist community and is one of the more astute observers of the existential dilemma faced by his generation described the tension as follows, "My generation...grew up with an inferiority complex relative to the secular sector, with respect to building the land, and also relative to the ultra-Orthodox—with respect to devotion."[83]

Political revolutions are typically followed by a trend toward normalization, and Israel certainly fits this basic pattern in many ways. With normalization after independence and the attendant reduction in the driving power of secular revolutionary Zionist values, aspects of the traditional, prerevolutionary religious ethos began to reappear among religious Zionists. Many among the younger generation had grown up in the religious youth movement of B'nai Akiba and had naturally internalized the paradox that was lived and managed by their parents. After independence, some began to question the rationalizations that they had grown up with. They resented their rejection by mainstream secular Zionism and their relegation to a secondary status. They also resented their lack of deep knowledge of Jewish tradition and involvement in learning. And they found the internalized tension inherent in the neomessianism of secular Zionism difficult to cope with in light of the traditional messianism inherent in Religious Zionism. A cadre of young people was ready to resolve the tension, and they did so through a kind of religious revitalization of Zionism.[84]

A small group of talented and energetic students formed in the early 1950s at Kfar Haro'eh, a religious Zionist farming settlement and residential center for Jewish learning founded in 1937 shortly after the death of Abraham Isaac Kook and named for him.[85] The purpose of this yeshiva located in a small farming village was not to turn out rabbis and scholars, according to Rabbi Shaul Yisraeli in his speech at its dedication ceremony,

---

[83] Aviezer Ravitzky, in *Haaretz*, July 22, 2005 (English Ed. Weekend), B7 (http://www.haaretz.com/general/a-crack-in-the-covenant-1.164705).

[84] Aran, "From Religious Zionism..." 259–281. See also, Ehud Sprinzak, *Ascendance*, 48–50, and a somewhat different perspective from Dov Schwartz, *Religious Zionism*, 95–97. For a history of the political developments that accompanied this movement within the religious Zionist community and the National Religious Party, see Yehudah Azrieli, *The Generation of the Knitted Kippot* (Hebrew) (n.p.: Avivim, 1990), 19–38.

[85] *Haro'eh*, meaning "the Seer," is an acronym for **Ha**Ra**v**'**A**vraham **Ha**cohen.

but rather was to produce activists who would build up the Land and make a Jewish commonwealth a reality.[86]

The students called their group *gachelet*, meaning "[burning] embers." In addition to conveying a sense of fiery activism, it was an acronym meaning "Nucleus of Pioneering Torah Students *(gar`in chalutzi lomdei torah).*" They lived in Kfar Haro'eh under the tutelage of Rabbi Moshe Tzvi Neriya, the activist and first editor of the B'nai Akibah Youth Movement Newsletter, *Zera`im*. Neriya founded and headed the school and was one of the chief spokesmen and outstanding personalities of Religious Zionism. His enthusiasm and learning encouraged the group's dedication and they loved him dearly, but the young members of Gachelet eventually rebelled against him along with the rest of the religious Zionist establishment. In fact, their youthful enthusiasm and idealist rebellion against the paradoxical compromises made by the movement succeeded in coopting him. They insisted that their beloved rabbi support the vision of his own teaching rather than succumb to the reality of the day.

The activists of Gachelet would go on to form new settlements and religious boarding schools in Israel before the territorial expansion of the 1967 War, including the influential *Hesder Yeshiva* system that combines traditional Torah study with military service. One of the Gachelet branches was formed in the first Hesder Yeshivah called Kerem Beyavneh ("vineyard in [the village of] Yavneh")[87] near the town of Ashdod. In what would turn out to be a fateful move, this group joined up with Mercaz Harav, the Jerusalem yeshiva of Rabbi Abraham Isaac Kook that had declined and become neglected and largely insignificant after the great rabbi's death. It was run by Kook's son, Rabbi Tzvi Yehudah Kook, whose status did not approach that of his father and whose reputation was not nearly as respected. But in a series of meetings held between the young activists and Rabbi Tzvi Yehudah, the rabbi left a profound impression on the group. These encounters, along with a leadership vacuum at Kerem Beyavneh, led to the convergence between the youthful energy of these idealists with a fitting mentor, and between Gachelet and Mercaz Harav. Aran describes this union.

> The *Gahelet* alumni generally maintain that they came "not to the yeshiva, but to the rabbi." This implies, of course, a negative judgment of the spirit which existed at "Mercaz" before their coming; but it

---

[86] "On the Essence of the Agricultural Yeshiva," *Zera`im* 20 (1938), 4–5.
[87] The significance of the ancient city of Yavneh is provided in chapter 3.

equally reveals the personal and intimate quality of their encounter with its principal. . . . To borrow a hasidic term, they made R. Zvi Yehuda their "rebbe." He became their discovery: a hidden genius, previously unappreciated, now revealed in all his glory as an exceptional personality. They surrounded him with a myth of their own creation: he became a towering figure of irresistible magnetism. His was a charisma that owed more to the veneration of his followers than to his own qualities.[88]

That enthusiastic and talented group of young people succeeded to energize what had become a sleepy institution of Jewish learning. Mercaz Harav was unique among Israel's yeshivas at the time in that it bridged the deep and total dedication to traditional Jewish learning with the mystic quality of living on and settling the Land of Israel. This yeshivah was the unique legacy of the great Rabbi Abraham Isaac Kook: an Orthodox yeshiva unself-consciously embracing the pioneering activism of Zionist settlement as a stage in the traditional religious expectation of messianic redemption.

But as we noted previously, that particular messianic perspective died out, at least in public discourse, with the death of Rabbi Kook. In the meantime, religious Zionists had effectively agreed to accept a second-class position in the Zionist Movement and a similarly inferior position vis-à-vis religious Orthodoxy. The chemistry of joining the young members of Gachelet with the living seed of "The Rav" seemed to ignite a new energy that would embrace both. As Samuel Heilman observed, "If Kook the Elder was abstract and mystical, Kook the Younger offered operational advice. The advice was to extract Zionism from the grip of secular culture, something that only religious activism could accomplish."[89] Regardless of his talents as an independent scholar or thinker, Rabbi Tzvi Yehudah succeeded in channeling the energy of a generation of enormously talented young people to engage in militant activism for the settlement-conquest of the Land of Israel.

The combination of youth movement activism in B'nai Akiba with deep Torah learning in the yeshiva environment provided the tools necessary to work on resolving the paradoxical position of Religious Zionism. The process had begun with the formation of Gachelet in the 1950s. A network of yeshivas was established subsequently in the 1960s, and then the creation

---

[88] Aran, "From Religious Zionism . . .," 275, and see Eliezer Goldman, "Controversy on Gush Emunim: Messianic Interpretation of Current Events," *Forum* 1977 1 (26), 37–38.

[89] Heilman, "Quiescent and Active Fundamentalisms," 187.

of Gush Emunim in the wake of the 1973 War. Through these institutions religious Zionist activists would demonstrate their total commitment to both worlds: Zionism through pioneering settlement and Orthodox Judaism through determined traditional learning and practice.

The cadre of young activists confronted the paradox of Religious Zionism in a variety of ways, but key among them was their open and comfortable understanding that the establishment of the State of Israel represented a stage in the traditional path to Redemption. The ingathering of the exiles, the return of the people to its land, and the establishment of a sovereign government were all traditional indicators of the impending messianic era. The state, therefore, was not merely a refuge, although it was that as well. The state became seen as a key milestone on the path to Redemption. Even the national bureaucracies and institutions that were formed within it were considered holy because they were constructed under the aegis of the Almighty through the establishment of the first independent Jewish commonwealth in nearly two millennia. Perhaps the most sacred of these holy institutions was the Israeli armed forces.[90]

As the core institution for producing a new form of "Haredi" Religious Zionism, Mercaz Harav became a symbol of a new and self-confident movement. But the emergence of this energizing trend was not restricted to Mercaz Harav. It flowered among the growing network of yeshivas and agricultural settlements, and it fulfilled a need among a generation of idealists who were dissatisfied with their erstwhile status and low aspirations. The energy was thus able to catch hold within the expanding network of religious and educational institutions that were developing under the aegis of the state through Mizrachi and the National Religious Party.

Not everyone in the movement was in favor of this trend. In fact, there was strong opposition among many in the leadership at the time and later. Yakov Drori, one of the founders of Yeshivat Kerem Beyavneh, protested what would later be called the "haredization" of religious Zionist youth and the lack of a leadership that would perpetuate the ideals and values

---

[90] Heilman, 188. A typical primary expression of this view may be found in Shlomo Aviner, *A People [that rises up]Like a Lion* (from Numbers 23:24) (Jerusalem: s.n., 1983), 179: "Thus said David, King of Israel [to Goliath]: 'But I come against you in the name of **The Lord of Armies, God of the ranks of Israel, whom you have defied**' (1 Samuel 17:25). The Holy One, Blessed be He is called Armies in reference to the armies of Israel, in reference to the IDF." [bold in original]. See also, Tzvi Yehudah Kook, *Sichot*, Genesis 366–367 [the four volumes of this publication are not numbered, but they were printed in the order of the books of the Torah. Genesis is therefore volume 1, Exodus volume 2, etc.] (Jerusalem: s.n., 1993–2002).

of "Torah and Labor" *(Torah va`avodah)* in the yeshiva.[91] But some youth leaders and rabbis such as Haim Druckman, who were sent to influence the youth leadership to change direction, were themselves won over to their point of view.[92] Druckman would become one of the most active and visible leaders in Gush Emunim.

The program that emerged from this development revitalized and spiritualized Religious Zionism, and it achieved this in part by recognizing as religious acts what had previously been considered secular activities. This was accomplished in a variety of ways, but one important avenue was through the use of traditional religious terminology. We have already observed above how secular Zionist activists had engaged in a similar process of valorization through language by applying traditional value-laden Hebrew terminology to secular nationalist goals in order to make activities that were not valued in Jewish tradition acceptable to traditional Jews. Necessary mundane activities were thus sacrilized through language in order to imbue them with Jewish meaning and make them "kosher"—so that Orthodox Jews could join with the secular Zionists. We noted in chapter 10, for example, how agricultural labor in the settlements was called `avodah*, the biblical term for sacrificial offerings to God in the Jerusalem Temple. Through this process, certain religious terms were secularized.

In the new trend, religious terminology that had previously been secularized was resanctified by applying transcendent religious meaning to it. We observed earlier how the idiom "conquest of the land" *(kibbush ha'aretz)* had been detached from its biblical military sense and applied by Labor Zionism to an ideological program of returning to agriculture and settlement. In the new discourse of Judaized Zionism, conquest would hearken back, based on the Talmud (as we learned in chapter 5), to Joshua's victories in capturing the Land of Canaan. But recall that reference to Joshua's victories in capturing the Land of Canaan was intended by the sages of the Talmud to limit the possibility of applying Commanded War in their own time. In contrast, the adherents of newly Judaized Zionism read the same reference to Joshua's wars as an example rather than a limitation, thus demonstrating that their current struggles are indeed part

[91] Yakov Drori, "Yeshivat Kerem Beyavneh: Clarification and Critique," *Amudim* 123 (Tishre/ September, 1956), 26–27. See also Yissachar Ben David, "Gush Emunim and its Opponents," *(Amudim* 363 [1975]), 148–150; Tzvi Yaron, "The Deterioration of Gush Emunim," (op cit), 151; Yakov Tzur, "Religious Zionism and Messianism " *(Amudim* 455 [1981]), 60–65; Shimon Glick, "The Tragedy of Gush Emunim," *(Tradition* 19:2 [1981]), 112–121.

[92] Aran, "From Religious Zionism...," 273.

of the divine plan. In the newly Judaized Zionism of the Settler Movement, the great advances marked by the establishment of the State are expressions of divinely ordained conquest, and especially the wars. The war for independence in 1948, for control of the biblical lands in 1967 (and the establishment of Jewish settlements in those areas), and the war for survival in 1973 were re-imagined as expressions of divinely ordained military conquest.

CHAPTER 15 | The 1980s

*Holy War and Its Excesses*

Whoever is with the Lord, come to me! (said by Moses to levitical
warriors to strike down the sinners of Israel)

EXODUS 32:26

## Rabbi Tzvi Yehudah and the Revitalizing Ideology of Conquest

In the previous chapter we examined some of the trends that emerged
within Religious Zionism to try to resolve its intrinsic tensions. These trends
include revitalization efforts that emerged among a generation of youth
disaffected with the ways in which their parents' generation expressed its
religiosity and Zionism. Key activists coalesced around the figure of Rabbi
Tzvi Yehudah Kook at the yeshiva of Mercaz Harav. A number of observers have been struck by Tzvi Yehudah's centrality.

> At first glance, [Rabbi Tzvi Yehuda Kook] would appear to have
> been an unlikely candidate to become a charismatic leader, and
> in fact, he only became one in the last stages of his life. Even his
> former students admit he was barely articulate, and that both his
> speech and writings were hard to follow. Yet he clearly cast a spell
> that created first of all a coterie of devoted disciples, and through
> them a much larger following. As in similar cases the reciprocal
> relationship between the charismatic leader and his disciples is criti-
> cal in explaining the mobilization and expansion of a revitalization

movement. When Rabbi Kook died at the age of 92 in 1982, he was mourned by thousands.[1]

Whether the attraction of Rabbi Tzvi Yehudah was his persona, his intimate association with his famous and beloved father, the acumen of his learning, or his interpretation of text and tradition, he represented an effective synthesis and resolution of the essential paradoxes in Religious Zionism for a generation of seekers. He was uncompromising on the essentials of messianic Zionism—not the neomessianism of the old secular pioneers, but a powerful messianism intrinsic to traditional Judaism combined with the fervor of modern activist Jewish nationalism directed toward the biblical Land of Israel.

Kook popularized a combination of ultra-Orthodox absolutism with an ideology of human activism inherent in modern nationalist movements. This equation produced a militant nationalist messianism, or what could also be considered a militant messianic nationalism. The traditional institution of the Three Vows had previously restrained most activist messianic inclinations associated with mass immigration to the Land of Israel or building an independent Jewish polity, but Kook taught that they had been cancelled. He taught that with God's sanction, the Jewish nation is on the final and inexorable path to Redemption through building up the Land of Israel—all of the Land of Israel. God's authority for this development must be recognized and cannot be understated. Not only does God sanction this redemptive moment of history, he decrees it. Any compromise in this journey is a renunciation of the divine plan and a violation of God's will. In a sense, Tzvi Yehudah simply carried the previously moderated and often unspoken messianic ideals of Religious Zionism to their logical conclusion.

For many idealistic religious Zionists, Rabbi Tzvi Yehudah Kook represented the absolute ideal. The "Übermensch" of Jewish tradition is the *tzaddik*, the entirely righteous individual on whose account God allows the world to endure. In the words of Rabbi Shlomo Aviner, editor of the multivolume collection of Tzvi Yehudah's oral discourse,[2]

---

[1] Myron Aaronoff, "The Institutionalisation and Cooptation of a Charismatic, Messianic, Religious-Political Revitalisation Movement," in *The Impact of Gush Emunim: Politics and Settlement in the West Bank* ed. David Newman (New York: St Martin's Press, 1985), 63. Dov Schwartz considers him a much more complex individual and considers his genius to be his ability to popularize the complex metaphysical notions of his father (Dov Schwartz, "A Theological Rationale for National-Messianic Thought: Rabbi Tzvi Yehudah Kook" [Hebrew], *Hatziyyonut* 22 [2000], 61–81).

[2] *The Discourses of Rabbi Tzvi Yehudah* (Hebrew). 4 volumes thus far (Jerusalem: s.n., 1993–2002).

In every generation there is a *Tzaddik* to the whole Israeli nation, a *Tzaddik* of the masses, a *Tzaddik* to all of the world. He is so universal in his influence, he is the foundation of the world itself.[3] These universally righteous men form a chain. From generation to generation, they funnel the Divine flow of life which advances the historical mission of Israel. This national *Tzaddik* is a unique personality, elevated over all of his generation. This is especially true today, in a generation which has witnessed the rebirth of our people and the restoration of our nation in our Land. For this national reawakening will bring the great, longed-for repentance, the *Tshuvah* of the entire nation of Israel, and, with it, the repentance of the world.[4] These *Tzaddikim* are unique. Harav Avraham Yitzhak Hacohen Kook, and Rav Tzvi Yehuda, his son, are the *Tzaddikim* of the redemption. The spirit of *Hashem*, which hovers over the world, and directs all of our history, is embodied in their souls.[5]

Most of Kook's later writings are collected from audiotapes of his talks at Mercaz Harav and from letters he wrote to his students and others in Israel. His earlier writings were collected and published in a series called *Linetivot Yisrael*.[6] In his early writings, even before the official establishment of the state, Rabbi Tzvi Yehudah, like his father, considered the Zionist enterprise to be the beginning of the messianic Redemption.

Any person among [the people of] Israel who does not close an eye to the words of the living God, ruler of the world whose written and oral Torah and whose appearance through divine providence to Israel and the world in this generation of ours, reveals and makes obvious the historical divine value of the One who Announces the generations,[7] of the beginning of the path to our Redemption and the redemption of our souls...has just to observe the special nature of this phase, step, and

---

[3] Proverbs 10:25.

[4] A. I. Kook, *Orot HaTshuva* 17:1.

[5] *Tshuvah* is the Hebrew term for repentance, and was kept in the original by the translator of this passage, as were the following terms: *Tzaddikim*, the plural of *Tzaddik*; *Harav*, meaning rabbi; and *Hashem*, literally, "the Name," a way to refer to God without using the name itself, which has become custom among a majority of the Orthodox and many other Jews as well (*Torat Eretz Yisrael: The Teachings of Harav Tzvi Yehudah Hacohen Kook*. Based on the Hebrew *Orations of Harav Tzvi Yehudah* compiled and edited by Rabbi Shlomo Aviner. Transl. Tzvi Fishman (Jerusalem: Torat Eretz Yisrael Publications, 1991), XVI.)

[6] Tzvi Yehudah Hacohen Kook, *Linetivot Yisrael: Collection of Articles* 3 Vols. (Hebrew) Jerusalem: s.n. 1989–1997.

[7] Isaiah 41:4.

stage that we have encountered now in the political maze of the government of the United States...[8]

Perhaps his most famous address occurred on the evening of Independence Day in 1967, a day before the tremendous escalation in militant rhetoric from Egypt and only three weeks before the outbreak of the war. This was his usual celebratory acknowledgment of Israel's independence, a public statement that was notable and at variance with most leaders in the ultra-Orthodox "yeshiva world" of the time. After the results of the war his words were considered prophetic, not least because he mourned the partition of Palestine in 1948 that removed Biblical Lands from Jewish access and control—a situation that was reversed in the 1967 war. His address has been termed a rare and dramatic discourse of a modern apocalyptic.[9]

Nineteen years ago on the same famous night, with the arrival of the [news of] the decision of the rulers of the nations of the world in favor of the revival of the State of Israel, when all the people flowed outside to celebrate in public the feelings of our joy, I could not go and join in the celebration. I sat alone....In those first hours I could not come to terms with what had happened, with that awesome news, because what had happened was 'My land they have divided!'[10] Yes, where is our Hevron—are we forgetting this? Where is our Shechem, and our Jericho? Where—have they been forgotten? And all the far side of the Jordan—it is ours, every clod of earth, every square inch, every district of the land and plot of land that belongs to the Land of Israel—are we allowed to give up even one millimeter of them? So my entire body was shocked, entirely wounded and torn into pieces— thus I could not be happy and celebrate. This was the situation nineteen years ago, on this same night at this same hour....[11]

[Kook continues:][12] There are important people who see the value of Independence Day *(yom medinateynu)* from the perspective of salvation

---

[8] *Linetivot Yisrael* 1:115. This was written on April 15, 1948, when the US was considering changing its position regarding the recognition of the State of Israel in the upcoming United Nations vote. Kook was certain that the United States would recognize the Jewish state and that this determinacy was a result of its messianic status.

[9] Dov Schwartz, *Challenge and Crisis*, 61.

[10] Joel 4:2.

[11] Rabbi Tzvi Yehudah Kook, "The Sanctity of the Holy People on the Sacred Land," *Shanah Beshanah* 1976, 268 (originally delivered orally in 1967).

[12] It is not clear from the *Shanah Beshanah* article whether this is a continuation of his Independence Day oration or whether this was added from his remarks on other occasions.

and rescue.[13] And in contrast to this [sense of rescue, they claim], its value as "Beginning of Redemption" (*atchalta dege 'ulah*) is in the category of divine mysteries (*kavshey derachamana*), and "hidden things of the Lord our God" (*nistarot...* ). On the contrary, the issues of redemption of Independence Day are not in the category of "hidden" at all, but rather, are revealed and explained.... [h]ow can we recognize when [the Redemption] is coming? By the Land of Israel giving forth its fruit beautifully, and, praised God, the produce of our Land is extremely beautiful...[14]

In his discourse, Kook often cites Nahmanides' famous command to settle the Land and not allow it to fall into the hand of foreigners.

Nahmanides continues: "And I say that the commandment that the sages emphasized, that [commandment] being living in The Land of Israel...All [consider it] a positive commandment, that being that we are commanded to inherit the Land and to settle it..." That is to say: the essence of the commandment is state conquest *(hakibbush hamamlakhti),* the national authority [representing] the entirety of [the people of] Israel in this sacred territory.[15] And from this general commandment comes the individual commandment that obligates every single Jew to live and settle in this sacred land. The sages, Abraham Bornstein and Yehoshua of Kutno[16] insisted on this point, defining the commandment of settling the Land of Israel as conquest *(kibbush)* and settlement and not as only settlement.[17]

Like his father, Tzvi Yehudah considered the signs of redemption to be visible everywhere. All are revelations of the living God. These include, in particular, the "miraculous divine revelation" associated with the victory of the 1967 War and the return of the people of Israel to the land of its ancestors.[18] "We believe, know and recognize that everything that happens to us in the Land is a miraculous revelation and divine guidance, appearing

---

[13] He is referring to the classic position of Mizrachi, which engaged in Zionism as a means to save Jewish lives and not as a messianic movement.

[14] *Shanah Beshanah* 1976, 270.

[15] *hashilton hale'umi haklal-yisra'eli beteritoria qedoshah zo.*

[16] Rabbi Abraham Bornstein of Sochaczew (d.1910), author of the well-known collection of responsa called the *Avney Nezer,* and Rabbi Yehoshua of Kutno, author of the collection of responsa, *Yeshu`ot Malko.* Kook refers to them in typical yeshiva style by the names of their well-known works, the *Avney Nezer* and the *Yeshu`ot Malko.*

[17] *Shanah Beshanah* 1976, 271.

[18] *Linetivot Yisrael* 3:102.

through the Eternal One of Israel who will not lie and will not change his mind,[19] for He is not man who changes his mind. Every step of life and our reconstruction [of it] here, whether holy or mundane, through spiritual and material means, and whether constructive or negative, through its improvement or decline, are all links in this revelatory chain, directed toward true redemption and eternal salvation."[20] No part of the biblical lands captured in the 1967 War can be given to non-Jews. They must remain always in the hands of Israel, and the state of Israel itself may not allow a referendum to decide whether they may be returned.[21]

Shortly before Egyptian President Sadat's visit to Jerusalem in 1977, Rabbi Tzvi Yehudah claimed,

> The territories of the Land of our Lives, of the areas of Judah and Samaria, the Golan and the Bashan and all of its expanses, from the holy land of Sinai, to the fullness of our settlements, the villages—all are our inheritance. They belong to all the many communities of our people, the House of Israel. No ruling of acquisition [or] thievery applies to them, and in accordance with the teaching and guidance of Nahmanides, Israel's father, it is effective and requires total implementation "for all generations," in full force.[22]

Tzvi Yehudah refers to Nahmanides regularly as the "father of Israel" *(avihem-shel-yisrael),* a term of great respect reserved for a select few of Israel's leaders and thinkers over the generations. The appellation is used especially in reference to Nahmanides' ruling that conquest/settlement is an eternal command. "Nahmanides, the father of Israel,[23] taught us in the *Book of Commandments*, that the commandment of conquering the Land—our land, deriving from the verse, 'And you shall inherit it and settle it'[24] is in force fully for all of us in every generation, and even during time of exile."[25]

---

[19] 1 Sam. 15:29.

[20] *Linetivot Yisrael* 3:121.

[21] *Linetivot Yisrael* 3:273–274; 3:299, 3:322, etc.

[22] *Linetivot Yisrael* 3:277. Dov Schwartz shows how Tzvi Yehudah fuses the holiness and chosenness of the People of Israel with the Land of Israel, thus making it impossible in his redemptive theology to give up even a tiny portion of the land ("A Theological Rationale..." 70–74).

[23] Kook cites the *Sha'agat-Aryeh* (Aryeh Lieb Ginzberg [d.1785]) and *Shabbat-Ha'aretz* (his father Abraham Isaac Kook) as the sources of this term for Nahmanides (*Linetivot Yisrael* 3:309).

[24] Deut. 11:31.

[25] *Linetivot Yisrael* 3:309.

According to Tzvi Yehudah, the exceptional ruling of *yehareg ve'al ya'avor*, meaning that one must even give one's life rather than transgress a divine commandment, must be applied to the commandment of conquest of the Land of Israel.[26] He notes that the sages forbade zealotry among Israel, even among exceptional people and even on behalf of God, but also points out that there is such a thing as a "pure zealot" *(haqana'i hatahor)*, which he applies as a positive epithet.[27]

Rabbi Tzvi Yehudah did not openly instigate violence in his writings, though he certainly called for revenge on occasion. One such occasion was in May 1980 when he delivered a eulogy for Rabbi Tzvi Glatt, who was shot and killed by Palestinian gunmen as he walked home from Shabbat worship services in Hebron. In this address he called emotionally for vengeance, but the agent that he called upon to avenge the killing of Glatt was neither his students nor the Israeli army, but God. The language of his soliloquy is full of rage, and the rage was directed at the non-Jewish world in general.

> "O God of vengeance, Lord; God of vengeance, come forth!" (Ps. 94:1). God is vengeance, among us and for the entirety of Israel, for all the people of Israel, for ever and ever. Rise up, Judge of the land! Bring vengeance on the gentiles *(hashev gemul 'al goyim)!*[28] Vengeance will be revealed, there is no doubt. It will most certainly be revealed, and from within us, on all the gentile nations *(goyim)*. The great vengeance will be revealed, uplifted, arisen. God is a God of retributions, who repays vengeance to His enemies! He will be lifted up, He is the One who lifts all the corners of the world. Revenge will be revealed. God is the God of revenge, the great revenge from all of Israel, from all the people of Israel, and from all of the great honor that must be revealed, that will be revealed, without any doubt, of the great uplifting, of the great compassion. You, our beloved and dear ones who have fallen, we will all be glorified through them, we all remember them, we all know them, we will all remember for ever and ever, for eternity. Their memory is for

---

[26] *Linetivot Yisrael* 3:293. This ruling traditionally applies only to three things: the intentional shedding of blood, public expressions of idolatry, and engaging in illicit sexual relations (Shulchan Arukh, Yoreh De'ah 157:1). Some have added commanded war as a requirement for defense. But no traditional authority, to my knowledge, has applied it to settlement or conquest.

[27] He states this in remembrance of Rabbi Yisrael Habas, founder of the weekly publication, *Hayesod*, which advocated the combination of Torah with 'holy land.' Kook refers to him as "the fighter for the wholeness of Israel, Torah, and the Holy Land" (*Halochem lishelemut yisra'el ve'oraita ve'ar'a qadisha* [*Linetivot Yisrael* 2:84]).

[28] Cf. Ps. 94:2, where the wording is actually *hashev gemul 'al ge'im*, meaning "bring vengeance on the arrogant."

all generations, for all the sacred generations. Sacred and pure for the splendor of Israel for ever and ever, for eternity, for all generations.[29]

Kook does not call here explicitly for revenge killings of Arabs, but he does call on God to avenge the victims. His rhetoric in this case is one of wrath and vengeance, and his words could be read by attentive students as calls for them personally to avenge the wrongful death of their comrade. Kook recognized that it was through war that Israel had achieved its gains. In May 1948, upon the beginning of the war that would bring Israel's independence, he wrote, "With the perfection of our military system...the perfection of the essence of our rebirth is evident. We are no longer considered to be only 'The People of the Book.' Instead we are recognized as 'The People of God,' the holy people, for whom the Book and the sword descended together from heaven."[30] And elsewhere, "War is not a nice thing, but the fact is that all the gains that we have made are through war: the state, Jerusalem and the place of the Temple. Therefore, one must not recoil so much from this. There is the commandment of Conquest of the Land according to the interpretation of Nahmanides...Our concerns are working themselves out step by step, not all at once. We hope that there will be fewer sacrifices in the future and fewer wars."[31] " 'God is a man of war,'[32] 'the One who makes wars and the One who causes the flowering of salvations.'[33] Through these wars begin our military revelations...Divine Providence is prepared through the brigades, the Jewish talents of today."[34]

Rabbi Kook explicitly states that the wars of Israel in the contemporary period are Commanded War, based on his understanding of Nahmanides. They are holy wars, authorized by God and initiated through settlement. Yet they are more than mere settlement, more even than

---

[29] Bramson, *The Last Days*, p. 249. There is a double-entendre in Kook's use of the term for nations: *goyim*. In biblical Hebrew, *goy* is a generic term for people or nation, and it applies to Israel as well as other peoples (Gen. 12:2, 18:18; Ex. 19:6; Deut. 26:5; 2 Sam. 7:23, etc.). In exilic Jewish discourse, which became well-established in the Yiddish vernacular of Ashkenaz, the term, "goy" (plural, "goyim") is a derogative term for gentile. His use of the idiom built out of Psalm 94 is not found in classical Jewish Midrash and commentary. It is a conscious play on words from the Psalm text (94:2), which has *hashev gemul `al ge'im*—"Bring vengeance upon the arrogant." His audience of traditional Jews would catch the word play and connect *goy* with *ge'* (*ge'eh*), suggesting that God is calling for revenge against the Gentiles who are, by definition (*goyim = ge'im*) equated with the arrogant.

[30] *Linetivot Yisrael*, pp.112–113, cited by Don-Yehiyah, "The Book and the Sword," 299.

[31] *Sichot* Exodus (Vol. 2), 137.

[32] Exodus 15:3.

[33] `oseh milchamot matzmiach yeshu`ot, from the daily morning worship service.

[34] *Sichot* Genesis, 367.

settlement-as-conquest. Israel's wars also include the forceful military re-acquisition of Israel's territory that had been forcefully taken away from its rightful Jewish owners. According to Kook, this is not "conquest," per se, for conquest refers to the acquisition of land from its lawful owners by force. On the contrary, the Land of Israel is in the process of being returned, even if by force, to its lawful owners by the hand of God.

Nahmanides establishes very clearly: The conquest of the Land of Israel is for us to establish control over it. This is Commanded War. This is a Torah commandment and there is no possibility of any other [interpretation]. There exists no people without a land, and the living and vital [people of] Israel must take hold of The Land. This commandment is eternal, as Nahmanides mentions three times. However, in earlier generations, even among generations of saints *(tzaddikim),* the commandment was not possible. Why? Because we were under physical duress [and therefore unable to carry it out].... The obligation is for all generations, but is impossible to carry out without certain instruments of war. Thus in earlier generations, there was no technical possibility of carrying out this commandment. Now, thank God, we have instruments of war, and this commandment is therefore again required of us. God makes kingdoms fall and makes kingdoms rise up. The Master of the Universe brought down [Ottoman] Turkey and established nations in its place [in the Land of Israel] that recognized the Bible, which belongs to the people of the Bible.[35] Through the Balfour Declaration, the Hebrew Regiment was formed, etc.[36] Slowly but surely, the opportunity was created to conquer the Land and the commandment was renewed.... The commandment includes inheriting and settling. Inheriting means conquest *(yerushah muvanah kibbush),* and carrying out the commandment of inheritance enables carrying out the commandment of settling. The commandment of settling the Land derives from the Torah so that [the Land] not become desolate. Therefore, it is necessary also to repair the spiritual desolation. It is impossible to avoid this commandment. Settling *(yeshiva)* is a term that means both Torah learning [i.e. a study yeshiva] and settling the Land [i.e. *yishuv ha'aretz*]. [The two words] are related in the Holy Tongue [of Hebrew]. The Great Hand [of God] in settlement extends through the spiritual authority of the Torah. Torah—

---

[35] *Ribbono shel `olam hipil et turkiya,vehikim bimkomam `amim shehikiru et hatanakh shehu shayakh la`am hatanakh...*

[36] Kook is referring to the Zion Mule Corps (see chapter 10 above).

war—settlement. These are a single triad, and we are blessed that we have authority over all of them.[37]

The words and sentiments of Rabbi Tzvi Yehudah have been collected into many volumes of his spoken and written discourses, most of which do not treat war at all. Taken out of the fuller context of his view of Jewish life and the destiny of the Jewish People, his words here may be mistaken to reflect a worldview that is only combative and violent. The fact is that many contemporary Israeli religious decisors and scholars, all of whom live in the real world of ongoing wars associated with the Jewish state, treat war in their writings because it has become a part of real life. No longer living in communities where warfare, including war for defense, is forbidden the Jews by the ruling powers, the exigencies of fighting and all the ethical and existential issues that are raised by it cannot be avoided as was the case in the Middle Ages. Consideration of war has become a necessary part of modern Jewish religious thought and practice.

The reality of Jews actually engaging in military combat after nearly two millennia of quiescence has been seen by some religious Zionist commentators as compelling evidence in and of itself that the divine Redemption is at hand. And of course, religious interpreters of history can base their views and interpretations on canonical biblical prophecies, the perceived parallels between Bible narratives and current events, and the comments of earlier and sometimes ancient exegetes who were relating to entirely different historical contexts. Kook's passion was for the People of Israel in the Land of Israel and for the anticipated arrival of a true and overwhelming messianic Redemption. But as in any act of reading, Kook's and his student's interpretations of scripture and tradition are influenced by the particularities of historical context.

He often cites Nahmanides' view in his talks and writings[38] in which he calls on his students to engage in conquest. Yet there is an enormous difference between the meaning of settlement-as-conquest in the generation of Nahmanides and the meaning he construes from this ideal in his generation. In the thirteenth century, it was impossible to carry out Nahmanides' sense of the divine command of conquest except through individual acts of immigration to the Land of Israel, a geographic entity that was governed

[37] Tzvi Yehudah Kook, "Between a People and Its Land," (Hebrew) excerpted from Conversations of Rabbi Tzvi Yehudah in Artzi 2 (1982), 18–19.

[38] Sichot Genesis, 136, 412; Exodus, 137; Numbers 29–31, 32, 166, 334–335, 376, 377; Linetivot Yisrael 3:262; "The Sanctity of the Holy People on the Sacred Land," Shanah Beshanah 1976, 270–271, etc.

by powerful foreign powers.[39] There was no possibility of realizing any kind of military or political conquest. The only possibility was a "conquest" of an individual or perhaps small community realized by coming to live and settle in a tiny portion of a land that could not possibly come under Jewish political control. Jewish control over the Land of Israel was imaginable only in the wildest of fantasies.

For Kook and his students, however, settlement-as-conquest was more communal, more militant, more military in nature, and far more realizable because of a radically different geopolitical situation. Moreover, Jews of his generation had the means to engage in genuine political and military communal actions that could have a significant political outcome. Also conceivable for Kook and his students while inconceivable for Nahmanides, success in settlement-as-conquest resulted in concrete large-scale physical achievements on the land: large collective farms and settlements, the growth of Jewish towns and cities, industry, transportation, and communication systems, and eventually Jewish self-government and even Jewish rule over non-Jews living in the state. All could be considered achievements that demonstrate concrete steps or phases on the path of Redemption, not only in the metaphysical sense of a divinely wrought Redemption, but also in the eventual formal Jewish political and military control of the entire Land of Israel.

A historical thirteenth century contextual reading of Nahmanides would find his view unremarkable. As noted in chapter 8, Nahmanides argued against Maimonides in order to preserve the Torah command of conquest by reducing the scope and the danger of the act, thereby making it humanly possible to carry out. He taught that the divine commandment of conquest, so plainly and repeatedly articulated in the Torah and so impossibly dangerous in his day as a military mission, could nevertheless be fulfilled through the achievable human act of moving to the Land of Israel and living there.[40] Nahmanides' interpretation was a means to resolve a particular problem, and his solution reflected his own historical and personal context. Politically powerless individuals could still carry out this divine command by engaging in a politically unthreatening act.

But a reading of Nahmanides' words in the historical context of nineteenth and twentieth-century national movements encourages a new

---

[39] In Nahmanides' generation, a powerful Muslim Mamluke state (1250–1517) ruled Jerusalem and Palestine from its capital in Cairo.

[40] Such a move might be achievable in theory, but it was certainly not easy. Travel in general was not safe in the thirteenth century, and with the ongoing Crusades and Muslim military counterattacks, travel for Jews could be especially precarious.

interpretation. Especially with an eye to the romantic European notion of ancient patrimony within the natural geography of the primeval homeland that is inherent in romantic nationalism, Nahmanides' words can take on a radical new significance. According to the new reading, the commandment of settlement-as-conquest is not merely a way to carry out a divine command as an individual. It is a means to carry out the national goals of an entire people.

The modern interpretation reverses the purpose of the Nahmanidean interpretation. No longer merely a cliché, conquest becomes a political and military reality, and this is how many of Kook's students understood the rabbi's reading of Nahmanides. Thus Rabbi Shlomo Aviner, one of Kook's closest students, once addressed officers of the Israel Defense Forces with these words: "We are obligated to endanger our lives: Nahmanides emphasizes that our obligation to the commandment [of settling the Land] exists even if observing it is bound up in wars. And in war, unfortunately, people kill and are killed. There is no promise in the Torah that in war to free the Land *(milchemet shichrur ha'aretz)* or conquest of the Land *(kibbush ha'aretz),* people will not be killed."[41] In an even more powerful statement directly relating to Nahmanides' view of war, Aviner wrote, "These words of Nahmanides parallel the modern concept of war of liberation."[42] The reversal and extension of Nahmanides' solution to the medieval problem has become part of Tzvi Yehudah Kook's legacy.

Rabbi Tzvi Yehudah Kook's views, his passion, his personal and family relationship with his sainted father, and the very fact that he ran the physical institution of a yeshiva that had room and desire for more students, were all factors in his becoming a central figure in the development that produced Gush Emunim and the Settler Movement. Despite his acknowledged centrality, however, Kook himself is not the central factor or cause of the great increase in militancy within Religious Zionism. As suggested throughout this study, it is not the particular individual or event, but rather the trajectories of historical circumstances that have re-activated holy war thinking among some sectors of the Jewish world. The continuing escalation of Palestinian violence after 1973, much in reaction to the increase in Jewish settlement in the territories, helped create a vicious cycle. The pressures of the United Nations and the political stresses caused by the Cold War, inter-Arab rivalries, as well as other factors all raised the tension

[41] Rabbi Shlomo Aviner, "Inheriting the Land and the Moral Problem," in *Artzi* 2 (May, 1982), 7.
[42] Rabbi Shlomo Aviner, "Our Redemption is Little by Little *(ge'ulateynu qim`a qim`a)*," *Amudim* 445 (December, 1983), 136.

and, to some religious Zionist observers, added to the signs of impending Redemption.

Kook became a principal figure around which trajectories of social, economic, political, military, and religious influence would come together. But there were other figures as well, and not only within the community of religious Zionists that had grown up on the milk of Mizrachi and pioneering settlements in Palestine and Israel. One important symbolic figure after 1967 is Rabbi Meir Kahane (d. 1990).

Ehud Sprinzak notes how Kahane's increased popularity was connected to the large swing to the right among the population of Israel in general in the 1970s, and that the shift was hardly influenced by Kahane himself.[43] But Kahane symbolized a radicalization and legitimating of violent behaviors among Jews during the 1970s and 1980s that reached a peak in the formation of the "Jewish underground."

The ascendance of Israel's radical right has been examined in detail by Sprinzak and others, and need not be rehearsed here. But it is nevertheless useful to point out how Kahane's repeated public reference to certain phrases and slogans caused ideas that had previously been anathema to become a part of common public discourse in Israel and among many Jews living outside of Israel. This is not to suggest that Meir Kahane himself conceived of the ideas that he espoused. He was an activist and publicist, not an original thinker. While others held most of his ideas prior to his public exclamations, both verbal and physical, he tended to carry them to their logical conclusion. And he organized a full range of angry and fearful emotions into a political movement. "It is not the *content* of [Kahane's] message that captures people's minds but rather the very fact that there is an ideology of some kind that offers a release and an outlet for the fears and the stored-up anger."[44]

He thus coined the term, T.N.T., an English acronym for a Hebrew slogan, *terror neged terror*, meaning "[Jewish] terror to counter [Arab] terror." As he did with his other undertakings, Kahane took a phenomenon already existing and moved it to a more intense and frantic level. Jewish violence and militancy had increased partly as a reaction to increased Arab violence long before Kahane. We have observed in chapter 11 that Jewish acts of terror had been used in the prestate period in an attempt to counter Arab violence against Jews. It was used also during the 1948 War in order to take control of Arab sectors of Palestine or to empty areas of

[43] Sprinzak, *The Ascendance of Israel's Radical Right*, 83–84.
[44] Ravitzky, Aviezer, "Roots of Kahanism: consciousness and Political Reality," *Jerusalem Quarterly* 39 (1986), 102 (italics in original).

their Arab inhabitants,[45] and we have examined in chapter 13 how acts of Israeli military retaliation in the 1950s would also be classified by international observers as terror. But in all these cases, such acts were not publicized and lauded as acceptable behaviors, even if occasionally considered necessary.

Kahane, however, publicly praised and extolled violence against non-Jews. Like most religious Zionists of his day, Kahane considered the establishment of the State of Israel to be part of the messianic process leading to ultimate Redemption. But the purpose of the Jewish State to Kahane was not limited to rescuing Jews from violence or even to represent a major signpost on the path to ultimate Redemption. According to Kahane, one of the state's most important purposes was to take revenge against the gentiles. "From the furnaces and from the ashes, a Jewish state arose—not because we had earned it but because the gentiles had; because God in His terrible anger had decided to mete out punishment to a world that had mocked and despised and degraded the Almighty God of Israel."[46] Terror against non-Jews, whether Soviets, Germans, Arabs, or Americans who abused or even threatened Jews, was therefore acceptable and even worthy of praise.[47]

Another term that became normalized under the influence of Kahane is "transfer," relating to the compulsory removal of Arabs from the territories acquired in the 1967 War and settling them in neighboring Arab countries. Until the advent of Kahane's party, "Kakh," such an idea could not be debated publicly, and for years Kahane's ideas were considered so racist that they were simply excluded from public discourse. But after being repeated so often in public venues and picked up and repeated in the press, "transfer" became a primary platform of a party that sent two representatives to the Knesset in 1988 after Kahane's own party was disqualified

---

[45] See, for example, Mustafa Abbasi, "The Battle for Safad in the War of 1948: a Revised Study," *International Journal of Middle East Studies* 36.1 (February, 2004), 21–47.

[46] Ravitzky, Aviezer, "Roots of Kahanism: consciousness and Political Reality," *Jerusalem Quarterly* 39 (1986), 93–94.

[47] This view is taken a significant step further a generation later. In an article justifying Barukh Goldstein's 1994 murder of twenty-nine people at prayer in a mosque at the "Cave of the Patriarchs" in Hebron, Rabbi Yitzhak Ginsburg argued that killing Gentiles in an act of terror can serve as a mystical technique (Yitzhak Ginsburg, *"Barukh Hagever,"* in Michael Ben Horin [ed.], *Barukh Hagever* [Jerusalem: n.p., 1995], 19–48; and analyzed at length by Don Seeman, "Violence, Ethics, and Divine Honor in Modern Jewish Thought," *Journal of the American Academy of Religion* 73:4 [December, 2005], 1015–1048). The neokabbalistic element in Jewish terror in the 1990s and after seems to be a development that occurred after the general revival of the holy war paradigm that is the core topic of this study (Nadav Shragai, "The Motive Behind Jewish Terror," in *Haaretz*, August 24, 2003—http://cosmos.ucc.ie/cs1064/jabowen/IPSC/php/art.php?aid=4005).

by an Election Law of Israeli Parliament that banned parties inciting racism. The possibility of accepting the idea of transfer, meaning an "agreed-upon" (though still compulsory)[48] relocation, only became palatable after Kahane's idea of a forced, one-sided "eviction" had already been bandied about for years previously.[49] Kahane himself was not the only cause of the radicalization. His views were possible only in a historical context that could allow for their acceptability.

We have noted often in this study of war in Judaism how Jewish notions do not emerge independently of history. Holy war is not a self-contained phenomenon uninfluenced by the environment, and Jewish expressions of holy war did not emerge as a result of a Jewish history disconnected from the history of the larger world in which Jews constantly interact. As with all human groups, historical developments do not occur in a vacuum. It would be an egregious error, therefore, to fail to mention that the same watershed events that marked changes in Jewish history in the Land of Israel also affected Palestinian and Arab history in Palestine and its adjacent lands, and vice versa.

Not only, therefore, was the 1948 War Israel's "War of Liberation," it was also the Palestinian's and Arab's "Catastrophe" *(nakba)*. Israel's humiliation in 1973 is hardly meaningful without noting that it was Egypt's triumph.[50] In the same way, the increase of antipathy among Jews toward Arabs in general and Palestinians in particular was influenced by the increased rhetoric and threats resulting from "the dramatic evolution of the PLO and the Palestinian nationalism associated with it" that is grounded by Sprinzak with the 1973 War.[51] And of course, influence moved in both directions as it always has in the case of modern Jewish-Arab relations in the Middle East.

Despite Rabbi Tzvi Yehudah's insistence that the Israeli acquisition of territory in 1967 was not political conquest but only taking delivery of the divine inheritance, by the end of the 1970s it appeared to many Israelis, as well as Palestinians, that settlement across the "Green Line" (marking unofficial borders between Israel and its neighbors according to the 1949 Armistice Agreement) was indeed a form of military conquest. And by this time, Jewish settlement in Judea and Samaria was no longer simple conquest in the Nahmanidean or Nahmanidean-Gordonean sense. It had evolved and transformed

---

[48] The logic of this is difficult to comprehend.

[49] Sprinzak, *Ascendance*, 172–176.

[50] Cairo hosts a museum dedicated to its triumph called "October War Panorama Museum" and known as "The October War Victory Museum."

[51] *Ascendance*, 83–87.

into something much closer to conquest in the modern military sense. Settlers were heavily armed by the state and full-scale protection of settlements was provided by Israeli military units with heavy armor. Jewish settlers and local Palestinians committed often lethal violence against one another at the individual, personal level,[52] while in the larger arena, Palestinian militias and trained fighting units battled with Israeli armed forces. To Jews engaged in this militant settlement of conquest, this was indeed a holy war. Jewish losses in Palestinian attacks were not in vain, but were *qorbanot*, sacrifices on behalf of the People of Israel in the Land of Israel, that recalled the sacrifices in the Jerusalem Temple.[53]

## Post 1973 Anxiety and the Radicalization of Settlement

The increased pace of settlement in the wake of the 1973 War naturally stimulated an increased rate of resistance among Palestinians, including violent resistance that was both spontaneous and organized. In 1977, a seismic political shift to the right in Israel brought the Likud party of Menachem Begin to power. At the top of the Likud party platform of 1977 is the Jewish right to all of the biblical Land of Israel:

> The right of the Jewish people to the land of Israel is eternal and indisputable and is linked with the right to security and peace; therefore, Judea and Samaria will not be handed to any foreign administration; between the Sea and the Jordan there will only be Israeli sovereignty. A plan which relinquishes parts of western Eretz Israel, undermines our right to the country, unavoidably leads to the establishment of a "Palestinian State," jeopardizes the security of the Jewish population, endangers the existence of the State of Israel, and frustrates any prospect of peace.[54]

---

[52] Weisburg, *Jewish Settler Violence*, 64–81.

[53] The term, *qorban/qorbanot* was and continues to be applied to all Jews killed on behalf of the homeland. The origin of its usage in Zionist discourse is unknown to me, but it was certainly used in reference to Jews who had died through martyrdom (*kiddush hashem*) since the period of the talmudic sages. All who lose loved ones in war hope that their deaths are not in vain, and sacrifice on behalf of the greater community is a common source of comfort. In the discourse of activist, militant Religious Zionism, the sense of sacrifice harkens back directly to biblical images and to the rabbinic imagery of martyrdom (*kiddush hashem*), which merits entry into the World to Come (Abraham Isaac Neriya, "Keeping the Commandments in the Time of Battle, *Shanah Beshanah* 1976, 311; Rabbi Yehudah Hertzel Henkin, "Those Who Fall as Martyrs," *Shanah Beshanah* 1984, 290–291).

[54] "The Likud Party Platform, 1977," in *Jewish Virtual Library* (http://www.jewishvirtuallibrary. org/jsource/Politics/LikudPlat1977.html. checked 12/09/08).

The cycle of increased Jewish settlement inflaming Palestinian resistance, which in turn provoked more settlement, could not be broken, not only because it became self-sustaining through a rhythm of reaction and sometimes escalation on both sides, but also because of internal political and religious forces within the Jewish and Arab communities. The internal issues within the Arab world and Palestinian communities are beyond the parameters of this study, but a brief review of the situation among religious Zionists will provide perspective to what has appeared to many outsiders as the frenetic and even chaotic actions of the settlers.

As mentioned previously, many Jews worldwide viewed the 1967 War as a miraculous victory. But for those raised on the religious ideas and symbolism of traditional Judaism and Religious Zionism, the astonishing success of the war was a true and divinely wrought miracle, a statement of divine support and assurance of the pending messianic coming. The drastic setback of the 1973 War, therefore, posed a serious dilemma, not only in military and political terms, but also in messianic terms. The emergence of Gush Emunim as an activist settlement movement was, in part, an attempt to correct for what was considered to be the lack of adequate Jewish response to the *messianic* message of 1967.[55] The failings of 1973 caused an increase in anxiety and even desperation among the activists of the emerging Settler Movement.

Rabbi Yehudah Amital (d. 2010), the head of the largest Hesder Yeshiva[56] (combining Torah study with military service), reflects the sense of crisis caused by the 1973 War in his book, *From Out of the Depths*. "This war is Commanded War in two respects—from the standpoint of 'saving Israel from the hand of an [attacking] enemy (Maimonides)... and war for the Land of Israel even without a danger of extermination is Commanded War.... Every war of Israel is a war for the unity of God[57]... Israel represents by its very existence the divine concept of the unity of God and the divine way of righteousness and justice. The meaning of the victory of Israel is the victory of the divine concept, and also, heaven forbid, the opposite."[58] This perception seems to position Israel as the only true representative of divine unity, the true God, thus pitting Israel against the

---

[55] Mordechai Nisan, "Gush Emunim: A Rational Perspective," *Forum* 36 (fall-winter, 1979), 15–23.

[56] Yeshivat Har Etziyon in the West Bank town of Alon Shevut.

[57] Cf. Maimonides, *Mishneh Torah*, *Kings* 7:15.

[58] Amital, *From Out of the Depths*, 18–19 (see also 55–61). Parentheses in original. The title derives from Psalm 130:1, but Rabbi Amital purposely alters the punctuation to render the traditional reading: "An ascension song: from the depths I called to You, God...," to "A song of ascensions from the depths: I called to you, God...."

entire world. Any war against Israel is a war against God. Such a position represents a classic representation of holy war.

Sprinzak considers Amital's book to have become "...the most inspiring document of the young Gush Emunim. Rabbi Amital's explanation for the 1973 war was that it was the final attempt of the gentiles to stop the inevitable Jewish redemption." Amital was a student of Rabbi Tzvi Yehudah and a hero of the Settler Movement, but he made a radical turn in his position after the emergence of increased settler violence against Palestinians, and especially after the Israeli invasion of Lebanon in 1982 and Israel's restoration to Egypt the same year of the Jewish settlement town in the Sinai Peninsula called Yamit.[59] His book, nevertheless, continues to be reprinted and remains available at the time of this writing, and his words have remained inspirational for many.

A spate of articles was published by thinkers in religious Zionist circles to work through the issues raised by the religious crisis brought about by the 1973 War. Inspirational pieces were included in religious journals such as *Torah Shebe`al Peh*[60] and *Shanah Beshanah*. In the 1976 edition of *Shanah Beshanah,* the editor, Rabbi Aharon Halevi Pitchenik, published the famous sermon of Rabbi Tzvi Yehudah that he delivered on the eve of Israel Independence Day in 1967. Pitchenik explains: "We are including here the words that were given by our master Rabbi Tzvi Yehuda Hacohen Kook, Rosh Yeshivah 'Mercaz Harav,' at the celebration of Independence Day, 1967, at the yeshiva as recorded by his students. Miraculous were these words that were said then, overlapping with the miraculous deeds that occurred about three weeks later in the Six Day War and the conquest of 'our Hevron, our Shechem, and our Jericho.'"[61]

A particularly powerful motivational sermon by the former Ashkenazic Chief Rabbi of Israel, Isser Yehuda Unterman, was also published there.

The words of the prophet have come true before our eyes: for the Lord of Armies has taken thought on behalf of His flock, the House of Judah;

---

[59] Elyashev Reichner, *By Faith Alone: The Story of Rabbi Yehuda Amital*, transl. Elli Fischer (New Milford, CT: Maggid, 2011).

[60] Rabbi Moshe Tzvi Neriya, "Our Right to the Land of Israel," *Torah Shebe`al Peh* 1974, 149–180 (written before the war but published as an inspirational article in its aftermath); Rabbi Chaim David HaLevi, "The Position of the'Yom Kippur' War among the Battles for the Redemption of Israel," *Torah Shebe`al Peh* 1975, 63–68. The entire 1979 *Torah Shebe`al Peh* conference (the journal accepts its articles out of its annual conference papers) was devoted to papers delivered under the title "Peace in the *Halakhah*." This included various positions on the possibility of returning certain of the territories to Arab control, clearly a response to the Camp David Accords signed in September, 1978.

[61] P. 267.

He will make them like majestic chargers in battle (Zechariah 10:3): And many more prophecies have been fulfilled entirely. The Children of Israel are being gathered slowly, like a flock of sheep that returns to its place, and with God's taking note of His flock, He has shown the House of Judah miraculous strength to defend itself against those who hate it, who have begun to push it [the House of Judah] from the Land, and it has achieved glory and splendor in its war. After this, there is no place for hesitation, but [rather] obligation to continue. The help of Heaven will not depart from us. Dear brothers, let us begin with energy to fortify our spiritual independence, that which is based on the eternal foundations of believing Judaism. And our full Redemption will soon come.[62]

The newsletters of the Religious Kibbutz Movement and B'nai Akiba Youth Movement were filled with motivational and inspirational articles immediately after the 1973 War, but they also included articles and letters that openly questioned some of the ideological assumptions and transcendent historical perspectives upon which the Settler Movement was based, and these invited sharp responses.[63] Only a few examples can be

---

[62] Rabbi Isser Yehuda Unterman, "The Prophecies Have Come About in their Entirety," *Shanah Beshanah*, 1978, 151. See also, Rabbi Benjamin Blech, "The Messianic Destiny of the State of Israel,"*Shanah Beshanah* 1976, 251–257; Rabbi Menachem M. Kasher, "Do not Fear, My Servant Jacob (Words of Encouragement and Keeping the Faith)," *Shanah Beshanah* 1979, 165–171: "Just as we do not understand the ways of God in the Holocaust, we know securely that there is absolutely no doubt that He is righteous and truthful. So also we do not understand His ways in the beginning of Redemption that is coming slowly, slowly [*qim`ah qim`ah*, a reference to an important passage in the JT Yoma 3:2 that the redemption of Israel will be 'at first, little by little, but in the end it will go along and burst into light'], but we believe that the prophecy of Ezekiel will be fulfilled: 'I gave you a new heart and will put into you a new spirit...' Here in our generation these prophecies are being fulfilled, and the time of the footsteps of the messiah are approaching, that most of the nations of the world have been marshaled together to wipe out the People of Israel, heaven forbid, and only in our day is the significance of the fulfilled prophecy understood, that most of the nations of the world stand on the side of the Arabs to destroy Israel and to isolate her... The believer who looks with discerning eyes on all that is occurring and has happened to Israel during the last 200 years, the extraordinary and unprecedented changes, destruction and renewal, ruin and re-growth, the bitter Holocaust and the fruitfulness of the Land of Israel, without doubt sees and says in his heart: the hand of God is with this... We are required to make clear to [the secular youth] immediately that all that has occurred to and is occurring to the People of Israel in its Land—the founding of the state, ingathering of the exiles, flowering and re-growth of the Jewish community and building up of the Land, and also the telling victories in all the battles of Israel, that all these are the hidden act of God" (166–170).

[63] The response of the two newsletters to the 1973 War was rather the reverse of the 1967 War. The B'nai Akiba Movement newsletter, *Zera`im*, which was edited at the time by the moderate activist and supporter of Gush Emunim, Rabbi Yakov Ariel, tended to include more ideological commentaries than *Amudim*, the newsletter of the Kibbutz Movement.

cited here, such as the article by a member of the religious Kibbutz Tirat Tzvi, which critiqued Gush Emunim for moving "from the rational to the mystical" and employing anti-democratic tactics in their activism. Yet he admired their commitment and activism and found them to have filled an ideological vacuum that nobody else was filling after the 1973 War.[64] The well-known scholar of Jewish liturgy and Midrash, Joseph Heinemann, offers a scathing critique of Tzvi Yehudah Kook's claim that "Definitions regarding belief are determined by those who are true to [or, perfect in] Torah and faith," a position that Heinemann considers entirely contrary to Judaism.[65] The arguments continue in the following three issues as Kook's student, Rabbi Shlomo Aviner, takes up his teacher's position contra Heinemann. *Amudim* dedicated a great deal of space in 1976 to the simmering arguments within Hapoel Hamizrachi and its communities over the direction of Religious Zionism with the emergence of Gush Emunim. Some of the contributors, in addition to those whose words are cited here, include such well-known figures as Daniel Lazar, Avraham Paltiel, and Yeshayahu Leibowitz.[66]

Despite the discomfort and occasional opposition of those who found the extra-legal tactics of Gush Emunim problematic, its powerful pioneering ethos, idealism, and activism were inspirational to many across the religious and political spectrum in Israel and the Jewish hinterland beyond. The Settler Movement became extremely successful as the vanguard for Zionist revivalism. It captured the enthusiasm of the new generation of religious Zionist activists, and not a few secular Jews as well. Yet at the very moment when settlement activism was making its mark, the entire

---

[64] Yisachar Ben-David, "'Gush Emunim' and its Detractors," *Amudim* 363 (1976), 148–150. In the same issue, a student and biographer of Rabbi Abraham Yitzak Kook, Tzvi Yaron, criticizes Rabbi Tzvi Yehudah (p. 151), drawing a sharp response from Tzvi Yehudah himself: "From the source of the divine Torah, which is the highest command for all of our ways, we are commanded to make settlements throughout the entire Land. The scribbles [of critics] making fun of this highest command of the commandment to settle [all of] this land of His, the inheritance of our fathers and our lives in it, is nothing but proof of spiritual poverty of its writers…" (*Amudim* 364 [1976], p.184). The ardent student of Rabbi Tzvi Yehudah, Rabbi Shlomo Aviner argues against Professor Yesha`yahu Leibowitz' critique of *Gush Emunim* a few weeks later ("On Our Redemption and on the Block of Our Faithful [*Gush Emunim*], Comments in Response to Prof. Isaiah Leibowitz," *Amudim* 366 [1976], 276–278), etc.

[65] Yoseph Heinemann, "Definitions Regarding Faith," *Amudim* 371 (1976), 448.

[66] In the United States there was much less discussion, because of a number of factors: the distance from the arena of conflict in Israel; the fact that the most ardent American Jewish advocates of activism had moved or planned to move to Israel; and because one of the leading rabbis of American Orthodoxy, Joseph B. Soloveitchik, was not supportive of settlement activism (Emanuel Rackman, "Violence and the Value of Life: The Halakhic View," in Salo Baron and George Wise [eds.], *Violence and Defense in the Jewish Experience* [Philadelphia: Jewish Publication Society, 1977], 137–140).

project was in danger of being turned on its head by the visit of Egyptian President Anwar Sadat to Jerusalem, where he addressed the Knesset in November, 1977. The Camp David Accords were signed less than a year later (in September, 1978), and the peace treaty between Israel and Egypt in Washington in March 1979.

The peace treaty required Israel to give up territories that had been previously controlled by Egypt but captured by Israel in the 1967 War. Giving up any territory animated the zealousness of settler activists and many who supported them, but there was some uncertainty about whether parts of the Sinai Peninsula that were to be returned were actually a part of the Land of Israel promised by God in the Torah to the Jewish people.[67]

There was little need to justify war in 1973 on the basis of Commanded War. The 1973 War itself was considered a war of national defense, which is always justifiable as Commanded War based on the Palestinian Talmud and Maimonides.[68] Security was a major issue in the postwar negotiations, but the elevation of emotions in the late 1970s was centered on the problem of giving away territory. To many Jews whether religious or secular, any return of territory was contrary to the Zionist project. But to those who considered Sinai (or portions of it) to have been divinely promised there was greater alarm, though it may be recalled that there was no great cry when the entire Sinai Peninsula was returned to Egypt after the 1956 War. The enormous consternation in the 1970s was the result of growing messianic conviction among a new generation of activist religious Zionists who feared that the nation was in danger of repudiating God's command to conquer—still meaning for many to settle—the Land of Israel as a necessary stage in the imminent messianic Redemption. The stakes thus appeared to be extremely high.

But not all religious Zionists were fully within the camp of the activists. Some who had grown up within the circle of the B'nai Akiba youth movement and Hapoel Hamizrachi advocated the return of territory for a real peace with the neighboring Arab states. A considerable community of observant Jews (many from non-European backgrounds) who did not grow up in the youth movements nevertheless counted themselves as committed religious Zionists. One of the most prominent leaders of this block

---

[67] See the legal examination of Rabbi Shlomo Goren, "The Sanctity of the Land of Israel According to Its Biblical Borders *Mahanayim* 31 (1957), 5–11. Cf. Rabbi Shilo Refa'el, "Conquering the Land of Egypt and Settling It," *Torah Shebe`al Peh* 17 (1975), 135–140, which examines the status of the areas within Egypt proper (across the Suez Canal) that were captured by the IDF in the 1973 War.

[68] See chapters 5 and 7.

was Rabbi Ovadia Yosef, the *Rishon Letziyon*—Chief Sefardi Rabbi of the State of Israel. In a surprising move following the Camp David Accords of September, 1978, Rabbi Ovadia ruled with scholarship and erudition that it was acceptable to relinquish political control of parts of the Land of Israel if surrendering territory would save Jewish lives.[69]

[I]f the heads and officers of the army, together with the government, determine that the issue of saving lives is inherent in the issue, that if territories from the Land of Israel are not returned there would be a danger of immediate war from neighboring Arabs, and from all sides the sword would bite, heaven forbid, and if by returning the territories to them the danger of war would be distanced from us, and there are possibilities for actual peace, it appears that according to all opinions [of sages and rabbis], it is permitted to return territories of the Land of Israel in order to achieve this goal, for you have nothing that takes precedence over saving lives.[70]

As Yosef himself notes in his article, this position clashes with those who claim that Jews should trust entirely in God that the territories will remain in Israel's hands. Those who place their trust entirely with God find support from those sages of the Talmud who criticized King Hezekiah for appeasing the Assyrians in hopes of preventing war, after which God destroyed the Assyrian camp (2 Kings, 18). But Rabbi Yosef counters that Jews must not depend on miracles to win wars because they may not be worthy of such miracles, or because the result of an error in judgment would simply be far too dangerous to the future of Israel.[71] He argues against the view that Nahmanides considered Commanded War obligatory in his own generation.

We may therefore conclude that even according to Nachmanides there is no obligation today to go to war and endanger ourselves in order to defend the conquered territories in opposition to the nations of the world, especially as we do not have a king, Sanhedrin, or the *urim vetumim*, which are prerequisite for war.... It may also be argued that even if the

---

[69] Rabbi Ovadia Yosef, "Returning Territories from the Land of Israel in Order to Save Lives," *Torah Shebe`al Peh* 1980, 12–21. A similar version of this article was translated into English as "Ceding Territory of the Land of Israel in Order to Save Lives," *Crossroads* 3 (1990), 11–28. The pagination of the Hebrew original is cited, followed by the pagination of the English translation.

[70] Yosef, "Returning Territories..." op. cit., 14/17.

[71] Yosef, 15/21.

opinion of Nahmanides is that the Torah commandment of conquering and defending the land applies today, the nature of our conquest in practice, where we do not have complete control of the territories, is not a fulfillment of the commandment... In particular, it must be noted that at present the roads in Judea, Samaria, and Gaza are dangerous, and are under no more than military rule, without the possibility of safe travel, let alone residence. This is clearly not the conquest, as a man acting within his own property, described by Nahmanides.[72]

A detailed critique of Rabbi Yosef's arguments and conclusions was made by Shaul Yisraeli, the intellectual and ideological leader of Religious Zionism.[73] Yisraeli concludes his analysis with the following words: "It is categorically prohibited to cede the territories which we liberated, by the grace of God, in a defensive war. Not only would this not diminish the danger of loss of life, it would actually increase it. Let us strengthen ourselves in faith in God, the Guardian of Israel, who will guide and keep us safe in difficult times, grant us salvation and redemption, and bless us speedily with the ingathering of the exiles of Israel."[74]

But Rabbi Yosef's legal opinion had already generated significant doubt and anxiety among many Orthodox Jews. Rabbi Yisraeli's explanation for his public refutation of Rabbi Yosef's opinion is revealing.

[T]he publication of [Rabbi Yosef's] statement caused a great deal of confusion, especially among observant Jews who look to rabbinic leaders for guidance. Several ministers [of state], claiming to be following his advice, issued extreme statements, declaring that we are indeed prepared to return the "conquered territories" (without mentioning Rav Yosef's stipulation).[75] These statements weaken our position even before the conditions for negotiations are ripe, and strengthen the left-wing politicians, whose aim is a shrunken State of Israel within the boundaries of the land of Israel, in order to obliterate the distinctiveness of the people and the Land of Israel. They are especially hostile to the thriving settlements which have been established in the territories since the Six Day War, without harming in any way the non-Jewish population.

---

[72] Yosef, 17–18/23–24.

[73] Shaul Yisraeli, "Ceding Territory Because of Mortal Danger," *Crossroads* 3 (1990), 29–46 (the earlier Hebrew article from which this is translated is unavailable to me).

[74] Yisraeli, "Ceding Territory...," 46.

[75] The stipulation is that military and diplomatic experts must be in agreement that such an act would indeed save many Jewish lives.

Their greatest joy would be to uproot them from their place. Since I believe that the Jewish law obligates us not to give in to pressure and threats of war, and not to cede sections of the Land of Israel to non-Jews, especially those areas inhabited by Jews, I have decided to publish my views. Torah, which is truth, cannot be merely argumentative, so I am confident that we will reach a harmonious conclusion, in the spirit of, "love truth and peace" (Zach. 8, 19).[76]

## 1978–1984: Emotional Climax: Jewish Terror and the Underground

As this interchange between rabbis Ovadia Yosef and Shaul Yisraeli indicates, the anxiety and tension that brought the Settler Movement into being after the 1973 War entered a climactic period beginning with the Camp David Accords in 1978. It reached a peak in the violent acts and eventual arrest of the Jewish underground in 1984, but even that shocking surge of deadly activism failed to cause a retreat among most sympathetic to the Settler Movement. This period marks the final stage in the revival of holy war in Judaism.[77]

The Camp David Accords, which were formalized in September of 1978, confirmed the worst fears of the activist religious Zionists who spearheaded the Settler Movement. Their messianic Zionist vision was based on Jewish possession of the lands defined as the Land of Israel, the most important territories of which had been miraculously restored to the People of Israel through God's design in the 1967 War. The initial loss of territory in the 1973 War was followed by the Camp David Accords, which required abandoning territory permanently. While the particular area under discussion was the Sinai Peninsula, most of which was beyond the reckoning of what constituted the sacred lands of the Bible, the precedence of giving away territory left everything in jeopardy. The peace treaty with Egypt was signed in the spring following the establishment of the Accords, and its formalization stimulated a distinct rise in settler activism. The rise in

---

[76] Yisraeli, "Ceding Territory...," 29–30 (un-numbered footnote).

[77] Some may criticize my choice in marking the emergence of the Underground as the final stage in the revival of Jewish holy war. There is, of course, no absolutely "final stage," because the complex notions described in this book are always being negotiated within religious culture and civilization, thereby continually remaining in a certain level of flux. But whether one places the watershed event that marks the transition earlier or later or chooses a different symbolic marker, my point still holds that a radical transition has occurred, and this in my view is the most obvious indicator of that transition.

settlement, in turn, caused an escalation of tension and violence between Jews and Arabs both within the borders of the state and in the West Bank. Other important events occurred during the same period. One of the most traumatic was the haunting symbolic act of Israel handing over the Jewish town of Yamit in the northern Sinai to Egypt in April of 1982 as required by the peace treaty. This was the first case of a Zionist or Israeli national organization voluntarily giving up a Jewish settlement and removing Jews from land acquired by Jews.[78] Israel's invasion of Lebanon, known in Israel as "Operation Peace for Galilee," began two months later.

The rise in tension, even to the point of anguish and desperation among some in the activist religious Zionist settler communities, led to violent expressions of radicalism and zealotry that looked quite like behaviors of believers in other religious traditions engaged in holy war.[79] This period marked a peak in extra-governmental, individual, and small-group bloodshed committed by Jews against Palestinians. The acts were naturally considered by the perpetrators to be justified given their interpretation of the historical and meta-historical situation. They were deemed reasonable responses to the threat against carrying out the divine command for the Jewish people to conquer, take possession, settle, and make blossom the Land of Israel. As noted several times previously, failure to carry out the divine imperative was believed not only to destroy the unique and unprecedented opportunity to experience the messianic redemption, but also likely to bring disaster to the Jewish people. Given the recent and indelible experience of the Holocaust, this was a possibility that had to be avoided at all costs.

There was little interest within the government during this period in policing the behaviors of the Jewish settlers. Disinterest in controlling Jewish violence was the result of several aspects of the general Israeli worldview and Israelis' overall perception of the situation. On the one hand, the view in general was that the settlers needed to be protected from local Palestinian residents rather than vice versa. On the other hand, it was assumed that using force against Arabs was not only acceptable, but even necessary because of "the Arab mentality" that many believed would respond

---

[78] No Jewish settlements were established in the areas that had been captured by Israel with the support of Great Britain and France in 1956 and returned after that war.

[79] See Peter Partner, *God of Battles: Holy Wars of Christianity and Islam* (Princeton: Princeton University Press, 1997); Karen Armstrong, *Holy War: The Crusades and their Impact on Today's World* (New York: Doubleday, 1988); Mark Juergensmeyer, *Terror in the Mind of God: The Global Rise of Religious Violence* (Berkeley: University of California, 2000); Charles Selengut, *Sacred Fury: Understanding Religious Violence* (Walnut Creek, CA: Alta Mira, 2003); Ami Pedahzur, *Jewish Terrorism in Israel* (New York: Columbia University, 2009).

positively only to force.[80] Related to this was the tacit feeling that Palestinians, who were perceived as engaging regularly in violent acts against Jewish settlers, deserved a dose of their own medicine. And finally, Jewish physicality and a certain level of brute force was overlooked because it epitomized part of the tough Sabra pioneering ethos that had been established by the heroic Zionist pioneers in the drive to establish the state. We have observed earlier how this ethos evolved as a modern response to the physical abuse and persecution of Jews in the nineteenth and early twentieth centuries, perceived to be attributed, in part, to their weak image. The ethos became more acute in response to the Holocaust. The slogan, "never again," became a reaction and sometimes an overreaction to real and perceived acts of anti-Jewish aggression.

We have observed how Jewish settlement in Palestine was a fundamental value in prestate Zionism. Settlement continued to be a central value after the establishment of the state, an essential slogan articulated repeatedly by successive Israeli governments as a proof of their loyalty to Zionist values. But despite support of the Israeli government for settlement expressed time after time by members of Parliament and government ministers, there was a palpable feeling among activists in the Settler Movement that the government had betrayed them by not encouraging massive Jewish settlement in the territories captured in 1967. They felt that their national leadership was failing to fulfill its Jewish and Zionist responsibility to protect them and their families as they took grave risks to carry out the classic Zionist commitment to settling the Land.

Many observant Jews were also frustrated by their view that the Israeli government was failing to carry out its transcendent duty to the Jewish people to fulfill the terms communicated by the Almighty through the signs so obvious to them. The ingathering of exiles, the establishment of a Jewish commonwealth on the Land deeded by God to Israel, the blooming of the desert, the glory of military victory—all these were considered

---

[80] Shortly before the 1973 war Raphael Patai published a controversial but influential book, *The Arab Mind* (New York: Charles Scribner's Sons), but any examination of the memoires and letters of Zionist leaders and activists such as Chaim Weizman and David Ben Gurion from the 1920s and 1930s would quickly reveal a general frustration and antipathy common among the Jews of Palestine toward Arab resistance to Zionism expressed in terms of an "Arab mentality." A recent study notes that Israeli political leaders "...did regularly portray themselves as juxtaposing Israeli pragmatic interests with Palestinian emotional needs, a rhetorical pattern that can still be discerned at the highest levels of political discourse whenever 'peace in the Middle East' is discussed" (Don Seeman, "Violence, Ethics, and Divine Honor in Modern Jewish Thought," in *Journal of the American Academy of Religion* Vol. 73, No. 4 [Dec. 2005], 1024). To be fair, such references to ethnic, national or religious mentality remain a well-known obstacle to conflict resolution in many quarters of the world.

signs pointing to the imminent Redemption. To give up when so near, and when the stakes were so high, was tantamount to treason.[81]

Those who actually engaged in acts of lethal terror against Palestinians during this period and who attempted to destroy that sacred Islamic edifice of the Dome of the Rock in Jerusalem were extremely few.[82] But as is usual in the case of religiously motivated terrorism, the small number of perpetrators tends to be backed by larger communities of supporters and even larger communities of sympathizers. And although the persons responsible were few and were opposed publicly by the leadership of the Settler Movement, there can be no doubt that they were acting out the logical conclusion of years of religious and ideological thinking and training. It is possible to suggest a variety of motivations for settler violence in the early to mid-1980s, but it is clear that their behaviors occurred within a context that was highly charged by religious ideology and fervor. These behaviors represent the revival, even if among only a small activist minority, of total, divinely authorized war against an enemy that had become entirely dehumanized because it was bent on preventing the realization of Redemption.

At 7:45 A.M. on the morning of June 3, 1980, the mayor of the West Bank city of Nablus, Bassam Shaka, walked out the door of his home and got into his car, parked out in the courtyard. When he started the ignition, it exploded, severing both his legs. At about the same time, the mayor of Ramallah, Karim Khalaf, lost one foot when he turned on the ignition of his car. The news spread immediately, so mayor Ibrahim Tawil of El-Bireh decided not to drive to work that day. He called the military government, which sent soldiers to his home. When an army sapper opened the garage door, another explosion severely wounded and blinded him.[83] Thus began a highly publicized wave of Jewish terror and vigilantism that ended with the arrest of the *machteret* or "Jewish underground," a small network of activists that terrorized Arabs and plotted to destroy Islam's third holiest religious shrine, the Dome of the Rock in Jerusalem.

The bombings of the Palestinian mayors, deadly firing of a rocket into a public Arab bus, murder of students in the Islamic College of Hebron,

---

[81] Sprinzak, *Ascendance*, 9, 322 note 30.

[82] For a recent study of extremist movements dedicated to rebuilding the Jerusalem Temple on the Temple Mount, see Motti Inbari, *Jewish Fundamentalism and the Temple Mount* (Albany: State University of New York, 2009); also, Inbari, "The Oslo Accords and the Temple Mount: A Case Study, The Movement for the Establishment of the Temple." *Hebrew Union College Annual* 74 (2003–2004), 279–323; Nadav Shragai, *The Temple Mount Conflict* (Hebrew, Jerusalem: Keter, 1995).

[83] Ami Pedahzur, *Jewish Terrorism in Israel* (New York: Columbia University, 2009), 39–41.

attempted bombings of Arab buses along with other planned acts of Jewish terror against Palestinians, and the plot to destroy the Dome of the Rock have been chronicled elsewhere and need not detain us here.[84] It is nevertheless important for our purposes to note that these acts were authorized, either directly or indirectly, by living rabbinic authorities.[85] Sprinzak observes that "[t]he confessions and testimonies of the members of the underground do not clarify whether the leading rabbis of Kiryat Arba were involved in the actions of the conspiracy, or, if so, how much. But they make clear that *only those operations approved by the rabbis took place.*...The rabbinical involvement in the terror acts that did and did not take place is of crucial importance. It tells us that the radicalization process that finally produced terrorism within Gush Emunim was not marginal but central. It was a byproduct of the movement's belief in its own redemptive role and in the necessity of settling Judea and Samaria at all costs. The idealistic people who began in 1968 to settle Judea and Samaria did not go there with violent intentions. They did not expect to become vigilantes, terrorists, or supporters of terrorism. Yet within twelve years the combination of messianic belief and a situation of continual national conflict with a built-in propensity for incremental violence resulted in extralegalism, vigilantism, selective terrorism, and, finally, indiscriminate mass terrorism."[86]

No respected rabbinic authorities publicly supported the violence of the underground, and the standard halakhic journals provided no articles to justify acts of terror. In fact, many rabbis publicly condemned them. But the fact remains that some rabbis who were steadfast and loyal to the religious, legal, and ideological tenets of Religious Zionism privately backed them, thus providing them with a certain religious legitimacy.

Religious justification for violent military conquest was prominent only in the more radical writings coming out of the movement, published

---

[84] Robert Friedman, *Zealots for Zion* (New Brunswick, NJ: Rutgers University, 1992); Ehud Sprinzak, *The Ascendance of Israel's Radical Right*; Ezra Rapaport, *Letters from Tel Mond Prison* (New York: The Free Press, 1996); Haggai Segal, *Dear Brothers: A History of the "Jewish Underground"* (Jerusalem: Keter, 1987), translated into English (Woodmere: Beit Shamai Publications, 1988); Nadav Shragai, *The Temple Mount Conflict* (Hebrew) (Jerusalem: Keter, 1995); Gershom Gorenberg, *The End of Days: Fundamentalism and the Struggle for the Temple Mount* (New York: Oxford University Press, 2000); Yoni Garb, "Messianism, Antinomism, and Power in Religious Zionism—the Case of the 'Jewish Underground,'" in Ayelet Bartal and Yehiel Kimchi (eds.), *The Religious Zionism: An Era of Changes—Studies in Memory of Zvulun Hammer* (Jerusalem: Bialik Institute, 2004), 323–363; Ami Pedahzur and Arie Perliger, *Jewish Terrorism in Israel* (New York: Columbia University, 2009), 45–68

[85] Some of their names are provided by Haggai Segal in his personal account of the underground (*Dear Brothers*).

[86] Sprinzak, *Ascendance...*, 99 (italics in original).

internally in certain yeshiva newsletters or other semipublic forums. Some of these appeared in the motivational magazines, *Artzi* and *Tzefiyah*.[87] But the language and the idea of military conquest in general had increasingly infiltrated the language of thinkers and teachers of the new pioneers that make up the Settler Movement and its supporters and, subsequently, increasingly in Zionist discourse in general.[88]

Holy war became part of this discourse. As noted earlier in the writings of Rabbi Yehudah Amital, one line of thinking among some settler theorists is the view, simply, that virtually *any* war engaged by Jews is divinely sanctioned. This would appear to contradict our observation in chapter 5 that the sages of the Talmud did not consider discretionary wars to be divinely authorized. Divinely sanctioned (that is, "holy") war is functionally defined in the Talmud as wars for which there can be no military deferments. Such wars are limited to the category of Commanded War, a category developed by the sages to severely limit the opportunities for Jews to engage in the dangerous and unstable act of holy war. The Talmud divides commanded wars into only two types: wars of defense, and wars of conquest defined as "Joshua's wars." But the wording of the Talmud can be interpreted in widely different ways. A narrow reading would understand "Joshua's wars" to refer specifically and only to the historical wars of conquest commanded by God to Joshua. A broad reading could understand the reference to indicate a category or type of war rather than a specific historical occurrence, thus extending the definition to any war that would bring the Land of Israel under Jewish jurisdiction. This reading identifies

---

[87] *Artzi* (1 and 2 [1982], 3 [1983], 4 [1986], 5 [1991]), is described by Ian Lustick as a "scholarly and ideologically oriented fundamentalist journal," though I would not consider it scholarly (Lustick, "Jewish Fundamentalism and the Israeli-Palestinian Impasse," in Silberstein, Laurence [ed.], *Jewish Fundamentalism in Comparative Perspective* (New York: New York University Press, 1993), 116, note 4), *Tzefiyah* is the magazine of a radical group that supported the underground and related issues and groups from the mid-1980s into the 1990s. Two issues were published in 1985 and occasionally thereafter (#3 was released in 1988, #5 in 1996). See Ehud Sprinzak, "The Emergence of the Israeli Radical Right," in *Comparative Politics*, January 1989, 187–188.

[88] Stuart Cohen notes how the Israel Defense Forces incorporates Jewish religious terminology, symbols and collective myths into its training and troop education in order to create a unified fighting force out of the divergent populations of religious and secular Jews of widely different backgrounds (*The Scroll or the Sword*. Amsterdam: Harwood, 1997, 42–45). This has a significant impact on the citizens of the state as a whole given the profound impact of the IDF on the personal lives of Israel's citizenry. "Traditional religious associations...serve as a social coagulant, and thus as a vehicle for fostering the feeling of affinity and reciprocity which have always been recognized to constitute essential criteria for military cohesion, and ultimately for effective battlefield performance" (Cohen, 53–54). Young soldiers are given an IDF-issued Bible with a cover letter pointing to the Bible as a means of invoking divine assistance in battle (citing Deut.20:4) and as the ultimate "deed of tenure and charter of ownership to our land and to the estate of our fathers." (Cohen, 56).

conquest of the Land of Israel as divinely authorized at any period of history when victory is possible.

One graduate of Mercaz Harav, Rabbi Yitzhak Kaufman, wrote a book of halakhic rulings related to Jewish military forces and war that was published in 1992. This was after the mid-1980s, the period that I mark as the final stage in the development of Jewish holy war ideology, and he, like many others, was powerfully influenced by it. In his book, he expands the category of divinely authorized wars to include not only Commanded Wars, but also Discretionary Wars: "Commanded and Discretionary Wars are [both] God's wars *(milchamot hashem)*. ... An Israelite king is permitted to require the people to initiate a Discretionary War with the goal of 'expanding the border of Israel and to increase his prestige and fame.'"[89] Kaufman teaches that an Israelite king can require the people to initiate a discretionary war for deterrence and even for the purpose of livelihood *(parnasah)*.[90] Moreover, although such wars are technically impossible because they require the existence of a type of rabbinical court that no longer exists (the Sanhedrin), such wars may nevertheless be initiated if the people agree voluntarily to engage in them, and we have observed above how religious adjudicators such as Chief Rabbi Isaac Herzog considered the elected Jewish government to have a status similar to that of the Sanhedrin.[91]

In his excursus on Commanded Wars, Kaufman lists nine subcategories, based on the premise suggested in the Palestinian Talmud that defensive war (war in which the enemy initiates against Israel) is Commanded War for which there can be no deferments.[92] These include, among others, a preemptive attack against a threatening enemy that is liable to cause Israeli casualties.

Kaufman defines *any* war over territory defined biblically as the Land of Israel to be Commanded War. This overrules any limitation suggested by either Talmud. "According to religious jurists *[leda`at haposkim],* any war to conquer *[likhbosh]* parts of the Land of Israel for the purpose of keeping them in our hands (and certainly with the goal of keeping the sections of the Land in which we are already settled) is considered Commanded War based on the commandment of settling the Land of Israel."[93]

---

[89] Yitzhak Kaufman, *The Army According to Halakhah: Laws of War and Army* (Hebrew). Jerusalem: 1992, Hebrew letter numbering system (second system in book) 1–2, note 2.

[90] See chapter six, above.

[91] See chapter 12.

[92] Kaufman 5–6. He uses the language of Maimonides (*Mishneh Torah, Kings* 5:1): "helping Israel from the hand of an [attacking] enemy."

[93] Kaufman 7–10 (parentheses in original). Cf. Rashi, who wrote on Sanhedrin 2a that "all war is called discretionary except for the war of Joshua to conquer the Land of Israel."

Not all thinkers and teachers among the Settler Movement take a militant position on the issue of conquest, but all must relate their position to the classic statement in Nahmanides' commentary to Maimonides' *Book of Commandments*. Rabbi Nachum Rabinovitch, the head of the *hesder yeshiva* Birkat Moshe in the settlement of Ma`aleh Adumim, does not read Nahmanides to mean that military conquest of the Land of Israel is necessarily Commanded War.[94] Harking back to the view of the Talmud, he understands Commanded War to have been limited to the actual military conquest of the Land of Israel under Joshua by virtue of it having been a command of the hour *(hora'at sha`ah)*. Commanded War as an initiated engagement (as opposed to defense against an attack), therefore, must be limited to that specific historical occasion only and does not represent an eternal command. He must therefore redefine the term, "conquest," not to mean war, but rather, acquisition. War in and of itself is forbidden. An exception was made for Joshua's conquest, but only at that particular time. The eternal command, then, is settling the land with the purpose of gaining ownership and control over it. It is not a military conquest.

This position stimulated a reaction among a number of thinkers in the activist religious Zionist camp. Rabbi Yakov Ariel, for example, refutes Rabinovitch's understanding of Nahmanides in at least two forums, claiming that Rabinovitch's position is an unacceptable innovation (*chiddush*) and that he fails to read Nahmanides correctly or follow the tradition properly.[95]

The simple and normative understanding of the words of Nahmanides is that war is an inseparable part of the commandment of settling the Land, and when the conditions require it, it is a commandment to be carried out in every generation. The public nature of this commandment is based upon this part of the commandment, which we have merited to carry out in our generation with the establishment of the State of Israel (from the discussions of Rabbi Tzvi Yehuda Kook on Independence Days in his yeshiva...), and anyone who takes the words of Nahmanides out of context is himself responsible for the idea.[96]

---

[94] Nachum Rabinovitch, *The Educated in War* (Hebrew: *melumedei milchamah*). Ma`aleh Adumim: 1994, 3–19. He makes this point also in his article, "The Method of Nahmanides and Maimonides on the Commandment of Inheriting the Land (Hebrew)," *Tehumin* 5 (1984), 180–186. Rabinovitch was nevertheless accused of making incendiary statements justifying the use of violence to stop the peace process, according to the co-directors of Rabbis for Human Rights, Rabbis Arik Ascherman and Jeremy Milgrom, in an appeal of September, 1996.

[95] Yakov Ariel, "The View of Nahmanides on Conquest of the Land" (Hebrew), in *Tehumin* 5 (1984), 174–179; idem, *In the Canopy of Torah: Responsa* (Hebrew) (Kefar Darom), 2003, 26–32.

[96] Idem, *In the Canopy of Torah*, 31 (parentheses in original).

The increased investment in linking Israel's modern wars to Commanded War parallels the intensification of belief that Redemption is imminent. The signs of approaching Redemption became increasingly obvious and more frequent. Certainly by the 1980s, but from 1967 if not earlier among some observers, it had become possible to observe the historical signposts of Redemption in seemingly odd ways.

It is simply that a series of historic events have brought the Jewish people into a position in which it is impossible not to feel that we are on the road that must lead to redemption. We have only to think of some of the events of the postwar era, following the apocalyptic terrors of Nazi Europe, to see how pregnant they are with significance. Had the necessity for free Jewish immigration into Palestine after 1945 not met with the implacable hostility of the Arabs, there might not have been a Jewish State in our time. Had President Truman's suggestion in 1946 to admit one hundred thousand displaced persons to Palestine been accepted by Britain and the Arabs, there would have been no UN Resolution. Had the Arabs not resisted that UN Resolution of 1947 the new Israel would have remained a tiny, truncated, insignificant pocket-state. Had Hussein in 1967 not thrown in his lot with the Arab anti-Israel confederacy (in defiance of Israel's plea), Judea and Samaria and Jerusalem might still have remained outside Jewish care and influence. Is it any wonder that believing Jews see in all this process the working of the Hand of God? History is bearing down on us.... Inexorably, if we have eyes to see and a heart to understand, we are led to acknowledge that, after two thousand years of wandering in the by-ways of exile, we have emerged on the high road of history which, however long it may yet be, must lead us eventually to Redemption. It is in this sense that we describe our own era as *"Reshit Zemichat Geulatenu* ("the beginning of the flowering of our Redemption").[97]

## Commanded War and Conquest of the Land of Israel in Our Time

We have observed in Part 3 how the meaning of conquest evolved and changed over the years in the discourse of prestate Zionism. It continued to

---

[97] Bernard M. Casper, "Reshit Zemichat Geulatenu," in *Religious Zionism after Forty Years of Statehood* ed. Shubert Spero and Yitzchak Pessin (Jerusalem: Mesilot, 1989), 66–69.

evolve during the two decades following the 1967 War. Conquest became more than agriculture, more than settlement and activism to restore the Land, and more than the military victory of Joshua over the prior inhabitants of the Land of Israel. By the mid-1980s, and particularly among more militant activists within the Settler Movement, conquest had taken on a far more aggressive and bellicose tone. Its meaning was transformed into something akin to the ancient, pre-Zionist, and indeed pre-Talmudic scriptural sense of divinely ordained, aggressive, and virtually unlimited military conquest of the biblical patrimony. In short, virtually all military operations had become narrowed to Commanded War, and Commanded War meant conquest.[98] Ironically, the very act of conquering became for many an indisputable heavenly sign of the inevitable coming of divinely ordained Redemption.

Some of the factors that facilitated this change, such as the decline of secular Zionist ideologies, rise in traditional yeshivah education among religious Zionists along with the growing anxiety among them over the role of Judaism in Zionism, and the rise in apprehension and fear over pressure (both within Israel and from outside Israel) to give back territories conquered in the 1967 War, have been discussed earlier in this volume. Other sources of motivation may also be mentioned, such as the great personal and emotional investment—including lost lives—of religiously observant Jews in settling land and building communities in the territories conquered in 1967. Dedication and sacrifice on behalf of pioneering settlement is an old and respected value in Zionism. To many in the general (nonreligious) Jewish public, the *religious* fervor of settler activists in their zeal to settle the Land was seen as a kind of revival of the old Zionist commitment that had been lost to post-independence normalization among so many nonreligious Israelis.

The pioneering zeal looked similar, but the motivation for that zeal was quite different and represents an enormous change from the ideology of activism in classical, secular Zionism. As a consequence, the re-spiritualized, religiously driven pioneering ethos of religious Zionism in the 1970s and 80s infiltrated and influenced public opinion far beyond the settler communities.

The increase in settlement activism stimulated increased violent resistance among Palestinians living in the territories, which caused an upsurge in the number of casualties among Jewish settlers and others (this was in

---

[98] Kalman Neuman arrives at the same conclusion based on analysis of modern halakhic responsa in a recent article, "The law of obligatory war and Israeli reality," in Levin and Shapira, *War and Peace in Jewish Tradition*, 2012, 186–199.

the days before the explosion of suicide bombings). The increased casualties, in turn, raised the hope and expectation for divinely wrought salvation. Ironically, even as Israel was becoming more economically and militarily powerful after the Camp David Accords and Peace Treaty with Egypt, it was becoming increasingly dangerous to live in the Jewish State. A desire for relief from suffering was palpable throughout the population, including among Jews not religiously observant, and many sought to find transcendent meaning in the pain and distress that they experienced simply by virtue of living in the Land of Israel. As noted above, one of the classic messages of Zionism proclaims that Jews will be safe only when they are in control of their own political destiny, when they normalize and fill all the roles of society from governed to governors, and from sanitation workers to soldiers. Ironically, however, one of the more dangerous places for Jews to live in the world lay between the borders of the state of Israel. Many in the secular camp became disillusioned with the reality of life in Israel and chose to leave and build their lives elsewhere, especially in Europe and the United States. Orthodox Israelis tended to stick it out even with all the stress, fear, and uncertainty that marked life there, because they were more likely to find transcendent meaning even in their suffering.

In Jewish religious tradition, significance and meaning for unexplained suffering can be found in the concept of "chastenings of love" *(yisurin shel ahavah)*. "It was taught: Rabbi Shimon Ben Yochai says: The Holy One gave three precious gifts to Israel, and all were given through suffering. These are the Torah, the Land of Israel, and the World to Come."[99] Israel will be redeemed through suffering,[100] and the greater the suffering, the greater the reward.

Not all Jewish suffering, however, is "chastenings of love." It can also derive from sin, but according to Jewish tradition the cause and effect of sin is communal and reflects communal responsibility. The community can be punished as a whole for the sins of a few, so the sin of bad government can result in divine punishment upon all of Israel. All therefore carry a measure of responsibility for the sins of the leaders. Religious Zionist activists worried about the possibility of divine retribution and were frustrated at what they perceived to be negligent lack of recognition of their views by Israeli governments and the public at large. Their frustration was intensified by a decided lack of public appreciation for

---

[99] BT Berakhot 5a-b.
[100] *Midrash on Psalms* (106:44).

what they considered their Zionist—not only religious—dedication and sacrifice. Increased anxiety in turn increased the likelihood of acting out mounting frustration through violence, not only against Palestinians but even against fellow Jews.[101]

The worry, anger, and resentment among the religious activists were responses to two general factors. One was the reality of the simple physical danger of living in Israel, and particularly in the areas captured in the 1967 War that tended to be densely populated by members of the Settler Movement and their sympathizers. The other was the danger that the secular opposition might succeed in reversing the forward movement on the path to Redemption. Due to these and other factors, spokespersons and public leaders of religious Zionism naturally increased use of religious language and rhetoric in their writings and public statements. Religious language and imagery thus began to increase in public discourse in general, including perspectives on the transcendent meaning of the Land of Israel and its conquest. Sprinzak noted that "[t]he radical right peaked during the great settlement years 1979–1984, which were also the years of the Lebanon War and the growth of Arab-Jewish friction throughout the entire Land of Israel."[102] While the political power of the religious right waxes and wanes in response to goings on within Israel and without, it succeeded in inserting religious paradigms into public discourse and moving the Israeli political center further to the right. One result of this shift has been that militant religious Zionist activists have largely succeeded in keeping dissenters within the community out of the public eye and their own ideas and perspectives in the center of public discussion. Two religious Zionist counter organizations, *Oz Veshalom* and *Netivot Shalom,* formed in the 1970s and early 1980s to oppose the position of the Settler Movement and have published a number of works taking positions specifically countering them and their ideology and policies,[103] but they have been unsuccessful in making a significant impact on the religious Zionist community as a whole.[104]

---

[101] Such acts are rare, but include the killing of Peace Now demonstrator Emil Grunzweig and the wounding of nine others by Yonah Avrushmi during the period of belligerent escalation in 1983 and the assassination of Prime Minister Rabin in 1995.

[102] Sprinzak, *Ascendence…*, 302.

[103] See, for example, Uriel Simon, *Seek Peace and Pursue it* (Hebrew) (Tel Aviv: Yediot, 2002); Tzvi Mazeh and Pinchas Leiser (eds.), *Drishat Shalom—Reading Peace and Justice in the Torah* (Hebrew) (Tel Aviv: Yediot, 2010). A third group was formed in 1987 by Rabbi Yehuda Amital called "Meimad," which later formed a party that elected a member to the Israeli Kenesset in 1999.

[104] On these movements, see Mordechai Bar-On, *In Pursuit of Peace: A History of the Israeli Peace Movement* (Washington, D.C.: Institute of Peace, 1996), 170–172; Fred David Levine, "Territory or Peace: Religious Zionism in Conflict," (New York: American Jewish Committee,

This is certainly the case with regard to the powerful religious symbolism of land and settlement that the Settler Movement so successfully implanted in the hearts of many Israelis. "Unlike the (secular) radical right of the 1930s and 1940s, the post-1967 radical right has had a major impact on the thinking of the entire nation.... It seems highly probable that even if the radical right is pushed to the political margins, it will continue to haunt the nation's collective psyche."[105]

Sprinzak was writing about the Israeli radical right in general, but he was careful to include the Israeli religious right in his observations. The generation of activist religious Zionists that came of age in the 1960s and then founded Gush Emunim and the Settler Movement finalized the revival of Jewish holy war by bringing it into the normative discourse of the Israeli public and gaining supporters far beyond their own numbers. This observation needs elucidation because the large Jewish secular population did not think of war and the conflict with Palestinians and neighboring nations according to the religious notions and terminology examined in this study. Many were nevertheless positively influenced by the pioneering ethos and sense of personal commitment and sacrifice that were exhibited by settler activists.

More important, however, staunchly secular Jews do not represent the entirety of modern Israel or even the majority. Very many in the large population of Jewish Israelis do not fit neatly into either of the quarreling religiously Orthodox or the secularist camps. Many in this large pool have become profoundly influenced by both the passion of religious Zionist activists and by the categories in which they think. Through the activists' internal conversations, writings, and public declarations and arguments, they successfully brought the ethos if not the halakhic religious category of Commanded War into public conversation. Their confidence in the divine imperative of Commanded War to conquer the Land of Israel for the People of Israel had become part of the discourse of Zionism in general by the 1980s and beyond, and this represented a major departure from the Zionist discourse of only two decades earlier. The increase in deliberation proceeded to normalize discussion about the contemporary conflict in transcendent terms in general and often also in terms of Commanded War, which made it more familiar and therefore more likely to be invoked.

---

Institute on American Jewish-Israeli Relations 1986); Hildegard Goss-Mayr and Jim Forest, "With Peacemakers in Wartime Israel," *International Fellowship of Reconciliation Report* (October, 1982), 3–7; Aviezer Ravitzky, Aaron Lichtenstein, David Kretzmer et. al., "You Must not Remain Indifferent," (*Netivot Shalom* Organization publication: "Rally at the Jerusalem Khan," February 7, 1988), 32 pages.

[105] Sprinzak, *Ascendence...*, 312–313 (parentheses added).

If Rabbi Yitzhak Kaufman could define *any* war over territory defined biblically as the Land of Israel to be Commanded War,[106] and Rabbi Yehuda Amital could consider *every* war of Israel Commanded War because it is war for the unity of God,[107] then it becomes clear that the notion became generalized to the extent that it could fit virtually any definition of the conflict between Israel and the Palestinians and neighboring countries. This represents a revival of holy war in Judaism. Of course not all Jews agreed with the pronouncements of these rabbis. Not all Jews even considered the construct of Commanded War valid. But virtually all traditionally minded Jews and most Jews living in Israel, whether religiously observant or not, became familiar with the term and with at least some of its implications. The revival of holy war was not a conscious program or political goal, but rather the product of an attempt to make sense of text and tradition in the light of contemporary events. It was the result of a religious and human response to a reality that was confusing and frightening, and also a response to social and political forces both locally and internationally that were beyond the ability of the political leadership of the state to manage.

---

[106] Yitzhak Kaufman, *The Army According to Halakhah*, 1–2, note 2.
[107] Yehudah Amital, *From Out of the Depths*, 18–19.

CONCLUSION | The Resurrection of Holy War

Holy war, which we have defined here as war authorized or even commanded by God, is a fundamental part of biblical religion and a core institution of the Hebrew Bible. Classic biblical cases of holy war often depict total war with great destruction and the loss of many lives. When God is understood to authorize or command war, warriors are confident that whatever the odds they can win because the "hand of God" is with them. War is always dangerous and potentially destabilizing. It eventually became too destabilizing and self-destructive to the Jewish people, especially when Jews lost political independence and most of the community came under the iron rule of the Roman Empire.

War had turned out to be too costly to keep in the political repertoire of Judaism. After two ruinous failures by Jewish zealots to remove Roman control of the Land of Israel by invoking war in the name of God, Jewish leaders tried to eliminate holy war from the range of actions available to the community. Their goal was to remove a deadly wild card that had proven so overwhelmingly disastrous. Some rabbinic thinkers began the process shortly after Jews had lost control over their national center in Jerusalem and the Land of Israel. Henceforth they would live as survivors in a world of Diaspora or, to use traditional Jewish religious terminology, exile *(galut)*.

While not all the sages of Rabbinic Judaism initially agreed, they eventually came to the conclusion that they must prevent holy war from being applied in their own time, and they did this through unique strategies of scriptural interpretation. It is unlikely that the strategies were conceived consciously with the specific purpose of solving the problem. More likely, they evolved in response to the historical, cultural, political, and intellectual developments that influenced their reading of sacred text and tradition.

In any event, the result of their exegesis was the tendering of two interpretive instruments, two safeguards that would prevent Jewish zealots from declaring holy war and thus endangering the continued survival of the community. One organized the many examples of war in the Bible and created a typology that reduced them to the two categories of Discretionary War and Commanded War, the latter a war commanded by God for which there could be no deferments. The rabbis then made it virtually impossible to invoke Commanded War aside from cases of self-defense. The second instrument was based on an interpretation of an obscure verse repeated three times in the biblical book called the Song of Songs (or in Christian Bibles, "The Song of Solomon") read by the rabbis as three separate vows invoked by God to serve as a decree that would govern the relationship between the Jewish People and the larger world of gentiles. The Jews were made to vow not to rebel against their gentile rulers or to move en masse to the Land of Israel, and the gentiles were made to vow not to treat the Jews too harshly in their rule over them. These two interpretive instruments made it virtually impossible for Jews to initiate war on behalf of the community for anything other than pure defense.

The rabbis' success was possible within a particular historical context. But times change, and the history of Jewish existential and political exile ended with the rise of modernity in the West and the concomitant emergence of nationalisms, including Jewish nationalism. Jewish nationalism in Zionism eventuated in the establishment of a Jewish State in part of the biblical Land of Israel that once again became the political domain of the Jewish people. Zionism was largely a secular national movement, but some Orthodox Jews became deeply engaged in this Jewish nationalism as well. The historical changes brought about by modernity, the development of Zionism, and the Holocaust enabled and, it may be argued, required the Orthodox Jewish community to reexamine the traditional rabbinic prohibition against Commanded War in the light of the needs of the times.

The safeguards established by the sages perhaps were never intended to be permanent. In any case, they have been effectively removed, at least for the majority of Orthodox Jews and also for a significant community of non-Orthodox Jews, but not without difficulty and not without disagreement. One of the clear lessons of this story is that the reading and interpretation of scripture are profoundly influenced by history. Strategies of exegesis emerge in response to exigencies of the hour. New readings, insights, and understandings enable interpretation to resolve critical or threatening issues and existential problems. It is all about exegesis, and exegesis is all about contemporary context.

When in 1947–1948 it became necessary to mobilize the entire Jewish community of Palestine to defend the declaration of Jewish statehood in the war that followed, Orthodox religious scholars struggled with the virtual ban on war established by the sages of the Talmud. The state survived its violent birth pangs and the Chief Rabbinate of the State of Israel succeeded in religious terms to sanction the integration of Orthodox Jews into the Israel Defense Forces.

We have observed in this study how ideologues and teachers of the religious Zionist B'nai Akiba Youth Movement in the prestate years promoted pioneering activism among their youth as more important than the traditional religious emphasis on Torah learning as superior to all other pursuits. Consistent with the ideologies and idealism that they absorbed from their modern, worldly environment, they combined elements of the secular, neomessianic Zionist ethos with traditional Judaism through exegetical strategies that encouraged activism in the larger Zionist project of settling the Land of Israel and establishing in it a Jewish homeland. After the establishment of the state and the normalization that followed, this particular balance of tradition and modernity was no longer suitable for some of the most talented and idealistic young religious Zionists, who sought more from their religion and their existence as Jewish Israelis who had returned to the ancient Land of Israel. A young idealistic group thus embarked on an intellectual and spiritual journey that would result in a new synthesis of modernity and religious tradition. Modern nationalist activism was combined with mystical religious fervor and traditional yeshiva learning to produce an ideology that would inspire a cadre of young people to dedicate their lives to a unique interpretation of the classic Jewish linkage between God, Torah, and Israel. This synthesis was profoundly influenced by the Holocaust and by the frustration and fear they experienced with the violent opposition of Arabs to the national goals of Zionism. It was also influenced by the frustration these idealistic leaders felt as their community was sidelined by the Israeli political establishment after independence.

The core of this community was deeply stimulated by the mystical thinking of Rabbi Abraham Isaac Kook and his son Rabbi Tzvi Yehudah, who considered the terrible upheavals of world war and Holocaust to be signs of an impending, divinely wrought Redemption. Religious Zionist thinkers and ideologues extrapolated this view to identify their own wars with the Palestinians and other Arabs as part of that trajectory of messianic birth pangs. The miraculous victory of the 1967 War with its unexpected acquisition of virtually all biblical lands became symbolic of the imminence of Redemption. Although never desired, war seemed to have become in their day a necessary part of—or perhaps trial on—the path to Salvation. With 1967, war became emblematic of the great potential of divinely blessed conquest and the resultant repossession of ancestral lands. After the painful failure of 1973, war also became symbolic of the disaster and ruin that would afflict the Jewish people if they failed to follow the divine imperative by not clinging fully and faithfully to the unprecedented opportunity for Redemption offered by God. Military engagement had become an expression of impending Redemption—or possible disaster if it would not be prosecuted properly.

If the government would not acquiesce in the process of redemption, then it was the responsibility of zealous believers to carry on without the government or to compel the government through action to retain the biblical patrimony at all costs, including war. Carrying on without the government meant engaging in settling the biblical lands with or without government blessing or support. Compelling the government through action to engage the enemy meant initiating violence and militancy that would escalate the conflict to force full military engagement and subsequently full control of the Land of Israel promised by God in the Torah of Israel to the People of Israel.

In this book we have followed the changes in of the meaning of settlement in Zionism—Nahmanidean and Gordonean, secular and religious, humanistic and messianic. Settlement of the Land, a technical term in Hebrew *(yishuv ha'aretz),* naturally and organically evolved among religious Zionists in response to the changing historical context and the interpretive strategies engaged to make sense of it. To some it has become military conquest. In its most radical expression, the players were to reenact, as it were, the conquest of Joshua, with modern Israeli settlers taking the part of the ancient Israelite *chalutzim*—meaning in the biblical context the armed Israelite vanguard of fighter-settlers who crossed the Jordan River to conquer the Land,[1] with the Palestinians taking the part of the Canaanites—the pagan natives who represented obstacles to the divinely ordained Israelite inheritance of the Land of Israel.

These images are extremely powerful in Jewish and Israeli worldviews formed through a combination of traditional and modern interpretations of Jewish history. The core ideology that drove the militant activists grew out of a Zionist worldview that combined elements of religious mysticism with romantic nationalism. The powerful combination influenced a cadre of secular activists on the political right to join with religious Zionists,

---

[1] See Numbers chapter 32, Joshua chapter 6.

and in fact the trajectories of influence intersected as Religious Zionism became increasingly influenced by right-wing national ideologies.

Israelis as a whole have been ambivalent about the dedication and behaviors of this new generation of pioneering settlers, the new-old *chalutzim*. That ambivalence played itself out in the action and inaction of government from the 1967 War to the exposure of the Jewish underground in the mid-1980s. A final reenactment of the ancient Israelite conquest, symbolized by the nearly successful attempt to destroy the Islamic holy shrine on the Temple Mount (which symbolized the pagan Canaanite shrines of yesteryear), was eventually thwarted by the combined forces of the Israeli government, opposition of Israelis opposed to the radical religious Zionist camp, international pressures, and some within the religious Zionist camp itself.

The path toward radicalization in Religious Zionism began as one of revitalization, but the steps or stations on that historic path were many. As always, history takes unexpected turns, and those turns were decoded and rationalized by those who were engaged in it. The 1967 War was a milestone that was invested with great meaning. The 1973 War was initially a terrible setback, but deeper existential meaning was discovered within it that fit it into the path toward redemption. Once the path was discerned, redemptive meaning could be assigned to earlier milestones as well. One could look earlier to the establishment of the State of Israel and the creation of a modern Jewish armed force, to the Holocaust, or still earlier to the First World War and the emergence of the Jewish national movement of Zionism. A few modern prophets, such as Rabbi Abraham Isaac Kook, were prescient enough to see meaning in these early events without the need for historical hindsight. But before 1967, most in the religious Zionist world had to be content with only a silent hope that the Zionist project might be more than simply a movement to provide shelter for hapless Jews.

All these events were interpreted by religious Zionists in Jewish terms, but they occurred within a much larger historical arena where other Jewish groups observed them differently and interpreted them in their own ways. But the religious Zionist community remained tightly knit and self-reinforcing, so despite its detractors even from within, a well-organized core succeeded in sustaining what was in some ways a hermetic interpretive stance. Partly in order to remain on track in the face of opposition, frustration, and anxiety, it radicalized and became even more inward-looking. While it once captured the imagination of many outside the community, its influence has declined. The radicalization of modern Jewish holy war ideology, however, has not ceased. It continues to exert a great influence within the community, but its impact on the Jewish world as a whole ebbs and flows. Samuel Heilman has observed this trend.

At their peak, the members of Gush Emunim and graduates of Mercaz Harav did indeed briefly capture the imagination and conscience of many Orthodox Jews, including some haredim who admitted in private that they were impressed (and therefore threatened) by these believers. And they even caught a wave of triumphalism that swept across the entire nation. They seemed to steal the pioneer spirit that had once been at the heart of the Israeli national character. But ultimately they did not succeed in shaping the national will. Instead their activism led to dissension. This first became apparent in the national conflict over withdrawal from Sinai. Later it was manifested in the widespread turmoil over the activities of the "Jewish underground," particularly those of the group that hoped to blow up the mosque on the Temple Mount and attacked the Islamic College as well as several Arab mayors in the territories. These events, coupled with the death of Rabbi Zvi Yehuda Kook and the subsequent absence of a unified ideological leadership, have undermined the active fundamentalists.[2]

Despite the ebb described by Heilman in 1994, settler activism has not decreased overall, and at the time of this writing the building of Jewish settlements in the biblical Land of Israel within the territories taken under Israeli control in 1967 has shown no signs of decline. There can never be complete control over the ways in which humans interpret the signs of history, nor should there be. Creative interpretation is a glorious fact of the human condition. It allows for innovative but sometimes dangerous ideas and programs to guide human interaction with history. Since the assassination of Prime Minister Yitzhak Rabin in 1995 we have witnessed a certain corrective among the general Israeli and larger Jewish public to the more radical notions of Jewish holy war that remain active within portions of the religious Zionist settler community. But as has been mentioned repeatedly in this study, Jewish history does not evolve in a vacuum. Like all history, it is interactive and bound up with the histories of other peoples. For there to be a truly significant reduction in the radical interpretations of Jewish history, there must also be a reduction in the radicalism of those among whom Jews live.

---

[2] Samuel C. Heilman, "Quiescent and Active Fundamentalisms: The Jewish Cases," 188–189.

# GLOSSARY

**Ashkenazi**   Jews deriving from medieval European acculturation

**Atchalta dege'ulah**   The beginning of the process of divine redemption

**Bavel**   The Jewish term for Mesopotamia in virtually all periods, from the time of the Babylonian Empire until the twentieth century

**Bavli**   Babylonian Talmud (the Talmud composed and redacted in Babylonia), Babylonian

**Chalutz**   Biblical: "girded with strength" or "equipped for war;" in Zionism, "pioneer"

**Eretz Yisrael**   The Land of Israel as defined by tradition interpretation of the Bible

**Etzel**   Acronym for *irgun tzeva'i le'umi*, "national military organization," a common term for the Irgun

**Fedayeen**   Arab military irregulars

**Green Line**   The unofficial demarcation lines set out in the 1949 Armistice Agreements between Israel and its neighbors, Egypt, Jordan, Lebanon, and Syria after the 1948 War

**Gush Emunim**   "Block of the Faithful," the name of an organization dedicated to establishing Jewish settlements beyond the "Green Line"

**Ha'aretz**   A term for the Land of Israel

**Haganah**   Prestate Jewish defense organization

**Haredi**   Non-Zionist or anti-Zionist Jewish Orthodoxy

**Hesder Yeshiva**   Combines traditional yeshiva learning with army training

**Iqveta de'meshicha**   The footsteps of the messiah (referring to the imminent divine redemption)

**Irgun**   A Jewish military organization that broke away from the Haganah and actively engaged in violent retaliation

**Kibbutz**   Jewish collective farm

**Kibbutz galuyot**   Ingathering [to the Land of Israel] of the exiles

**Land of Israel**   Lands considered by religious scholars to have been granted to the Jewish people by God as articulated in boundaries provided in the Hebrew Bible

**Machteret**   *(Hamachteret hayehudit)* the Jewish terrorist underground brought to light in the 1980s

**Medinat yisrael**   The State of Israel

**Milchemet mitzvah**   (Divinely) commanded war

**Milchemet reshut**   Discretionary (not divinely commanded) war

**Mizrachi**   Literally, "eastern," refers to (1) the historical Zionist movement representing Orthodox Jews and Judaism in the Zionist Movement, (2) the Jewish population of modern Israel that derives from the Middle East and North Africa

**Moshav**   Jewish semi-collective settlement

**New Yishuv**   The new communities of pre-state Palestine established primarily by Zionists

**Old Yishuv**   The traditional Jewish community of pre-state Palestine

**Palmach**   Front-line fighting force of the Haganah

**Pikuach nefesh**   "Saving of life," a principle in Jewish law in which a religious injunction is disregarded in order to save a life

**Rav**   Rabbi

**Rebbe**   A term for a charismatic Hasidic rabbi

**Rosh Hashanah**   New year

**Rosh yeshiva**   Rabbinic headmaster of the yeshiva

**Sabra**   A modern Jew born within the borders of the Land of Israel

**Shekhina**   The divine presence

**Sefardi**   Jews deriving from medieval Spanish acculturation

**Teshuvah**   Repentance

**Urim vetumim**   Items imbedded within the breastplate of the Temple High Priest that were used for a kind of limited divination

**Yerushalmi**   The Talmud of the Land of Israel ("Jerusalem" or "Palestinian" Talmud)

**Yeshiva**   School for the study of traditional Jewish texts and traditions

**Yishuv**   Jewish community of prestate Palestine

**Yishuv ha'aretz**   Settling the land

# BIBLIOGRAPHY

Abbasi, Mustafa, "The Battle for Safad in the War of 1948: a Revised Study." *International Journal of Middle East Studies* 36.1 (February, 2004), 21–47.

Abramov, S. Zalman, *Perpetual Dilemma: Jewish Religion in the Jewish State.* Jerusalem: World Union for Progressive Judaism, 1976.

Abu Dawud, *Sunan.* Cairo: Dar al-Misriyya al-Lubnaniyya, 1988/1408.

Admonit, Tzuriel, "From Tzuriel's Correspondence." *Amudim* #257–258 (July–August, 1967), 334–335.

Aescoly, Aharon Ze'ev, *Jewish Messianic Movements. Sources & Documents on Messianism in Jewish History: From the Bar Kokhba Revolt until Recent Times* (2 vols.). Hebrew, Jerusalem: Bialik Inst. 1956.

Aho, James, *Religious Mythology and the Art of War: Comparative Religious Symbolisms of Military Violence.* Westport, CT: Greenwood, 1981.

Albright, William Foxwell, *Yahweh and the Gods of Canaan.* Garden City, NY: Doubleday, 1968.

Almog, Shmuel, "Messianism as a Challenge to Zionism," in Tzvi Baras (ed.) *Zionism and Eschatology.* Jerusalem: Zalman Shazar Center, 1983, 433–438.

Almog, Shmuel, *Zionism and History: The Rise of a New Jewish Consciousness.* Jerusalem: Magnes Press, 1987.

Alon, Gedaliah, "Did the Jewish Nation and Its Sages Cause the Hasmoneans to be Forgotten?" in Gedaliah Alon, *Studies in Jewish History* (Hebrew) Vol. 1 (1967), 15–25, translated as "Did the Jewish People and Its Sages Cause the Hasmoneans to Be Forgotten?" in Gedaliah Alon, *Jews, Judaism and the Classical World.* Jerusalem: Magnes Press, 1977.

Alon, Gedaliah, "Rabban Johanan B. Zakkai's Removal to Jabneh," in Gedaliah Alon, *Jews, Judaism and the Classical World* (Jerusalem: Magnes, 1977), 269–313.

Alon, Gedaliah, *The Jews in Their Land in the Talmudic Age*, translated and edited by Gershon Levi. Cambridge, MA: Harvard University, 1980.

Alter, Robert, "The Masada Complex," *Commentary* 56, #1 (July, 1973).

Amital, Yehuda, *From out of the Depths.* Jerusalem 1974; reprinted Alon-Shevut: Har Etzion Association, 1986.

Anderson, Benedict, *Imagined Communities: Reflections on the Origin and Spread of Nationalism*. London: Verso, 1991.

Anonymous, *The Mitzvah to Live in Eretz Israel*. Beer Sheva: Beit Yosef Institute, 2005.

Applebaum, Shimon, *Prolegomena to the Study of the Second Jewish Revolt*. Oxford: British Archaeological Reports, Supplement 7, 1976.

Aran, G. "From Religious Zionism to Zionist Religion." Goldscheider, Calvin, and Neusner, Jacob (eds.), *Social Foundations of Judaism* (Englewood Cliffs, NJ: Prentice Hall, 1990), 259–281.

Ariel, Israel, *Atlas of the Land of Israel: Its Boundaries According to the Sources* (Hebrew). Jerusalem: Cana, 1988.

Ariel, Yakov, "The View of Nahmanides on Conquest of the Land" (Hebrew), *Techumin* 5 (1984), 174–179.

Ariel, Yakov, *In the Canopy of Torah (be'ohalah shel Torah): Responsa* (Hebrew). Kefar Darom: Institute for Torah and Land, 2003.

Armstrong, Karen, *Holy War: The Crusades and their Impact on Today's World*. New York: Doubleday 1988.

Aronoff, Myron J. "The Institutionalization and Cooptation of a Charismatic, Messianic, Religious-Political Revitalization Movement," in Newman, David (ed.), *The Impact of Gush Emunim: Politics and Settlement in the West Bank*. NY: St Martin's Press, 1985, 46–69.

Astren, Fred, *Kara'ite Judaism and Historical Understanding*. Columbia, S.C.: University of South Carolina Press, 2004.

Bradley Shavit Artson, *Love Peace and Pursue Peace*. New York: United Synagogue of America, 1988.

Aviad, Janet, "The Contemporary Israeli Pursuit of the Millennium." *Religion* 14 (1984), 199–222.

Aviner, Shlomo, "On Our Redemption and On the Block of Our Faithful (*Gush Emunim*), comments in response to Prof. Isaiah Leibowitz." *Amudim* 366 (1976), 276–278.

Aviner, Shlomo, "Inheriting the Land and the Moral Problem." *Artzi* 2 (May, 1982), 4–13.

Aviner, Shlomo, *A People [Rising Up] like a Lion* (Hebrew). Jerusalem, 1983.

Aviner, Shlomo, "Our Redemption Is Little by Little (*ge'ulateynu qim`a qim`a*)," *Amudim* 445 (December, 1983), 135–137.

Avineri, Shlomo, *The Making of Modern Zionism*. New York: Basic, 1981.

Avineri, Shlomo, "Zionism and the Jewish Religious Tradition," in Almog, Shmuel, Reinharz, Jehuda, and Shapira, Anita (eds.), *Zionism and Religion*. Hanover, NH: Brandeis University Press, 1998, 1–9.

Avi-Yona, *The Jews of Palestine: A Political History from the Bar Kokhba War to the Arab Conquest*. New York: Schocken, 1976.

Avruch, Kevin, "Traditionalizing Israeli Nationalism: The Development of Gush Emunim." *Political Psychology* 1:1 (spring, 1979), 47–57.

Azrieli, Yehudah, *The Generation of the Knitted Kippot* (Hebrew). n.p.: Avivim, 1990, 19–38.

Baer, Yitzhak, *Galut*. New York: Schocken, 1947.

Balakh, Benjamin, "The Messianic Destiny of the State of Israel," *Shanah Beshanah* 1976, 251–257.

Bar Kokhva, Bezalel, *Judas Maccabaeus: The Jewish Struggle Against the Seleucids* Cambridge, England: Cambridge University Press UK, 2002.

Baron, Salo, *A Social and Religious History of the Jews.* 18 vols. Philadelphia: Jewish Publication Society of America, 1957–1983.

Baron, Salo, and Wise, George (eds.), *Violence and Defense in the Jewish Experience.* Philadelphia: Jewish Publication Society, 1977.

Barrett, Lois, *The Way God Fights: War and Peace in the Old Testament. Peace and Justice* 1. Scottdale, PA: Herald, 1987.

Bartal, Israel, "Responses to Modernity: Haskalah, Orthodoxy, and Nationalism in Eastern Europe," in Almog, Shmuel, Reinharz, Jehuda, and Shapira, Anita (eds.), *Zionism and Religion.* Hanover, NH: Brandeis University Press, 1998, 13–24.

Bar Zohar, Michael, *The Longest Month* (Hebrew). Tel Aviv: Levin Epstein, 1968.

Bauckham, Richard, "Jews and Jewish Christians in the Land of Israel at the Time of the Bar Kochba War, with Special Reference to the *Apocalypse of Peter*," in Graham Stanton and Guy Stroumsa, *Tolerance and Intolerance in Early Judaism and Christianity.* Cambridge: Cambridge University, 1998, 228–238.

Baumer, Judith Tydor, *The 'Bergson Boys' and the Origins of Contemporary Zionist Militancy*, transl. Dena Ordan. Syracuse, NY: Syracuse University, 2005.

Baumgarten, A. I., "The Akiban Opposition," *HUCA* 50 (1979), 179–197.

Begin, Menahem, *The Revolt.* New York: Nash, 1977.

Belfer, Ella, "The Land of Israel and Historical Dialectics in the Thought of Rav Kook: Zionism and Messianism," in Lawrence Kaplan and David Shatz (eds.), *Rabbi Abraham Isaac Kook and Jewish Spirituality.* NY: New York University, 1995, 257–275.

Ben David, Yissachar, "Gush Emunim and its Detractors." *Amudim* 363 (1975), 148–150.

Ben-Gurion, David and Bransten, Thomas, *Recollections of David Ben-Gurion.* London: MacDonald, 1970.

Benosovsky, Aryeh, "The Law of War and the Participation of Women in War." *Hatorah Vehamedinah* #5 (1953), 62–71.

Ben-Sasson, H. H., *History of the Jewish People.* Cambridge, MA: Harvard University Press, 1994.

Ben-Shalom, Y. "The Status of Bar Kokhba at the Head of the Nation and the Support of the Sages for the Rebellion" (Hebrew). *Cathedra* 29 (1984), 13–28.

Ben-Yehuda, Nahman, *The Masada Myth: Collective Memory and Mythmaking in Israel.* Madison: University of Wisconsin Press, 1995.

Biale, David, *Power and Powerlessness in Jewish History* (NY: Schocken, 1986)

Bickerman, Elias, *From Ezra to the Last of the Maccabees.* New York: Schocken, 1966.

Bickerman, Elias, *The Jews in the Greek Age.* Cambridge, MA: Harvard University Press, 1988.

Blau, Joseph, *Reform Judaism: A Historical Perspective.* New York: Ktav, 1973.

Bleich, J. David, *Contemporary Halakhic Problems.* New York: Ktav, 1977.

Bleich, J. David, "Judea and Samaria: Settlement and Return." *Tradition* 18 (summer, 1979), 44–78.

Bleich, J. David, "Preemptive War in Jewish Law." *Tradition* 21 (spring, 1983), 3–41.

Bleich, J. David, *Contemporary Halakhic Problems*, Vol. 2. New York: Ktav, 1983.

Blidstein, Gerald (Yakov), *Political Concepts in Maimonidean Halakhah* (Hebrew) 2nd and expanded edition. Ramat Gan: Bar Ilan University, 2001.

Blidstein, Gerald (Yakov), "Holy War in Maimonidean Law," in Joel L. Kraemer, ed., *Perspectives on Maimonides.* New York: Littman Library and Oxford University Press, 1991, 209–220.

Blidstein, Yakov, "The Treatment of Hostile Civilian Populations: The Contemporary Halakhic Discussion in Israel," *Israel Studies*, 1:2 (Fall, 1996), 27–44.

Blum, Eli, Shlomo Bar-On, et. al., *Arakhim bemivchan milchamah* (*Values under the Trial of War: Morality and War in the View of Judaism*), the family and friends of Ram Mizrachi, *z"l* from the military preparatory yeshivah "Har Etzion," n.d.

Blumenfeld, Meir, "On the Vow Not to Go Up As a Wall." *Shanah Beshanah* 1974, 151–155.

Boyarin, Daniel, *Unheroic Conduct: The Rise of Heterosexuality and the Invention of the Jewish Man.* Berkeley and Los Angeles: University of California, 1997.

Bramson, Yosef, *The Last Days: The End is Hastening* (Hebrew). Jerusalem: 2nd ed. Daf-Chen, 1987.

Brandon, Samuel, G. F., "Zealots" in EJ2 16:949.

Braude, William (transl.), *Pesikta Rabbati* (2 Vols.) New Haven: Yale, 1968.

Braslavi (Braslavski), Josef, *War and Defense among the Jews of the Land of Israel from after the Bar Kokhba Rebellion to the First Crusade* (Hebrew). Ein Harod, 1943.

Broyde, Michael J., "Just Wars, Just Battles and Just Conduct in Jewish Law: Jewish Law is Not a Suicide Pact!*," in Schiffman, Lawrence, and Wolowelsky, Joel, *War and Peace in the Jewish Tradition.* New York: Yeshivah University, 2007, 1–43.

Burns, E. L. M., "The Israeli Policy of Retaliation," in Burns, *Between Arab and Israeli.* London: George G. Harrap, 1962, 58–68.

Cahan, Yakov, *Kitvey Yakov Cahan* (2 vols.), Tel Aviv, 1948.

Caputo, Nina, *Nahmanides in Medieval Catalonia: History, Community and Messianism.* South Bend, IN: University of Notre Dame, 2008.

Casper, Bernard, "Reshit Zemichat Geulatenu" (English), in Shubert Spero and Yitzchak Pessin, eds. *Religious Zionism After 40 Years of Statehood.* Jerusalem: Mesilot, 1989, 59–72.

Chavel, Charles, *Ramban, His Life and Teachings* ( New York: Feldheim, 1960).

Chavel, (Charles) Chayim Dov (ed.), *The Writings of our Rabbi Moses ben Nachman.* Hebrew, 2 vols. Jerusalem: Mosad Harav Kook, 1964.

Chavel, Charles (transl.), *The Commandments* 2 vols. London: Soncino, 1967.

Chazan, Robert, *Barcelona and Beyond.* Berkeley and Los Angeles: University of California, 1992.

Cohen, Gerson D. "Esau as Symbol in Early Medieval Thought," in Alexander Altmann, ed. *Jewish Medieval and Renaissance Studies.* Cambridge, MA: Harvard University Press, 1967, 19–48.

Cohen, Shaye, *From the Maccabees to the Mishnah.* Philadelphia: Westminster, 1987.

Cohen, Shear Yashuv, "The Call for Peace in Israelite Wars." *Torah Shebe`al-peh* 1980, 74–81.

Cohen, Stuart, *The Scroll or the Sword.* Amsterdam: Harwood, 1997.

Cohen, Yonah, "The Six Day War." *Shanah Beshanah* 1968, 269–321.

Cox, Harvey, *Fire From Heaven: The Rise of Pentecostal Spirituality and the Reshaping of Religion in the Twenty-first Century.* Jackson, TN: Perseus, 1994.

Craigie, Peter, *The Problem of War in the Old Testament.* Grand Rapids, MI: William B. Eerdmans, 1978.

Cromer, Gerald, "Withdrawal and Conquest: Two Aspects of Haredi Response to Modernity," in Laurence Silberstein (ed.), *Jewish Fundamentalism in Comparative Perspective.* New York: New York University Press, 1993, 164–180.

Cromer, Gerald, "Amalek as Other, Other as Amalek: Interpreting a Violent Biblical Narrative." *Qualitative Sociology* 24.2 (2001), 191–202.

de Lange, Nicholas, and Freud-Kandel, Miri (eds.), *Modern Judaism: An Oxford Guide.* Oxford: Oxford University Press, 2005.

de Leon, Yitzhak ben Eliezer, The *Megillat Esther* (commentary in the traditional printed page of Maimonides, *Book of Commandments.*

Don-Yehiya, Eliezer, "The Impact and Origins of Gush Emunim." *Middle Eastern Studies* 23:2 (April 1987), 215–234.

Don-Yehiya, Eliezer, "Religion and Political Terrorism: Orthodox Jews and Retaliation during the 1936–39 'Arab Revolt'" (Hebrew). *Zionism* 17 (1993), 155–190.

Don-Yehiya, Eliezer, "The Book and the Sword: The Nationalist Yeshivot and Political Radicalism in Israel," in Martin Marty and R. Scott Appleby, *Accounting for Fundamentalisms*, vol. 4 Chicago: U. of Chicago Press, 1994, 264–302.

Don-Yehiya, Eliezer, "Traditionalist Strands," in Nicholas de Lange and Miri Freud-Kandel (eds.), *Modern Judaism: An Oxford Guide.* Oxford: Oxford University Press, 2005, 93–105.

Drori, Yakov, "Yeshivat Kerem Beyavneh: Clarification and Critique." *Amudim* 123 (Tishre/September, 1956), 26–27.

Dubin, Lois, C., "Enlightenment and Emancipation," in Nicholas de Lange and Miri Freud-Kandel (eds.), *Modern Judaism: An Oxford Guide.* Oxford: Oxford University Press, 2005, 29–41.

Dunlop, Douglas, *The History of the Jewish Khazars.* Princeton, N.J.: Princeton University Press, 1954.

Durkheim, Emile, *The Elementary Forms of the Religious Life*, transl. Joseph Ward Swain. London: George Allen and Unwin, 1915.

Eisen, Robert, *The Peace and Violence of Judaism: From the Bible to Modern Zionism.* New York: Oxford University Press, 2011.

Eisenstein, J. D. (ed.), *Otzar Massa'ot.* New York: Eisenstein, 1926.

Elbogen, Ismar, *Jewish Liturgy*, translation by Ramond Scheindlin based on the 1913 German edition and 1972 Hebrew edition. Philadelphia: Jewish Publication Society, 1993.

Ellenson, David, *After Emancipation: Jewish Religious Responses to Modernity.* Cincinnati: Hebrew Union College Press, 2004.

Emden, Jacob, *Amudey shamayim sulam beit el lehaga'on hechasid yavetz z"l.* Hama`ayan 7 (1967), 1–3.

Englard, Yitzhak, "The Halakhic Problem of Giving Back Territories from the Land of Israel: Law and Ideology (Hebrew). *Haperaklit* 41 (1993), 13–34.

Epstein, Isadore., *Abraham Yitzhak Hacohen Kook: His Life and Times.* 1951.

Feiner, Shmuel, *New Perspectives on the Haskalah* (Oxford: Littman Library, 2004).

Feldman, Louis, "Josephus' Portrayal of the Hasmoneans Compared with I Maccabees," in Fausto Parente and Joseph Sievers (eds.), *Josephus and the History of the Greco-Roman Period: Essays in Memory of Morton Smith.* Leiden: Brill, 1994, 41–68.

Feldman, Louis, *"Remember Amalek!" Vengeance, Zealotry, and Group Destruction in the Bible According to Philo, Pseudo-Philo, and Josephus.* Cincinnati: Hebrew Union College, 2004.

Felder, Gedalia, "War and Army in the Light of the *Halakhah.*" *Torah Shebe`al Peh* 1982, 118–127.

Firestone, Reuven, *Jihad: The Origin of Holy War in Islam.* New York: Oxford University Press, 1999.

Firestone, Reuven, "Conceptions of Holy War in Biblical and Qur'anic Tradition." *The Journal of Religious Ethics* 24 (1996), 801–824.

Firestone, Reuven, "Holy War Idea in the Biblical Tradition," in Palmer-Fernandez, G. (ed.), *Encyclopedia of Religion and War* (1st ed.). New York: Berkshire/Routledge, 2004, 180–85.

Firestone, Reuven, "Holy War in Modern Judaism? 'Mitzvah War' and the Problem of the 'Three Vows,'" in the *Journal of the American Academy of Religion* 74(4) December, 2006, 954–982.

Fishbane, Michael, *Biblical Interpretation in Ancient Israel.* Oxford: Clarendon. 1985.

Fishman, Tzvi (transl.), *Torat Eretz Yisrael: The Teachings of Harav Tzvi Yehuda Hacohen Kook Based on the Hebrew Orations of Harav Tzvi Yehuda compiled and edited by Shlomo Aviner.* Jerusalem: Torat Eretz Yisrael Publications, 1991

Flusser, David, "Heroism and Martyrdom." *Machanayim* 87 (1964), 76–79.

Flusser, David (ed.), *Sefer Yosifon.* Jerusalem: Mercaz Zalman Shazar, 1978.

Fox, Everett (transl), *The Five Books of Moses.* New York: Schocken, 1983.

Frank, Daniel, *Search Scripture Well: Karaite Exegetes and the Origins of the Jewish Bible Commentary in the Islamic East.* Leiden: Brill, 2004.

Freud-Kandel, Miri, "Modernist Movements," in Nicholas de Lange and Miri Freud-Kandel (eds.), *Modern Judaism: An Oxford Guide.* Oxford: Oxford University Press, 2005.

Friedland, Roger, and Richard D. Hecht,, "The Politics of Sacred Place: Jerusalem's Temple Mount/*al-haram al-sharif*," in Jamie Scott and Pauls Simpson-Houseley, *Sacred Places and Profane Spaces.* New York: Greenwood Press, 1991, 21–61.

Friedlander, M. (transl.), *Guide for the Perplexed by Moses Maimonides.* New York: Dover, 1956.

Friedman, Menahem, "Jewish Zealots: Conservative versus Innovative," in Silberstein, Laurence (ed.), *Jewish Fundamentalism in Comparative Perspective.* NY: New York University Press, 1983, 148–163.

Friedman, Robert, *Zealots for Zion: Inside Israel's West Bank Settlement Movement* (New Brunswick, NJ: Rutgers University), 1992.

Gershuni, Yehudah, "On the Issue of the Command to Wipe Out Amalek." *Hatorah Vehamedinah* #9 (1958), 76–81.

Gershuni, Yehudah, "Discretionary War and commanded war" [Hebrew]. *Shanah Beshanah* 1971, 147–156.

Gillerman, Sharon, "Samson in Vienna: The Politics of Jewish Masculinity." *Jewish Social Studies*, Vol. 9 No.2 (2003), 65–97.

Ginzberg, H. L., "Dates and Characteristics of the Parts [of the Book of Daniel]." *Encyclopedia Judaica* 5:1281–1286.

Glatzer, Nahum, "The Attitude Toward Rome in Third-Century Judaism," in Nahum Glatzer, *Essays in Jewish Thought*. Tuscaloosa, AL: University of Alabama Press, 1978, 1–14.

Glick, Shimon, "The Tragedy of Gush Emunim." *Tradition* 19:2 (1981), 112–121.

Golden, Peter B., *Khazar Studies*. Budapest: Akadémiai Kiadó, 1980.

Goldin, Judah, (transl.) *The Fathers According to Rabbi Nathan*. New Haven: Yale University Press, 1955.

Goldman, Eliezer, "Controversy on Gush Emunim: Messianic Interpretation of Current Events." *Forum* 1977 #1 (26), 37–38.

Goldscheider, Calvin, and Neusner, Jacob (eds.), *Social Foundations of Judaism*. Englewood Cliffs, NJ: Prentice Hall, 1990.

Goldstein, Jonathan, A., *I Maccabees: Anchor Bible Vol. 41*. Garden City: Doubleday, 1981.

Goldstein, Jonathan, A., *II Maccabees, Anchor Bible*. New York: Doubleday, 1989.

Golinkin, David, *Insight Israel: The View from Schechter*. Jerusalem: Schechter Institute, 2005.

Goren, Shlomo, "The Sanctity of the Land of Israel According to its Borders in the Torah." *Machanayim* 31 (*Erev Chanukkah*/December) 1957, 5–11.

Goren, Shlomo, "Commanded War and Discretionary War." *Machanayim* 69 (1962), 5–15.

Goren, Shlomo, "Army and War in the Light of the Halakhah." *Machanayim* 97 (1965), 6–15.

Goren, Shlomo, "Army and War in the Light of the Halakhah." *Machanayim* #121 (1969), 7–18.

Goren, Shlomo, *The Law of the State* (*Torat Hamedinah*). Jerusalem: Ha'idra Rabba, 1996.

Goren, Shlomo, *The Teaching of the State* (*Mishnat Hamedinah*). Jerusalem: Ha'idra Rabba, 1999.

Gorenberg, Gershom, *The End of Days: Fundamentalism and the Struggle for the Temple Mount*. New York: Oxford University Press, 2000.

Avraham Grossman, *Rashi: Religious Beliefs and Social Views* (Hebrew). Alon Shevut: Tevunot, 2007.

Gruen, Erich, "Hellenistic Judaism," in David Biale (ed.), *Cultures of the Jews: A New History*. New York: Schocken, 2002, 77–132.

Hailperin, Herman, *Rashi and the Christian Scholars*. Pittsburgh: University of Pittsburgh, 1963.

Halevi, Chaim David, "The Meaning of the 'Yom Kippur' War among the Battles of the Redemption of Israel." *Torah Shebe`al Peh* 17 (1975), 63–78.

Halevi, Chaim David, "The Ruling of 'If he intends to kill you, kill him first' in Our Public Lives." *Techumin* 1 (1980), 343–348.

Halevi, Yehuda, *The Kosari of R. Yehuda Halevi*, transl. Yehuda Even Shmuel (Hebrew). Tel Aviv: Dvir, 1972.

Halkin, Abraham, and Cohen, Boaz, *Moses Maimonides' Epistle to Yemen: The Arabic Original and the three Hebrew Versions*. New York: American Academy for Jewish Research, 1952.

Halliday, Fred, *Religion and Nation in the Middle East*. Boulder, CO: Lynne Reinner, 2000.

Halperin, Avraham, "The State of Israel in Religious Thought and the Education of Our Generation" (Hebrew). *Amudim* #242 (April, 1966), 247–254.

Hanbali, Mujir al-Din al-`Ulaymi al-, *Al-Uns al-Jalil bitarikh al-Quds wal-Khalil* 2 vols. Amman: Maktabat Dandis, 1999.

Harris, Jay (ed.), *Maimonides After 800 Years*. Cambridge, MA: Harvard University, 2007.

Hartom, Menachem, "Suggestions of Rabbi Hartom." *Amudim* 257–258 (July–August), 335–338.

Hasan-Rokem, Galit, *Web of Life: Folklore and Midrash in Rabbinic Literature,* Trans. Batya Stein. Stanford, CA: Stanford University, 2000.

Hashmi, S. (ed.), *Just Wars, Holy wars, and Jihads: Christian, Jewish, Muslim Encounters and Exchanges*. New York: Oxford, 2012.

Hasson, Isaac, *Fada'il al-Bayt al-Muqaddas*. Jerusalem: Magnes, 1979.

Heft, James L.S.M., *John XXII and Papal Teaching Authority*. Lewiston, NY: Edwin Mellen Press, 1986.

Heilman, Samuel, "Quiescent and Active Fundamentalisms: The Jewish Cases," in Martin Marty and R. Scott Appleby, *Accounting for Fundamentalisms*, vol. 4 Chicago: U. of Chicago Press, 1994, 173–196.

Heineman, Isaac, "*Maimuni und die arabischen Einheitsleher.*" *MGWJ* 79 (1935).

Heinemann, Yosef, "Definitions Regarding Faith." *Amudim* 371 (1976), 448.

Hengel, Martin, *The Zealots: Investigations into the Jewish Freedom Movement in the Period from Herod I until A.D. 70*, transl. by David W. Smith. Edinburgh: T & T Clark, 1989.

Henkin, Yehudah Herzl, "On Settling the Land of Israel." *Shanah Beshanah* 1983, 331–334.

Henkin, Yehudah Herzl, "Those Who Fall as Martyrs." *Shanah Beshanah* 1984, 290–292.

Herr, Moshe David, "The Problem of War on the Sabbath in the Second Temple and the Talmudic Periods." *Tarbitz* 30 (1961), 242–256, 342–356 (Hebrew).

Herr, Moshe David, "A Problem of Periodization: The Second Temple and the Mishna and Talmud Periods in Jewish History" (Hebrew), in Aharon Mirsky, Avraham Grossman and Yose Kaplan, *Exile and Diaspora: Studies in the History of the Jewish People Presented to Professor Haim Beinart on the Occasion of His Seventieth Birthday*. Jerusalem: Ben-Zvi, 1988, 64–74.

Hershman, Abraham (transl.), *The Code of Maimonides*. New Haven: Yale University Press, 1949.

Hertzberg, Arthur, *The Zionist Idea*. New York: Atheneum, 1971.

Herzl, Theodor, *Old-New Land*. New York: Bloch, 1960.

Herzog, Isaac, *Collected Writings of Rabbi Yitzhaq Isaac Halevi Herzog, Chief Rabbi of Israel* (Hebrew). Jerusalem: Mosad Harav Kook/Rabbi Herzog Memorial, n.d.

Herzog, Isaac, "On the Founding of the State and Its Wars." *Techumin* 4 (1983), 13–24.

Hezser, Catherine, *The Social Structure of the Rabbinic Movement in Roman Palestine*. Tübingen: Mohr Siebeck, 1997, 53–77.

Higger, Moshe, *Sheva Massekhtot Ketannot*. New York: Bloch, 1930.

Hoffman, Lawrence (ed.), *The Land of Israel: Jewish Perspectives*. South Bend, IN: Notre Dame, 1986.

Holzer, Elie, "The Evolving Meaning of the Three Oaths Within Religious Zionism" (Hebrew), *Daat: Journal of Jewish Philosophy and Kabbalah*, 47 (Summer, 2001), 129–145.

Holzer, Elie, "Attitudes Towards the Use of Military Force in Ideological Currents of Religious Zionism," in Lawrence Schiffman and Joel Wolowelsky, eds., *War and Peace in the Jewish Tradition*. New York: Yeshivah University, 2007, 341–413.

Horowitz, Elliot, *Reckless Rites: Purim and the Legacy of Jewish Violence*. Princeton: Princeton University, 2006.

Horowitz, Elliott, "From the Generation of Moses to the Generation of the Messiah: The Jews Confront 'Amalek' and his Incarnations." (Heb). *Zion* 64 (1999), 425–454

Ilan, Mordechai, "Whether Sanctified for Its Own Time [Or] Sanctified Forever." *Torah Shebe`al Peh* 10 (1968), 62–73.

Inbar, Efraim, "War in Jewish Tradition." *The Jerusalem Journal of International Relations* 9 (1987), 83–99.

Inbari, Motti, "The Oslo Accords and the Temple Mount: A Case Study, The Movement for the Establishment of the Temple." *Hebrew Union College Annual* 74 (2003–2004), 279–323.

Inbari, Motti. *Jewish Fundamentalism and the Temple Mount*. Albany: State University of New York, 2009.

Ish-Shalom, Michael, *Christian Travels to the Land of Israel*. Hebrew, Tel Aviv: Am Oved, 1979.

Jawziyya, Shams al-Din Ibn Qayyim al-, *Ahkam ahl al-dhimma* (ed. Sabhi Salih). Beirut: Dar al-`ilm lil-milaliyin, 1983.

John, Robert and Hadawi, Sami, *The Palestine Diary* 2 vols. New York: New World Press, 1970.

Johnson, James Turner, *Ideology, Reason, and the Limitation of War*. Princeton: Princeton University Press, 1975.

Jones, Gwilyn, H., "The Concept of Holy War." In *The World of Ancient Israel: Sociological, Anthropological and Political Perspectives*, ed. R. E. Clements. Cambridge: Cambridge University. 1989, 299–302.

Josephus, Flavius, *Wars, Antiquities.* trans., William Whiston, Grand Rapids: Kregel, 1960.

Josephus, *The Jewish War*, trans., G. A. Williamson, revised with new introduction, notes and appendixes, by E. Mary Smallwood. New York: Dorset, 1981.

Juergensmeyer, Mark, *Terror in the Mind of God: The Global Rise of Religious Violence*. Berkeley: University of California, 2000.

Kalmin, Richard, "Rabbinic Traditions about Roman Persecutions of the Jews: A Reconsideration." *JJS* LIV no. 1 (2003), 21–50.

Kanarfogel, Efrayim, "The Aliyah of the 'Three Hundred Rabbis,'" in *Jewish Quarterly Review* 76 (1986), 191–212.

Kaplan, Tzvi, "The Western Wall in Halakhah." *Shanah Beshanah* 1968, 168–181.

Karpel, Moti, *The Revolution of Belief: The Decline of Zionism and the Rise of the Alternative of Belief* (Hebrew). Alon Shevut, 2003.

Kasher, Menachem, "A Legal Opinion on the Vow that Israel Not Go Up as a Wall to the Land of Israel." *Shanah Beshanah* 1977, 213–228.

Kasher, Menachem, "Do Not Fear Jacob My Servant! (Words of Encouragement and Keeping the Faith)." *Shanah Beshanah* 1979, 165–171.

Katz, Yakov (Jacob), "On Elucidating the Conception of the Harbingers of Zionism" (Hebrew). *Shivat Tziyon* 1 (1950), 91–105.

Katz, Jacob, *Out of the Ghetto: The Social Background of Jewish Emancipation 1770–1870*. New York: Schocken, 1973.

Kaufman, Yitzhak, *The Army According to Halakhah: Laws of War and Army* (Hebrew). Jerusalem: 1992.

Kelsay, John, *Arguing the Just War in Islam*. Cambridge, MA: Harvard University Press, 2007.

Kersel, G., (ed.), *Rabbi Yehuda Alkalai and Rabbi Tzvi Hirsch Kalischer: Selected Writings* (Hebrew). Tel Aviv: Mitzpeh, n.d.

Khadduri, Majid, *War and Peace in the Law of Islam*. Baltimore: Johns Hopkins, 1955.

Killebrew, Ann, *Biblical Peoples and Ethnicity*. Atlanta: Society for Biblical Literature, 2005.

Kimelman, Reuven, "The Ethics of National Power: Government and War from the Sources of Judaism," in Daniel Elazar (ed.), *Authority, Power and Leadership in the Jewish Polity*. Lanham: University Press of America, 1991, 247–294.

Kimelman, Reuven, "War," in Steven T. Katz, *Frontiers of Jewish Thought*. Washington, D.C.: B'nai B'rith Books, 1992, 309–332.

Kimelman, Reuven, "Laws of War and its Limits" (Hebrew), in Isaiah M. Gafni and Aviezer Ravitzky, *Sanctity of Life and Martyrdom*. Jerusalem: Zalman Shazar Center, 1992, 233–254.

Kimmerling, Baruch and Migdal, Joel, *Palestinians: The Making of a People*. New York: Free Press, 1993.

Kolatt, Israel, "Zionism and Messianism" (Hebrew), in Tzvi Baras (ed.) *Zionism and Eschatology*. Jerusalem: Zalman Shazar Centre, 1983, 419–431.

Kolatt, Israel, "Religion, Society, and State during the Period of the National Home," in Almog, Shmuel, Reinharz, Jehuda, and Shapira, Anita (eds.), *Zionism and Religion*. Hanover, NH: Brandeis University Press, 1998, 273–301.

Kolkheim, Uzi, "The Vision of the 'Revealed End' in the Perspective of the Generations," (Hebrew) in Refa'el, Yitzhak and Shragai, Sh. Z (eds.), *Sefer Hatzionut Hadatit* 2 vols. Jerusalem: Mosad Harav Kook, 1977, I, 96–110.

Kolsky, Thomas, *Jews Against Zionism: The American Council for Judaism 1942–1948*. Philadelphia: Temple University, 1990.

Kook, Abraham Isaac, *Orot*. Jerusalem: Mossad Harav Kook, 1993.

Kook, Abraham Isaac, *Orot*. Translated into English by Bezalel Naor. Northvale, NJ: Jason Aaronson, 1993.

Kook, Tzvi Yehudah, "On Questions of the Liberated Territories by the IDF." *Shanah Beshanah* 1968, 108–109.

Kook, Tzvi Yehudah, "The Sanctity of the Holy People on the Holy Land." *Shanah Beshanah* 1976, 267–274. Reprinted in Tirosh, Yosef, *Religious Zionism and the State: A Collection of Articles on the 30th Year of the State*. Jerusalem: World Zionist Organization, 1978, 140–146.

Kook, Tzvi Yehudah, "Between a People and Its Land," excerpted from *Conversations of Rabbi Tzvi Yehudah*. *Artzi* 2 (1982), 15–23.

Kook, Tzvi Yehudah, *Torat Eretz Yisrael: The Teachings of Harav Tzvi Yehudah Haco-hen Kook Based on the Hebrew Orations of Harav Tzvi Yehudah compiled and edited by Rabbi Shlomo Aviner*. Transl. Tzvi Fishman. Jerusalem: Torat Eretz Yisrael Publications, 1991.

Kook, Tzvi Yehudah, "Clarification About the Claim of the Three Vows" (Hebrew), in *Lenetivot Yisrael* 3 vols. Jerusalem: n.p., 1997.

Kook, Tzvi Yehudah, *Discourse (sichot) of Rabbi Tzvi Yehudah*, ed. Shlomo Aviner. 4 Vols (to date). Jerusalem: n.p. 1993–2002.

Kraemer, Joel, ed., *Perspectives on Maimonides*. New York: Littman Library and Oxford University Press, 1991.

Kumaraswamy, P. R. (ed.), *Revisiting the Yom Kippur War*. London: Frank Cass, 2000.

Lamm, Norman, "Amalek and the Seven Nations: A Case of Law vs. Morality," in Lawrence Schiffman and Joel Wolowelsky, eds., *War and Peace in the Jewish Tradition*. New York: Yeshivah University, 2007, 201–238.

Landa, S. Z., & Rabinowitz, J. (eds.), *Or Layesharim*. Warsaw, 1900.

Laqueur, Walter, *The Road to War 1967: The Origins of the Arab-Israeli Conflict*. London: Weidenfeld and Nicolson, 1969.

Laquer, Walter, *A History of Zionism*. New York: Schocken, 1976.

Lassner, Jacob and Troen, S. Ilan, *Jews and Muslims in the Arab World: Haunted by Pasts Real and Imagined*. New York: Rowman and Littlefield, 2007.

Leibman, Charles, and don-Yehiya, Eliezer, *Civil Religion in Israel*. Berkeley: University of California Press, 1984.

Leibman, Charles, and Cohen, Asher, "A Case of Fundamentalism in Contempo-rary Israel," in Leibman, Charles, ed., *Religion, Democracy, and Israeli Society*. Amsterdam: Harwood, 1997, 57–76.

Leibman, Charles, ed., *Religion, Democracy, and Israeli Society*. Amsterdam: Harwood, 1997.

Leibowitz, Yeshayahu, "After Qibya." *Beterem*, 1953/1954, 168–173.

Lemche, Niels Peter, *The Canaanites and their Land*. Sheffield, England: JSOT, 1991.

Levin, Yigal, "The Wars of Joshua: Weaning Away from the Divine," in Yigal Levin and Amnon Shapira, *War and Peace in Jewish Tradition: From the Biblical World to the Present*. London: Routledge, 2012, 37–50.

Levin, Yuval, and Shapira, Amnon, *War and Peace in Jewish Tradition: From the Biblical World to the Present*. London: Routledge, 2012.

Levinger, Moshe, "The Flowering of Our Redemption." *Amudim* #256, June 1967, 304.

Lewis, Bernard, *History Remembered, Recovered, Invented*. Princeton: Princeton University Press, 1976.

Liber, Maurice, *Rashi*. Philadelphia: Jewish Publication Society, 1906/1938.

Lichtenstein, Aaron, *The Seven Laws of Noah*. New York: Z. Berman, 1987.

Lifshitz, Joseph Isaac, "War and aesthetics in Jewish law," in Yigal Levin and Amnon Shapira, *War and Peace in Jewish Tradition*. London: Routledge, 2012, 103–115.

Lind, Millard C. *Yahweh is a Warrior: The Theology of Warfare in Ancient Israel*. Scottdale, PA: Herald, 1980.

Litvinoff, Barnet, *The Letters and Papers of Chaim Weizman*, 2 Vols. New Brunswick, N.J.: Rutgers University Press, 1984.

Lustick, Ian, "Jewish Fundamentalism and the Israeli-Palestinian Impasse," in Silberstein, Laurence (ed.), *Jewish Fundamentalism in Comparative Perspective*. New York: New York University Press, 1983, 104–116.

Luz, Ehud, *Parallels Meet: Religion and Nationalism in the Early Zionist Movement*. Philadelphia: JPS, 1988.

Luz, Ehud, *Wrestling with an Angel: Power, Morality, and Jewish Identity*, transl. Michael Swirsky (New Haven: Yale, 2003).

Luz, Ehud, "The Limits of Toleration: The Challenge of Cooperation between the Observant and the Nonobservant during the Hibbat Zion Period, 1882–1895," in Almog, Shmuel, Reinharz, Jehuda, and Shapira, Anita (eds.), *Zionism and Religion*. Hanover, NH: Brandeis University Press, 1998, 44–54.

Maimon (Fishman), Y. L. Hacohen, in *Hatziyonut Hadatit Vehitpatchutah*.

Marcus, Ralph, *Jewish Antiquities* [Greek/English text], vol. 7. London: William Henemann, LTD, 1943 and reprinted 1961.

Marks, Richard G., *The Image of Bar Kokhba in Traditional Jewish Literature*. Pennsylvania State University Press, 1994.

Marty, Marty, and R. Scott Appleby, *Accounting for Fundamentalisms*, vol. 4 Chicago: U. of Chicago Press, 1994.

Mendels, Doron, *The Rise and Fall of Jewish Nationalism*. Grand Rapids, MI: Eerdmans, 1992.

Mendes-Flohr, Paul, and Reinharz, Jehuda (eds.), *The Jew in the Modern World*, 2nd ed. New York: Oxford Univ. Press, 1995.

Meyer, Michael, *Response to Modernity a History of the Reform Movement in Judaism*. New York: Oxford Univ. Press, 1988.

Millar, Fergus, "The Jews of the Graeco-Roman Diaspora Between Paganism and Christianity, AD 312–438," in Judith Lieu, John North and Tessa Rajak (eds.) *The Jews Among Pagans and Christians in the Roman Empire*. London: Routledge, 1992, 97–123.

Mor, Menachem, *The Bar Kokhba Revolt: Its Extent and Effect*. Jerusalem: Yad Ben-Tzvi, 1991.

Mor, Menahem, and Le Beau, Brian (eds.) *Pilgrims and Travelers to the Holy Land*. Omaha: Creighton University Press, 1996.

Morgenstern, Arie, *Messianism and the Settlement of Eretz-Israel in the First Half of the Nineteenth Century* (Hebrew). Jerusalem: Yad Yitzhak ben Tzvi, 1985.

Morgenstern, Arie, "Dispersion and the Longing for Zion, 1240–1840," *Azure* 12 (2002), 71–132.

Morris, Benny, *Israel's Border Wars*. Oxford: Oxford University Press, 1993.

Myers, Jody, *Seeking Zion: Modernity and Messianic Activism in the Writings of Tsevi Hirsch Kalischer*. Oxford: Littman Library, 2003.

Nahlon, Aharon, "The Religious Significance of the State of Israel," *Amudim* #242 April 1966.

Naor, Bezalel, (translator), *Orot*. Northvale, NJ: Jason Aaronson, 1993.

Near, Henry, *The Image of the Pioneer in North America and Pre-State Jewish Palestine*. Haifa: Institute for Study and Research of the Kibbutz and the Cooperative Idea at the University of Haifa Discussion Paper No. 69, January 1987.

Nehorai, Michael Tzvi, "Rav Reines and Rav Kook: Two Approaches to Zionism," in (no ed. listed), *The World of Rav Kook's Thought*. Jerusalem: Avi Chai, 1991.

Nemoy, Leon, *Karaite Anthology*. New Haven: Yale, 1980.

Neriya, Moshe Tzvi, "Upon Your Ramparts, Jerusalem." *Zera`im* 324 (Av/August-September, 1967), 3.

Neriya, Moshe Tzvi, "Jerusalem the Sacred City and of the Temple (Holiness of the *Shechinah* and Holiness of the Separation)." *Torah Shebe`al Peh* 10 (1968), 74–85.

Neriya, Moshe Tzvi, "Our Right to the Land of Israel." *Torah Shebe`al Peh* 1974, 149–180.

Neriya, Avraham Yitzhaq, "Keeping Commandments in the Time of Battle. *Shanah Beshanah* 1976, 309–316.

Neuman, Kalman, "The Law of Obligatory War and Israeli Reality," in Yigal Levin and Amnon Shapira, *War and Peace in Jewish Tradition: From the Biblical World to the Present*. London: Routledge, 2012, 186–199.

Neusner, Jacob, *Messiah in Context: Israel's History and Destiny in Formative Judaism*. Philadelphia, Penn.: Fortress Press, 1984.

Newman, Aryeh, "The Centrality of Eretz Yisrael in Nachmanides." *Tradition* 10 (summer, 1968), 21–30.

Newman, David (ed.), *The Impact of Gush Emunim: Politics and Settlement in the West Bank*. New York: St Martin's Press, 1985.

Newman, David, "Gush Emunim Between Fundamentalism and Pragmatism." *The Jerusalem Quarterly* 39 (1986), 33–43.

Niditch, Susan, *War in the Hebrew Bible: A Study in the Ethics of Violence* (New York: Oxford, 1993).

Nisan, Mordechai, "Gush Emunim: A Rational Perspective," *Forum* 36 (Fall-winter, 1979), 15–23.

Novak, David, *The Image of the Non-Jew in Judaism: An Historical and Constructive Study of the Noahide Laws*. New York: Edwin Mellen, 1983.

O'Dea, Janet, "Gush Emunim: Roots and Ambiguities: The Perspective of the Sociology of Religion." *Forum on the Jewish People, Zionism and Israel* 2 (25) (1976), 39–50.

Ohana, David, *Political Theologies in the Holy Land: Israeli Messianism and its Critics*. New York: Routledge, 2010.

Oppenheimer, Aharon, *The Bar Kokhba Revolt* (Hebrew). Jerusalem: Zalman Shazar Center, 1980.

Oppenheimer, Aharon, and Rappaport, Uriel, *The Bar Kokhba Revolt: New Studies*. 1984.

Oppenheimer, Aharon, "Sanctity of Life and Martyrdom in the Wake of the Bar Kokhba Revolt" (Hebrew), in Yesha'ya Gafni and Aviezer Ravitzky (eds.), *Sanctity of Life and Martyrdom* (Jerusalem: Zalman Shazar Center, 1993), 85–97.

Oppenheimer, Aharon, "The Ban of Circumcision as a Cause of the Revolt: A Reconsideration," in Peter Schäfer (ed), *The Bar Kokhba War Reconsidered*. Tübingen: Mohr/Siebeck, 2003, 55–69.

Oren, Michael, *Six Days of War: June 1967 and the Making of the Modern Middle East*. Oxford: Oxford University, 2002.

Partner, Peter, *God of Battles: Holy Wars of Christianity and Islam*. Princeton: Princeton University Press, 1997.

Patterson, J. H., *With the Zionists in Gallipoli*. New York: George H. Doran, 1916.

Pearl, Chaim, *Rashi*. New York: Grove, 1988.

Pedahzur, Ami and Perliger, Arie, *Jewish Terrorism in Israel*. New York: Columbia University, 2009.

Pedersen, Johannes, *Israel: Its Life and Culture* III-IV. London: Cumberlege: Oxford University Press, 1940 (translated and reprinted from the Danish edition of 1934.

Peters, Rudolf, *Jihad in Classical and Modern Islam*. Princeton: Markus Wiener, 1996.

Plaut, Gunther, *The Rise of Reform Judaism: A Sourcebook of its European Origins*. New York: Wold Union for Progressive Judaism, 1963.

*Polliack*, Meira, *Karaite Judaism: A Guide to Its History and Literary Sources*. Leiden: Brill, 2003.

Rabinowitz, Abraham Tzvi, "Ethical Considerations on the Topic of War," in Blum, Eli, Shlomo Bar-On, et. al., *Arakhim bemivchan milchamah* (*Values under the Trial of War: Morality and War in the View of Judaism*), the family and friends of Ram Mizrachi, *z"l* from the military preparatory yeshivah "Har Etzion," n.d.

Rabinowitz, Nachum Eliezer, "The Method of Nahmanides and Maimonides on the Commandment of Inheriting the Land (Hebrew)." *Techumin* 5 (1984), 180–186.

Rabinowitz, Nachum Eliezer, *The Educated in War* (*Melumadey milchamah*). Ma'aleh Adumim: Ma'aliyot, 1994.

Rackman, Emanuel, "Violence and the Value of Life: The Halakhic View," in Salo Baron and George Wise (eds.), *Violence and Defense in the Jewish Experience* (Philadelphia: Jewish Publication Society, 1977), 116–141.

Rapaport, Ezra, *Letters from Tel Mond Prison*. New York: The Free Press, 1996.

Ravitzky, Aviezer, "Roots of Kahanism: consciousness and Political Reality." *Jerusalem Quarterly* 39 (1986), 90–108.

Ravitzky, Aviezer, "Religious Radicalism and Political Messianism in Israel," in Sivan, Emmanuel, and Friedman, Menachem (eds.), *Religious Radicalism and Politics in the Middle East*. Albany, NY: SUNY Press, 1990, 11–37.

Ravitzky, Aviezer, *Messianism, Zionism, and Jewish Religious Radicalism*, transl. Michael Swirsky and Jonathan Chipman. Chicago: U. of Chicago Press, 1997.

Refa'el, Shilo, "Conquering the Land of Egypt and Settling It." *Torah Shebe'al Peh* 17 (1975), 135–140.

Refa'el, Yitzhak and Shragai, Sh. Z (eds.), *Sefer Hatzionut Hadatit* 2 vols. Jerusalem: Mosad Harav Kook, 1977.

Reichner, Elyashev, *By Faith Alone: The Story of Rabbi Yehuda Amital*, transl. Elli Fischer. New Milford, CT: Maggid, 2011.

Reinharz, Jehuda, "Zionism and Orthodoxy: A Marriage of Convenience," in Almog, Shmuel, Reinharz, Jehuda, and Shapira, Anita (eds.), *Zionism and Religion*. Hanover, NH: Brandeis University Press, 1998, 116–139.

Reiser, Stewart, *The Politics of Leverage: The National Religious Party of Israel and its Influence on Foreign Policy*. Cambridge, MA: Harvard University Press, 1984.

Rivlin, "The Law of the Land of Israel in the Teaching of Nahmanides (700 years since his *aliyah*)." *Shanah Beshanah* 1968, 203–212.

Sachar, Howard Morley, *A History of Israel* third edition revised and updated. New York: Knopf, 2007.

Safran, Nadav, *From War to War: The Arab Israeli Confrontation 1948–1967*. New York: Pegasus, 1967.

Sagi, Avi, *Judaism: Between Religion and Morality* (Hebrew). Tel Aviv: Hakibbutz Hameuchad, 1998.

Salmon, Yosef, "Tradition and Modernity in the Beginning of Religious Zionist Thought (Hebrew)," in (no ed.). *Zionist Ideology and Policy: Collected Essays*. Jerusalem: The Zalman Shazar Center, 1978, 21–37.

Salmon, Yosef, "Zionism and Anti-Zionism in Traditional Judaism in Eastern Europe," in Almog, Shmuel, Reinharz, Jehuda, and Shapira, Anita (eds.), *Zionism and Religion*. Hanover, NH: Brandeis University Press, 1998, 25–43.

Samson David, and Tzi Fishman, *HaRav Avraham Yitzhak Hacohen Kook: War and Peace*. Jerusalem: Torah Eretz Yisrael Publications, 1997.

Saperstein, Marc, "The Land of Israel in pre-Modern Jewish Thought: A History of Two Rabbinic Statements," in Lawrence A. Hoffman (ed.), *The Land of Israel: Jewish Perspectives*. South Bend, IN: Notre Dame, 1986, 188–209.

Schäfer, Peter, "The Causes of the Bar Kokhba Revolt," in Jakob Petuchowsky and Ezra Fleischer (eds.), *Studies in Aggadah, Targum and Jewish Liturgy in Memory of Joseph Heinemann*. Jerusalem: Magnes, 1981, 74–94.

Schäfer, Peter, "Hadrian's Policy in Judaea and the Bar Kokhba Revolt: A Reassessment," in Philip R. Davies and Richard T. White (eds.), *A Tribute to Geza Vermes. Essays on Jewish and Christian Literature and History*. Sheffield: JSOT Press, 1990, 281–303.

Schäfer, Peter, *The Bar Kokhba War Reconsidered*: New Perspectives on the Second Jewish Revolt Against Rome. *Tübingen*: Mohr Siebeck, 2003.

Schechter, Solomon (Ed.), *Avoth de Rabbi Nathan* (Hebrew). Edited from Manuscripts with an Introduction, Notes and Appendices. Vienna, 1886, republished New York: Feldheim, 1945.

Schepansky, Israel, *Eretz-Israel in the Responsa Literature* (3 Vols. Hebrew) (Jerusalem: Mosad Harav Kook, 1978.

Schiffman, Lawrence, "War in Apocalyptic Thought," in Lawrence Schiffman and Joel Wolowelsky, eds., *War and Peace in the Jewish Tradition*. New York: Yeshivah University, 2007, 477–495.

Schiffman, Lawrence, and Wolowelsky, Joel, *War and Peace in the Jewish Tradition*. New York: Yeshivah University, 2007.

Schindler, Pesach (transl.) *Restoration of Zion as a Response During the Holocaust: Em Habanim Semecha*, by Yissakhar Shlomo Taikhtel (Teichthal). New York: Ktav, 1999.

Scholem, Gershom, *The Messianic Idea in Judaism*. London: George Allen & Unwin, 1971.

Schur, Nathan, *History of the Samaritans*. Frankfurt am Main, Peter Lang, 1989.

Schur, Nathan, *Twenty Centuries of Christian Pilgrimage to the Holy Land*. Tel Aviv: Dvir, 1992.

Schurer, Emil (revised & edited by Geza Vermes & Fergus Millar), *The History of the Jewish People in the Age of Jesus Christ*. New York: Continuum, 1987.

Schwally, Friedrich, *Der Heilige Krieg in alten Israel*. Leipzig: Deiterich Stolz, 1901.

Schwartz, Daniel R., "The Other in I and II Maccabees," in Stanton and Stroumsa, *Tolerance and Intolerance in Early Judaism and Christianity*. Cambridge: Cambridge University, 1998, 30–37.

Schwartz, Dov, *The Land of Israel in Religious Zionist Thought* (Hebrew) Tel Aviv: Am Oved, 1997.

Schwartz, Dov, "A Theological Rationale for National-Messianic Thought: Rabbi Tzvi Yehudah Kook" (Hebrew), *Hatziyonut* 22 (2000), 61–81.

Schwartz, Dov, *Meshichiut: Faith at the Crossroads; a Theological Profile of Religious Zionism* (trans. Batya Stein). Leiden: Brill, 2002.

Schwartz, Dov, *Religious Zionism: History and Ideology.* Boston: Academic Studies Press, 2009.

Schwartz, Seth, *Imperialism and Jewish Society, 200 B.C.E. to 640 C.E.* Princeton: Princeton University Press, 2001.

Scott, Jamie, and Pauls Simpson-Houseley, *Sacred Places and Profane Spaces.* New York: Greenwood Press, 1991.

Seeman, Don, "Violence, Ethics, and Divine Honor in Modern Jewish Thought," in *Journal of the American Academy of Religion* Vol. 73, No. 4 (Dec. 2005), 1015–1048.

Segal, Haggai, *Dear Brothers: The West Bank Jewish Underground.* Jerusalem: Keter, 1987, translated into English, Woodmere: Beit Shamai Publications, 1988.

Segev, Tom, *One Palestine, Complete: Jews and Arabs under the British Mandate* transl. Haim Watzman. New York: Metropolitan, 2000.

Segev, Tom, *1967: Israel, the War, and the Year that Transformed the Middle East,* transl. Jessica Cohen. New York: Macmillan, 2007.

Selengut, Charles, *Sacred Fury: Understanding Religious Violence.* Walnut Creek, CA: Alta Mira, 2003.

Shapira, Anita. *Struggle and Disappointment:* Hebrew Labor 1929–1939 (Hebrew). Tel Aviv: Hakibbutz Hame'uchad, 1977.

Shapira, Anita, *Land and Power: The Zionist Resort to Force* 1881–1948. Oxford: Oxford University Press, 1992.

Shapira, Anita, "Religious Motifs of the Labor Movement," in Almog, Shmuel, Reinharz, Jehuda, and Shapira, Anita (eds.), *Zionism and Religion.* Hanover, NH: Brandeis University Press, 1998, 251–272.

Sharabi, Hisham, "Prelude to War: The Crisis of May-June 1967," in Ibrahim Abu-Lughod (ed.), *the Arab-Israeli Confrontation of June 1967: An Arab Perspective.* Evanston, IL: Northwestern University, 1970, 49–65.

Sheleg, Ya'ir, *The New Religious: A Contemporary Look at the Religious Society of Israel.* Hebrew, Jerusalem: Keter, 2000.

Shemesh, Moshe, "Did Shuqayri Call for 'Throwing the Jews into the Sea'?" *Israel Studies* 8.2 (2003) 70–81.

Shimoni, Gideon, *The Zionist Ideology.* Waltham, MA: Brandeis University Press, 1995.

Shragai, Shlomo Zalman, *Immediacy and Eternity (sha`ah venetzach).* Jerusalem: Mosad Harav Kook, 1960.

Shragai, Shlomo Zalman, "Ascension to the Land: Eternal Command," *Shanah Beshanah* (Hebrew) 1969, 275–278.

Signer, Michael, "The Land of Israel in Medieval Jewish Exegetical and Polemical Literature," in Lawrence Hoffman (ed.), *The Land of Israel: Jewish Perspectives.* South Bend, IN: Notre Dame, 1986, 220–233.

Silberstein, Lawrence (ed.), *Jewish Fundamentalism in Comparative Perspective.* New York: New York University Press, 1993.

Silver, Abba Hillel, *A History of Messianic Speculation in Israel: From the First through the Seventeenth Centuries.* Boston: Beacon, 1927.

Shochat, Azriel, Baskin, Judith, and Slutzky, Yehuda, "Haskalah," *Encyclopedia Judaica*, 2nd ed., 2007, 8:434–444.

Smend, Rudolf, *Yahweh War and Tribal Confederation: Reflections on Israel's Earliest History*. Nashville: Abingdon. 1970.

Smith, Jonathan Z., *To Take Place*. Chicago: University of Chicago, 1993.

Sobel, Lester (ed.), *Israel and the Arabs: The October 1973 War*. New York: Facts on File, 1974.

Soloveitchik, Aharon, "On *Milchemet Mitzvah* in the Land of Israel at this Time." *Shanah Beshanah* 1974, 136–146.

Sorkin, David, *The Berlin Haskalah and German Religious Thought: Orphans of Knowledge*. Portland, OR: Valentine Mitchel, 2000.

Sorkin, David, *Moses Mendelssohn and the Religious Enlightenment*. London: Peter Halban, 2004.

Sprinzak, Ehud, "The Emergence of the Israeli Radical Right," in *Comparative Politics*, January 1989, 171–192.

Sprinzak, Ehud, *The Ascendance of Israel's Radical Right*. New York: Oxford: 1991.

Stanislawski, Michael, *Zionism and the Fin de Siècle: Cosmopolitanism and Nationalism from Nordau to Jabotinsky*. Berkeley and Los Angeles: University of California, 2001.

Stanton, Graham, and Stroumsa, Guy (eds.), *Tolerance and Intolerance in Early Judaism and Christianity*. Cambridge: Cambridge University, 1998.

Stemberger, Günter, *Jews and Christians in the Holy Land*, transl. Ruth Tuschling. Edinburgh: T & T Clark, 2000.

Stern, Ephraim and Eshel, Hanan (eds.), *The Samaritans* (Hebrew). Jerusalem: Ben-Zvi, 2002.

Stern, Menahem, *Greek and Latin Authors on Jews and Judaism* 3 vols. Jerusalem: Israel Academy of Sciences, 1974.

Stern, Philip D., *The Biblical Herem: A Window on Israel's Religious Experience*. *Atlanta*: Scholars Press, 1991.

Stolz, Fritz, *Jawhes and Israels Krieg*. Abhandlungen zur Theologie des Alten and Neuen Testaments 60. Zurich: Theologischer Verlag, 1972.

Sullivan. Francis A., Magisterium: Teaching Authority in the Catholic Church. Paulist Press, 1984.

Tabari, Muhammad ibn Jarir, al-, *Jami` al-bayan `an ta'wil ayat al-Qur'an*. Beirut: Dar al-Fikr, 1984.

Tabory, Joseph, "The Piety of Politics: Jewish Prayers for the State of Israel," *Liturgy in the Life of the Synagogue: Studies in the History of Jewish Prayer* (ed. Ruth Langer and Steven Fine). Winona Lake: Eisenbrauns, 2005, pp. 225–246.

Ta-Shema, Israel, "Aspects of Heroism in the Halakhah." *Machanayim* 87 (1964), 72–75.

Taikhtel, Yisachar Shlomo, *Em Habanim Semechah*. Jerusalem: Kol Mevaser, 1998. Translated by Pesach Schindler as *Restoration of Zion as a Response During the Holocaust: Em Habanim Semeha*. New York: Ktav, 1999.

Teitelbaum, Yoel, *On the Redemption and Recompense* (Hebrew). Jerusalem, 1982.

Tekhoresh, K. P., "Discretionary, Commanded and Required War"*Hatorah Vehamedinah* #2 (1950), 89–98.

Tirosh, Yosef, *Religious Zionism and the State: A Collection of Articles on the 30th Year of the State* (Hebrew). Jerusalem: World Zionist Organization, 1978.

Troen, Ilan, "Frontier Myths and their Applications in American and Israel: A Transnational Perspective." *Israel Studies* 5.1 (Spring, 2000), 301–329.

Troen, S. Ilan, *Imagining Zion: Dreams, Designs, and Realities in a Century of Jewish Settlement.* New Haven: Yale University Press, 2003.

Tubb, Jonathan, *Canaanites.* Norman, OK: U. of Oklahoma, 1998.

Twersky, Isadore, *Introduction to the Code of Maimonides.* New Haven: Yale University Press, 1980.

Twersky, Isadore, (ed.), *Rabbi Moses ben Nahman (Ramban): Explorations in His Religious and Literary Virtuosity.* Cambridge, MA: Harvard University, 1983.

Tzur, Yakov, "Religious Zionism and Messianism." *Amudim* #455 (1981), 60–65.

Unna, Moshe, "Ha-Po'el Ha-Mizrachi," in *Encylopedia Judaica* 7:1320–1324.

Unterman, Isser Yehuda, "The Acquisition (*qinyan*) of the Nation Is not Open for Trading." *Shanah Beshanah* 1968, 103–105.

Unterman, Isser Yehuda, "The Prophecies Have Come About in Their Entirety." *Shanah Beshanah* 1978, 145–151.

Urbach, Ephraim, *The Sages.* Cambridge, MA: Harvard University Press, 1987.

Urbach, Uri, and Chagai Segal, *And Today They Use It to Wrap Up Fish: Prophecy about Destruction and Miracles: 1967–1992* (Hebrew). Beit El: Sifriat Beit El, 1992.

Van Henten, Jan Willem, "II Maccabees as a History of Liberation," in *Jews and Gentiles in the Holy Land in the Days of the Second Temple, the Mishnah and the Talmud*, ed. Menachem Mor and Aharon Oppenheimer, Jack Pastor and Daniel Schwartz. Jerusalem: Yad Ben-Zvi, 2003, 63–86.

Vital, David, *Zionism: The Formative Years.* Oxford: Clarendon Press, 1982.

von Clausewitz, Carl, *On War*, transl. J. J. Graham. London: N. Trübner, 1874, new and revised edition with introduction and notes by F. N. Maude, 1909 in three volumes.

von Rad, Gerhard, *Holy War in Ancient Israel*, translated by Marva J. Dawn, 1951, reprint, with a new introduction and annotated bibliography. Grand Rapids, MI: William B. Eerdmans, 1991.

Wach, Joachim, *The Sociology of Religion.* Chicago: University of Chicago, 1944.

Walzer, Michael, "The Idea of Holy War in Ancient Israel." *Journal of Religious Ethics* 22.2 (1992): 215–227.

Walzer, Michael, Menachem Lorberbaum, Noam Zohar and Ari Ackerman, *The Jewish Political Tradition* Vol. 2: *Membership.* New Haven: Yale University Press, 2003.

Wanefsky, Joseph, *Rabbi Jacob Reines; His Life and Thought.* New York: Philosophical Library, 1970.

Wasserstrom, Steven, *Between Muslim and Jew.* Princeton: Princeton University Press, 1995.

Weber, Max, *The Sociology of Religion*, translated by Ephraim Fischoff. Boston: Beacon, 1963.

Weinfeld, Moshe, "Divine Intervention in War in Ancient Israel and in the Ancient Near East," in *History, Historiography and Interpretation: Studies in Biblical and Cuneiform Literatures*, ed. Moshe Weinfeld and Hayim Tadmor. Jerusalem: Magnes, 1983, 121–147.

Weinfeld, Moshe, *The Promise of the Land*. Berkeley and Los Angeles: UCLA, 1993.

Weippert, Manfred, " 'Heiliger Krieg' in Israel und Assyrien: Kritische Anmerkungen zu Gerhard von Rads Konzept des 'Heiligen Krieges im alten Israel.' " *Zeitschrift fur die altestamentiche Wissenschaft* 82 (1972): 460–493.

Weisburd, David, *Jewish Settler Violence: Deviance and Social Reaction*. Philadelphia: University of Pennsylvania Press, 1989.

Weitzman, Steven, *Surviving Sacrilege: Cultural Persistence in Jewish Antiquity*. Cambridge, MA: Harvard, 2005.

Wellhausen, Julius, *Prolegomena to the History of Ancient Israel*. Reprint 1957, Cleveland: One World.

Wilken, Robert, *The Land Called Holy: Palestine in Christian History and Thought*. New Haven: Yale, 1992.

Wilkes, George R., "Religious War in the Works of Maimonides and its Reception Amongst Jews in Christian Lands," in Sohail Hashmi, ed. *Just Wars, Holy Wars, and Jihads: Christian, Jewish, Muslim Encounters and Exchanges*. Oxford: Oxford University Press, 2012.

Wright, Thomas, *Early Travels in Palestine*. New York: Ktav, 1968.

Ya`ari, Abraham, "Has the Heroism of the Hasmoneans been Truly Forgotten?" *Machanayim* 63 (1962), 138–149.

Yadin, Yigal, *Bar Kokhba: The Rediscovery of the legendary hero of the Second Jewish Revolt against Rome*. New York: Random House, 1971.

Yadin, Yigal, *Masada: Herod's Fortress and the Zealots' Last Stand* (Jerusalem: Steimatzky's, 1966.

Yaron, Zvi, "Kook, Abraham Isaac," *Encyclopedia Judaica* 10:1182–1187.

Yaron, Zvi, "The Deterioration of Gush Emunim." *Amudim* 363 (1975), 151.

Yaron, Zvi, *The Philosophy of Rabbi Kook* (Avner Tomaschoff, transl.). Jerusalem: World Zionist Organization, 1991.

Yisraeli, Shaul, "The Kibiya Affair in the Light of *Halakhah*." *Hatorah Vehamedinah* #5 (1953), 71–113.

Yisraeli, Shaul, "To Hold On to the Liberated Territories with All Our Might." *Shanah Beshanah* 1968, 106–109.

Yisraeli, Shaul, "Commanded War and Discretionary War." *Torah Shebe`al Peh* 10 (1968), 46–50.

Yisraeli, Shaul, *Sefer Eretz Chemdah*. Jerusalem: Mossad Harav Kook, Fourth Printing: 1999.

Yisraeli, Shaul, "Ceding Territory Because of Mortal Danger," *Crossroads* 3 (1990), 29–46.

Yosef, Ovadia, "Returning Territories from the Land of Israel on Account of Saving Lives." *Torah Shebe`al-peh* 1980, 12–21 (translated into English as "Ceding Territory of the Land of Israel in Order to Save Lives." *Crossroads* 3 [1990], 11–28).

Zerubavel, Yael, "The Death of Memory and the Memory of Death: Masada and the Holocaust," *Representations* 45 (Winter, 1994), 72–100.

Zakovitz, Ya'ir, *Introduction to Internal Biblical Commentary* (Hebrew). Even-Yehuda, Israel 1992.

Zion, Noam, and Specter, Barbara, *A Different Light*, NY and Jerusalem, Shalom Hartman Institute, 2000.

Zur, Yaakov , "German Jewish Orthodoxy's Attitude toward Zionism," in Almog, Shmuel, Reinharz, Jehuda, and Shapira, Anita (eds.), *Zionism and Religion*. Hanover, NH: Brandeis University Press, 1998, 107–115.

*Traditional Hebrew language texts*

*Babylonian Talmud* (traditional edition)
*Bereshit Rabbah*
*Exodus Rabba*
*Palestinian Talmud* (traditional edition)
*Lamentations Rabba*
*Mekhilta deRabbi Yishmael* (Ed. Horovitz-Rabin [Jerusalem: Wahrman, 1970].
*Mekhilta deRabbi Yishmael* (Ed. Lauterbach [Philadephia, Jewish Publication Society, 1936].
*Midrash Tanchuma* (Buber)
*Mishnah*
*Pesiqta deRav Kahana* (Mandelbaum, Jewish Theological Seminary, 1987)
*Pesiqta Rabbati* (Ish Shalom, Vienna)
*Rashi's Commentaries on the Torah*. Ed. Chayim Dov Chavel (Hebrew). Jerusalem: Mosad Harav Kook, 1995.
*Shulchan Arukh*
*Seder Eliayu Zuta.*
*Seder Rav Amram Gaon* (Warsaw, 1865).
*Seder Rav Amram Gaon*, ed. Daniel Goldschmidt (Jerusalem: Mosad Harav Kook, 1971).
*Sifrei Devarim*
*Song of Songs Rabba* (trad. Vilna ed. Bar Ilan University).
*Targum Yonatan* (midrashic Aramaic translation of the Hebrew Bible found in traditional Rabbinic Bibles).
*Targum Onkelos* (mostly contextual Aramaic translation of the Hebrew Bible found in Rabbinic Bibles).
*Tosefta* (Leiberman)
*Tosefta* (Zuckermandel)
*Yalqut Shim`oni* (Multiple volumes and dates). Jerusalem. Mosad Harav Kook.
Maimonides, Moses, *Commentary on the Mishnah*, Ed. Yosef David Kapach. Jerusalem: Mosad Harav Kook, 1965
Maimonides, Moses, *Book of Commandments, with the commentary of Nachmanides*. Hebrew, Ed. Rabbi Chayim Dov Chavel. Jerusalem: Mosad Harav Kook, 1981.

# INDEX

anti-Zionist Orthodox Jews, 12, 90, 104,
    154, 203, 238n55
apocalyptic literature, 173
Apocrypha, 69
Arab Higher Committee, 191
"Arab mentality," 306–307, 307n80
*Arab Mind, The* (Patai), 307n80
Arab Revolt (1936–1939), 160–161,
    189–197
Arabs, Palestinian
    1936–1939 Arab Revolt, 160–161,
        189–197
    class solidarity with, 187–189
    fear of, 210
    *fedayeen,* 230–232, 236, 236n46
    influence of Settler Movement, 314–315
    *nakba,* 296
    tolerance towards, 199–200
    "transfer" of, 295–296
    and violence, 189–190, 230–232,
        235–238 (*see also* violence)
Arafat, Yassir, 103–104n17
Arameans, 18
Aram Zobah, 18, 82, 116–118, 241–242
Aran, Gideon, 224, 273, 277
*aratzot teme'ot* (polluted lands of exile),
    145
archaeological discoveries, 244–245, 246
Ariel, Yakov (Stieglitz), 254, 263n50, 312
arm or limb, symbolism of, 61n64 *see*
        *also* "hand of God" imagery
*Artzi* (journal), 310, 310n87
ascension to the Land of Israel
    in 13th century, 292
    "as a wall" *(kechomah),* 75, 96,
        205–206, 209, 213–214, 262–263,
        263n50
    defined, 75n17
    and forcing hand of God, 147–151
    "in a wall" (*bechomah*), 91–93, 135,
        144, 147–150, 165, 234, 256,
        262–263, 263n50
    Nahmanides, 127–134
    Rashi on, 234
    *see also* emigration to the Land of
        Israel; Three Vows; Zionism

Ashkenazi Chief Rabbis. *see* Goren,
    Shlomo; Herzog, Isaac Halevi;
    Kook, Abraham Isaac; Unterman,
    Isser Yehuda
assassination of Yitzhak Rabin, 7,
    316n101, 324
assimilation, 142–143, 147
Assyrians, 303
atonement, prayers of, 46, 58–59, 58n57
Augustus, 43
*Avelei Tsiyyon* immigrants, 128n4
Averroes (Muhammad Ibn Rushd),
    118n30
Aviad, Janet, 269
*avihem-shel-yisrael* (father of Israel), 287
Aviner, Shlomo, 283–284, 293, 301,
    301n64
Avi-Yonah, Michael, 91n24
Avner, 174
`avodah (sacrificial offerings), 164–165,
    280
*avodat ha'adama* (working the land),
    273–274
Avrushmi, Yonah, 316n101

*Ba`alei tosefot* (Ashkenazi schools of the
    Rhineland), 114
*ba`aley trisin* (shield-bearers), 92
Babylonia and Babylonian Empire, 18,
    20, 208n16, 263
Babylonian Talmud
    on categories of war, 74, 83–88, 113,
        115–116, 216
    on fighting on the Sabbath, 216
    on Hanukkah, 27, 37
    on "ingathering of exiles," 223n3
    *see also* Palestinian Talmud
Baer, Yitzhak, 96
Balfour Declaration, 169n19, 228, 260,
    290
*baraitot* (outside materials), 71 *see also*
    tannaitic literature
*barayta* (tannaitic passage of Mishnah), 37
*Bar Giora* (secret defense group), 189
Bar-Ilan, Meir, 195–196 *see also* Berlin,
    Meir

Bar Kokhba Rebellion
about, 50–62, 68
as Commanded War, 3
condemnation of, 95–96
mythologizing of, 186
reevaluation of, 244–245
Bar Kosiba, Simon, 50, 54 *see also* Bar
Kokhba Rebellion
*bavel* (Babylonia), 208n16 *see also*
Babylonia and Babylonian Empire
*bayit* (shelter, house), 78
*bayit chadash* (new house), 78
*bechomah* ("in a wall"), 91–93, 135, 144,
147–150, 165, 234, 256, 262–263,
263n50
Begin, Menachem, 183, 297
"beginning of the flowering of our
Redemption, the" (*reshit
tzemichat ge'ulateynu*), 227–229,
313 *see also* Redemption
Beitar, 52, 55–57
Ben Gurion, David, 180, 221n1, 231, 237
Ben Yochai, Shimon, 315
Ben Yosef, Shlomo, 192n41
Berdichevsky, Micha Joseph, 48–49, 181,
187
Berlin, Meir, 151 *see also* Bar-Ilan, Meir
Bernstein, Yeshayahu, 194n51
*biryonim* (thugs), 62, 67, 175, 175n33
Blidstein, Gerald, 120, 233
Block of Faithful movement. *see Gush
Emunim* movement
Bloi (Rabbi), 194
B'nai Akiba youth movement, 182,
300–301, 321
Bodenheimer, Max, 186
*Book of Commandments* (Maimonides),
123–125
borders
biblical, 119n31, 225, 239, 285, 297
settlement of the Land beyond, 244
of State of Israel, 230, 235–238
*see also* violence
Bornstein, Abraham, 286, 286n16
Borochov, Ber, 164
Breitbart, Zishe, 175

brigands (*leistai*), 43, 43n3
British Mandate
and Jewish militant activism, 192,
192nn41–42
and the Three Vows, 264
two state solution, 161
and the White Paper, 194, 198
Britt, Zevulun Leib, 151
Burma Road, 271, 271n76

Cahan, Yakov, 185n22
Camp David Accords, 302, 305
Canaanites/Canaan, 17, 82, 104–106 *see
also* seven Canaanite nations
Cassius Dio, 51
Catastrophe (*nakba*), 296
Catholic Church, 2
*chalutzim* (Zionist pioneers), 164, 164n6,
180
chastenings of love (*yisurin shel ahavah*),
315
Children of Efrayim, 95–96, 95n34
Christiani, Pablo, 127
Christianity, 70, 173n28
class solidarity with Palestinian Arabs,
187–189
*Code of Jewish Law* (Maimonides), 117
Cohen, Geula, 271, 273
Cohen, Shaye, 68
Cohen, She'ar Yashuv, 103, 209
Cohen, Stuart, 310n88
Commanded War (*milchemet mitzvah*)
1956 Sinai Campaign as, 242–243
1973 War as, 298, 302
about, 3–5
against Amalek, 99–104, 116–125,
214–215
authorization of, 106–107, 215–217
Babylonian Talmud on, 74, 83–88, 113,
117
and counter-terrorism against Arabs,
197
defensive war as, 74–75n14, 214–215,
302
and deferments, 79–85, 117, 217
defined by rabbis, 74, 310